Moral Economy and Popular Protest

Also by Adrian Randall

AN ATLAS OF INDUSTRIAL PROTEST IN BRITAIN, 1750–1984
(*with Andrew Charlesworth, Dave Gilbert, Humphrey Southall and Chris Wrigley*)

BEFORE THE LUDDITES: Custom, Community and Machinery in the
English Woollen Industry, 1776–1809

MARKETS, MARKET CULTURE AND POPULAR PROTEST IN EIGHTEENTH-
CENTURY BRITAIN AND IRELAND (*editor with Andrew Charlesworth*)

Also by Andrew Charlesworth

AN ATLAS OF INDUSTRIAL PROTEST IN BRITAIN, 1750–1984
(*with Adrian Randall, Dave Gilbert, Humphrey Southall and Chris Wrigley*)

ATLAS OF RURAL PROTEST IN BRITAIN

MARKETS, MARKET CULTURE AND POPULAR PROTEST IN EIGHTEENTH-
CENTURY BRITAIN AND IRELAND (*editor with Adrian Randall*)

Moral Economy and Popular Protest

Crowds, Conflict and Authority

Edited by

Adrian Randall
Professor of English Social History
University of Birmingham

and

Andrew Charlesworth
Reader in Human Geography
Cheltenham and Gloucester College of Higher Education
Cheltenham

Published by PALGRAVE
Houndmills, Basingstoke, Hampshire RG21 6XS and
175 Fifth Avenue, New York, N.Y. 10010
Companies and representatives throughout the world

PALGRAVE is the new global academic imprint of
St. Martin's Press LLC Scholarly and Reference Division and
Palgrave Publishers Ltd (formerly Macmillan Press Ltd).

Outside North America
ISBN 0–333–67184–8

In North America
ISBN 0–312–22592–X

This book is printed on paper suitable for recycling and
made from fully managed and sustained forest sources.

A catalogue record for this book is available from the British Library.

Library of Congress Catalog Card Number: 99–15312

Printed and bound in Great Britain by
Antony Rowe Ltd, Chippenham and Eastbourne

To the memory of Edward Thompson, 1924–93

Contents

Preface   *ix*

Notes on the Contributors   *xii*

1   The moral economy: riots, markets and social conflict   1
    Adrian Randall and Andrew Charlesworth

2   The food riots of 1347 and the medieval moral economy   33
    Buchanan Sharp

3   The pragmatic economy, the politics of provisions and the
    'invention' of the food riot tradition in 1740   55
    John Bohstedt

4   Moral economy, political economy and law   93
    Douglas Hay

5   Food riots revisited: popular protest and moral economy
    in nineteenth-century India   123
    David Arnold

6. Moral economy, political economy and the
    American bourgeois revolution   147
    Edward Countryman

7   Industrial disputes, wage bargaining and the
    moral economy   166
    John Rule

8   The moral economy as an argument and as a fight   187
    James C. Scott

9   The moral economy of the English countryside   209
    Roger Wells

Index   273

Preface

This book is the belated product of a conference held at the University of Birmingham in 1992 to mark the coming of age of Edward Thompson's concept of 'the moral economy'. Some 31 prominent scholars from the UK, North America and Europe attended this conference, the most warmly welcomed of all being Edward Thompson himself who delivered an after-dinner paper on the first evening. While his health had been poor for some time, he obviously relished the vigorous cut and thrust which characterised the debates and discussions of the following two days. And, while he made it clear that his days in the archives would now be much curtailed, it was clear that the intellectual and polemical vigour which had always characterised his approach to life still burned as bright as ever.

Little did we then realise that his participation in this conference would prove to be a valedictory one for Edward. Less than eighteen months later, he died peacefully in his garden at Wick Episcopi. From the correspondence which followed the sad news of his death, it was clear that all involved in the conference felt an enormous sense of shock and loss, a loss not only of one of the most significant and inspirational historians of the post-war generation but of a highly regarded human being and friend.

Thompson's work has been the subject of many appraisals and reappraisals, both during his life time and after. However, we make no apology for bringing together this volume of essays on the subject of the moral economy. This, perhaps the most fecund of all his many imaginative and persuasive insights into the study of social, economic and political relations, has, surprisingly, received much less attention than his many other contributions to the development of social history: for example, Kaye and McClelland's extensive assessment of E. P. Thompson's historical writings lacks any real reference to it.[1] It was this which, among other reasons, prompted the holding of the conference.

Perhaps one of the reasons for this lack of engagement by 'Thompson watchers' with the case of the moral economy is the way in which the concept has been taken up, utilised and reshaped by scholars across an extraordinarily wide range of disciplines and subject areas.

As the reader of this volume will discover, the reach of the moral economy has proved wide indeed. As the conference in Birmingham made clear, the moral economy has a life which transcends its creator, a fact that he happily acknowledged in his last published statement on the subject: 'it has come of age and I am no longer answerable for its actions. It will be interesting to see how it goes on.'[2]

This volume was not conceived as a valediction for Edward Thompson nor is it now intended to be one. As the conference proposed, these contributions are much more than a taking stock, a retrospective look. They also point us forward both critically and conceptually. Their engagement with the concept Thompson formulated in his seminal article in 1971 is as rigorous and as critical as he himself would have expected. He would have enjoyed the argument. It is in this spirit that the authors wish to dedicate the book to his memory.

Many people deserve our thanks for their parts in running the conference or in shaping this book. We must thank the Nuffield Foundation for their award of a small grant towards the costs of setting up and running the conference. Their involvement in this way was apposite, given that the Nuffield Foundation had provided a grant towards the archival research on which the original 1971 paper was based. It was also fitting that one of the research assistants so funded – Jeanette Neeson – was a participant at the conference. We would also like to take this opportunity to thank both the British Academy for their generous support which enabled the attendance of certain overseas participants and Martin Eve of Merlin Books who provided welcome support for the event. We must also record our collective thanks to Mrs Diane Martin of the Department of Economic and Social History at the University of Birmingham who proved herself an outstanding secretary to the conference and to the staff at the Manor House who made us so comfortable. Tim Farmiloe of Macmillan has been an extraordinarily patient editor and unfailingly encouraging in the face of endless delays in the final completion of this volume. Finally, but by no means least in importance, the editors and authors would like to acknowledge their debt to all those who attended the conference for the many perceptive and challenging contributions they made towards the shaping of the ideas which are developed here. Thank you all.

ADRIAN RANDALL
ANDREW CHARLESWORTH

Notes

1. H. Kaye and K. McClelland (eds), *E. P. Thompson: Critical Perspectives* (Cambridge: Polity, 1990). Edward Thompson and his works have also been extensively reviewed by, among others, B. D. Palmer, *The Making of E. P. Thompson: Marxism, Humanism and History* (London: Macmillan, 1981); L. Hunt (ed.), *The New Cultural History* (Berkeley, Cal.: University of California, 1989); and R. Wells, 'E. P. Thompson, *Customs in Common* and moral economy', *Journal of Peasant Studies*, 21, 2(1994), pp. 263–307.
2. E. P. Thompson, *Customs in Common* (London: Merlin, 1991), p. 351.

Notes on the Contributors

David Arnold is Professor of South Asian Studies at the School of Oriental and African Studies, London. He has published widely on the political and social history of nineteenth- and early twentieth-century India and is currently working on the history of science, technology and medicine in South Asia. His most recent publications include *Colonizing the Body: State Medicine and Epidemic Disease in Nineteenth-Century India* (Berkeley, Cal.: University of California Press 1993), and *The Problem of Nature: Environment, Culture and European Expansion* (Oxford: Oxford University Press, 1996).

John Bohstedt is Associate Professor and Associate Head of the History Department at the University of Tennessee, Knoxville. He is the author of *Riots and Community Politics in England and Wales 1790–1810* (Cambridge, Mass.: Harvard University Press, 1983) and co-author of *Social Protest and the Politics of Provisions in Britain, France, England and the Twentieth Century World* (forthcoming).

Andrew Charlesworth is Reader in Human Geography at Cheltenham and Gloucester College of Higher Education. He is the editor and co-author of the *Atlas of Rural Protest in Britain* (London: Croom Helm, 1983) and has written extensively on social protest in Britain between 1500 and 1900. He is, with Adrian Randall, editor and co-author of *Markets, Market Culture and Popular Protest in Eighteenth-Century Britain and Ireland* (Liverpool: Liverpool University Press, 1996) and, with Adrian Randall, David Gilbert, Humphrey Southall and Chris Wrigley, author of the *Atlas of Industrial Protest in Britain, 1750–1984*.

Edward Countryman is Professor in the Clements Department of History at Southern Methodist University, Dallas, He has published two books and many articles on the American Revolution. His most recent book, *Americans: A Collision of Histories*, expresses his current interest in the emergence of American identity out of American conflict. He is now beginning a study of black, white and red people in Mississippi between 1770 and 1860.

Douglas Hay is Associate Professor of Law and History at York University, Toronto. He has co-edited and contributed to *Albion's Fatal*

Tree: Crime and Society in Eighteenth-Century England (London, 1975); *Labour, Law and Crime in Historical Perspective* (London, 1987); *Policing and Prosecution in Britain 1750–1850* (Oxford, 1989). He has recently published, with Nicholas Rogers, *Eighteenth-Century English Society: Shuttles and Swords* (Oxford, 1997).

Adrian Randall is Professor of English Social History at the University of Birmingham. He is the author of *Before the Luddites* (Cambridge, 1991) and, with Andrew Charlesworth, editor and co-author of *Markets, Market Culture and Popular Protest in Eighteenth-Century Britain and Ireland* (Liverpool, 1996). He has written extensively on labour, technology and social protest in eighteenth- and nineteenth-century England.

John Rule is Professor of History at the Univesity of Southampton. He is the author of *The Vital Century: England's Developing Economy 1714–1815* and *Albion's People: English Society 1714–1815* (both 1992). With R. Malcolmson he edited *Protest and Survival: Essays for E. P. Thompson* (London: Merlin, 1993), and has published widely on early labour history.

Buchanan Sharp is Professor of History at the University of California, Santa Cruz. He is author of *In Contempt of All Authority: Rural Artisans and Riot in the West of England 1586–1660* (Berkeley, Cal.: 1980). He is currently working on a study of early English food riots, 1347–1547.

James C. Scott is the Eugene Meyer Professor of Political Science and Anthropology at Yale University, directs the Program in Agrarian Studies there and raises sheep. He is author of *The Moral Economy and the Peasant* (New Haven, Conn.: Yale Univesity Press, 1976); *Weapons of the Weak: Everyday Forms of Peasant Resistance* (New Haven, Conn.: Yale University Press, 1985); *Domination and the Arts of Resistance* (New Haven, Conn.: Yale University Press, 1990); and *Seeing Like a State* (New Haven, Conn.: Yale Univesity Press, 1998).

Roger Wells is Professor of History at Canterbury Christ Church College. He is the author of *Insurrection: The British Experience 1795–1803* (Gloucester: Alan Sutton, 1983), *Wretched Faces: Famine in Wartime England 1793–1801* (Gloucester: Alan Sutton, 1988) and numerous articles on modern British social history. He also edited *Victorian Village* (1992) and, with Mick Reed, *Class, Conflict and Protest in the English Countryside 1770–1880* (London: Frank Cass, 1990).

1
The Moral Economy: Riot, Markets and Social Conflict

Adrian Randall and Andrew Charlesworth

In 1971 *Past and Present* published a paper by E. P. Thompson which was to become seminal for a number of areas of research in social history and social anthropology, for 'The moral economy of the English crowd in the eighteenth century' fundamentally redefined the way in which social historians investigated and interpreted popular protest. In his paper, Thompson sought to rescue the study of eighteenth-century food riots from 'crass economic reductionism'. Such riots, he believed, could not be regarded simply as 'rebellions of the belly' since they displayed an order and focus which could not be explained by a simple desperation for food. Food riots, he argued, were 'a highly complex form of direct popular action, disciplined and with clear objectives', the actions of the crowd being 'informed by the belief that they were defending traditional rights or customs'. These rights and customs were in turn derived from 'the paternalist model of the marketing and manufacturing process', a model which had real if eroded existence in a body of statute law, common law and customary usage. This paternalist model, much of it dating back to Tudor times, demanded that foodstuffs should be marketed at or near their place of origin, that all transactions should be transparent and in the market-place and that the needs of the poor should always take precedence over those of dealers and middlemen. Practices such as the sale of crops by sample and the sale of standing crops which enabled corn dealers to bypass the local market were proscribed, as were forestalling and engrossing, means by which an 'artificial' scarcity might be created. The poor, argued Thompson, accepted and invoked this model as a 'legitimising notion' to justify popular intervention whenever, but particularly in times of scarcity, they believed such offences were taking place. These values and actions, Thompson believed, denoted a community consensus which 'can be said to constitute the moral economy of the poor'.[1]

In delineating this concept of the moral economy, Thompson provided a model and an analytical framework that has been readily taken up not only by scholars of eighteenth-century market protests but also in fields far beyond, giving rise to an increasingly rich, fertile and extensive debate. Thus over the past two decades a voluminous series of studies of different forms of protest about food in both Western Europe and in the Third World have tested and extended many aspects of Thompson's original model and, in so doing, have both deepened and widened our understanding of them.[2] In this respect alone, it would be difficult to think of another paper which has had such an impact on modern social history. The concept of the moral economy has additionally been picked up as an explanatory tool by historians studying labour protests in the eighteenth and nineteenth centuries and by historians interested in customary rights. The debate on the moral economy has likewise impinged upon economic history and the history of economic thought, in particular because Thompson couched the concept of moral economy in a dialectic tension with that of market economy. Historical understanding of the changing nature of market practices within the context of the development of regional, national and international food markets has been augmented by a recognition that food may not be viewed simply as another tradable commodity but carries, as Thompson insisted, a social and political baggage which cannot easily be detached. The extension of the concept of the moral economy to the Third World has in turn led on to a consideration of the relationship between popular protest and government strategies in times of famine. In particular, Sen's important theory of food entitlement, although not directly drawn from Thompson, has become engaged with aspects of moral economy in these debates.[3] Moreover, social anthropologists of the Third World, most notably James C. Scott, have found the notion of moral economy a very useful tool in locating a modern peasantry's view of its reciprocal economic and social relations with both landlords and the state and with kin and co-villagers. As Scott makes clear, the issue of social conflict 'is not just a problem of calories and income but is a question of peasant perceptions of social justice, of rights and obligations, of reciprocity'.[4] Thompson's paper has, in short, provided the raw material for a debate which has spread far beyond its original focus.

Thompson himself broadly welcomed this development in his essay, 'The moral economy reviewed', published in his *Customs in Common* in 1991, recognising that, while he remained father of the concept, 'the term has long forgotten its paternity...it has come of age and I am no longer responsible for its actions'. Yet this did not impede him from an extensive and robust review of the uses and misuses of his original concept. As that essay shows, he remained far from persuaded by some of the ways in which the moral economy had been taken up and utilised by others, including some who are contributors to this book. Nevertheless, as Thompson wrote, the debate on the moral economy 'is an agenda for forward research'.[5] The contributions in this volume are intended as such, both critically examining Thompson's original (and revised) ideas and seeking to enquire how the concept of the moral economy may best be further deployed. They should be read as contributions to an ongoing debate.

In introducing this collection, we are not seeking to provide a definitive review of the moral economy and its multifaceted use by historians, anthropologists, sociologists, Third World specialists and the like.[6] Rather, our intention here is to provide an extended reflection on the issues raised by the concept in order to contextualise the themes covered by the studies in this volume. These have focused around three areas of debate, delineated because they remain closest to Thompson's original usage of the term: the moral economic framework within which food riots occurred in Europe, but particularly in England, in the eighteenth century; the dialectic tension between moral and market economy *Weltanschauung*; and the issue of the applicability of the concept of moral economy once taken beyond its original context of eighteenth-century food riots.

Food Riots and a Moral Economy Perspective

While food riots were by far the most typical form of popular protest in eighteenth-century Europe, they had a long history. For England their origins have generally been located in the sixteenth century[7] but, as Sharp demonstrates in Chapter 2, food riots were also to be found in medieval England, displaying many of the characteristics of later disturbances. In the succeeding centuries and across a variety of localities, an extended repertoire of crowd actions was developed: price-fixing in the marketplace; the compulsion of farmers to bring food to the marketplace; the stoppage of foodstuffs in transit; and the seizure and/or destruction of foodstuffs. We should note that, in 1971, historians had but limited knowledge of this picture. Thompson's researches on food rioting had begun in the early 1960s as part of a wider comparative study into the nature of eighteenth-century food protests in both England and France, a study which was to have involved Thompson,

Richard Cobb and Gwyn Williams.[8] That collaborative work was never completed, though each wrote separately on the topic, but Thompson's delineation of the concept of the 'moral economy of the poor' was doubtless informed by their discussions. Furthermore, in Thompson's case his research was grounded in his emerging exploration of eighteenth-century English plebeian culture. From the start, he saw food rioting, like its accompanying dearth, as (in Appadurai's words) 'a special sort of lens for examining society in normal times'.[9] Riots might be atypical events, but they unmasked many of the values of a common people which in other times went unvoiced. Riot revealed their underlying assumptions about social and economic relations.

Thompson saw that riots did not occur simply as a result of scarcity or price rises. They were, he showed, the consequence of sudden and, to the consumer, suspicious price rises and shortages which smacked of illicit market manipulation by those who had the power to withhold food or who sought to find more lucrative markets for it elsewhere. Protests erupted when these actions were allowed to continue unchecked. Informed by the value system of the moral economy, popular protest was directed not merely towards securing a subsistence at prices which could be afforded but, as importantly, at preventing abuses and punishing those who perpetrated them. For Thompson, the moral economy was not a static, tradition-bound entity. It was a selective reconstruction of paternalist legislation which became more, rather than less, sophisticated in the eighteenth century. The guarantors of this developing moral economy were, for the most part, the crowd; hence the title of his original paper. It was the crowd which most actively resisted changes in marketing practice and the crowd which ensured that those who sought to break old market customs and culture encountered real and effective intimidation or retribution. These actions were underwritten and legitimised by the community character of protest for, Thompson believed, the moral economy was not the value system of the few: it was the value system of an entire plebeian society.

Thompson's thesis and his interpretation of eighteenth-century English food riots has encountered many critics, unpersuaded of his claims that food riots were manifestations of wider moral values or of social and economic norms of behaviour.[10] Were rioters really so orderly, so community-minded? Did they in fact share any sort of value system beyond the desperate determination to obtain food? There is not enough room here to follow up all these critiques – Chapter 3 by John Bohstedt is highly critical of parts of Thompson's model – but attention may be drawn to some.

The origin, development and behaviour of those involved in food riots has long engaged historians critical of Thompson's model. The frequent point of origin of food riots was, as might be expected, the marketplace or the roadside and the immediate participants in the drama were frequently small-scale hucksters and women. Much has been made about the 'myth' of the female riot but, as Thompson himself made clear, the food riot was neither gendered nor easily typologised.[11] Yet for all these proto-riots, the context was the same: fast rising prices; a strong belief that these reflected not the 'reality' of the market situation but trader greed; and some minor flashpoint, such as one purchaser refusing to pay, strong language, a scuffle or a barrow overturned. That these fracas more frequently involved women reflected the fact that they, more than men, were in most cases the primary managers of the family economy. Their targets were often other women: bread sellers, butter vendors, potato sellers. Noticeably, the victims of this sort of action rarely received any money for the produce taken.[12] These sorts of disturbance may well have been much more frequent than our current evidential knowledge suggests, given that they were less likely to have resulted in recorded prosecutions. Where they *were* recorded, it is often because they led on to wider and more concerted actions. Some communities possessed a particularly dynamic culture of protest which could rapidly be invoked and the fracas turned into riot. Once raised, the crowd in such places proved both 'structured' and formidable.

The rioting crowd were generally keen to involve as many as possible in the process of asserting common 'rights' and customary practice. Dallaway noted of the Gloucestershire food riots in 1766: 'The rioters come into our workshops and force all the men willing or unwilling to join them.'[13] The crowd at Oxford likewise swept up supporters for their actions, while the Kingswood colliers, a notoriously united riot force, were reported to be touring Wiltshire in 1753 after their violent defeat at the hands of the Bristol tradesmen in order to reinforce their strength for a return.[14] In 1766 a mob led by William Russell marched along the turnpike towards Newbury, rounding up workers on their way, urging: '"come one and all to Newbury in a body to make the price of bread cheaper". And they all joined to the number of 50 with sticks and as they came into the town they gave three huzzas, in order to raise a greater mob.' In 1795 the colliers from Hook marched into Haverfordwest, raising others on their route, and entered the High Street chanting 'one and all, one and all'.[15] This requirement for community involvement in dispensing community justice gave rise to some contemporary concern at the nature of leadership. Thus the fact that the crowds were so well informed, finding magazines of wheat and cheese which the authorities and landlords sometimes genuinely believed non-existent, and so well co-ordinated in their actions, as often as not avoiding the troops brought in to confront them, caused some to believe that there must be a military presence guiding them and pressing a majority of reluctant members into action. Yet there is little evidence that the mobber bands were either run by those with a military background or were principally made up of unwilling participants, even if some chose this line of defence at their trials.[16] Such pleas suited the authorities but the more perceptive magistrates realised that the mobs were held together by common purpose, not by bully boys. That purpose was not simply to obtain food at reasonable prices: it was also to reassert 'justice'.

The behaviour of the food rioting crowd has likewise prompted debate. Thompson argued that the crowd's actions were marked by their orderliness, suggesting restraint, care and complex motivation. Thus, he argued, the crowd often paid for foodstuffs which they had commandeered while the level of gratuitous 'theft' was low. Critics have challenged the notion that rioters exhibited order or restraint, arguing that riots were frequently violent.[17] However, there is an inherent difficulty in characterising food riots as either 'violent' or 'restrained', for clearly they could be both at the same time. Others have pointed to the criminality of rioters, noting that the majority of those prosecuted were charged with theft.[18] That is certainly true, but we must note that the forced sale of any commodity at a price lower than that demanded by the seller was, of necessity, defined as theft. The law could not be seen to sanction the consumer determining the market price in such a direct fashion. Yet 'regulators' did not see price-fixing as criminal. Careful reading of both sources and context is necessary before we place too much weight on the bare results of prosecution. Besides, prosecution, being always a private matter, depended upon both identification and context. When the mob was in the ascendent, civil action might be kept low key. Alternatively, when troops eventually provided some protection and the balance of power shifted, victims might feel more confident to prosecute. At such times it might also be easier to capture perpetrators. The legal evidence has to be utilised with caution.

In times of disorder there were clearly plentiful opportunities for the criminal to take advantage of the situation to purloin and filch. Indeed, in such circumstances they might even provide a lead.

Thus Wendy Thwaites notes that a group of horse thieves was apparently prominent in the disorders in and around Oxford in 1757. Yet there is no such suggestion that the riots in that county in 1795 and 1800, riots which took a very similar form, were led by criminals.[19] Likewise, personal grudges could easily be settled under cover of popular sanction of avowed market criminals. But against these examples, we must contrast the large number of instances where the crowd behaved with what can only be described as quite extraordinary probity. We may note, among others, the way in which a band of Gloucestershire 'regulators', coming from a farmhouse where they had discovered hidden wheat, not only positively responded to accusations that they had stolen some silver spoons by voluntarily searching all their members but, moreover, when they discovered the culprit, took him to the otherwise impotent magistracy and demanded his immediate incarceration.[20]

Clearly any civil disorder carries potential for a spectrum of action and motivation. The preponderance of moral economic behaviour nevertheless remains remarkable, particularly when set against a backcloth of increasingly extreme conditions of dearth and, as Wells argues for 1795–1800, even famine.[21] Thus, to take another example from Gloucestershire in 1766, we find that, in the same week as the 'spoons' incident, a crowd numbering over one thousand marched with flags, bands and banners some thirteen miles from Stroudwater to Cirencester, a major entrepôt between the corn country and the London market. There they staged an enormous forced sale of tons of corn, cheese and bacon. Nearly all food taken was paid for, if at the prices deemed fair by the crowd rather than at the inflated 'market' rate which the owners of the foodstuffs would have otherwise demanded.[22] But the point is that the crowd had no need to pay anything. They paid because they did not believe they were stealing and they did not act as thieves. As Dallaway, the High Sheriff of the county, recorded of these extensive riots, they 'pilfered very little'.[23]

Not all foodstuffs seized by rioters were even taken away. Flour and grain would often be destroyed in a public demonstration of communal punishment of those deemed guilty of immoral practices. This occurred most frequently at mills, as, for example, at Painswick in Gloucestershire, at Fisherton and Beckington in Wiltshire and at Greenham near Thatcham in Berkshire in 1766, where Richard Winter was accused of having 'flung away and destroyed the wheat flower'.[24] Given the very real pressures upon all consumers to find and to be able to afford their subsistence, such events are inexplicable except as reflections of a very deep belief in the values of the moral economy and in the need to make clear examples of those who transgressed its rules. Recognition that the rioters were both enforcers and avengers of a wider legitimacy was reflected in the way in which millers, bakers and farmers would sometimes take out advertisements to emphasise that *they* had not contravened the moral economy of the crowd by forestalling or engrossing grains and other foods. Thus B. Wingrove, a Bath corn miller, declared in 1766, 'I have this day made my oath that I never exported flour, corn or any thing whatever, in my life; neither do I sell any flour wholesale'. Gloucester bakers likewise publicised their claim that high prices in November 1795 were not of their making but the result of the 'extortion' of the dealers and farmers, while the following February they denounced jobbers as 'mere speculators' who had 'a very pernicious effect on the fair market'.[25] In so acting, they not only sought to protect their own property from attack: they also underlined the legitimacy of the crowd's actions against those who were deemed guilty.

Much of the debate on the moral economy in action has concentrated upon gentry/populace relations, ignoring the middling sort. This has been focused upon by Thompson's critics, with some validity.[26] Certainly, the middling sort played but little part in his 1971 paper. This has given rise to the view that the moral economy was exclusively a plebeian value system and one repudiated by the emerging middle class. However, recently some historians have addressed themselves to just this issue. Their findings are very suggestive. Thus, two recent studies of the middling sort in major regional trading and manufacturing cities (Bristol and Norwich) in times of food rioting indicate that, far from the values and attitudes of the moral economy being the preserve of the crowd, these values were also held by many in the superior urban classes.[27] While the middling sort usually possessed the opportunity, via the power of money, to exercise some choice, either by buying alternative commodities or by having access to stored food, they were far from endorsing the consequences of an unregulated food market. If the middling sort rarely joined in with market protesters,[28] their hostility to the jobber, forestaller and regrater in times of food scarcity was by no means negligible. Both Renton and Poole direct us to look again at the role of the press as both the moulders and reflectors of middling-sort opinion, teetering at times on the edge of endorsing protest against forestallers while concerned to maintain order. More such studies need to be carried out before we can ascertain whether the moral economy of the crowd may indeed have had a significantly wider social audience than Thompson suggested.

Even though the eighteenth century was a particularly riotous era, riot was, of course, not an everyday occurrence. This has been seized upon by critics of the moral economy thesis who have argued that food riots *per se* were too infrequent and scattered across the country to have sustained even a tradition of food rioting, let alone sustained the development of a more sophisticated moral economic outlook over the course of the eighteenth century. They point, as Williams has done, to the 'blank' areas on maps which record rioting and to the large preponderance of years without any such riots.[29] Such arguments, however, ignore the fact that 'riots' are notoriously difficult to locate and count.[30] This problem is further complicated by the fact that some historians register each 'event', while others record all incidents happening in an area over a period of time as one 'riot', as does Bohstedt in Chapter 3.[31] Furthermore, we should note that a full-blown market riot might not be necessary to secure the crowd's aim. A minor market fracas or peaceable demonstration – in the form of placards, threatening letters or simply an orderly deputation – might well alert the authorities to the need to intervene, to regulate or to punish those who were transparently breaking established market rules and culture. In some places, this was all the prompting that was needed, given the previous histories of vigorous crowd action. Such incidents would rarely leave any record.

This raises the question of why some communities were more willing to protest than were others. We have argued elsewhere that such communities were characterised by a high percentage of manufacturing workers and/or miners and were places where a strong collective labour consciousness had been forged by long and continuing experience of capitalist relations. Such communities had experience of large-scale conflicts over a wider range of problems than just food prices. They evinced a rich and constantly regenerating heritage of different forms of protest, stretching from minor mêlées over the market women's baskets to wide-ranging quarterings of the country in search of hidden granaries, through various forms of industrial protest and action to disorders occasioned by conflicts over gleaning rights, rights to collect fuel from local woodland and rights of commoners. In these and in other ways, a repertoire of protest forms was developed. Thus, 'the defence of particular customs became experiences that justified and reinforced belief in the moral economy and gave the crowd further resolve to go on to the streets to assert other customary rights when occasion arises, thereby further enriching the tradition'.[32] The impact of such an assertive crowd went far beyond a single event, both temporally and geographically. In regions such as industrial Cornwall, the Forest of

Dean, Essex, Stroudwater and west Wiltshire, history showed that the crowd was a force to be reckoned with. Even if they remained 'quiet' at any one stage, their latent power of protest could not be discounted. The threat they posed to public order, to the commercial life of town or city and to the 'face' and standing of the local ruling elite in the eyes of the Lord Lieutenant and Westminster meant that account had to be taken of popular attitudes.

The progression of protest, however, was not dependent entirely upon the crowd. It also depended upon the way in which the authorities, landlords and farmers behaved in the face of protest or, perhaps more often, in the face of incipient protest. The actions of the crowd were, we must remember, directed two ways: not only against the farmers, merchants and badgers to persuade or coerce them into making food available; but also towards the authorities whom the crowd expected to intervene in the market to ensure both supply and fairness. As Thompson saw, most eighteenth-century food riots were ultimately contained and managed by a theatre of concession and regulation which the model of the moral economy demanded and which food rioters expected.[33] The role of the authorities was a crucial one and seen by the crowd as such. As Thompson has observed, there was a field of force between crowd and gentry which was informed by the moral economy. The crowd were able to coerce their rulers into action on their behalf. But this action was prompted by more than fear, by more than the need to maintain law and order in the self-denied absence of an effective system of policing. The moral economy was the obverse of paternalism and the crowd was able to challenge their rulers to fulfil the role which they had assigned to themselves.

For the local authorities, riot, as Thompson pointed out, 'was a calamity'.[34] It was best avoided by pre-emptive action. Therefore periods of disturbance frequently brought forth well-publicised revivals of market regulation, pronouncements against illegal practices and notices from landlords ordering tenants to supply the poor at low prices or threatening immediate eviction for those discovered to be jobbing. Thus, in 1766 John Pitt, Hardwicke's steward, acidly noted how, once riot broke out,

> associations to prosecute [factors] were set on foot. Badgers, who would have brought corn into the country, were refused to be licensed for fear they should carry it out. Resolutions were agreed at all the meetings that all buyings and sellings but in open market were illegal ... you could not buy an egg or a pound of butter but at the tingling of a bell and on a particular spot.

To Pitt's displeasure, he was instructed by his employer to order tenants to release grain on to the market at the crowd's price. The *Bath Chronicle* noted:

A gentleman of fortune in this neighbourhood sent into market of Saturday last a quantity of wheat and ordered it to be sold at 5s a bushell. The same gentleman has warned out one of his tenants for being a jobber in cattle, etc, and is determined that no person concerned in jobbing cattle, corn, cheese, etc, shall rent any part of his estate.

Wiltshire landlords took similar action. After riots in Salisbury, some prominent farmers sent wheat to market 'and caused it to be published around the city by cryer that the poor might be served at 5s. 6d. and some at 5s.' Colonel Bathurst of Clarendon Park publicly ordered his bailiff to supply the local poor with wheat at 5s. a bushel while, at Urchfont, the Earl of Chatham ordered wheat to be sold at 4s. 6d. Similar actions were taken by Devizes and Chippenham gentry.[35] Such actions made little commercial sense, but they made for very good politics. If they prevented disorder, it was a price well worth paying. It often took a degree of prompting before the gentry donned their paternal hat and set about the task of reimposing order, not with a stick but with an olive branch. But, grudging or not, their actions confirmed the legitimacy of their own paternalist justification of the political order and, in turn, of the crowd's own actions. Moreover, every time this theatre of governance took place, it reinforced the crowd's belief in the moral economy.

This 'theatre' of riot has given rise to debate concerning the development of the 'classic' food riot. Chapter 3 by John Bohstedt in this volume addresses itself to this issue.[36] It is an interesting question whether or not food riots developed in form towards some sort of apogee. Certainly, we can discern evolution and development over time but whether a particular pattern of change can be shown to obtain over a wide geography is open to question. We are not inclined to think so. Riots reflected local and regional circumstances which were never exactly replicated across the country or even across time. There was no master plan. Riot was a dynamic force. Once triggered, riots might develop a momentum of their own. Why they were triggered and why in some places they developed beyond mere market fracas into something approaching *levées-en-masse* brings us to the critical question of developing community economic and political relations which is at the heart of the debate on the development and demise of the moral economy.[37] It is here that future research needs to be directed if we are to progress our knowledge and understanding of the forms, *mentalités* and management of eighteenth-century food riots. To do this, Edward Thompson's methodology of placing accounts of protest in a context of 'thick description' needs to be taken forwards towards attempting a 'total history' of riotous, and non-riotous, communities, a history which will take account of the changing social, economic and political context from which protest emanated and of the rich variety of forms which protest took. In particular, this involves moving away from the compartmentalisation of protest. While division of protests into different 'types' – food, industrial, political, customary, and so on – may be neater, it obscures our understanding of the very linkages which overarched them. More, it fails to take account of the fact that the participants in such dramas lived lives which were not neatly pigeon-holed. Unless we recognise this, we risk missing key moments or misunderstanding the motivations of those studied under the 'special sort of lens' of riot studies.

The Market, Markets and Market Cultures

The context of the moral economy thesis centres upon the consequences of changes in marketing practice in the eighteenth century occasioned by the so called 'rise of a national market'.[38] This debate has been informed on the one hand by historians of transport and of the agrarian economy and on the other by historians of economic thought. It has also, we might add, been coloured by the ideological ascendency of *laissez-faire* capitalism in the 1980s and 1990s, a very different ideological climate to that prevailing in the 1960s when Thompson was working on his original paper.

The impact of the establishment of a national market in grain, it is asserted, both engendered the demise of the old local market structure and created new opportunities for consumers, while the growing sway of the 'science' of political economy gave rise to new ways of understanding and conceptualising economic, and social, relations. These changes may, on the one hand, have engendered protest but on the other they provided the chance to evolve new values and attitudes. Thus Root, comparing food markets in eighteenth-century England and France, argues that, unlike the national market, the moral economic model served only 'narrow regional and occupational groups at the expense of general welfare'. The moral economic model, therefore, far from being a widespread popular value system, in fact characterised a selfish localism, the displacement of which advantaged a much wider consumer public.[39] Similarly, Bohstedt and Williams argue that, as the national market came to displace old narrow local economy, it also displaced the moral economy because people came to repudiate regulation for the opportunities of participation in a wider capitalist marketing system.[40]

Clearly there was significant change taking place in the marketing of food in later eighteenth-century England and, as Arnold shows in Chapter 5, in nineteenth-century India: both societies were peculiarly prone to food riots. Rapid population growth, improved communications, industrialisation and war were all factors which transformed the British national picture and meant that the extensive food riots of 1795 and 1800–1 would prove the last of their kind. While food riots were still evident in the nineteenth century, they were no longer the force they had formerly been. Yet, before we succumb to the view that this decline reflected a transformation in popular attitudes towards the 'new' 'national' market, we should first ask how far the consumer's real experience in the market actually changed, and at what speed, as the eighteenth century drew to a close.

There can be no doubt that the transport revolution opened up new regions to a trade in foodstuffs, above all grains, which burgeoned in the second half of the eighteenth century, aided by the results of the first great wave of parliamentary enclosure.[41] The development of ever-increasing volumes of grain shipments around the country depended upon a growing body of dealers and merchants whose operations became increasingly extensive. Such middlemen had been the objects of deep popular mistrust and resentment since the medieval period, possibly before. As their activities increased in the middle and later years of the eighteenth century, they were the first target of popular hostility, especially whenever prices rose rapidly and unaccountably. Thus, in 1765, the *Bath Journal* reported, 'We are informed that papers tending to inflame the minds of the people against the corn-jobbers have been stuck up in most of the market towns in this neighbourhood'.[42] Certainly, the food rioters in 1766, in 1795 and in 1800–1 all exhibited a common animosity towards middlemen, dealers and anyone suspected of 'exporting' grain. Grain and other foodstuffs in transit were frequently the target for crowd action. Dean miners regularly stopped grain barges on the Severn, to the consternation of the authorities, while at ports ships were frequently boarded and unloaded.[43] In inland areas, grain wagons were intercepted, while Wiltshire food rioters in 1766 were reported to be 'burning and pulling down the mills of those whom they know to be concerned in sending meal to Bristol for Exportation, a term become as shocking as that of a Bounty to starve the poor'.[44] The threat which such men's activities posed for local marketing structures and practices was significant, yet, in periods of relatively good harvests, might pass unchallenged, if not unnoticed, for a time. It was only when crisis or some apparent glaring injustice arose that trouble developed. At such times, the experience of middlemen, some of them plainly commodity speculators,[45] was an ambivalent one. On the one hand they were recognised as a necessary part of a trading and transport structure, in part created by the land-lords in order to boost their rentals. Yet those self-same landlords, wearing their magistrates' hats, would rapidly condemn them as fore-stallers and regraters when the need arose.

However, while changes were happening, there is no clear picture as to how they actually impacted upon the lived experience of the local consumer in the local market. Certainly everywhere there is evidence of the growth in the number of small shops as the so-called 'consumer revolution' developed.[46] As the century drew to a close, the poor increasingly obtained their bread ready-baked from bakers or hucksters, but the relative decline of the practice of buying grain, having it milled and then baked for the owner by a baker cannot be quantified. Certainly the ordinary consumer continued to purchase grain in signif-icant, if declining, quantities into the early nineteenth century.[47]

The rise of the dealer, of the purchase of standing crops or of gath-ered crops direct from the farm, all contributed to bring pressure upon the old pitching markets, as complaints in the 1760s indicate. Yet we must remember that the latter could easily be reinvigorated by crisis. Thus, as noted above, in Gloucestershire in 1766 pitching markets were rapidly revived when rioting swept through the county, indicating both that the mechanisms had not fallen into complete desuetude and that the authorities recognised that public opinion regarded such forms as the only acceptable way of conducting food marketing. The Chippenham market had continued to use the bell to signify its open-ing and closing but a cabal of engrossing farmers ensured that little grain was available for sale: 'though t'is true, to avoid the penalty of the law, they bring [corn] to market, yet the bargain is made before and the market is but a farce'. When riots broke out in 1766, the gentlemen of the town formed an association to stop corn being sold by sample and offered a reward of a guinea for information against anyone found so doing. The market was soon operating according to the old regula-tions, and supplying wheat at 5s. a bushel.[48]

The formality of the pitching market, the use of bells to signal the opening and closing of transactions, the differentiation of purchasers to prioritise small consumers from large ones, is easily portrayed as antediluvian or quaint. However, we might note that the practice was reflected in other markets unconnected to food: for example, the woollen cloth halls of the West Riding, where master clothiers brought their woven and fulled but unfinished cloths for sale, were all elaborately regulated by bells. This was by no means an industry or a region characterised by economic ossification. Aside from cotton, the Yorkshire woollen industry was the fastest growing part of the economy in late eighteenth-century Britain.[49] The model of regulated trading was a part of wider social and economic experience.

If the pitching market had a more lengthy and vigorous life than some have suggested, other indicators point to a much slower rate of general marketing change than some economic histories have suggested. The persistence of local grain measures in many regional markets, in spite of the obvious difficulties they created both for dealers and for those larger farmers seeking to produce for the national market, indicates that local custom and trust were more powerful agencies than simple marketing models might indicate. The failure of the regular attempts by the authorities to enforce compliance with the Statute of Winchester in parts of the West Midlands and in the West of England suggests that, rise of a national market or not, localism remained a vigorous factor in restraining change. This was amply demonstrated in Tetbury in 1768 when opposition to the Winchester measure erupted in a remarkable community protest:

> Wednesday last, an old venerable bushel containing nine gallons and a half adorned with trophies, was ordered into our market with drums and trumpet, bells and bonfire; and then conducted to the parish church, amidst the acclamation of all orders and degrees of men, regular and secular, and there suspended, to the terror and amazement of the farmers on the top of our lofty steeple.[50]

In west Wales too, hostility was strong, as was seen in Carmarthen in 1795 when a crowd assembled in the market, 'forcibly carried away the Winchester measure belonging to the corporation, and bore it away in triumph to a neighbouring iron forge, where they burnt it to pieces'.[51] Such resistance cannot simply be ascribed to backwardness or remoteness from national influences, for many of the markets which witnessed protest were themselves major national entrepôts in the grain trade. It was only from 1812 that this local resistance faded.[52]

If old corn measures were still to be found in major markets, local regulatory market mechanisms continued to inform practice in many important regional centres. Eighteenth-century Coventry had an elaborate system of corporate control, while a regulatory model of food marketing informed the actions of the civic authorities in Norwich, in Oxford and even among the free trading burghers of Bristol, a port city whose politics otherwise remained firmly in favour of freedom of trade but which was more than willing to utilise the power of the corporation to regulate markets to ensure food supplies and safeguard social peace in times of stress.[53] Here the Assize of Bread, what Clapham called 'a kind of economic common law',[54] provided another immediate, practicable and omnipresent model of interventionism and regulation in the food market. Its maintenance remained important throughout the French wars, and even in London it was not until 1822 that the Assize was finally abolished.[55] The impact of these mechanisms was to reinforce the model of regulation and the moral economy as the 'just' and appropriate mechanism for the distribution of staple foodstuffs. Many justices shared this view. Wells notes of the 1795 riots, 'Magistrates ... frequently revealed their own sympathies by supporting the crowd with formal injunctions.'[56]

Likewise, the role the state itself played in the management and manipulation of the grain market in the eighteenth century, and for the earlier period, demands careful attention for it could have major impacts upon the marketing and availability of grain. The subtle utilisation of the eighteenth-century corn laws to maintain domestic prices through the bounty-assisted export of grain surpluses could at times go horribly wrong, as was shown in 1766 when failure to suspend the bounty system encouraged dealers to 'drain the country' in a time of impending acute shortage.[57] Later governments sought to control the availability and distribution of grain on a wide scale. This was particularly seen in the attempt to regulate the balance of grain between the English and Irish markets in 1799–1801.[58] And, at the very highest levels of state when Kenyon was Lord Chief Justice, as Hay shows in Chapter 4, there was concern that the courts should act firmly to protect the interests of the consumer. Kenyon's intervention in the crisis of 1795/6 had direct bearing on the way markets operated, encouraging the bench to prosecute forestallers and regraters. This had a particular impact in Staffordshire where the bench embarked upon a major campaign of enforcement.[59] The crowd were far from the only group seeking to manipulate the ways in which food markets operated throughout the century.

All these examples suggest that the transformation from a model primarily based upon local partly regulated exchange to a national consumer-driven unregulated market was neither fast nor uniform. They also raise fundamental questions about the assertions that the crowd in general approved of such changes in marketing practice. For example, Williams criticises Thompson's portrayal of the crowd as hostile to the rise of an unregulated market in grain. It was, he argues, the 'imperatives of the market economy', not of a moral economy, which determined their actions. The crowd could in no way be described as hostile to the new market system 'since they were, and had long been, members of the same market system'.[60] Bohstedt likewise notes a popular approval for the 'promise' of the liberated market.[61] Yet what that 'promise' might have been seen as being is by no means clear.

Such arguments, as Thompson pointed out,[62] smack as much of ideology as of recovery of the real experience of consumers, for we must remember that, for them, the market, in whichever model form, was (and had long been) the only game in town. They could obtain their subsistence in no other way. The 'market' was not something new in the mid- and later eighteenth century. Markets of one sort or another had long since dominated the lives of all descriptions of labourers and petty producers. Small town artisans and labour aristocrats, out-parish weavers, remote-dwelling colliers and tinners, all had ample knowledge of and experience in markets, a point reiterated by John Rule in Chapter 7.[63] They sold their labour in a labour market, they sold their commodities in product markets and they bought their staple food – bread – in food markets, either as grain to be ground by millers on commission, as flour or as freshly baked bread from bakers or hucksters. Markets were an integral part of everyone's daily lives. This was why a market culture had developed which proved so ubiquitous and tenacious in defence of established and popularly-sanctioned mechanisms. The market was a matrix within which a range of actions, aspirations and values were housed. The moral economy market model was therefore not an *alternative* to a capitalist market but a model of a capitalist market subject to careful regulation. It was in reality no more entirely 'regulated' than the market structure which supplanted it later was entirely 'free'. All markets embody aspects of both for, in truth, they reflect shifting balances of power between those with commodities to sell, those wishing to buy them and the state which requires that commerce should enrich and not threaten political security. Crowd, authorities and dealers recognised this. It was only the new political economists who sought to abstract markets and divorce them both from the people who cut the deals and from the context in which they cut them.

There is not enough space here to pursue the debate between Thompson and historians of economic thought concerning the ideological provenance and 'morality' of the new political economy. While the latter have criticised Thompson for misrepresenting 'the Smithian position', their own position remains, as Thompson noted, confined to the development of ideas within the world of academic salons.[64] Interesting though they may be *per se*, it was only at the point when these ideas began to influence or to legitimate action, at national or at local level, that we may say they impacted upon real markets as distinct from theoretical ones.

In truth, this impact was by no means rapid. While *The Wealth of Nations* proved the most systematic and comprehensive argument in favour of 'freedom', the debate over the liberalisation of the grain market long pre-dated it.[65] Yet there is little evidence that any of this debate had much impact upon the way in which those charged with responsibility for the preservation of public order either behaved in their dealings in the marketplace or understood the functioning of the market. Indeed, while history shows *laissez-faire* ideology ultimately to have triumphed, it was far from dominating the market in ideas before the turn of the century. Recent research upon the voluminous pamphlet material on the subject of the provision of food in the years 1750–1810 in fact reveals a surprisingly vigorous retention of the old moral economic models.[66] The case for a removal of regulation remained the view of a minority. This was not only true of benighted provincials. As Hay shows in Chapter 4, the 'intellectual' context of the Waddington case, heard at the highest legal level, was far from being one in which the forces for free markets were predominant in the closing years of the century.

To conclude, there was no clear bi-polar split between a world run on moral economic lines and one based upon the new political economy. Markets, like societies, are places of negotiation and compromise. What we discern is not seismic change but a process of gradual shift. This should not occasion surprise, least of all in eighteenth-century England. Seismic change, it was feared, might produce revolution. The authorities were not about to take that sort of risk, particularly when their power rested on a nice balance between coercion and negotiation held within the tenacious tentacles of custom. Change certainly came, particularly after 1800, but 'the imperatives of the market economy' were less important than the political context of war with revolutionary

France and escalating fears of Jacobinism at home in motivating the state towards rapid abandonment of old regulatory modes and models. The triumph of political economy owed more to politics than to economics.[67]

A Ubiquitous Value System?

A third area of debate concerning the moral economy thesis revolves around the question of whether or not the concept may properly and prudently be applied outside the chronological and geographical context of its origin, namely interpreting food riots in eighteenth-century England. Was the moral economy not merely a strategic philosophy concerning the morality of food distribution mechanisms but also a concept applicable to other areas of economic life and to other forms of popular protest? Was it indeed a value system to be found not only in eighteenth-century Britain but also in developing societies more widely?

Thompson was by no means sure. While acknowledging that others had taken his model and applied it to other areas of social and economic conflict, he was at best half-hearted in his endorsement of some attempts and applications. Noting his use of the term in the short discussion of food riots in *The Making of the English Working Class* published in 1963, Thompson argued in *Customs in Common* that his employment of the term thereafter had been confined to food riot situations:

It is not only that there is an identifiable bundle of beliefs, usages and forms associated with the marketing of food in time of dearth which it is convenient to bind together in a common term, but the deep emotions stirred by dearth, the claims which the crowd made upon the authorities in such crises, and the outrage provoked by profiteering in life-threatening emergencies, imparted a particular 'moral' charge to protest. All of this, taken together, is what I understand by moral economy.

He continues, 'If the term is to be extended to other contexts, then it must be redefined or there will be some loss of focus.'[68]

We can certainly agree that there is no merit in utilising the term 'moral economy' as a catch-all simply to denote 'tradition' or mere conservatism of any one social or economic group. Neither would we dispute the peculiar importance which was attached to food, above all to bread, the very staff of life. Certainly, the need to provision the poor was seen as a major 'moral' and political concern of the state across Europe, certainly from medieval times as Sharp shows in Chapter 2, and it remains to this day a pressing matter for many Third World countries.[69] The consequence in Britain was a paternal model of political economy which reflected the belief that, while the rights of property were generally inviolable, other rights or entitlements might, in the circumstances of the food market, be deemed to be of superior importance.

The moral economy was, though, more than just 'a bundle of beliefs, usages and forms'. Its strength, and what turned a 'value system' into a dynamic and regenerating force, was the fact that it was underpinned by the sanction of law, both statute and common. The key empowering and legitimising factor behind the moral economy of the crowd was the fact that they knew that the law provided the consumer with certain protections against rapacious farmers, dealers and factors, as Hay argues in Chapter 4.[70] The existence of legal controls and sanctions determined the parameters within which the various protagonists in food riots operated, giving the crowd their confidence to act and to demand reciprocal actions. Thus, food rioters frequently proclaimed they were acting in the name of the law or of the King. 'Many that are under sentence of death', wrote John Pitt, a fierce critic of the 1766 Gloucestershire food rioters, 'thought they were doing a meritorious act at the very moment they were forfeiting their lives'.[71] In other circumstances, actions like these would have seemed extremely presumptuous, not to say hazardous. Had protesting industrial workers, for example, regularly seized the property of their employers and sold it on amongst themselves, there can be little doubt that the state would have reacted very harshly indeed. The old statutes and common law precedents concerning food marketing created the space in which protest could thrive.

It was not simply the existence of laws or the readiness of the crowd to riot which made the moral economy so potent an ideology, however. It was the willingness of the courts, magistracy and gentleman to enforce the law, even if it were done in an increasingly unenthusiastic fashion, which made it work. The moral economy was as much about the negotiation of power as about actual rights. The bases of this power lay in the relative strengths, and weaknesses, of crowd and authorities and in the willingness of each to accede to aspects of the other's demands. Here we see the real theatre of riot, the theatre of negotiation described by Thompson, in action. When one party stopped playing by the old rules, indeed ceased to believe in the efficacy of the old rules, the moral economy of the crowd was fatally threatened. Riot and moral economic action drew upon, as Thompson said, values and attitudes which were common to governors and governed alike.

How far can these characteristics – conflicting economic interests, a basis in statute or customary law for regulation and for balancing different rights, authorities willing to intervene and regulate – be discerned in other theatres of social and economic conflict? Two such areas can be examined here.

Large-scale industrial disputes in eighteenth-century England shared certain characteristics with the food riot. Industrial workers, particularly weavers, tinners and colliers were prominent among food rioters.[72] This has led some historians of labour to make use of the moral economy model in their interpretation of industrial action and attitudes. Of these Thompson conceded that he was 'more than half persuaded' by Randall's use of the term in describing the 'industrial moral economy' of the Gloucestershire handloom weavers. 'But where are we to draw the line?' Not that far, in fact, as his critique of Reddy's use of the term in an industrial context showed.[73] This is a view reinforced by Rule in Chapter 7 who suggests a rather different philosophical basis for the *mentalités* of the artisans. Yet Thompson himself was not quite so limited in his utilisation of the term in *The Making of the English Working Class*. Here, as well as the use noted concerning food riots, he also referred to 'the moral economy of the "trade"' of those involved in Luddism. Of the small master clothiers of Yorkshire, he wrote 'The small masters who supported the "Institution", or "Clothiers' Community", between 1802 and 1806 had at their backs a general theory of moral economy', while further noting that 'the tradition of the just price and the fair wage lived longer among "the lower orders" than is sometimes supposed. They saw *laissez faire*, not as freedom, but as "foul imposition".' And indeed, in the 1971 'moral economy' paper itself Thompson referred to 'the paternal model of the marketing *and manufacturing* process' (our italics) which informed the crowd's 'belief that they were defending traditional rights or customs'.[74]

We might remind ourselves that the woollen industry was much circumscribed by a very large body of regulatory legislation of ancient lineage. In the case of the Gloucestershire weavers in 1756, their appeals were directly to this legal corpus for redress. When the existing law could not be made to work, they successfully sought a new act and attempted, successfully, to apply it through the courts, if only for a time. This legal basis also underlay the campaign by the weavers of Gloucestershire, Wiltshire and Somerset and by the master clothiers of Yorkshire in 1803 to protect their 'rights' from the new mill owners who, recognising in the old statutes mechanisms which could be utilised to impede their own objective of transforming the woollen industry, were seeking to have all the old legislation repealed as 'obsolete'.[75] The woollen industry was in some respects a special case but other trades too had a body of law to protect them, as the example of the Spitalfields silk weavers shows. Thus Steinberg refers to the Spitalfields Acts as 'one pillar of a moral economy of trade and community relations championed by the [Spitalfields] weavers'. Their actions in defence of their trade had much in common with food riots.[76] A similar case might also be advanced to account for the attitudes behind the Apprenticeship Campaign fought by the artisans in the years from 1809 to 1813. Here again we see values expressed which support a view of industrial relations in which the rights of capital and of labour were to be considered of equal worth, to be equally upheld by the local and national authorities, if necessary via the courts.[77] The Lancashire Weavers' Association in 1799 spiritedly rejected the political economy of an unregulated labour market and demanded a legislative mechanism to fix wage rates: 'The price of Labour neither is, nor ought to be, governed by the demand...we believe the legislature might adopt regulations which would make the demand both regular and increasing,'[78] Were these, as Thompson once seemed to suggest, aspects of moral economy?

The debate over whether the concept of moral economy can be used to interpret the attitudes of industrial groups defending customary economies raises the question as to whether the moral economy was specifically a value system of workers who had yet to acquire a 'labour consciousness'. Rule's chapter suggests this sort of line of argument, seeing in the arguments advanced by the artisans in trade disputes a *mentalité*, aggressive rather than defensive, which is markedly different to that of the moral economy. Artisans may certainly be seen as having a stronger trade consciousness than other working groups by virtue of their higher skill, their combinational strength, their 'exclusivity'. And yet. We must not overdo the picture of the isolated craftsman, safe in his (for it is always his) trade, concerned both to keep out the unskilled and to extort ever better conditions from employers through a judicious use of the ratchet of 'custom'. Certainly the trades preserved their position by a careful regulation of recruitment. Allowing only one son to be apprenticed in a shop at any one time, only one apprentice per journeyman, kept numbers limited and the masters always on the look-out for labour. But the 'privilege' which preserved jobs for one son, usually the eldest, also often excluded other younger sons.

They had, perforce, to find trades elsewhere. In the textile industries, for example, this usually meant weaving. This should warn us to be cautious about neat compartmentalisation of the labour force into skilled/unskilled categories and assuming in consequence that there was no social, or riotous, intercourse between. Kinship cut across trades. And all labour, skilled or otherwise, depended upon the market for their food supply. All were conscious of their common status as consumers.

If there was an industrial moral economy, was there an agrarian one? Historians of eighteenth- and early nineteenth-century rural England have utilised the concept of the moral economy as an explanatory tool with which to comprehend the conflicts of the countryside, most notably by Snell. He argued that popular attitudes to settlement rights, to the poor law and to yearly hiring formed 'a consistent part of those "moral economy" values analysed by E. P. Thompson'. Thompson was very critical of this appropriation of the concept[79] but others too have seen the countryside as the last redoubt of old paternal values and of moral economic actions. Thus Bushaway has taken up the moral economy concept under the guise of 'customary society' to show the ways in which the old reciprocities of the paternalist/moral economy matrix continued to inform values in the countryside well into the nineteenth century.[80] While Mandler has argued that old paternalist attitudes among the gentry had been supplanted by a new attitude by the 1830s,[81] social historians have seen in the Swing riots of 1830 parallels with earlier food riots: the collection of support under banners and flags; the limited, property-directed, violence; the strong sense of order and legitimacy; the appeals to, and the coercion of, the gentry to act against 'immoral' practices.[82] This case is developed in depth in Chapter 9 by Wells who, noting Thompson's identification of the need to specify the moral economy within a 'particular historical formation', reinforces Snell's belief in a rural moral economy.

If the moral economy survived into the nineteenth century among rural labourers and some industrial workers, it might be wondered how far it influenced or retarded the development of popular political ideas and attitudes. O'Brien's use of the term in 1837, as noted by Thompson,[83] was more an evocation of a departed, and perhaps idealised, domestic system of production than of a tradition of paternal regulation; he would certainly not have entertained support for a political system dependent upon gentlemanly paternalism. Nevertheless, the model of a state which regulated the power of rampant industrial capital, that bore due attention towards the suffering of the poor, that ensured a proper distribution of provisions, was one to which many radicals would subscribe. Indeed, in the writings of men such as Cobbett and Oastler, echoes of the old moral economy may be caught among the attacks upon a new rapacious capitalist ethic.[84] They can be heard too from the determinedly non-political pen of Gloucestershire handloom weaver Timothy Exell whose *History* of the weavers written in 1838 reiterated demands for regulation and a return to older moral economic values.[85]

If the extension of the moral economy thesis to other aspects of eighteenth- and early nineteenth-century English economic and political relations gives rise to debate, this is even more the case when the concept is applied outside the contextual confines of English history. To quote Michael Adas, 'a pattern identified in one society and historical period may not be transferable, at least without major modifications, to others that are fundamentally different'.[86] Yet it is here we find the most radical and exciting extension of Thompson's original concept.

In the case of North America, the problem of transferability might not be deemed too wide a stretch, given the very strong links which existed in culture and attitude between the colonies and Britain. Countryman asks in Chapter 6 how far the values of the moral economy were translated across the Atlantic into the different soil and distinctive social conditions which existed there. He suggests a legacy may be discerned in the politics of revolutionary America.

The American colonies were rarely severely short of food. The same could not be said for nineteenth-century India where very extensive food riots broke out across the sub-continent on numerous occasions. Given their very different context and evolution, Arnold none the less asks in Chapter 5 if food riots in fact have a substance and motivation which is common across both continents and time. The attitude of the British ruling class certainly provided a common factor here, as in Ireland, though by the nineteenth century the official policy of the colonial state had become firmly entrenched in the principles of *laissez-faire* and, in India, in a policy of strict non-interference. Yet, as Arnold shows, this policy could not always survive in the face of incipient riot or impending dearth. He raises here interesting questions concerning the utilisation of paternal action as a counterweight to actual or threatened disorder which have real resonance for those examining English food riots. Likewise, the Indian exploration raises issues concerning the transitional nature of the food riot and the moral economy. These issues might with advantage be pursued by those examining the sudden decline of food riots in Britain after 1812.

If studies of food riots in India and of the impact of the moral economy in eighteenth-century North America might be seen as having some commonality with Thompson's principal focus, the same cannot be said of those studies which seek to apply the moral economy model to an examination of modern peasant societies. Indeed, it is in the use of the concept by anthropologists and development theorists, working upon modern peasant societies, that we see the widest departure from the original context in which Thompson placed his original delineation. Thompson himself was, given his scepticism towards the extension of the concept to other eighteenth-century protests, surprisingly positive about this development:

> Much of the very interesting discussion which is now extending under the rubric of 'moral economy' from African and Asian to Latin American or to Irish Studies has little to do with my (1971) usage but is concerned with the social dialectic of unequal mutuality (need and obligation) which lies at the centre of most societies. The term 'moral economy' has won acceptance because it is less cumbersome than other terms.[87]

At the forefront of this application of the moral economy is the work of James C. Scott.[88] His contribution to this volume, Chapter 8, places the moral economy and its various facets, the reciprocal 'micro-politics of class relations', customary practices and patterns of paternalism, at the centre of his account of the power relations which determine the pattern of peasant life. In particular, he shows that the poor are not prepared to accept the loss of customary rights and subsistence expectations tamely, Utilising the 'weapons of the weak', pressure could be applied in many and subtle ways upon both landlords and authorities in order to safeguard popular versions of entitlements in the face of predatory attack. This emphasis upon entitlements as something popularly defined rather than simply as a legal and economistic notion likewise powerfully confronts the argument put forward by Sen concerning the response to famine in the twentieth century.[89] Moreover, Scott points the way for historians of eighteenth-century England to explore in greater depth the ways in which crowd, landlords, dealers and authorities interacted in times when riot did not break out. As suggested above, it is in these smaller details that we may discover new aspects of moral economic action.

Conclusion

The reader of this volume will make up his or her own mind as to whether Thompson's concept of the moral economy continues to retain its validity and, indeed, whether it can with advantage be extended further into new aspects of the economic and social relations concerning subsistence. However one answers these questions, what is striking is the way in which, some 25 years on, the moral economy thesis is still at the centre of debates, still at the cutting edge of ways in which to understand and decipher economic and social relations in periods of transition. That it should still have such a power a quarter of a century after its publication is testimony both to the formidable intellect which fathered it and to the inspirational qualities found within it. As one participant at the Moral Economy conference in Birmingham put it, the moral economy is a veritable 'Heineken' of a concept:[90] it refreshes those parts that other concepts cannot reach. We will drink to that.

...mpson, 'The moral economy of the English crowd in the eighteenth century', *Past and Present*, 50 (1971), quotations from pp. 77, 78, 79, 83. The article is reprinted in E.P. Thompson, *Customs in Common* (London: Merlin, 1991).
2. Principal national studies are J. Bohstedt, *Riots and Community Politics in England and Wales 1790–1810* (Cambridge, Mass.: Harvard University Press, 1983); A. Charlesworth (ed.), *An Atlas of Rural Protest in Britain 1548–1900* (London: Croom Helm, 1983) ch. 3; R. Wells, *Wretched Faces: Famine in Wartime England 1793–1801* (Gloucester: Alan Sutton, 1988); R. C. Cobb, *The Police and the People: French Popular Protest Movements 1789–1820* (Oxford: Oxford University Press 1970); C. Tilly, *The Contentious French: Four Centuries of Popular Struggle* (Cambridge, Mass.: Harvard University Press, 1987); M. Gailus, *Straase und Brot: Sozialer Protest in den deustchen Staaten unter besonderer Beruckksichtigung Preussens, 1847–1849* (Gottingen: Vandenhoek & Ruprecht, 1990); R. Bin Wong, 'Food riots in the Quing dynasty', *Journal of Asian Studies*, xli (1982), pp. 767–88; for an account of post-1945 food riots in the Third World see J. Walton and D. Seddon, *Free Markets and Food Riots: the Politics of Global Adjustment* (Oxford: Blackwell, 1994).
3. A. Sen, *Poverty and Famines: An Essay on Entitlement and Deprivation* (Oxford: Oxford University Press, 1981). For a powerful critique of Sen, see C. Gore, 'Entitlement relations and "unruly" social practices: a comment on the work of Amartya Sen', *Journal of Development Studies*, 29 (1993), pp. 429–60. This paper was given at the Moral Economy Conference.
4. J. C. Scott, *The Moral Economy of the Peasant: Rebellion and Subsistence in Southeast Asia* (New Haven, Conn.: Yale University Press, 1976), p. vii.
5. Thompson, *Customs in Common*, p. 351.

6. For an excellent overview, see R. Wells, 'E. P. Thompson, *Customs in Common* and moral economy', *Journal of Peasant Studies*, 21 (1994), p. 297.
7. See, for example, J. Walter, 'Grain riots and popular attitudes to the law: Maldon and the crisis of 1629', in J. Brewer and J. Styles (eds), *An Ungovernable People: The English and their Law in the Seventeenth and Eighteenth Centuries* (London: Hutchinson, 1980), ch. 2.
8. Thompson, *Customs in Common*, pp. 259–60. The three separate studies that emerged were Thompson's 'Moral economy' paper; Cobb, *The Police and the People* (1970); and G. A. Williams, *Artisans and Sans-culottes* (London: Edward Arnold, 1968).
9. A. Appadurai, 'How moral is South Asia's economy – a review article', *Journal of Asian studies*, xliii (1984), p. 482.
10. Principal critics include D. E. Williams, 'Morals, markets and the English crowd in 1766', *Past and Present*, 104 (1984), pp. 56–73; J. Bohstedt, 'The moral economy and the discipline of historical context', *Journal of Social History*, Winter 1992, pp. 265–84; J. Stevenson, 'The "moral economy" of the English crowd: myth and reality', in A. Fletcher and J. Stevenson (eds), *Order and Disorder in Early Modern England* (Cambridge: Cambridge University Press, 1985).
11. On women and food riots, see M. I. Thomis and J. Grimmett, *Women in Protest, 1800–1850* (London: Croom Helm, 1982), ch. 2; J. Bohstedt, 'Gender, household and community politics: women in English riots, 1790–1810', *Past and Present*, 120 (1988), pp. 88–122, which refers to 'the myth of the feminine food riot' (pp. 90, 93); and Thompson, *Customs in Common*, pp. 305–36 for a forceful critique of Bohstedt.
12. In the riots in Gloucestershire and Wiltshire in 1766 none of the incidents in which only women were involved saw the victims receive any money for bread or other foodstuffs seized. Dallaway (High Sheriff of Gloucestershire) noted that the Gloucestershire regulators 'will not now suffer women and boys to go with them' to avoid accusations of pilfering. Public Record Office (hereafter PRO), P.C. 1/8/41, Dallaway to Conway, 20 September 1766.
13. PRO, P.C. 1/8/41, Dallaway to Conway, 17 September 1766.
14. W. Thwaites, 'Oxford food riots: a community and its markets', in A. J. Randall and A. Charlesworth (eds), *Markets, Market Culture and Popular Protest in Eighteenth-century Britain and Ireland* (Liverpool: Liverpool University Press, 1996), pp. 37–162; S. Poole, 'Scarcity and the civic tradition: market management in Bristol, 1709–1815', idem., p. 98.
15. PRO, T.S. 11/995/3707, evidence of Edward Titcomb; PRO, H.O. 42/35, Philips to Portland, 24 August 1795. We are grateful to James Taylor and Chris Rogers for these examples.
16. W. J. Shelton, *English Hunger and Industrial Disorders* (London: Macmillan, 1973), p.124, notes and supports this view that army and militia veterans led the mobs because 'the restraint and honesty of the mobs in the early stages of the riots suggest a rudimentary organisation and leadership which would have proved beyond the capacity of untrained rustics'. Cf. A. J. Randall, 'The Gloucestershire food riots of 1766' in *Midland History*, X (1985), p. 84.
17. See, for example, Bohstedt, Chapter 3, note 34.

18. Shelton, for example, identifies a deterioration in the standards of honesty of the crowd as riots spread or continued: Shelton, *English Hunger*, pp. 124–5.

19. Thwaites, 'Oxford food riots', pp. 147–9, 152–6.

20. British Library (hereafter BL), Hardwicke Mss, Pitt to Hardwicke, 29 September 1766.

21. Wells, *Wretched Faces*, ch. 4.

22. PRO, P.C. 1/8/41, Bathurst to Conway, received 23 September 1766; W.O. 4/80, D'Oyle to Bathurst, 6 October 1766; T.S. 11/1128, cases against Sawyer, Onion, Belcher, Haines.

23. PRO, P.C. 1/8/41, Dallaway to Conway, 20 September 1766. Pitt noted to Hardwicke, 'Their chief direction seems to be against the corn being carried out of the land and this leads them to the flour.' B. M., Hardwicke Mss, Pitt to Hardwicke, 29 September 1766.

24. PRO, P.C. 1/8/41, Dallaway to Conway, 17 September 1766; *Salisbury and Winchester Gazette*, 22, 29 September 1766; *Aris's Birmingham Gazette*, 22, 29 September 1766; B.M., Hardwicke Mss, Harris to Hardwicke, 3 October 1766; PRO, T.S. 11/995/3707, evidence of Robert Goaty; see also Thompson, 'Moral economy', pp. 114–5.

25. *Bath Journal*, 29 September 1766; *Gloucester Journal*, 2 November 1795; 8 February 1796.

26. See, for example, D. E. Williams, 'Morals, markets and the English crowd', pp. 71–2; Bohstedt, 'The moral economy and the discipline of historical context', p. 279.

27. On Bristol, see Poole, 'Scarcity and the civic tradition': on Norwich, see S. Renton, 'The moral economy of the English middling sort in the eighteenth-century: the case of Norwich in 1766 and 1767', both in Randall and Charlesworth (eds), *Markets, Market Culture and Popular Protest*.

28. This was not always the case. Thus, in January 1801, John Ladd, the mayor of the little town of Newport in Pembrokeshire, himself led a crowd, which had assembled to protest against high prices, off on a visit to the home of the two local magistrates. Finding them away, the mob returned towards Newport but Ladd persuaded them to reassemble in the town, with all their friends and their money, on the following market day, when grain would be supplied at low prices. He was later arrested for his trouble and held in gaol for three following market days: D. Jones, *Before Rebecca: Popular Protests in Wales, 1793–1835* (London: Allen Lane, 1973), pp. 25–6.

29. D. E. Williams, 'Morals, markets and the English crowd', p. 70. See also Stevenson, 'The "moral economy" of the English crowd', p. 67.

30. See R. Wells, 'Counting riots in eighteenth-century England', *Bulletin of the Society for the Study of Labour History*, XXXVII (1978), pp. 68–72. The author-ities had very good reason for ensuring that market disturbances received little publicity, a view shared by the local press. Thus, after recording the earliest food riots in the country in early September 1766, the *Gloucester Journal* then maintained a silence on the subject until 6 October: 'We have hitherto been unwilling to speak of the late conduct of our unhappy neigh-bours in the manufacturing part of this county.'

31. See Chapter 3 note 21: 'I count … as one event all crowd violence that takes place in contiguous districts within the same week.' We would argue that, while recognising that there were frequently common personnel from local incident to incident, lumping together all events over 'contiguous districts'

in this way runs the very real risk of conflating very different circumstances, participants and actions.

32. A. Charlesworth and A. J. Randall, 'Comment: morals, markets and the English crowd in 1766', in *Past and Present*, 114 (1987), p. 208.
33. E. P. Thompson, 'Eighteenth-century English society: class struggle without class?', *Social History*, 3 (1978), p. 151. This element of 'theatre' is echoed by Bohstedt in J. Bohstedt, *Riots and Community Politics*, pp. 27–68.
34. Thompson, 'Moral economy', p. 122. See also p. 126, 'riot was a social calamity'.
35. B. M., Hardwicke Mss, Pitt to Harwicke, 29 September 1766; *Bath Chronicle*, 20 October 1766; *Salisbury and Winchester Journal*, 22 September, 13, 27 October 1766; *Bath Chronicle*, 30 October 1766. Not all such actions stemmed from political pragmatism. Some, perhaps many, gentlemen strongly endorsed the paternal model and took positive actions to alleviate food crises. Like others in September 1800, Rev. William Holland of Over Stowey in Somerset lamented the rising cost of grain, but he determined 'to thresh out a few bushells and divide it into pecks at a low price'. His hopes that other farmers in the parish would follow were disappointed. 'I wish I could prevail on the Farmers to sell their wheat to the Parish at the rate of ten shillings a bushell', his diary noted in October: J. Ayres (ed.), *Paupers and Pig Killers: The Diary of William Holland, a Somerset Parson, 1799–1818* (Hardmondsworth: Penguin, 1984), pp. 46, 47–8.
36. For a definition of 'the classic food riot', see also Bohstedt, *Riots and Community Politics*, pp. 27–68.
37. Charlesworth and Randall, 'Comment: morals, markets', pp. 206–9; and see also A. Charlesworth, 'From the moral economy of Devon to the political economy of Manchester, 1790–1812', *Social History*, 18, 2 (1993), pp. 205–17.
38. For a useful overview of this process, see M. Daunton, *Progress and Poverty: An Economic and Social History of Britain 1700–1850* (Oxford: Oxford University Press, 1995), pp. 320–7.
39. H. Root, *The Fountain of Privilege* (Berkeley, Cal.: University of California Press, 1994), p. 85.
40. Williams, 'Morals, markets and the English crowd', p. 73; Bohstedt, 'The moral economy and the discipline of historical context', p. 268.
41. See, for example, J. A. Chartres, 'The marketing of agricultural produce', in J. Thirsk (ed.), *Agricultural History of England and Wales, Vol. 5, 1640–1750* (Cambridge: Cambridge University Press, 1985); R. Perren, 'Markets and marketing', in G. E. Mingay (ed.), *Agrarian History of England and Wales, Vol. 6, 1750–1850* (Cambridge: Cambridge University Press, 1989).
42. *Bath Journal*, 25 March 1765.
43. Sir George Onesipherous Paul lamented in 1795, 'they think it justifiable to seize this vessel and sell the corn': WO 1/1091, Paul to War Office 20 July 1795. Magistrates at Fishguard, on the other hand, appear to have condoned the seizure of butter from a ship in the port in 1795, where the rudder was removed from the vessel on the 'recommendation of the magistrates': PRO, H.O. 42/37, Knox to Portland, 29 December 1975.
44. *Aris's Birmingham Gazette*, 29 September 1766.
45. A rare direct insight into the operations of such speculators can be seen in the account of the way in which the Dublin corn merchant firm of Jebb & Co. attempted to manipulate the Irish market at a time of extreme dearth

in 1799–1801 in R. Wells, 'The Irish famine of 1799–1801: market culture, moral economies and social protest', in Randall and Charlesworth, *Markets, Market Culture and Popular Protest*, pp. 175–6.

46. See, for example, N. McKendrick, J. Brewer and J. H. Plumb, *The Birth of a Consumer Society: The Commercialization of Eighteenth-Century England* (London: Europa, 1982); and J. Brewer and R. Porter (eds), *Consumption and the World of Goods* (London: Routledge, 1993).

47. W. Thwaites, 'The corn market and economic change: Oxford in the eighteenth century', *Midland History*, XVI (1991), pp. 103–25. Cobbett, in 1821, railed: 'How, wasteful, then and indeed how shameful, for a labourer's wife to go to the baker's shop.' He recognised that, 'In London, or in any very large town', obtaining and storing fuel might be difficult, 'but in all other situations there appears to me to be hardly any excuse for not making bread at home': W. Cobbett, *Cottage Economy* (London, 1822: reprinted by Cedric Chivers, 1975), pp. 54, 62–3.

48. B. M., Hardwicke Mss, Pitt to Hardwicke, 29 September 1766; Montague to Shelburne, 30 October 1766, *Calendar of Home Office Papers, 1766–1769* (London, 1897), p. 91; *Salisbury and Winchester Journal*, 13 October 1766; PRO, W.O. 4/80, Barrington to Bonham, 30 September 1766.

49. On the woollen industry of Yorkshire, see P. Hudson, *The Genesis of Industrial Capital: A Study of the West Riding Wool Textile Industry 1750–1850* (Cambridge: Cambridge University Press, 1986); R.G. Wilson, 'The supremacy of the Yorkshire cloth industry in the eighteenth century' in N. B. Harte and K. G. Ponting (eds), *Textile History and Economic History* (Manchester: Manchester University Press, 1973); W.B. Crump, *The Leeds Woollen Industry* (Leeds: Thoresby Society, 1931); A. J. Randall, *Before the Luddites: Custom, Community and Machinery in the English Woollen Industry 1776–1809* (Cambridge: Cambridge University Press, 1991).

50. *Gloucester Journal*, 25 April 1768.

51. *Felix Farley's Bristol Journal*, 7 March 1795.

52. For a wider discussion of this opposition, see R. Sheldon, Randall, Charlesworth and Walsh, 'Popular protest and the persistence of customary corn measures: resistance to the Winchester corn bushel in the English West', in Randall and Charlesworth, *Markets, Market Culture and Popular Protest*.

53. Renton, 'The moral economy of the English middling sort'; Thwaites, 'Oxford food riots'; Poole, 'Scarcity and the civic tradition'; all in Randall and Charlesworth (eds), *Markets, Market Culture and Popular Protest*.

54. Sir J. H. Clapham, *An Economic History of Modern Britain: The Early Railway Age* (Cambridge: Cambridge University Press, 1950), p. 344.

55. Stevenson, 'The "moral economy"', p. 230.

56. Wells, *Wretched Faces*, p. 110.

57. Shelton, *English Hunger and Industrial Disorders*, ch. 1; D.E. Williams, '1766', in A. Charlesworth (ed.), *Atlas of Rural Protest*, pp. 88–92.

58. Wells, 'The Irish famine of 1799–1801', in Randall and Charlesworth, (eds), *Markets, Market Culture and Popular Protest*.

59. See Hay, Chapter 4 below. Also Staffordshire C.R.O., Q/SB/1795; Wells, *Wretched Faces*, pp. 83–5.

60. D.E. Williams, 'Morals, markets and the English crowd in 1766', pp. 73, 70.

61. J. Bohstedt, 'The moral economy and the discipline of historical context', p. 268.

62. Thompson, *Customs in Common*, pp. 267–8.
63. On the role of the market in the lives of the manufacturing classes, see J. G. Rule, *The Experience of Labour in Eighteenth-Century Industry* (London: Croom Helm, 1981), ch. 8.
64. See, for example, A.W. Coats, 'Contrary moralities: plebs, paternalists and political economists', *Past and Present* 54 (1972), pp. 130–3; E. Fox-Genovese, 'The many faces of moral economy', *Past and Present*, 58 (1973), pp. 62–3; I. Hont and M. Ignatieff (eds), *Wealth and Virtue* (Cambridge: Cambridge University Press, 1983), pp. 14–20; cf. Thompson, *Customs in Common*, pp. 268–85.
65. Perhaps the most important contribution to this line of thinking was Charles Smith, *Three Tracts on the Corn Trade* (London, 1758–9), an elegant and sustained assault on regulation in the corn market.
66. This is an area currently being researched by Richard Sheldon for his PhD thesis, 'The politics of bread in eighteenth-century Britain', University of Birmingham.
67. On the political context of the changing attitude to the politics of provision, see R. Wells, *Insurrection: the British Experience 1795–1803* (Gloucester: Alan Sutton, 1983), ch. 12; and R. Wells, *Wretched Faces*, Pt III.
68. Thompson, *Customs in Common*, pp. 337–8.
69. See, in particular, Walton and Seddon, *Free Markets and Food Riots*.
70. Interestingly, Thompson did not include this legal backbone to the moral economy in his most recent reiteration of the key elements of the concept, cited above: *Customs in Common*, p. 338.
71. BL, Hardwicke Mss, Pitt to Hardwicke, 20 December 1766.
72. J. Stevenson, *Popular Disturbances in England 1700–1832* (London: Longman, 1979), pp. 119–21; Charlesworth and Randall, 'Comment: morals, markets', pp. 202–5.
73. Thompson, *Customs in Common*, pp. 338–41; A. J. Randall, 'The industrial moral economy of the Gloucestershire weavers in the eighteenth century', in J. Rule (ed.), *British Trade Unionism 1750–1850: The Formative Years* (London: Longman, 1988); W.R. Reddy, *The Rise of Market Culture* (Cambridge: Cambridge University Press, 1984).
74. E. P. Thompson, *The Making of the English Working Class*, pp. 601, 599, 600–1; 'Moral economy', p. 83.
75. Randall, 'The industrial moral economy of the Gloucestershire weavers'; Randall, *Before the Luddites*, ch. 6.
76. M. W. Steinberg, 'New canons or loose cannons? The post-Marxist challenge to neo-Marxism', *Political Power and Social Theory*, 8 (1993), pp. 221–70. 'This moral economy was validated in their relations with the district's petty-bourgeois authorities, who affirmed the weavers' status as respectable citizens and supported their claims to governmental assistance...The culture of the moral economy was a collective construction in which the weavers produced validations of their perceived rights in these relations': p. 239.
77. I. J. Prothero, *Artisans and Politics in Early Nineteenth-Century London: John Gast and his Times* (Folkestone: Dawson, 1979), ch. 3.
78. *Manchester Gazette*, 14 December 1799, cited in Bohstedt, *Riots and Community Politics*, p. 141.

79. K. Snell, *Annals of the Labouring Poor: Social Change and Agrarian England 1660–1900* (Cambridge: Cambridge University Press, 1985), in particular see pp. 99–103; see also Thompson's response in *Customs in Common*, pp. 339–40.

80. R. W. Bushaway, *By Rite: Custom, Ceremony and Community in England 1700–1880* (London: Junction Books, 1982).

81. P. Mandler, 'The making of the New Poor Law redivivus', *Past and Present*, 117 (1987), pp. 131–157.

82. R. Wells, 'Social protest, class, conflict and consciousness in the English countryside, 1700–1880', and A. Charlesworth, 'The development of the English rural proletariat and social protest, 1700–1850: a comment', both in M. Reed and R. Wells (eds), *Class, Conflict and Protest in the English Countryside, 1700–1880* (London: Cass, 1990); A. J. Randall and E. Newman, 'Protest, proletarians and paternalists: social conflict in rural Wiltshire, 1830–1850' in *Rural History*, 6, 2 (1995), pp. 205–27.

83. Thompson, *Customs in Common*, p. 337.

84. On Cobbett, see Ian Dyck, 'William Cobbett and the rural radical platform', *Social History*, 18, 2 (1993), pp. 185–204; J. Sambrook, *William Cobbett* (London: Routledge, 1973); on Oastler, see C. Driver, *Tory Radical: The Life of Richard Oastler* (Oxford: Oxford University Press, 1946).

85. T. Exell, *A Brief History of the Weavers of the County of Gloucester* (Stroud, 1838).

86. Michael Adas, '"Moral economy" or "contest state"?: Elite demands and the origins of peasant protest in Southeast Asia', *Journal of Social History*, 13, 4 (1980), p. 540.

87. Thompson, *Customs in Common*, p. 344.

88. J. C. Scott, *The Moral Economy of the Peasant*; this work was then extended and deepened in his later works: *Weapons of the Weak: Everyday Forms of Peasant Resistance* (New Haven, Conn.: Yale University Press, 1985) and *Domination and the Arts of Resistance: Hidden Transcripts* (New Haven, Conn.: Yale University Press, 1990).

89. Sen, *Poverty and Famines*. For another powerful critique of Sen, see also Gore, 'Entitlement relations and "unruly" social practices', *Journal of Development Studies*, 29 (1993), pp. 429–60. As Arnold, Ch. 5 below, notes, Sen modified his original 'entitlement' thesis in J. Drèze and A. Sen, *Hunger and Public Action* (Oxford: Oxford University Press, 1989).

90. A long-running advertisement for Heineken lager, voiced-over by Victor Borg, graphically demonstrated the alleged powers of the beverage to 'refresh those parts which other beers cannot reach'. The fact that all participants at the conference 'got' the joke is devastating testimony to our age.

2
The Food Riots of 1347 and the Medieval Moral Economy

Buchanan Sharp

In his classic article, 'The moral economy of the English crowd in the eighteenth century', Edward Thompson recognised that memories, or invocations, of an earlier age of state-sanctioned market regulations served to legitimate eighteenth-century crowd actions in the face of dearth or rising food prices. The invocation of Tudor and Stuart paternalism, as faded and tattered as it had become or perhaps always had been, was used to compel local authorities to enforce half-forgotten market regulations. When magistrates failed to act then the crowd acted in their stead, literally taking the law into their own hands.[1] It was not, however, one of Thompson's central concerns to explore in detail the substance and context of those earlier regulations. Rather he focused his attention on the values embedded within the common history and experience of local communities that underpinned the capacity of crowds to take direct action in the face of dearth.

In the years since the appearance of Thompson's article in 1971 other historians have extended our knowledge of market regulations and popular responses to dearth in the sixteenth and seventeenth centuries.[2] This knowledge now makes much clearer the extent to which the ideas underlying the moral economy of the eighteenth-century crowd were derived from the earlier regulatory age. Such ideas included, among others: prohibition on outward shipment of grain, so that food would be available at a reasonable and affordable price; insistence that all buying and selling of grain take place openly and publicly in known marketplaces, with the poor to be served first; prohibition on private out of market dealing in grain; and close supervision and regulation of the activities of millers, bakers, carriers, and other dealers in relatively large amounts of grain who were likely, for their own gain, to exploit and thereby intensify scarcity through forestalling and other sharp practices.

Since the ideas for remedial responses to grain scarcity that animated the eighteenth-century crowd were virtually identical to the emergency market regulations which Tudor and early Stuart governments implemented in times of dearth, it is certainly possible to argue that statutes, royal proclamations and conciliar directives contributed as much to the content of the moral economy as did the community-based experiences and traditions of the crowd. This is not to say that the motives and aims of official policy were identical with those of the people who engaged in riot and other dearth-related protests. Nor does it mean that state paternalism was the equivalent of the moral economy of the crowd. But it is clear that the notions on which the concept of the moral economy is based were worked out in a complex, tension filled, and sometimes conflictual relationship between central authority, local magistrates and the inhabitants of local communities.

While modern scholarship has successfully pushed our knowledge of the moral economy into the sixteenth and seventeenth centuries, in going no further back in the exploration of the subject it has created the impression that the Tudor period was both the first age of sustained regulation of the grain trade, culminating in the Book of Orders of 1587, and the first century of English food riots.[3] The possibility that there were food riots in England earlier than 1527 has been raised by just one medievalist, to my knowledge, who only raised the possibility to dismiss it.[4]

Whatever the current views of modern historians, there actually were food riots in late medieval England and they raise many of the same questions about crowd behaviour, market regulation and prevailing attitudes towards the buying and selling of grain as do the protests of the period from the sixteenth through to the eighteenth centuries. There are also striking similarities between the late medieval and early modern periods in at least three areas: the actions of rioters, the location of riots, and government response to dearth. To illustrate these points I intend to focus chiefly on one cluster of mid-fourteenth-century food riots.

In the late spring and early summer of 1347 there were food riots at five different locations in England: Bristol; King's Lynn and Thetford in Norfolk; Boston in Lincolnshire; and unidentified ports in Kent. Our knowledge of the riots comes from the contents of special commissions of oyer and terminer issued to try the rioters. Typically, a special commission assigned a group of prominent individuals, a mixed bag of judges and local notables, to hear a specific complaint. Thus for the food riots of 1347 a different commission was issued in reponse to each outbreak, except that the commission to try the protesters at Lynn also included authority to try those responsible for the disorders at Thetford. Such commissions 'were initiated at the suit of the injured party, and were obtainable from Chancery, like writs *de cursu*, on the Chancellor's own authority.'⁵ To begin the process it was necessary for the injured party to submit a petition or complaint, addressed to the king, his council or the Chancellor, stating his case: the commission was then issued on payment of the appropriate fee. Beyond assigning justices to hear the matter at issue, the commission, at least in the fourteenth and fifteenth centuries, contained a statement of the complainant's case.⁶

In effect our main evidence for the 1347 riots, and it must be said for a number of other medieval food riots, comes from the complaints of merchants whose ships were ransacked and grain seized by rioters. We can all agree that such evidence is not likely to be the most objective but, leaving aside generalised and possibly hyperbolic statements about the level of violence involved in the protests or the threat they posed to the lives and properties of the 'good men' of the various communities where the riots occurred, it is striking that the behaviour of the rioters described in the commissions matches well with the better documented behaviour of early modern food rioters.

The first of the 1347 riots took place at Bristol, in late May or early June, certainly before 6 June. Earlier in the year, around 28 April, William Casse, a Bordeaux wine merchant, had obtained a royal licence to ship 700 quarters of wheat from Bristol to Gascony. At the same time, the king had ordered the mayor and bailiffs of Bristol to let Casse have suitable ships to carry the grain to his lieges in Bordeaux and had commanded all admirals and local officials to let the grain pass to its destination without hindrance.⁷ On the day of the riot, according to the commission of oyer and terminer, a crowd assumed the royal power, elected a captain, issued proclamations, boarded the ships in Bristol harbour and, with armed force, took the grain away.⁸

At King's Lynn on 16 June 1347 a crowd boarded two ships loaded with corn licensed for shipment to Gascony. The licensee was John de Wesenham, the king's butler, a sometime customs farmer and prominent citizen of Lynn, who was heavily involved in the wool and grain trades.⁹ On 2 June 1347 Wesenham had obtained licences to export 600 quarters of grain in the ships and intended to return with wine for the king.¹⁰ Once on board, the crowd, assuming royal power, unloaded the ships 'against the will of the owners' and put the grain up for sale 'at their own price'. The protesters also seized and sold other shipments of corn being brought into Lynn to be marketed and then 'on their authority' sentenced the owners or carriers to the pillory, 'without process of law'. Finally, the crowd was accused of arresting the mayor and other inhabitants of the town and of issuing quasi-royal proclamations.[11]

According to the commission of oyer and terminer issued to try the rioters at Lynn, the events there inspired the inhabitants of Thetford, and other unnamed towns in Norfolk, to similar actions. Unfortunately the actual actions are undocumented. The disorders in Kent are also poorly documented. A commission of oyer and terminer was issued to hear charges that, at some time before 1 September 1347, crowds prevented grain, which was intended to supply Edward III and his army in France, from leaving unnamed ports in the county, but little else can be discovered.[12]

Finally, there is the Boston riot dating from late June 1347. At Boston a crowd led by an elected captain, Thomas of Okeham, cordwainer, boarded ships loaded with grain and seized their cargoes. As in the Bristol and Lynn cases the shippers, four London merchants, had obtained the King's licence to export the grain, no doubt to Gascony. The crowd was also accused of taking corn and other merchandise from the townspeople. To assemble together and co-ordinate their actions the rioters arranged for the ringing of the common bell, undoubtedly the market bell. Like the protesters at Lynn, the Boston rioters were charged with making quasi-royal proclamations, including one that those inhabitants who had left the town because of the disorders had to return by a given deadline or their houses would be destroyed.[13]

The immediate context for this outbreak of disorder is a combination of elements including a rapid, short-term increase in grain exports shipped to sustain Edward III's supporters in Gascony, purveyance for military purposes, and a bad harvest in 1346. To take the last point first, the precise regional extent and depth of the 1346 harvest deficiency is unclear. The only medieval dearth that has been the subject of a modern scholarly study is the great famine of 1315–22,[14] but available data indicates a sharp rise in the prices of all grain during the harvest year 1346–7, a rise which was sustained into the following year, 1347–8.[15]

Certainly the dearth experienced in 1346–7 was nowhere near the magnitude of the disastrous years 1315–22. What made the period 1315–22 so difficult was the number of bad harvests over a relatively short time. If we follow Bruce Campbell and include the deficient harvest of 1314 as marking the beginning of the great famine, then in the nine years 1314–22 'dearth had occurred in no fewer than six'.[16] In contrast the harvest failure of 1346 came at the end of a long period of largely abundant harvests. During the years 1333–45 there were no major dearths and only two marginally deficient harvests, in 1339 and 1343.[17] None the less Campbell has concluded that the dearth of 1346–7 had a much greater adverse impact on the peasantry than could be expected from one bad year following a succession of largely good harvests. This conclusion is based on the evidence of land transactions in Coltishall, Norfolk, which indicate that the peasant survival strategy during dearth, of selling land to buy food, became increasingly common in the course of the first half of the fourteenth century.[18]

The larger implication of Campbell's argument is that, contrary to the Postan thesis, the catastrophic years 1315–22 did not put a permanent brake on population increase. Instead population resumed its upward course in the better years of the 1330s and 1340s, thereby accelerating the marginalisation and impoverishment of a larger proportion of the rural population and making more people vulnerable to the negative effects of a single harvest failure. If Campbell is right in his argument that 'the progressive build-up of population may have pressed hard upon resources' until the eve of the Black Death, then one wonders if it is only a coincidence that the first recorded English food riots occurred in 1347.[19]

Whatever the impact of the harvest deficiency of 1346–7 on peasant producers, its effects on consumers were magnified by the export of grain to Gascony, the only overseas destination in 1347 for which recorded export licences have survived. For that year licences were issued to ship a total of 15 950 quarters of grain, with licences for 13 050 quarters concentrated in May and June. Such large shipments concentrated in a short period of time must have driven up prices in the areas from which the grain was obtained, especially towards the end of a poor harvest year when grain stocks would have been declining. Of the 13 050 quarters of grain licensed for export to Gascony in May and June 1347, 11 850 were shipped from three ports: King's Lynn, London and Hull.[20]

King's Lynn was one of the leading grain exporting centres in England from the early fourteenth century through to at least the early eighteenth. The town's rise to importance as a grain port began in the late thirteenth or early fourteenth century when it became the main outfall of the system of East Anglian rivers which fed the Great Ouse. This was a result of natural changes in the courses of those rivers aided by the cutting of artificial channels.[21] Towards Lynn the river system directed grain from some of the most productive arable land in England, spread over as many as eight counties, but concentrated particularly in Norfolk.[22] From Lynn the grain was either shipped coastwards, north as far as Newcastle and south as far as London or Portsmouth, or exported to various European destinations depending, in part, upon royal political and diplomatic considerations.

For thirteenth- and early fourteenth-century East Anglian grain producers with a surplus to sell on the market, all roads and rivers led to Lynn. Customary tenants of the Abbey and Bishopric of Ely, for example, were required to do carrying service to move grain – on their backs, by pack horse or by cart – to places on the rivers like Thetford, where it was collected and moved by boat to market at King's Lynn. Ely was also entitled to further tenant services that included transporting grain and other victuals by water to various locations on the East Anglian river system or to the final destination at Lynn. Other great ecclesiastical landlords, such as Ramsey Abbey which had extensive estates across a number of East Anglian counties, shipped large quantities of grain to Lynn.[23]

Just a moment's reflection on the weight of a cargo of grain reveals the importance of river transport. A bushel of grain weighs 56 lb, while 8 bushels, one quarter, weigh 448 lb, or four hundredweight. According to T. S. Willan, a led pack horse in the early modern period could carry two hundredweight.[24] Thus two pack horses were required to carry one quarter of grain. Over the course of any given year, but especially in the weeks after harvest, thousands of quarters of grain must have been transported towards Lynn from its hinterland, either to be shipped out immediately or stored for the short term in the granaries of merchants. One can visualise pack horses and horse-drawn carts making numerous short trips with relatively small loads to the river settlements where the larger cargoes were assembled and then sent down river on boats. What is difficult for the modern observer to imagine, given grain's bulk, is carriage of grain over any distance in panniers slung on the backs of peasants.

The full extent of grain movements from King's Lynn, or any other port in medieval England, will never be known. No systematic record of domestic coastal grain shipments was kept until the mid-sixteenth century. Furthermore, there is no way of knowing how much grain was exported illegally at any time during the late middle ages. For the second half of the sixteenth century Neville Williams has shown, on good evidence, that illegal exports of grain from Norfolk ports must have at least equalled the amount of legal exports that were duly licensed and on which customs duties were paid.[25] There is no reason to believe that customs officials were any more willing or able to control smuggling in the fourteenth century than in the sixteenth. Finally, the nature of surviving medieval customs accounts renders problematic any attempt to determine the amount of grain exported in any given year from a particular port.[26]

The fullest evidence we have for grain exports from Lynn and other ports in the period prior to the 1347 riots comes from licences to export enrolled on the Patent Rolls, supplemented by royal mandates sent to local officials ordering them to permit specific licensed shipments to sail. Even this evidence does not provide a complete account of exports. It is clear from the evidence of the mandates that not all licences were enrolled.[27] Moreover, other Chancery enrolments such as the Gascon and Treaty Rolls, which I have not yet searched, are known to contain copies of export licences. The figures that I have so far accumulated must, therefore, be regarded as incomplete and subject to future upward revision. For the year 1347 all the licences enrolled on the Patent Rolls that authorise export from Lynn are concentrated in one month, 1 May–2 June, when a total of 4600 quarters of grain was licensed for shipment to Gascony.[28] This month was matched in known exports from Lynn by only one other period in the 1340s, namely 17 December 1342–16 January 1343, when 4900 quarters of grain, plus five other shiploads and a further unspecified amount, were licensed for shipment to Flanders.[29]

In addition to Lynn, Hull and London were major shippers of grain to Gascony in the spring of 1347. During May and June 1347, 2600 quarters of grain were licensed for shipment from Hull, while other sources indicate that Hull sent 5057 quarters of grain overseas in the period 20 November 1346–10 August 1347, all of it to Gascony.[30] From the port of London, 4650 quarters plus three other shiploads were licensed for Gascony in May and June.[31] We do not know the precise source of the grain shipped from London. Already the capital was being supplied from a variety of areas, including the Thames valley, Hertfordshire, Kent, Essex and East Anglia.[32] We can be certain, however, that a substantial proportion of the grain exported in 1347 had first been shipped to London from Lynn and from ports in Kent.

The explanation of Gascony's need is simple. It was a classic monoculture region that could not feed itself, but depended on the import of grain and other foodstuffs in return for the wine it produced and sold overseas, particularly in England. In 1346–7 warfare between the French and English crowns was being conducted on at least two fronts, Gascony and northern France. Gascony, which was under English lordship, was invaded by a French army in 1345 and was the location of intermittent fighting until the summer of 1347.[33] The provisioning needs of Anglo-Gascon forces undoubtedly made it necessary to send even more grain than usual to the duchy; a number of the export licenses make it clear that the cargoes were intended to meet military requirements but most simply refer to the needs of the king's lieges.[34]

The English military campaign in northern France, led personally by Edward III, resulted in the victory at Crécy on 26 August and was soon followed by the eleven-month siege of Calais, which ultimately fell early in August 1347. To sustain the king's campaign, large quantities of foodstuffs were purveyed in England and shipped from Lynn, Hull, Boston, London and Maldon (in Essex) to Portsmouth for movement to France. For example, at least 731 quarters of flour, 243 quarters of oats, and 60 quarters of peas and beans, plus other victuals, purveyed in Cambridgeshire, Huntingdonshire and Northamptonshire were shipped through Lynn.[35]

With the context of overseas shipment of grain in mind let us turn to the actions of the King's Lynn protesters in 1347. While the export of grain from Lynn, particularly the 4600 quarters in May and early June 1347, probably drove up local prices, an even more important trigger for protest must have been the sight of such large quantities of grain being sent to foreign parts over a relatively short period. Visible export clearly created fears or expectations of dearth among the townspeople. The crowd's actions in taking the grain from the ships and selling it at their own price indicate that prices in the market were rising above a level that was popularly regarded as just.

Further indicators of possible rising prices and fear of dearth at Lynn are the crowd's seizure and sale of grain being brought into the town to be marketed, presumably having been transported by road or river from the agricultural hinterland, and the condemnation to the pillory of the owners or carriers of such grain. This latter act reflects a popular belief that sellers of grain were obtaining excessive returns from high market prices. The crowd may also have believed that the people bringing grain to Lynn were forestallers, who had bought it from the original producers before it reached market and intended to profit by selling on a rising market themselves; sentence to the pillory was one legal punishment for fourteenth-century forestallers.[36] The tactic of seizing grain, both leaving and entering the town, was obviously designed to prevent future shortages and price rises through further export. It is worth recalling that the Lynn protests triggered similar actions at Thetford, a community on the Little Ouse, where grain was collected for transport to Lynn. Here again frequent outward grain shipments must have raised the possibility of local scarcity and thereby provoked remedial action by the populace.

Unfortunately, we cannot put much contextual flesh on the bare bones of the Boston riot. There are no licences for export of grain from the port in 1347 recorded on the Patent Rolls, another indication that enrolment was a hit or miss affair; the commission of oyer and terminer notes that the merchants whose ships were plundered at Boston had been licensed to export the grain. There is certainly evidence of grain exports in other years. For example, in 1346 a licence was issued for the export of 1000 quarters of grain from Boston to Spain at the request of the king's daughter Joan.[37] For the campaign in northern France in 1346–7 at least 552 quarters of flour, 300 quarters of oats, and 100 quarters of peas and beans, plus other victuals, which had been purveyed in Lincolnshire, were shipped from Boston and Hull to Portsmouth.[38] While it is surprising that records of grain export from Boston in 1347 are scarce, the actions of the protesters in stopping shipments leaving the harbour were much like those of the Lynn rioters and indicate a fear of local scarcity and high prices if export continued. Boston is on the other side of the Wash from Lynn; it may well be that fear of scarcity at Boston and the accompanying riot were stirred by news of the Lynn protest.

The effects of purveyance appear to provide the context for the riots in Kentish ports. While there is evidence for the purveyance of grain and other victuals in Kent during 1346 and 1347, there are no available figures on actual amounts. None the less, during the siege of Calais (4 September 1346–4 August 1347) Sandwich became a major collecting and shipping point for purveyed grain and other victuals to supply English forces.[39] The importance of Kentish ports in this regard is further indicated by the royal mandate of 25 October 1346 that prohibited the export of grain from Sandwich and the other Cinque ports except to Calais.[40] It is clear from the language of the commission of oyer and terminer issued to deal with the food riots in Kent that the rioters were trying to stop the flow of supplies to the English army, which was led by the king in person. The protesters forcibly 'prevented some of the king's servants and others assigned' to the task from shipping 'victuals for the sustenance of the king and his lieges in the war with France'. The commission also contains an interesting admission regarding the situation in Kent. The justices were assigned to try not only the protesters but also purveyors and others who, by virtue of their offices, extorted victuals, 'ransoms and fines at will'. The document's association of food riots in Kentish ports and the 'oppressions' of purveyors can hardly be coincidental.[41] By 11 March 1348 a royal letter to the sheriff of Kent admitted that grain and other victuals were scarce in the county because of shipments to Calais.[42]

In the late middle ages and the early modern period Bristol was the major outlet for the agricultural produce and manufactures of the West Midlands shipped down the river Severn. The town depended on the river not only for its own food supply but for the grain cargoes it sent to the coast and overseas. Grain came down river by boat from Tewkesbury, Worcester, Shrewsbury and Gloucester.[43] Illegal export in a bad harvest year appears to provide the most plausible explanation for the Bristol riot of 1347. There certainly was purveyance in the counties of the Severn valley during 1346–7 but we do not know a great deal about its effects. On 3 May 1346 a commission was issued to Richard Talbot, steward of the King's household, to investigate the oppressive behaviour of sheriffs and other officials in the counties of Gloucester, Hereford and Worcester, among others, who extorted money from the wealthy in return for exemptions from purveyance while they took corn and victuals for the king from 'poor and simple men' who could not afford to part with them.[44]

By the spring of 1347 there are signs of grain scarcity in Gloucestershire caused, or at least aggravated, by transportation out of the area. On 30 May, around the time of the Bristol riot, royal letters sent to the sheriff of Gloucestershire and to the mayor and bailiffs of Gloucester indicate scarcity in the town. According to the letters the 'men of Gloucester town' had petitioned the king that merchants, both with and without royal warrant, had bought up so much corn in Gloucestershire that dearth had resulted, thereby impoverishing the populace who, 'unless a remedy is speedily supplied...will succumb'. As a remedial measure the letters ordered a proclamation in both the town and the county of Gloucester placing a prohibition on the export of grain, except for properly licensed shipments to 'the king's lieges' in Gascony.[45] One properly licensed grain shipment was the 700 quarters that William Casse intended to export to Bordeaux, the only 1347 grain cargo outward bound from Bristol for which a licence is recorded.[46]

After Casse's grain cargo was taken by the Bristol crowd, three royal letters on his behalf were issued on 6 June 1347. The sheriff of Gloucestershire and the bailiffs of Gloucester were instructed to allow a replacement cargo of grain to move down the Severn to Bristol and then on to Bordeaux, notwithstanding the earlier order to prohibit the export of grain. Local magistrates in Gloucester had taken the opportunity offered by the order of 30 May to arrest and stop the movement down river of Casse's new cargo. At the same time, the king ordered the mayor and bailiffs of Bristol to allow Casse to ship the replacement 700 quarters of grain from Bristol to Bordeaux.[47] Soon, however, the Crown became concerned about illegal export from the Severn. On 16 February 1348, a commission was appointed to enquire into such export and arrest those responsible. According to the commission, merchants daily shipped corn down river in boats from Tewkesbury and other places, claiming that the cargoes were for sale at Bristol. Instead, the grain was transferred to ships anchored outside Bristol harbour and then shipped overseas illegally to the king's enemies. In addition to their other tasks, the commissioners were to survey all boats loaded with grain going past Gloucester and take sureties from the shippers that the cargoes were bound only for Bristol.[48]

We do not know in any detail the nationwide extent or the regional variations of the grain scarcity in 1346–7. Nor do we know with any certainty the degree to which it was caused by a deficient harvest, grain export, purveyance or some combination of the three. But by late summer and autumn of 1347 the Crown was persuaded, no doubt in part by the riots, that the scarcity was the product of excessive export. Apparently, some time in August, a royal mandate ordered that two shiploads of grain licensed for shipment from London to Bordeaux should be stayed, unloaded, and sold because of growing dearth in the capital.[49] Another mandate in August to the sheriffs of London ordered that limits be imposed on the activities of purveyors because they had caused scarcity in the city.[50] Finally, in October, a prohibition was imposed on the export of grain from England, except to Calais, unless licensed by the king and his council.[51] The express justification for the prohibition was that the export of great quantities of grain had produced scarcity in the kingdom. One indication of the clampdown on the grain trade is that from late July 1347 to the end of the year no licences permitting export of grain from England are recorded on the Patent Rolls. None the less, it took a while given other pressing needs for the Crown to respond to the grain shortage. On a number of occasions, from mid-June through to July 1347, royal orders were issued, in the face of known scarcity, to permit shipments of grain from London to Gascony, largely for political and military purposes.[52]

The 1347 prohibition on export raises the question of official regulation of the grain market in the late middle ages, a large topic which will only be touched upon briefly here. One useful way of approaching the topic is to stand back from the details and think of some of the larger implications of the riots. The crowd actions of 1347 reported in the surviving sources – stopping transport of grain, seizing shipments and selling grain at their own price – fit well with eighteenth-century crowd behaviour as described in Thompson's moral economy article, and more generally with the behaviour of English food rioters at any time from the sixteenth century onwards. Moreover we can see reflected in the actions of the 1347 food rioters the role that the law and royal government had begun to play in the regulation of grain marketing.

In the Lynn riot the crowd's act of 'adjudging' to the pillory those persons who brought grain into the town to sell reflects popular knowledge of existing law regarding the crime of forestalling. In a recent penetrating article on the statute of forestallers, R. H. Britnell has demonstrated that the statute, with its definition of the crime as the buying of grain and other victuals before they reached market with the intention of reselling them at a profit, began as a clause in a series of directions for the clerks of the Marshalsea in 1274–5. By the late years of Edward I that clause had been raised to the status of a statute.[53] Then 'in October 1304 commissions of oyer and terminer were appointed to examine complaints that forestallers were intercepting victuals and other goods, and consequently raising prices, in Norwich, Great Yarmouth and Ipswich'.[54] During the early years of Edward II's reign another series of commissions was issued to enforce the law on forestalling along with other market regulations. According to Britnell, a major consequence of those commissions was that 'from the beginning of Edward II's reign, then, the suppression of forestalling was an obligation to the Crown'.[55] As provided in the statute, one punishment inflicted on repeat offenders was sentence to the pillory.

Perhaps an even more significant reflection of the Crown's role in regulating the grain market is to be found in other actions of the 1347 rioters. Recall that the rioters at Bristol, Lynn and Boston were charged with assuming the royal power and with issuing proclamations. I read those two charges as closely connected, if not idenitcal. It was in making proclamations in the king's name that the rioters assumed or, as the law would have it, accroached the royal power.[56] The assumption of royal power probably involved uttering, in the king's name, prohibitions to stop the export of grain and orders to seize and unload the cargo. What lies behind such behaviour is knowledge that the king's government took some hand in the regulation of the grain trade; in turn that knowledge sanctioned popular direct action. Without an already established tradition of monarchical regulation through proclamations, the crowd actions of 1347, as reported in the commissions of oyer and terminer, would be meaningless.

In fact during the fourteenth century the Crown regularly issued proclamations imposing prohibitions on grain export, with various kinds of conditions attached to them. The texts of these proclamations often included a statement of the reason for the issuance, the most common being to prevent grain reaching the King's foreign enemies or to alleviate scarcity at home. During the reign of Edward II (1307–27) at least seven such prohibitions were issued, all of which contain political or military justifications, either to prevent grain from reaching the Scots or to direct grain supplies northwards in support of military operations against the Scots.[57] Two of the seven also mention scarcity in England: these are the proclamations of 1 September 1315 and 14 February 1317 which put heavy emphasis on the bad weather and rains that adversely affected harvests as justification for the prohibitions on export.[58] The proclamation of 1 September 1315 marks the beginning not only of a famine year but also of a longer period of recurrent dearth, deprivation and high mortality that ran until 1322.[59] In further response to dearth Edward II, in December 1315, wrote to both the King of France and the Duke of Brittany requesting that merchants of Newcastle upon Tyne be allowed to buy grain in their lands and ship it home. At the same time, the English king ordered the seneschal of Ponthieu, one of his possessions in France, to permit the same merchants to buy grain there.[60] In 1316 Edward II extended his protection and safe conduct for a year, then increased to two years, to all foreign merchants, except those of Scotland and Flanders, to encourage them to bring grain to England.[61]

During the reign of Edward III (1327–77) at least twenty-seven separate proclamations were issued imposing prohibitions on grain export.[62] Unlike the proclamations of the previous reign, grain scarcity in England had now become the single most frequently announced justification. Only five of Edward III's proclamations, three of them from 1336, provide political or military justification, once again to prohibit grain from reaching the Scots or to direct grain north in support of royal campaigns.[63] In contrast, nine of the proclamations refer to scarcity, caused either by a poor harvest or by excessive transportation overseas.[64] Although the other thirteen of Edward III's proclamations contain no express justification in their texts, eight of them were issued in known scarcity years.[65] This evidence certainly conveys the impression that regulation of grain export by proclamation had become a standard response to signs of dearth in the reign of Edward III.

In the years immediately preceding the riots of 1347 the Crown issued two proclamations prohibiting grain export. The first, on 24 December 1342, prohibited the export of grain without the king's special licence. A year later the prohibition was renewed, naming the locations to which licensed export was permitted – Gascony, Ireland, Flanders, Brittany, Brabant, Spain, Holland, Zealand and Germany – all places either in the English king's friendship or under his lordship.[66] This second proclamation, of December 1343, states that a great deal of grain had been shipped out of the country, thereby alluding to the possibility of scarcity. Although the harvest of 1343 was somewhat deficient, it is probable that export more than harvest failure posed a greater threat to domestic supplies.[67]

For the years 1342–7 there is evidence of continuing efforts to enforce the prohibitions on export. Royal mandates were sometimes sent to bailiffs or sheriffs commanding them to seize unlicensed grain shipments and arrest the ships and their masters.[68] Another routinely enforced requirement of the proclamations of 1342 and 1343 was that each exporter of a licensed cargo had to swear an oath and find sureties that he would ship only to foreign destinations allowed by the proclamation. The bond would be discharged when the merchant returned and submitted to the Chancery a letter or certificate, testifying to the arrival and disposal of the cargo, sealed by a bailiff or other magistrate of the foreign destination. Local magistrates and customs officials were regularly reminded not to allow grain cargoes to sail until the shippers found sureties as to their destination.[69] By the beginning of 1344, the government of Edward III was persuaded that the terms of the proclamation were being routinely disregarded. Therefore commissions were issued regularly, until at least 1349, to a number of individuals to arrest ships carrying unlicensed corn, or other goods upon which customs had not been paid, and to certify the arrests to the Chancery.[70]

Although such commissioners may have had an occasional success, as in January 1344 when Saier Lorimer arrested two ships loaded with unlicensed grain, it is doubtful that they could stem the tide of illegal exports.[71] But the effectiveness of regulations is not the issue. What mattered was the public and known intentions of the Crown. Since proclamations were publicly proclaimed at the county court and the market cross of the towns in each shire, the populace knew those intentions.[72] Moreover, the continued attempt over five years to implement a regulatory policy based on two royal proclamations, despite the exceptions contained within them, may have created a general impression that a more stringent prohibition was in force than actually was the case. Or perhaps that was the intentional misreading of the situation on the part of local magistrates who occasionally stopped licensed shipments of grain with the claim that an export prohibition was in force. Such a locally stayed shipment was only allowed to proceed on receipt of a royal mandate ordering its release because the cargo was properly licensed for shipment and the shipper had found sureties guaranteeing the cargo's final destination.[73] One such cargo of 900 quarters of grain, stayed at Sandwich and then released by royal order for its destination at Bordeaux on 3 October 1346, was shipped by William Casse, another of whose cargoes was seized by the Bristol rioters in 1347.[74]

Keeping in mind this background of royal attempts to impose controls on grain export, especially in the 1340s, one can understand why the protesters of 1347 apparently made proclamations in the king's name to prohibit export, arrest ships and seize grain. Their actions were sanctioned by a history of regulation of the grain trade through proclamations that reached back at least to the first decade of the fourteenth century. The 1347 protesters could have plausibly argued that, in the face of dearth and rising prices, they were acting either in support of a royal proclamation or in place of one which ought to have been in force. Eventually, in October 1347, the Crown found itself in agreement with the protesters and issued its more stringent prohibition on grain export, except to Calais, without the king's special licence on the advice of the council.[75]

In reflecting upon proclamations prohibiting export, one must realise that no prohibition was ever absolute, no matter how bad the harvest or how widespread the fear that scarcity was the result of excessive export. There was always the possibility of exceptions granted through the king's power to issue export licences, usually for a price. Such exceptions were based on a number of different considerations. There was the diplomatic necessity to support foreign allies in an age when England was engaged in major military operations in Scotland and France. Then those military operations needed to be victualled, in part, by directing licensed shipments of grain to the campaign's location. The English king's own subjects in Gascony and Calais required provisioning. During the late fourteenth century both places were often exempted from export prohibitions.[76] Finally, powerful commercial interests and sources of loans, represented by the likes of John de Wesenham and the equally wealthy Lynn merchant Thomas de Melchebourn, were regularly rewarded with export licences.[77] While licensed shipments contributed to the likelihood of local scarcity, so too did the Crown's overseas shipment of purveyed grain and other victuals in support of military campaigns.

Such apparent paradoxes or contradictions in royal policy are regularly encountered by historians who study the enforcement of social and economic regulations in England during the sixteenth and seventeenth centuries. Often, paternalist social policies were under-mined or redirected to become revenue raising schemes. For example, one historian of sixteenth-century Norfolk has argued, with some justi-fication, that Elizabethan licensing of grain exports in the dearth years of the 1590s was a money-making scheme, akin to the sale or granting of monopolies, rather than an attempt to limit export in order to alle-viate domestic scarcity.[78]

The outbreak of food riots in and around ports in 1347 should come as no surprise to early modern historians. Ports shipping grain remained one of the likeliest locations for such protests into the eighteenth century. During other periods of grain scarcity in the late fourteenth and early fifteenth centuries, ports and their hinterlands, especially in East Anglia, experienced riots or other dearth-related disturbances: Yarmouth, Norfolk in 1375; various locations in Norfolk and Suffolk in 1410–11; Ipswich and Southwold, Suffolk, in 1438.[79]

Rivers, which were important routes for the transportation of grain, were also likely scenes of food riots. The Severn, in particular, was regu-larly the scene of protest actions from late medieval times until the end of the eighteenth century. Whenever grain scarcity threatened in the late fourteenth or early fifteenth centuries, the inhabitants of both the town and county of Gloucester attempted to stop and seize grain car-goes moving down river.[80] The people of the Forest of Dean were a par-ticularly riotous lot. In the late middle ages the forest was already an important mining and iron producing area that did not grow enough grain to feed its population but depended on grain shipments from elsewhere. With some frequency in the early fifteenth century the inhabitants of Dean plundered boats carrying grain down the Severn from Worcester, Tewkesbury and Gloucester towards Bristol.[81]

In the late fourteenth and early fifteenth centuries, just as food riot remained one popular response to dearth, so did the issuance of royal proclamations prohibiting export continue to be a standard official response.[82] This kind of regulation by proclamation, with accompany-ing bonds and licences, survived to be the main method by which Tudor and early Stuart monarchs attempted to control the coastal and export trades in grain.[83] Beginning with the dearth of 1347, however, the Crown's response to grain scarcity went well beyond proclamations to prohibit export.

In the reigns of the first two Edwards, and occasionally in the earlier years of Edward III's reign, commissions to enquire into forestalling had been appointed but it is not clear that these particular measures were directly related to the effects of dearth.[84] Then in May 1347 a commission of oyer and terminer was appointed on complaints from the inhabitants of the city of Exeter that the corn scarcity there was caused by forestallers.[85] On 8 October 1370, following a poor harvest, royal instructions were sent to the sheriffs of Kent, Essex, Hertford, Cambridge, Huntingdon, Bedford, Buckingham and Lincoln to proclaim in the markets and fairs within their bailiwicks that forestalling of grain was forbidden. According to the proclamation, forestalling was driving up prices and causing dearth 'to the manifest impoverishment of the people'. It was made clear to the sheriffs that grain was only to be bought and sold in open market.[86] Two days later commissions were appointed to enquire into the names of the forestallers in those same counties.[87] In 1375 the Crown commissioned the justices of the peace in thirteen major grain-producing counties to enquire into the activities of merchants whose export of grain overseas was reputed to be the cause of that year's dearth.[88] During yet another dearth year, 1391, the king ordered the first known inquiries, at Tamworth and Winchester, into the amount of hoarded grain in private houses and granaries, with instructions that the hoarders were to be punished and their grain sold in local marketplaces.[89]

The hard years 1437–40 produced a range of royal responses in addition to proclamations prohibiting export. On 1 September 1437, at a time when the price of grain had risen because of bad weather, the sheriff of Hampshire was ordered to issue a proclamation forbidding forestalling in the county, on pain of imprisonment and forfeiture of the forestalled grain.[90] In December 1438, commissions were issued to enquire into, and punish according to the statute, forestallers of grain who bought large amounts of grain in Kent and Buckinghamshire, 'notwithstanding the dearness and scarcity of wheat and other kinds of corn for no small time in the realm owing to the bad weather, in their desire for unjust gain.'[91] A few days later other commissions were appointed regarding the extortions and deceptions of millers, 'having no regard to the dearness of corn', in Essex, Middlesex and Surrey.[92]

One striking aspect of the royal response to dearth from the late fourteenth century onwards is the increasing use of paternalist language in the documents. During the scarcity of 1391 grain was regularly allowed to be imported free of customs duty 'for the public good and the relief of the populace'.[93] In the great dearth of 1437–40 'the common good' was frequently invoked in regulatory proclamations.[94]

At the same time grain merchants were condemned as 'greedy for extravagant gain'.[95] In 1438 forestallers of grain in Kent and Buckinghamshire, who profited from scarcity, were characterised as 'without bowels of pity'.[96] While I have not yet worked out the full extent or implications of late medieval governmental attempts to regulate the grain trade in response to scarcity, everything I have discovered so far indicates that English monarchs in the fourteenth and early fifteenth centuries laid the foundation upon which the later Tudor–Stuart regulatory apparatus was erected.

Notes

1. E. P. Thompson, 'The moral economy of the English crowd in the eighteenth century', reprinted in his *Customs in Common* (London: Merlin Press, 1991), pp. 193–4, 208–12, 224–9.
2. In 'The moral economy reviewed', in *Customs in Common*, Thompson provides a convenient list of that recent scholarship on p. 264, n. 1.
3. J. Stevenson, *Popular Disturbances in England 1700–1870* (London: Longman, 1979), p. 91; P. Slack, *Poverty and Policy in Tudor and Stuart England* (London: Longman, 1988), pp. 116–17; J. Guy, *Tudor England* (Oxford: Oxford University Press, 1990), p. 171.
4. C. Dyer, *Standards of Living in the Later Middle Ages: Social Change in England c. 1200–1520* (Cambridge: Cambridge University Press, 1989), p. 272.
5. E. Powell, 'Special Oyer and Terminer Proceedings 1262–1443' (typescript list in the Round Room of the PRO, Chancery Lane, 1984), p. 2.
6. Powell, 'Proceedings', p. 2; R. W. Kaeuper, 'Law and order in fourteenth century England: The evidence of Special Commissions of Oyer and Terminer', *Speculum*, 54 (1979), pp. 747–52, 757–8.
7. *Calendar of Patent Rolls (hereafter CPR) 1345–48* (London: HMSO, 1894–1910), p. 280; for the identification of Casse as the plundered merchant and a trader in Bordeaux wine see *Calendar of Close Rolls (hereafter CCR) 1346–49* (London: HMSO, 1892–1939), pp. 224, 458–9, 464.
8. *CPR 1345–48*, p. 392. In all instances I have checked the calendar version of the commissions against the originals on the Patent Rolls. I will only refer to the calendar in the footnotes unless there is additional material from the originals. A full transcript of the commission on the Lynn riot is in *Foedera* (London: Record Commission, 1816–30), v. 3 pt. 1, p. 126.
9. Information on Wesenham can be found in N. S. B. Gras, *The Evolution of the English Corn Market from the Twelfth to the Eighteenth Century* (Cambridge, Mass.: Harvard University Press, 1915), p. 173; and E. B. Fryde, 'The English farmers of the customs 1343–51', *Transactions of the Royal Historical Society*, 5th. ser. 9 (1959), pp. 1–17.
10. *CPR 1345–48*, p. 283; Wesenham is identified as the plundered merchant in *CPR 1345–48*, p. 376.
11. *CPR 1345–48*, p. 388; the date of the riot comes from PRO, JUST1/612/5, the record of the trial of the Lynn rioters before the justices of oyer and terminer.

12. *CPR 1345–48*, pp. 398–9.
13. *CPR 1345–48*, p. 381; see also PRO, K.B. 27/354 rex roll, m. 1v.
14. I. Kershaw, 'The Great Famine and the agrarian crisis in England 1315–1322', *Past and Present*, 59 (1973), pp. 3–50.
15. D. L. Farmer, 'Prices and wages', in H.E. Hallam (ed.), *The Agrarian History of England and Wales 1042–1350* (Cambridge: Cambridge University Press, 1988), p. 791; Dyer, *Standards of Living*, p. 262.
16. B. M. S. Campbell, 'Population pressure, inheritance and land market in a fourteenth-century peasant community', in R. M. Smith (ed.), *Land, Kinship and Life-Cycle* (Cambridge: Cambridge University Press, 1984), p. 114; see also Farmer, 'Prices and wages', pp. 790–1.
17. Campbell, 'Population pressure', pp. 115–16; Farmer, 'Prices and wages', p. 791.
18. Campbell, 'Population pressure', pp. 115–20.
19. Campbell, 'Population pressure', p. 120.
20. *CPR 1345–48*, pp. 216, 219, 225, 246, 251, 280–3, 287, 291, 350; *CCR 1346–49*, pp. 219, 224, 226, 228, 308.
21. H. C. Darby, *The Medieval Fenland* (Newton Abbot: David & Charles, 1974), pp. 93–100; N. J. Williams, *The Maritime Trade of the East Anglian Ports 1550–1590* (Oxford: Oxford University Press, 1988), pp. 54–5.
22. Campbell, 'Population pressure', pp. 89–92; Williams, *Maritime Trade*, pp. 54–5.
23. D.L. Farmer, 'Marketing the produce of the countryside, 1200–1500' in E. Miller (ed.), *The Agrarian History of England and Wales 1348–1500* (Cambridge: Cambridge University Press, 1991), pp. 347–9, 354; E. Miller, *The Abbey and Bishopric of Ely* (Cambridge: Cambridge University Press, 1951), pp. 84–5; Darby, *The Medieval Fenland*, pp. 101–3; Gras, *English Corn Market*, pp. 174–6.
24. R.E. Zupko, *A Dictionary of English Weights and Measures* (Madison: University of Wisconsin Press, 1968), p. 25 notes that the Winchester bushel of wheat 'was supposed to weigh' 56 tower lb or 56 avoirdupois lb; T. S. Willan, *The Inland Trade: Studies in English Internal Trade in the Sixteenth and Seventeenth Centuries* (Manchester: Manchester University Press, 1976), pp. 11–12.
25. Williams, *Maritime Trade*, pp. 18–19, 25–33, 35–49, 72.
26. In *English Corn Market*, appendix C, pp. 281–96, Gras offers statistics on corn exports 1303–1690 which are drawn, at least for the period before 1565, largely from PRO, E. 122 (Customs Accounts). These accounts were submitted to the Exchequer by collectors and other officials in each port; unfortunately only a small fraction of the total number survives. The fragmentary nature of the sources explains the considerable gaps in Gras's annual figures for every port. There is a complete series of enrolled customs accounts in PRO, E. 356 but they do not list quantities for goods, like grain, which were liable only for poundage and petty customs; see H. L. Gray, 'Tables of Enrolled Customs and Subsidy Accounts, 1399 to 1482', in E. Power and M. M. Postan (eds), *Studies in English Trade in the Fifteenth Century* (London: Routledge, 1951), p. 323.
27. In *CCR 1341–43*, pp. 627–8, 694–5 and *CCR 1343–46*, pp. 81–2, 116, 205, 274–5, 390–1, for the period December 1342–June 1344, there are 23 royal

orders to local officials in a variety of ports to allow export of particular cargoes of grain with sureties as to destinations. Only one of those cargoes is
mentioned on the Patent Rolls as licensed: *CPR 1340–43*, p. 579.
28. *CPR 1345–48*, pp. 281–3.
29. *CCR 1341–43*, pp. 627–8, 694–5.
30. *CPR 1345–48*, pp. 281–3; Gras, *English Corn Market*, p. 287.
31. *CPR 1345–48*, pp. 281–3, 291; *CPR 1346–49*, pp. 219, 224, 226, 228.
32. Farmer, 'Marketing the produce', pp. 367–73.
33. M. McKisack, *The Fourteenth Century 1307–1399* (Oxford: Clarendon Press,
1959), pp. 132–7.
34. Mention of military needs are found in *CCR 1346–49*, pp. 219, 226; *CPR
1345–48*, pp. 216, 219, 225.
35. H. J. Hewitt, *The Organization of War under Edward III 1338–1362*
(Manchester: Manchester University Press, 1966), p. 55.
36. R. H. Britnell, 'Forstall, forestalling and the Statute of Forestallers', *The
English Historical Review*, CII (1987), pp. 94, 96, 102.
37. *CPR 1345–48*, p. 201.
38. Hewitt, *Organization of War*, p. 55.
39. Hewitt, *Organization of War*, p. 57.
40 *Foedera*, v. 3 pt.1, p. 92.
41. *CPR 1345–48*, pp. 398–9.
42. *CCR 1346–49*, p. 502.
43. R. H. Hilton, *A Medieval Society: The West Midlands at the End of
the Thirteenth Century* (New York: Wiley, 1966), pp. 194–7, 207–17;
E. M. Carus-Wilson, 'The overseas trade of Bristol' in Power and Postan
(eds), *Studies in English Trade*, pp. 185–9.
44. *CPR 1345–48*, p. 113.
45. *CCR 1346–49*, p. 281.
46. *CPR 1345–48*, p. 280.
47. *CCR 1346–49*, p. 224.
48. *CPR 1345–48*, pp. 67–8, 165.
49. *CPR 1345–48*, p. 372.
50. *CCR 1346–49*, p. 375.
51. *CCR 1346–49*, p. 403; a full text is in *Foedera*, v. 3 pt. 1, p. 139.
52. *CCR 1346–49*, pp. 226, 228, 308.
53. Britnell, 'Statute of Forestallers', pp. 89–102.
54. Britnell, 'Statute of Forestallers', pp. 99–100.
55. Britnell, 'Statute of Forestallers', pp. 100–1.
56. J. G. Bellamy, *The Law of Treason in England in the Later Middle Ages*
(Cambridge: Cambridge University Press, 1970), pp. 66–8, 218. On these
pages Bellamy not only discusses the offences of accroaching the king's
power and misprision but he illustrates his discussion with the examples of
the Bristol, Lynn and Boston riots. Since Bellamy was only interested in the
development of the treason laws, a big enough topic it must be admitted,
he missed the fact that he had fallen on what are, arguably, the first
recorded English food riots. No other modern scholar, to my knowledge,
has made reference to the riots except myself, briefly, in B. Sharp, 'Popular
protest in Seventeenth Century England' in B. Reay (ed.), *Popular Culture in
Seventeenth Century England* (London: Croom Helm, 1985), pp. 280–1.

57. *CCR 1307–13*, pp. 225, 337, 338; *CCR 1313–18*, pp. 308–9, 445, 558; *CCR 1318–23*, p. 134. See also full texts in *Foedera*, v. 2 pt.1, pp. 115, 120, 276.
58. *CCR 1313–18*, pp. 308, 445.
59. Kershaw, 'The Great Famine', pp. 3–50.
60. *CCR 1313–18*, pp. 318–19; see also *Foedera*, v. 2 pt 1, p. 282.
61. *CPR 1313–17*, pp. 440, 450.
62. *CCR 1330–33*, p. 159; *CCR 1333–37*, pp. 82, 98, 675, 683, 731; *CCR 1341–43*, p. 666; *CCR 1343–46*, pp. 267–8; *CCR 1346–49*, p. 403; *CCR 1349–54*, pp. 199–200, 233, 274, 402–3, 593; *CCR 1354–60*, pp. 190, 298, 401–3; *CCR 1360–64*, pp. 138, 334, 436, 542–3; *CCR 1364–68*, pp. 288, 370–1; *CCR 1369–74*, pp. 114–15; *CCR 1374–77*, pp. 103, 208. See also the full texts in *Foedera*, v. 2 pt. 2, pp. 850, 855, 954–5; *Foedera*, v. 3 pt. 1, pp. 92, 139, 199, 207, 250–1, 298, 553; *Foedera*, v. 3 pt. 2, pp. 603, 683, 710, 797, 823, 1016, 1026. In putting together this list I have included the proclamations that cover the entire country or at least the major grain exporting ports but excluded those that relate only to a single county or a few ports.
63. *CCR 1333–37*, pp. 98, 675, 683, 731; *CCR 1364–68*, pp. 370–1.
64. *CCR 1330–33*, p. 159; *CCR 1343–46*, pp. 267–8; *CCR 1346–49*, p. 403; *CCR 1349–50*, pp. 199–200, 402–3; *CCR 1354–60*, pp. 401–3; *CCR 1360–64*, pp. 138, 334; *CCR 1364–68*, p. 288.
65. The eight proclamations in scarcity years are *CCR 1349–54*, p. 233 (23 June 1350), p. 274 (27 October 1350), p. 593 (28 January 1353); *CCR 1360–64*, p. 436 (26 November 1362), pp. 542–3 (8 October 1363); *CCR 1369–74*, pp. 114–16 (26 November 1369); *CCR 1374–77*, p. 103 (2 November 1374), p. 208 (1 March 1375). In identifying scarcity years I have relied on Dyer, *Standards of Living*, pp. 262–3.
66. *CCR 1341–43*, p. 266; *CCR 1343–46*, pp. 267–8.
67. In the tables in Farmer, 'Prices and Wages', p. 791, overall grain prices for the harvest year 1343–4 are 8% above the mean; in contrast overall prices in the harvest year 1346–47 are 31% above the mean.
68. *CCR 1341–43*, p. 691; *CCR 1343–46*, pp. 99, 207, 261, 410–11.
69. See, for example *CCR 1341–43*, p. 628; *CCR 1343–46*, pp. 81–2, 205, 207; *CCR 1346–49*, p. 116.
70. *CPR 1343–45*, pp. 186–7, 279, 286, 403, 421–2; *CPR 1345–48*, pp. 30, 97, 304; *CPR 1348–50*, p. 311.
71. *CCR 1343–46*, p. 261.
72. For references to proclamations at the county court, see *CCR 1307–13*, p. 225; in all towns and ports, see *Foedera* v. 3 pt. 2, p. 710; at the market cross, see G. R. Owst, *Preaching in England* (New York: Russell & Russell, 1965), p. 196; in fairs, markets, hundreds, market towns, see *CCR 1369–74*, pp. 193–4.
73. *CCR 1341–43*, p. 694; *CCR 1346–49*, pp. 116–17, 308.
74. *CCR 1346–49*, p. 116. While this mandate refers to 90 quarters of wheat, the licence in *CPR 1345–48*, p. 198 states 900 quarters.
75. *CCR 1346–49*, p. 403.
76. Hewitt, *Organization of War*, p. 62; see also pp. 60–3 for a discussion of the victualling needs of Calais and Gascony.
77. For licences in the years 1347–50 see *CPR 1345–48*, pp. 281–3; *CPR 1348–50*, pp. 287, 469; see also Gras, *English Corn Market*, pp. 172–3.

78. A. Hassell Smith, *County and Court: Government and Politics in Norfolk, 1558–1603* (Oxford: Clarendon Press, 1974), pp. 18–19, 137–8; see also Williams, *Maritime Trade*, 33–40.
79. *CPR 1374–77*, p. 160; *CPR 1408–13*, pp. 222–3, 316, 375; *CPR 1436–41*, p. 199.
80. *CPR 1374–77*, pp. 324–5; *CCR 1399–1402*, pp. 14–47; *CPR 1399–1401*, p. 516; *CCR 1422–29*, p. 551.
81. *CPR 1399–1401*, p. 516; *CPR 1408–13*, p. 175; *Rotuli Parliamentorum* (hereafter *RP*), 6 vols (London, 1767–77) v. 3, pp. 475–8; *RP*, v. 4, pp. 345–6.
82. See, for example, *CPR 1389–92*, p. 80; *CCR 1405–9*, pp. 482, 485, 527; *CCR 1435–41*, pp. 89, 138, 157.
83. Williams, *Maritime Trade*, pp. 33–40; G. R. Elton, *Star Chamber Stories* (London: Methuen, 1958), pp. 78–133.
84. Britnell, 'Statute of Forestallers', pp. 99–100; *CPR 1334–38*, p. 445; *CPR 1338–40*, p. 64; *CPR 1343–45*, pp. 398, 426.
85. *CPR 1345–48*, p. 320; see also pp. 387–8, a commission to enquire into forestalling in Nottingham, 12 July 1347.
86. *CCR 1369–74*, pp. 193–4; 'manifest impoverishment' comes from the original, PRO, C. 54/208 m. 8d.
87. *CPR 1367–70*, pp. 474–5.
88. *CPR 1374–77*, p. 146; some of the returns are in *Calendar of Inquisitions Miscellaneous (Chancery) 1348–77* (London: HMSO, 1937), pp. 371–2, 376–8.
89. *CCR 1389–92*, p. 250; *CPR 1388–92*, p. 441.
90. *CCR 1435–41*, p. 157; *CPR 1436–41*, p. 145.
91. *CPR 1436–41*, p. 266; PRO, C. 145/308/3 is a return of the inquiry held at Canterbury, Kent.
92. *CPR 1436–41*, p. 267.
93. *CCR 1389–92*, pp. 257, 265, 332–3, 348, 388, 390. My translations of the originals in PRO, C. 54/232, m. 12, m.9, m.16d., m.10d.; c. 54/233 m. 35, m. 34 is 'public good' not 'common weal'.
94. *CCR 1435–41*, pp. 138, 157; translation checked against originals in PRO, C. 54/288 m. 20d.
95. *CCR 1435–41*, p. 195; translation checked against original in PRO, C. 54/289 m. 33.
96. *CPR 1436–41*, p. 266.

3

The Pragmatic Economy, the Politics of Provisions and the 'Invention' of the Food Riot Tradition in 1740

John Bohstedt

E. P. Thompson's brilliant essay on 'The Moral Economy of the English Crowd in the Eighteenth Century' richly illuminated the significance of food riots: food supplies and prices provided primary moral issues of grassroots politics in the last half of the eighteenth century.

I agree with Thompson that the overlap between commoner's and authorities' rhetoric created a political space for 'bargaining by riot' over the claims of consumer needs and property rights, hunger and order. However, Thompson exaggerated food rioters' traditionalism, and hence misconstrued their motives and actions. *↳⊙ of Thompson*

Two decades' study of food marketing and riots call for major changes in Thompson's accounts of the market and of rioters' behaviour. We would be better thinking in terms of a 'pragmatic economy', *-↗ Sensible* in which both rioters and magistrates acted with an eye to political *& realistic* calculation and experience, rather than hoary traditions.[1]

This chapter will explore the 'moral economy' of eighteenth-century food riots by focusing on their formative period, 1740–66, and especially on the first nationwide rioting in 1740, which comprised about 45 incidents ranging from Pembroke to Colchester, from Rhuddlan to Great Yarmouth, and from Dover to Derby and Dewsbury and Durham. It appears that in this formative generation the food riot 'tradition' or repertoire was largely 'invented', and it *evolved* over the last half of the eighteenth century into a complex 'politics of provisions', in which riots, repression and relief interacted. In the pioneering food riots of 1740 both rioters and magistrates were only beginning to improvise the ground rules of a 'politics of provision', not acting out a 200-year old script.

↳what. is this?

7 Do others look at different periods? Such as Walter.

The Moral Economy of Eighteenth-Century English Food Rioters

In his original formulation, Thompson insisted that the issues of fair prices and profits lay at the core of a 'moral economy'. He argued that 'an older moral economy ... taught the immorality of ... forcing up the price of provisions by profiteering'. In his classic article, Thompson argued that food rioters' actions implied:

> the belief that they were defending traditional rights or customs ... [and] a popular consensus as to what were legitimate and ... illegitimate practices in marketing, milling, and baking, etc. in its turn ... grounded upon a consistent traditional view of social norms and obligations, of the proper economic functions of several parties within the community, which taken together can be said to constitute the moral economy of the poor. An outrage to these moral assumptions, quite as much as actual deprivation, was the usual occasion for direct action.

Thompson argued that 'the crowd derived its sense of legitimation, in fact, from the paternalist model', from their 'selective reconstruction' of the traditional market regulations of 'paternalist' officials. He counterposed 'the old moral economy of provision' based on the needs of consumers to 'the new political economy of the free market'. Food riots were part of 'the conservative culture of the plebs' which resisted 'in the name of "custom", those economic innovations and rationalisations ... ([such] as enclosure, work-discipline, free market relations in grain) ... [This] innovation of capitalist process' was experienced as violation of custom. As legitimating warrants, 'food rioters appeal[ed] back to the Book of Orders and to legislation against forestallers, etc., artisans appeal[ed] back to certain parts (e.g. apprenticeship regulation) of the Tudor regulatory labour code'. 'Hence we can read eighteenth-century social history as a succession of confrontations between an innovative market economy and the customary moral economy of the plebs.'[2]

Three Centuries of Provision Politics

The chief problem with Thompson's thesis is that a market economy was far from new in the eighteenth century. The artisans, women and labourers who made up food riot crowds were just the people most immersed in market relations as wage earners, household managers and consumers. In the course of three centuries, food riots became the flywheel of a *provision politics* not because of a clash between 'an innovative market economy' and traditional plebeian beliefs and official regulations so much as because of the convergence of two things: a set of long-term economic trends that increased widespread vulnerability to harvest failure *and* eligibility to riot; and the post-Restoration Government's policy favouring food export, a policy too slowly reversed under the new conditions of the mid-eighteenth century.

Our first century (*c*.1550–1650) was a high-pressure century.[3] The national population nearly doubled, while the proportion of town dwellers and wage-earners, hence consumers, rose as patches of rural industry and agriculture began to commercialise. Those changes increased the numbers of harvest-sensitive consumers who depended on markets for a substantial portion of their food supplies. To meet these needs the food marketing system grew along dual lines: many small market towns serving localities and hinterlands, and a growing wholesale interregional trade.[4] As growing masses of workers came to depend on markets for their food, England became increasingly vulnerable to harvest failure and to food riots: a few in the mid-sixteenth century, a few more in 1586–87 and the 1590s, rising to a peak in the 1620s, especially 1629–31 (which witnessed 30 riots) when trade depression coincided with harvest failures, a double blow at purchasing power.[5] Partly motivated by fear of riots, the Tudor Council issued Books of Orders in 1587 (reissued in 1594, 1595, 1608, 1622 and 1630), directing local magistrates to search out available supplies of food and require farmers and dealers to bring them to market to sell to the poor. At the same time royal proclamations banned exports and ordered punishment of forestallers, regraters and engrossers. Setting prices was not a part of this official paternalism.[6]

The scattered food riots of this first century were mainly confined to ports and old-established centres of woollen production in southern England.[7] Wrightson and Walter argue that poor people typically petitioned magistrates rather than rioted. But occasional riots did prompt magistrates to remedial action that reaffirmed the beneficence of the social order.[8] Much more frequently, struggles over subsistence entitlements took the form of enclosure riots rather than food riots. I take as authoritative John Walter's judgement: 'If crises of subsistence were largely absent from early modern England so were crises of disorder...years of harvest failure were not marked by widespread and frequent food riots.'[9]

Our second century, following the Civil Wars – roughly 1650–1740 – was one of low demographic pressure. Rioting became rarer and, not coincidentally, so did market regulation. Pressure on food supplies eased as agricultural productivity grew faster than stagnating population.[10] All the while an increasing proportion of the population was becoming land-poor and harvest-sensitive, as rural industry grew and larger farms were consolidated. However, though more people seemed vulnerable to dearth, this middle century witnessed very little crisis mortality or hunger rioting. The only significant clusters were two dozen riots spread over 1693–95, and seven each in 1709 and 1727–28.[11] The rarity of riots was probably due to contradictory trends in entitlements. The widespread establishment of the Poor Law in thousands of parishes established the pervasive assumption that the poor were entitled to relief, and real expenditure per capita doubled between 1700 and 1750.[12] However, putting a safety net under paupers did not assure the security of those artisans and labourers, typical rioters, who would devote a lot of energy, and even riot, just to avoid becoming paupers! On that score, John Walter has suggested that riots were rare because of the social economy of dearth: that is, non-market protections against market prices. For instance, the working poor might be shielded from market food prices by customary common or gleaning rights; charities; and especially by non-pecuniary relationships with landlords or employers, offering credit, low prices at the farm gate, and board for live-in servants and apprentices. So potential rioters might be deterred by either relief or dependency on local elites. Walter believes that by the mid-eighteenth century, such social protections against dearth were wearing thin, and coming to be defined as discretionary rather than obligatory. He suggests that the elites' control of such protections meant that the poor could claim their 'entitlements' to relief only at the price of sinking more deeply into webs of dependence.[13]

Meanwhile, after the Civil Wars, governments had backed away from consumer-oriented intervention in marketing, and instead tried to help producers by offering bounties to encourage exports. The prerogative power to suspend exports of grain was not renewed in Restoration legislation, and such interference with subjects' property was counter to the constitutional principles of the Bill of Rights of 1689. So exportation was suspended, necessarily by parliamentary statute, only in 1699 and 1709.[14] This was a major reversal of the Tudor–Stuart paternalism, but it seemed tolerable in a period of farm surpluses and low prices (and little rioting). At the same time, in the absence of central government prodding, magisterial intervention in local marketing probably slackened.[15]

The upshot was, when rioting 'blossomed' from 1740 onwards, neither rioters nor magistrates could build upon strong traditions of

either riotous bargaining or market regulation. In the widespread rioting of 1740, both seemed to be improvising, often clumsily.

Our third century, from 1740 to c.1820, was the golden age of food
riot. By 1700 or 1750 national market in wheat, at least, connected
supply regions with greatest demand. Food exportation had been
encouraged by government bounties since 1672. The export trade gathered steam from 1700 on, but continental demand for English corn
remained stagnant until the 1730s when export levels rapidly tripled
those of the 1720s.[16] Record exports drew loads of grain on to roads
and waterways. The national wholesaling apparatus created since 1700
to gather and ship grain also supplied a growing interregional market
as agricultural and manufacturing regions specialised. The government's policy of promoting exports was on a collision course with the
population pressure on food production, especially in the swelling
industrial districts. Now when dearth struck, the concentrations of
corn and cheese moving towards distant domestic or continental customers provided great targets of opportunity for hungry crowds, and
provoked bitter resentments even though they were not new. That was
so particularly because the government did not act quickly to stop
exports in times of crisis as the early Stuarts had. Now that England
had become a large exporter, the failure to shift the gears of national
policy in mid-century was the biggest factor in the rioting.[17]

In this high-pressure century, rapid population growth put pressure
on food supplies, and, together with urbanisation and regional economic specialisation, this increased the numbers of wage-earners
dependent on wages and markets for their food.[18] But the quality of
their social status was as important as their numbers. More than in the
previous century they had the *optimum degree of social independence to
riot*. On the one hand Walter's informal personal shields continued to
decay: live-in farm servants and apprentices decreased, while gleaning
and common rights were challenged,[19] so more people became
vulnerable to dearth. At the same time, the common people became
more 'eligible' for riot. First, growing pockets of manufacturing workers
were free of the dependency networks of social control more common
to agrarian communities, and second, many of those worker communities – colliers everywhere, tinners in Cornwall, textile workers in the
West Country – began to develop the solidarities that would give them
a formidable if informal franchise in the politics of provisions.[20]

Rather abruptly riots grew into a sturdy and nationwide tradition:
about 45 riots in 1740; about 110 riots in 1756–57; a similar number
in 1766; a few dozen in the 1770s and 1780s; and then around 150
riots in both 1795–96 and 1800–1; but surprisingly only a few dozen in

? Just focus on the 45 in 1748

1810–13, and even fewer in 1816–18.[21] It is from this period that we have wide evidence of labour combinations, as well as riots.

Both combinations and riots often relied on implicit reciprocities with magistrates. Growing social independence did not mean a complete break with the gentry. Workers still appealed to magistrates for mediation in labour disputes, and food rioters sometimes sought out magistrates to negotiate with. The patronage networks of parliamentary boroughs often provided a framework within which familiar parties could bargain. The rhetoric of the moral economy still provided a meeting ground on which to negotiate social peace. Magistrates and gentlemen still condemned wicked merchants (forestallers, regraters and engrossers), but mainly for symbolic effect.[22] They spent much more effort obtaining and distributing relief supplies than trying to regulate the markets, according to S. I. Mitchell's study of Cheshire magistrates between 1757 and 1812.[23] Very broadly speaking, by 1801 the politics of provisions had spawned a viable protocol of riot, by which I mean both rioters and magistrates restrained their use of force while riots succeeded in prompting relief by the gentry, at least in many places. But the beginning in 1740 was much rougher since rioters and magistrates were 'inventing' a nationwide 'tradition'.

The 'Invention' of the Food Riot Tradition in 1740

The riots of 1740, because they were the first national wave, deserve more study than they have hitherto received.[24] How far did any precedents for rioters' and magistrates' actions appear, and where did they come from? Our *long-term* trends – population resurgence, commercialisation, decay of social 'insulation' – doubtless *contributed* to the first national wave of food riots in 1740. But the proximate cause of those riots was the massive and visible exportation of foodstuffs in a very hard year. The winter of 1739–40 was one of the severest on record, and 'many poor People' perished from cold and hunger despite 'great … Acts of Charity'.[25] Harvests failed and corn prices rose sharply. Even worse, substantial quantities of corn were shipped to the Continent to meet both domestic and military demand in the spring of 1740. The beginning of the war with Spain and impressment hurt shipping and employment, and economic depression plus high food and fuel prices increased the numbers of the poor and hungry, and the numbers of burials in London. The dip in national marriage rates was the second-greatest in the eighteenth century.[26] The hard times elicited many 'retail' (individual) charitable efforts, including coal hand-outs, in London and other towns, though they ended with the winter season.[27] In the spring, as riots against exportation broke out, the Privy Council consulted its law officers about the corn laws but in late June merely issued a proclamation ordering magistrates to scrutinise exports and to enforce the old Tudor statutes against forestalling, regrating and engrossing. That seems to have been window-dressing intended to 'chill' exportation and perhaps popular excitement. The *Leeds Mercury* and other newspapers took the bait and reported that the government had banned exports, but specialists in the trade knew better. Merchants scrambled to ship grain away. The government did not act to ban exportation of corn until November 1740;[28] hence tangible 'exports' of grain both from neighbourhoods and to overseas markets provoked the riots of 1740. People blamed exports for the high prices; they said nothing about precedents or novelties.

The rioting of 1740 began at Dewsbury in the West Riding of Yorkshire. No known food riots had taken place in the north of England before this time.[29] Dewsbury was in the heart of the growing West Riding woollen district between Leeds and Huddersfield, though its independent clothier-farmers made the district ordinarily self-sufficient in grain.[30] On the last Saturday in April, 1740, about 400 men and women from Dewsbury and the surrounding villages assembled 'to prevent the Badgers [Dealers] from making Wheat Meal or Flower, to send into other Counties [especially Lancashire], alledging that such Practice would cause a Scarcity in Yorkshire, and much advance the Price of Corn'. They also felt that '(one of the mills being much employ'd in grinding for the Badgers), the Poor People could not have their corn ground without a Bribe to the Miller'.[31] They spotted a badger's wagonload of flour on its way to Lancashire and seized it, but the owner had decoyed them with bran dust which they threw on to the highway. They marched on to Dewsbury mill to get the meal and flour but, finding it well secured, they rested overnight in the woods. Next day they unroofed the millhouse, demolished the bolting engine, and carried off 20 packs of flour, throwing some of it into the river. Reinforced by recruits 'invited ... by Open Proclamation made in the Church yard', the rioters crossed the river to Thornhill mill to destroy bolting machines and seize flour, and even the beef and bacon of the poor mill assistant. One account designated the crowd 'a great posse', for indeed the 'power of the county' vested in the people was ambivalent when food supplies were at stake.[32]

In this pioneering phase of provision politics, 'negotiations' were crude and one-dimensional: the magistrates sought merely to disperse crowds rather than to recognise their grievances. The rioters were confronted by Sir John Kaye, MP for York, and Sir Samuel Armytage, High Sheriff of the County. The crowd explained their goal was 'to prevent Corn being carryed out of the Country, which they pretended occasioned a great Scarcity amongst them'. These high officials read the Riot Act proclamation ordering them to disperse, but the crowd 'threw Stones and other Things at them'. Sir John did invite the crowd to his mansion on Monday where the assembled justices would 'hear their Complaints and redress their Grievances, *if any'* (my italics). So the next day about 1000 rioters arrived 'by Beat of Drum and Colours carried before them, in defiance of Authority'. Instead of offering remedies, the gentlemen again called on them to disperse, and the High Sheriff did not even show up. The people felt let down, for they marched off 'with Huzza's, crying, They neither car'd for the High Sheriff, nor the Justices of the Peace'.

They marched on to demolish bolting machines and seize corn and meal at three more mills and then besieged a storehouse, where the owner, Joseph Pollard, wounded several with 'hail shot', and sent several prisoners to the Wakefield House of Correction. The next afternoon, beating a drum, the rioters marched into Wakefield to a Captain Burton's house. Burton took a good stick in his hand and demanded 'by what authority they came in so tumultuous a manner?' They replied, 'We are come to relieve our Men which you have Prisoners, and have 'em we will', adding 'they would pull down Pollard's House, and hang him up and skin him like a Cat'. At this Captain Burton knocked down several and seized others. Order was restored that evening when troops arrived, and ultimately nineteen prisoners were sent under strong guard to York Castle. At the July Assizes, no fewer than ten men were transported for seven years, while four men were jailed for a year for riot and attempted rescue. This was a hard-nosed Yorkshire collision rather than a politick negotiation: defiance, damage, and grain seizures on one side, incomprehension and stiff punishments on the other. Apparently there were no elite efforts to provide relief. Sir John Kaye had his reputation for stinginess at elections to preserve![33]

The rioters of this formative generation of 1740–66 did not distinguish themselves by the discipline and respect for property emphasised by Thompson and others. Nor does their behaviour sustain Thompson's contention that 'the central action was setting the price'.[34] Seizure of grain and damage to mills and granaries were much more typical. The riots were about physical supplies more than market morality.

It is significant that the first riot in 1740 began with bolting mills, which were again major targets in 1756–57 and 1766. They may have been new in some areas, but they were attacked primarily because of their connection with exportation as well as with 'engrossing' and adulteration. 'Boulting mills' (otherwise called dressing or bunting mills) were machines powered by the main mill-drive that sifted fine flour for export into the commercial trade. Eusebius Silvester, writing in 1757, explained that dressing mills were attacked by the 'poor mistaken and undistinguishing populace', because they had permitted the millers to become monopolists, 'the Stockjobbers of Bread the...staff of life'. He blamed high prices on that 'monopoly' of the millers or mealmen (as he called them), for it imposed several profits between farmer and consumer.[35] Indeed, those sifting machines had transformed millers from local tradesmen into great manufacturers and wholesale flour merchants. The mills were not new in 1740. They had spread outward from London since the seventeenth century, when a law against them had been passed.[36] Rioters attacked them as a practical way to stop the export of flour and to procure food, and thus practised true Luddism by wrecking machines not because they were new, but as a way to stop production in a dispute.[37]

At Nottingham in 1740 the country people and then 'the Town Mob' threatened to destroy a bolting mill at Radford 'where corn is ground for a considerable corn factor in Nottingham', and forced a country farmer to leave his wagon of wheat in the town.[38] Sometimes the rioting spread from an initially provocative shipment 'up' the distribution chain to the granaries and mills where the corn and flour was processed. At Colchester in May and June 1740, dearth and 'want of employment' in the woollen industry made the poor fear that exportation would drain the countryside. The magistrates ordered dragoons to guard corn wagons to the water landing after several had been attacked. In the following weeks crowds spread out to the granaries at Manningtree in the Stour estuary, to nearby mills where they threw about and seized flour and meal, and then to the bolting mills at Bures and Bailington. At the Essex Summer Assizes four people were transported for riotously entering mills and seizing wheat at Saffron Walden and near Colchester, and three women were acquitted.[39] At Kettering in 1740 popular opposition to the 'transportation' of corn in mid-May led to the town crier crying a 'mach of futball' of 500 men a side, but the real 'design was to pull down Ed Betey Jermaine's Mills'.[40]

Exportation was the central motif in the press's and magistrates' reports of the food riots of 1740, as they spread nationwide for the first time, from Rhuddlan to Yarmouth, from Pembroke to Colchester, and from Dover to Newcastle. In 27 (60 percent) of the approximately 45 riots, the rioters' chief action and/or expressed motive was to stop exportation or transport by attacking storehouses or shipments by road or water.[41] Indeed, exportation was linked to the English food rioters' banner cry: 'We'd rather be hanged than starved.' Thus the women of Stockton 'swear they will dye before any corn shall be exported for that they had better be killed or hanged than starved'. The rioters of Rhuddlan mistakenly insisted that the corn was being sent to 'their enemies the Spaniards & they would choose to die fighting against them & rather to be hanged than starved!'[42]

Rather than marketplace eruptions of popular regulation, these early riots often featured great invasions of town by outsiders, especially colliers. The miners of North Wales had already been aroused by 'exports' to Chester and Liverpool in the hard times of 1709 and 1728–29. On 21 May 1740, Trelogan colliers told of being called up from their pits to go to Y Foryd, a landing near Rhuddlan, to stop corn exportation. That morning hundreds of men, women and children armed with staves and clubs marched into Rhuddlan and seized a wagon of wheat being shipped to Liverpool. The price of corn had suddenly doubled and they had heard 'that it was stopd in other parts of England from being shipd off'. Now, they told the Tory magistrate,

> they and their families were starving for want of bread … little corn was brought to the markets, so that they could not get it for money, & … great quantities were sent from thence to Sea, which they were resolved to stop from going out of the country whilst they were in want.

They would only disperse when he promised to ban exports and release arrested rioters. That Sunday churchyards rang with the proclamation that Rhuddlan merchants had promised to stop exporting corn.[43]

The violent Newcastle riot of 1740 also began with women protesting against high prices and grain shipments. The rioting reached its climax when the rioters demanded to unload a ship loaded with rye at the town quay.[44] At nearby Stockton,

> great numbers of people continue[d] to assemble … and obstinately oppose the shipping of any corn at that port; and tho' a detachment of soldiers has been sent thither … this means is not found to be at all effectual, for the fear among the populace of wanting bread surmounts the Dread of an armed force.

The merchants offered them large quantities of corn at cut prices but the disorder continued, especially because the county's MPs failed to dissuade merchants from shipping off more corn.[45]

At Peterborough women 'rose in a tumultuous manner, rioted the farmers out of their sacks, and strowed their corn in the street'.[46] This was hardly a simple marketplace dust-up, however: rioters also seized 'great quantities' of grain from boats and barges on the river and threatened to murder people and pull down their houses.[47] At Wellingborough one of the rioters declared that corn was seized to prevent it being exported or engrossed. Another rioter justified her actions 'under the false and mistaken notion [perhaps based on the June proclamation "against exports"] that it was lawful to seize and detain the said wheat supposing it to be bought up for Transportation to the prejudice of the poor of this Town'.[48] These two statements were the only occasions in 1740 that plebeians may have referred to older laws and regulations.

At Dover a nefarious French twist was added: the report to the Duke of Newcastle was that 'the French merchants ride about the country & bye up all the wheat and barley they can find', to raise its price, and 'the French export most of it to Spain'. The women of Dover cut the sacks of farmers bringing grain to the port, seized most of the corn and scattered some of it in the streets, and then pelted the teams and drivers for three miles out of town. If that did not stop them, they said they would board the ships and unload them. Continental demand had stripped the coast bare.[49] On the three occasions when presumably hungry rioters scattered corn in the streets, was it intentional punishment of wrong-doers, as many historians have assumed? Was it anger at hoarders or exporters? Was it 'breakage' from the rough seizure and distribution? We cannot be sure.

When price-fixing did take place it was usually connected with blocking export rather than with regulating a marketplace. At Yarmouth a mob plundered a vessel about to sail overseas, and forced the dealers to sell the corn at 2s. a bushel. At Colchester a merchant attempted to bargain with George Mallard, who brandished a sword in leading a crowd to plunder a boat. But offers of drink and half-pecks of corn were refused and the crowd broke open the sacks despite the attempts of their would-be leader to 'supervise' them. At Pembroke colliers smashed their way into a vessel bound for Bristol and seized the corn, after which they came into the market 'to demand corn at their own price'. In the Isle of Ely a crowd of fenmen from Upwell marched into Wisbech, broke corn merchants' windows, seized grain from granaries 'to prevent its exportation', fixed prices for its sale to bakers whom they also 'regulated', and extorted from £30 to £80 in 'donations' from shopkeepers and householders, before returning to Upwell with commandeered wagons carrying most of the grain. When the rioters were arrested a rescue was feared because of 'the same discontented spirit and temper about the exportation of corn here and thereabouts'.[50]

At Norwich the following week the magistrates also feared riots 'on pretence of preventing Corn from being exported into forreign parts'. In addition the master weavers had lowered their journeymen's wages. On the Sunday morning the fishmongers raised the price of mackerel, causing a 'sort of riot'. The next day a thousand of the common people pinned a note on the door of every baker in the city: 'Wheat at sixteen shillings a comb.' They forced bakers to sell their corn at cut prices, and then broke open several granaries and seized great quantities of corn. The magistrates' immediate promise to stop exports bought a temporary peace. Later that week crowds stopped a keel of wheat and rye on the river and divided it up, and then for days extorted money and drink from the townspeople and farmers.[51] Crowds also blocked 'exports' by road.[52] When a Kinver miller came to Envill (Staffordshire) to buy ten bags of corn at 'the house of one Daniel Appleby' a small crowd of women and a man rang some pans and stopped the pack horse before he could leave town, and cut the bags so that the corn was strewn in the streets.[53]

Sometimes rioters brought intercepted food back into the market-place to make a public ceremony of dividing it up. When farmers at Newport Pagnell tried to disguise their corn as cheese, some cunning old women intercepted the wagons outside the town. 'Unwilling so much corn should go out of the kingdom, [the old women] swore they would lose their lives before they would part with it', and rallied 300 women to overpower the farmers, and bring the corn back into town amidst great rejoicing. There they set a guard on it and then a 'grand Council' was called to settle how to distribute it.[54]

Interregional trade ran afoul of local provision politics at Derby too. The *Derby Mercury* reported (inaccurately) that the Privy Council had ordered the enforcement of 'the laws against exportation'. Derby was apparently a transshipment point for processing corn which had come up the Trent on its way from the east to the West Midlands industrial areas. Despite the magistrates' warnings about engrossing, two millers sent wagons of flour off towards Leek, Staffordshire, in early July. They were intercepted by a crowd. A magistrate stopped them as 'the Women [were] filling their Aprons, Bags, or other things they brought to carry it away in', and persuaded them to bring it back to the marketplace, two women leading the forehorse, and the mob shouting in great triumph. Once there, however, they resumed 'ransacking' and carrying it away. The millers, William Evans and his partner, advertised in the *Mercury* (presumably speaking to potential rioters and sympathisers) that they had been falsely accused of exporting great quantities of flour into foreign parts. They declared all the flour they produced was sold in England. They dealt only with a baker in Manchester, and two bakers in Leek to whom they sent 'some little'. But the 'chief part' of the flour they made was sold in their own neighbourhood, and they had bought only a little wheat in Derby in the previous six months.[55]

It will be clear by now that the rioters of 1740 were more interested in seizing food than regulating markets. In North Wales mobs of all sizes roamed the countryside between Holywell and Conway for more than a week, ransacking shops, a mill and houses, carrying off grain, shop goods, pewter and raisins, and demanding money. Markets were disrupted, not regulated. The only sale of grain reported was not a disciplined *taxation populaire*, but a disposal of looted grain for cash at an inn, after which one of the lucky rioters spent his share of the proceeds eating and drinking at the inn, a fantasy rather like winning the lottery. The crowd at Mold had put the corn they seized in the Town House to await distribution, but the military prevented that.[56]

Geographically and occupationally the rioters came from emerging industrial worker communities or else from town artisans and labourers, though we have much less information on their identities than for later riots. In general the riots of 1740 took place in arable/surplus areas or their ports, not deficit regions.[57] Rioters did not protest at empty barns. The distribution of riots was only partly shaped by specific economic regions:[58] round Dewsbury in the West Riding but not across the whole woollen district; in the Vale of Clywd in North Wales, structured as much by political rivalries as by economic geography; in traditional haunts of riots, like the textile district round Colchester and the counties of Northamptonshire and Staffordshire, and the coal districts of the north-east. Strikingly missing from action in 1740 were the traditionally riotous West Country woollen workers, Cornish tinners and Oxford townspeople. Colliers formed nuclei of crowds at Pembroke, Newcastle, the Vale of Clywd, and at scattered episodes in Staffordshire. They were called upon as shock troops at Stockton. In Pembroke and the Vale of Clywd, mine owners moved to relieve their own workers.[59] This may confirm Ashton and Sykes' proposition that larger coal owners could afford to supply their men, but the smaller works' men were left on their own, often to riot.[60] Indeed, the Kingswood colliers seems to have been habitually in the latter position, marching into Bristol to make demands on the city officials in 1740 and in many other crises.[61] Otherwise textile workers appeared in Essex and Dewsbury. Women were identified in a fair share of riots (13), as in 1756 and 1766, participating fully in them, but not dominating them. The broader impression is that riot crowds typically comprised both men and women.

L7 Can' Say something about this?

The Contribution of Parliamentary Patronage to Food Riots

If neither rioters nor magistrates seem guided by established traditions of food riots or market regulation, they could draw upon the experience of many riots over other issues.[62] But lacking a tradition (socialised experience) of negotiating specifically about provisions, magistrates seemed to lack imagination. (The events of 1740 are not an advertisement for the 'cunning of the ruling class'.) There were relatively few episodes in 1740 in which magistrates had anything to offer rioters, by contrast with the 'paternalists' of 1756, 1766 and the end of the century, who preached against forestallers, imposed the Assize of Bread, persuaded farmers and tenants to bring their corn to market at reasonable prices, and started relief subscriptions. Very little of this was done in 1740.

 However, other folkways supplied precedents, especially those from elections and political patronage. Where 'negotiations' of a sort did take place – where the rioters received something besides stony silence or naked steel – it was often in parliamentary boroughs, where officials were more used to dealing with plebeian constituents. We have already seen how the MP for Yorkshire, Sir John Kaye, invited the rioters to parley at Dewsbury. Indeed at a climactic point in the Stockton rioting, the two County Durham MPs turned the tide by selling 600 bushels of corn cheaply to the poor, and announcing a local ban on exportation. Merchants had offered an additional 1000 bushels.[63] It was evidently 1740's only relief effort on a community scale. At the borough of Colchester, where unemployment in the woollen industry compounded the high prices of food, the magistrates promised a crowd they would ask the Government for an export ban.[64] The Norwich magistrates also responded to riots with handbills proclaiming that they would strictly enforce the Privy Council's orders 'for preventing the Exportation of Corn', and after some shootings had escalated violence, 'plenipo [tentiaries]' of rioters and officials negotiated a truce.[65]

In a few other cases, corporate officials balanced 'rhetorical paternalism' with warnings against riot. The most elaborate gesture towards the old market sins was at the borough of Derby. Following the June proclamation against forestalling, regrating and engrossing, and the subsequent riot, the magistrates, bearing the town mace with elaborate ceremony, marched to the steps of the Town Hall to proclaim that forestallers, engrossers and rioters would be punished by quarter sessions. Later that week the two millers who had shipped the flour were charged with engrossing at the Quarter Sessions, but the grand jury refused to indict. However, two women were transported for the riot.[66] Since Justice was class-based, her scales were not blind! When the Kingswood colliers marched towards Bristol to complain to city officials about high prices, the magistrates called out a guard of soldiers and constables. The Mayor at least spoke to their delegates and promised to try to keep a tight lid on the bakers' prices, but he also asked the Secretary of State to alert the military should force be needed.[67] Furthermore, reviving paternalism prompted the Bishop of Durham, *custos rotulorum* of the county, to preach a Christian homily at the July Quarter Sessions about a moral economy in which the various elements of society would serve each other. This it was wicked to withhold grain but also to riot.[68]

The most structured bargaining in 1740 took place in Newcastle upon Tyne.[69] On one side were the coalminers or pitmen, the river keelmen, and the Crowley ironworkers, a formidable corps of proletarians experienced in forceful collective bargaining with large-scale capitalists. Many of them were freemen, voters, and experienced factional bludgeon-men in the ancient corporate town and large parliamentary borough of Newcastle. The entrenched borough elite was riven by party and business rivalries, and dominated by Alderman Matthew Ridley, expected to run for Parliament in 1741 to replace his recently deceased father, a long-time political czar. The colliers marched into town with drum, horn and flying colours to protest about the prices and exports, and seized corn from inns and carts and piled it in the marketplace. The magistrates sensibly decided to negotiate, the corn merchants agreed to reduce their prices, and the demonstrators stacked their corn in the public weigh-house. The next day, however, finding the shops closed, the crowd began to seize bread, attack granaries, and reduce prices to the previous year's levels. After a stand-off lasting several days, the tension exploded in a scuffle, a shooting, and the thorough sacking of the town Guildhall. It took three companies of soldiers to restore order. Until the merchants closed their shops, this had been the most orderly negotiation of the year. Indeed the Newcastle authorities went on to prohibit exports of local grain; it was a partial success for the rioters. Alderman Ridley was also reported to have provided corn for his employees; the shadow of the impending election of 1741 cannot be discounted.

In the Vale of Clywd in North Wales, parliamentary rivalries and patronage also structured riot politics. Sir Thomas Mostyn, Tory MP for Flintshire, was the proprietor of collieries at Mostyn and Bychton, and his colliers were led into riot by their stewards. On their first visit to Rhuddlan (above) they had seized a wagon of corn bound for Liverpool. On their second foray, they acted like an election mob, stopping first at Mostyn Hall to get ancient helberds, pikes and a rusty musket, more potent as livery than as weapons. They shouted 'A Mostyn!' as they marched into Rhuddlan, stronghold of the area's only Whig MP, Sir George Wynne, where they seized more corn 'designed for Exportation'. This time they were hunting three Whiggish merchants, George Colley, Ned Williams, innkeeper of the Blackmoor's Head, and John Evans, clerk to the vicar, all of them 'considerable Dealers in and Exporters of Corn'. Forewarned, the three of them hid under hedges, but the crowds attacked their houses and storehouses, breaking their windows and even Colley's looking glass and parlour pictures, drinking their beer and wine, and seizing oats and wheat from their stores: 'If Colley's house had not been *insured* they would have fired it.' Colley had had five of them arrested on their previous visit, and they vowed to quarter Colley and parade his parts on pikes or else 'they would cutt his head off and set [it] upon Dyserth finger post and tye his guts about it'. They swore 'they would lay Rhuddlan in ashes and their threatening [was] more to be dreaded because they were sober' [*sic*]. Colley charged that Mostyn's agents had protected three 'Tory' merchants from the mob, who 'were set on by Gentlemen', so 'it's plain it's a concerted thing'.[70] The Whig justice David Foulkes added that, 'Sir Robt Grosvenor's smelters...I understand were all there [at Rhuddlan].' Grosvenor was another of the dominant Tories in the region. The magistrates themselves were split by party. When the rioters forced a large corn merchant to sign a bond not to export corn, they decided against one justice, who 'was not of their party', and resolved to take him to the Tory justice, Humphrey Parry, who was popularly claimed to have sanctioned the rioting to stop corn going to sea. A third MP, Sir Watkin William Wynn, a powerful, reactionary Tory and a fervent Jacobite, was nicknamed 'the Prince of Wales'. The Member for Denbighshire had been saluted by crowds crying out as they marched along, 'King Watkin forever'. But when a crowd of Wrexham 'freeholders and Tradesmen' demanded he distribute some meal, and he refused, they devastated him with the cry, 'Myddleton for ever and down with Watkin', and promised retribution at election time.[71]

Parliamentary politics even entered into peacekeeping. When the magistrates at Pembroke arrested a couple of colliers they were soon obliged to let them go. William Owen, Whig MP for Pembroke, felt the riots were mitigated by the 'vast exportation' and 'extravagant prices' when 'the people were starving for want', and not likely to continue since the corn was gone, and 'the owners of the collieries [had begun] to supply the men with corn'. As for quartering the troops on the town, he complained, 'I assure you my pocket must pay for this ye next election'. Owen, whose family controlled the county for decades, was no stranger to mobs. When he was opposed in the election of 1741, his opponent found himself blocked on the steps of the hall 'by a great number of persons armed with pitchforks and other offensive weapons'.[72] At Stockton, gentlemen had to yield up several prisoners to the crowd; the Sheriff explained to the Bishop, 'I presume my friend Hedworth so near a new election wou'd not be overforward to think of soldiers'.[73]

Roughly speaking, then, the more parliamentary rivalry and patronage, the more 'negotiation' was likely and the greater chance of success for the rioters.[74] (The above examples of negotiation in parliamentary constituencies comprise one-fifth of the riots.) It suggests that, as eighteenth-century electoral violence declined, it may have passed on some traditions of 'patronage' to food riots.[75]

Primitive Peacekeeping

Without a distinctive food riot protocol to guide them, the magistrates' first recourse was to order the rioters to disperse, half a dozen times, by reading the Riot Act proclamation. Sometimes the rioters dispersed, sometimes they did not. The magistrates next thought of suppression. A few times they reached out naively for the ancient *posse comitatus*, the power of the county, the mobilisation of the people themselves to put down treason and disorder.[76] Under order from the magistrates, the ageing sheriff of County Durham climbed out of his sick bed to summon the posse (all men in the county) to meet him at Sedgefield to march to Stockton to put down rioting. But he was certain it was a bad idea: if he led them to confront a mob, there would be a general battle and much bloodshed, but if no mob appeared, he had no power to keep them in being. At the appointed rendezvous, a horn sounded and an ambivalent crowd appeared: the question was, whose posse were they? Some hoped to protect their own lives and property, but they were hostile both to the authorities and to exportation. They went to Stockton, restored 'order', but then melted away near Durham, permitting their prisoners to be rescued. The sheriff doubted the posse could be called out again, for those who had stayed home laughed at those who had gone.[77] The magistrate at Rhuddlan managed to see the fatal ambiguity of the posse in advance. After procuring a 'Warrant writ to raise the power of the county … [he] consulted two lawyers … but upon consideration that all the Country were of the same way of thinking [as the mob] we thought it in vain'.[78]

Old-fashioned dependencies or cash might still rally an effective posse (as in 1756): after fenmen from Upwell had plundered Wisbech, gentlemen of the town raised £200, hired 500 mercenaries and marched out to Upwell to seize 60 suspects and strike terror into the rest.[79] Doubtless the town–country antagonism helped. In Northamptonshire, townspeople and the servants of the Earl of Northampton and other gentlemen overcame a crowd and arrested thirty-three.[80]

At other times improvised peacekeeping backfired and inflamed conflict. At Newcastle after factionalism hindered the calling up of the town guard, the ever-ready Alderman Ridley appeared with a private army of 60 horsemen and 300 foot, all bearing oak cudgels and wearing green boughs in their hats, like an election mob. A gentleman fired into the crowd, touching off the sacking of the Guildhall in retaliation.[81] Similarly, it seems to have been overheated citizens who started the shooting at Norwich that resulted in six deaths.

In nine of the 45 incidents magistrates called on troops to restore order. There were two chief problems with troops: first, the logistics were very clumsy. In principle, a magistrate was supposed to request troops from the Secretary of State, who would rule on the request (in many cases after consulting the Privy Council) and pass it on to the Secretary at War, who would then issue the order, perhaps through the commander in chief's office to the troops in the field.[82] Thus it took some days for the troops to arrive in Dewsbury, Newcastle, North Wales. Meanwhile 'the people were up'. Second, troops might restore order, but not authority. In the twilight of dependency, it was still assumed that gentlemen ought to be able to govern their neighbours by influence and reciprocity, and the use of troops stripped the velvet glove from the iron fist, as Secretaries of State were all too fond of reminding harried magistrates. In 1740 peacekeeping was also bedevilled by the spectre of Porteous. Only two years before, Captain John Porteous had commanded a military detachment that fired into an Edinburgh crowd, killing seventeen. Porteous was convicted of murder and condemned to hang. Worse, before sentence could be carried out he was lynched by a mob.[83] It was a double-edged warning to every peace officer in Britain. After the rioting in North Wales had been suppressed, a magistrate told the government that if the troops were pulled out too soon, he would go with them as a volunteer soldier, 'rather than stay at home to be Porteous'd by those Ruffians'. The Sheriff of County Durham had a contentious debate with the magistrates over who should order troops to fire: 'the thoughts of shedding blood & being tried for itt to me I own was terrible'. Bristol and Newcastle officials also shuddered at the appalling Porteous precedent.[84]

The Politics of Justice

Reinforcing the impression of inexperienced and hamfisted peacekeeping was a draconian 'politics of justice': that is, judicial processes with a public message. My impression is that rioters in 1740 received sentences proportionately much harsher than those at the end of the century. Although only two rioters were hanged for the riots of 1740,[85] no fewer than 47 men and 6 women were transported (in 19 of the 45 riots for which there is some evidence), most of them for seven years. The harshness of these sentences conveys something of the shock of the elites, and also the rarity of short imprisonment.[86] Six men were sentenced to short gaol terms, while seventeen men and four women were held in gaol pending bail, two men and eight women were sentenced to be publicly whipped, and eleven men and seven women were fined.[87] There is some gender bias in these sentences: for instance, of 43 people identified in the rioting at Dewsbury, not one of the twelve women in the group was convicted; most were not brought to trial. It should also be noted that in 1740 as later, quite a few rioters spent months in gaol awaiting trial at the Assizes so that even when charges were dismissed, they had served a punitive and deterrent span of time.[88]

Of course, arrests, convictions and harsh sentences were meant to make examples to deter more rioting; such politics of justice was hardly new. A royal judge declined old William Fisher's petition for mercy:

> considering that Great disturbances had happened in the Northern as well as other parts of the Kingdom on the account or under the Pretence of the high Price of Corn; I thought it might be proper for

the sake of example, to Order Him and eight other persons ... to be all transported.[89]

But deterrence was diluted as Dewsbury rioters absconded before they could be apprehended, and one justice regretted that two 'notorious' rioters 'were not capitally convicted', 'owing to the extraordinary Lenity of the jury'.[90] The prize for overkill went to the gentlemen of Wisbech who seized *sixty* fenmen for riot, and actually got fourteen of them sentenced of death. Higher officials clucked:

> Surely it has not been prudent in the Wisbech justices to take up such a multitude of them when the seizing and making examples of the Captain, the Lieutenant and the Commodore, as they stile themselves, and a few more of the Chiefe of them, would have sufficiently terrified the rest.[91]

The Wisbech officials backpedalled, asking the Privy Council for pardons at least for some, for now that the public peace had been restored 'there could be no service to the district to hang so many', and indeed such severity would 'probably raise a general Discontent and Murmuring against Those, who from a Spirit of Zeal for his Majesty's Service, as well as for the sake of their own preservation ... suppressed the late Riot, and apprehended the Offenders.' In the event all were pardoned and 'merely transported.[92] Later in the century that sort of calculation would typically be made more discreetly before cases came to trial. There was one additional wrinkle in the 'politics of justice'. By early 1741, after the nine men had been transported, some of the victims of the Dewsbury riots persisted in the prosecution of one active rioter, for they were 'now more desirous to have [monetary] Satisfaction for their losses than to inflict any further corporal punishment', and their quarry, John Robinson the younger, a Soothill clothier and the son of an innkeeper, was 'a man of substance'.[93]

Some of the crudeness of these early riots contrasts with the protocol of riot of the end of the century. Since ambiguities surrounded troops and posses, magistrates often let riots run their course. Partly for lack of troops, partly for lack of redress, riots in 1740 (and in 1756 and 1766) often included crowds marching over several days and parishes, somewhat less 'compact' in the dramatic unities than the later riots. At the same time the politics of justice awaited further refinement. In sum the politics of provisions of this formative generation, especially in 1740, were much rougher in all respects than the more rehearsed socio-dramas of the 1790s. It is tempting to interpret the intervening three generations of food riots as witnessing the transition from a declining social economy of retail (individual) protection to a more routine provision of wholesale shields against communal distress by 1800. The riots of 1740 perhaps indicated where the gap was the widest.

Were Food Riots a Response to 'an innovative market economy'?

If food riots and moral economy/paternalist beliefs were as entrenched in defence of tradition as Thompson argued, those traditions and beliefs ought to have been manifest in the first national waves of riots in 1740, 1756–57 and 1766. The stories of 1740 suggest otherwise. Were food riots *typically* provoked by innovations in marketing practices? With one exception, there is little evidence that they were. As one such innovation Thompson discusses sale by 'samples' in inns or markets that was replacing the public offering of grain in bulk in the open marketplace.[94] But the chronology does not fit the inception of nationwide riots in 1740. Thompson quotes the most prominent (and rare) paternalist pamphlet of the first half of the century to the effect that sale by samples had replaced bulk marketing by *c.*1700 in one town. It has become general practice by 1750.[95] Did sale by samples provoke riots? Thompson presents evidence of several verbal protests against the practice between 1710 and 1733 when there were very few food riots. But sale by sample was implicated in only one riot, at Oxford in 1757.[96] Another example of innovation cited by Thompson was the Winchester bushel, an official attempt at a standard measure since Charles II. For the Winchester bushel, Thompson provides evidence of three complaints, but no riots.[97] The bolting mill was the one innovation that did figure in riots although it was not emphasised by Thompson. Otherwise market innovations were implicated in fewer than ten riots across the whole century, hardly *typical* amidst 700 riots.

Nor can eighteenth-century food rioters be seen as innocent consumers outraged by profits. Their normative model of exchange was hardly the idyllic marketplace of Thompson's 'moral economy' where producers met consumers as 'servants of the community'[98] under the watchful eye of a paternal magistrate. Industrial workers (who rioted most) often bought their groceries, flour and bread not from farmers, but from shops and bakeries after it had passed through the hands of merchants, millers and bakers, profit-makers all.[99] Marketplace were the place to purchase perishables: fresh produce, eggs, butter, fruits, *why?*

vegetables and meat, usually from small dealers, butchers and farmer's wives. These vendors were not attacked very often. In inland port cities such as Chester and Oxford, corn was sold mainly in the inns by mid-century, or else in the corn market, but to processors, especially bakers, not consumers.[100]

Rioters did not attack shops or bakers very often. For one thing, rioters knew shopkeepers were not making much profit, while bakers were under considerable constraints as the Assize of Bread was revived in eighteenth-century dearths. It also seems likely that many consumers depended on shopkeepers for credit and on bakers' ovens to bake dough made up at home,[101] so they could not afford to alienate them.

Thompson claimed that 'an outrage to ... moral assumptions, quite as much as actual deprivation, was the usual occasion for direct action'.[102] The evidence suggests otherwise: dearth – 'actual deprivation' by scarcity and high prices – prompted rioters to attack the mills, granaries and waterside warehouses of the big corn and cheese dealers, and to seize food. Like the English bank robber who robbed banks because that's where the money is, food rioters went where the food was. Judging from the rioters' words and actions, getting food was primary, punishing 'hoarding' a distant second. At least in the early food riot crises (1740–66) crowds 'regulating' marketplaces comprised only a small fraction of food riots. By emphasising capitalist innovations, 'setting the price', and marketplace regulations and riots, Thompson distorted the real patterns of eighteenth-century riots to make a case for a popularly-held anti-capitalist ethos that the social history of food riots does not sustain. Rioters aimed much more at intercepting exports, attacking mills and storehouses and seizing food than at regulating markets.

Scarcity certainly created intense short-term competition for supplies – and riots – as Roger Wells' study of the 1790s has abundantly shown.[103] In 1800, the people of Sidmouth expressed 'their mortification far unparalleled' when they watched local wheat being 'purchased *under* the price [they] had offered and drawn off to some distant parish'.[104] The careful researches of Wendy Thwaites have shown that in the scarcity of 1795 dealers from Birmingham, Derbyshire and Lancashire *extended* their search for foodstuffs into Oxfordshire.[105] But an interregional market network that ebbed and flowed with supply and demand had been gradually developing since the sixteenth century, especially as industrial districts emerged. Indeed it was just there, in the places most immersed in the market capitalism of production and consumption,

that riots occurred. This does not fit Thompson's thesis of a confrontation between 'an older moral economy' and 'an innovative market
economy'.

Riots and Paternalist Traditions

Thompson argued that food rioters exhibited a 'pattern of behaviour
for whose origin we must look back several hundred of years', which
'reproduce[d] ... the emergency measures in time of scarcity whose
operation, in the years between 1580 and 1630, were codified in the
Book of Orders'. He also declared, 'The central action in this pattern is ...
the action of "setting the price"'.[106] Certainly this emphasis on price-
setting underpins his theory that food riots were reactions to innovative capitalist practices.

There are several problems with this contention. First, food rioters'
premier tactic was not 'setting the price' until long after food riots
became an established tradition.[107] Second, the Tudor–Stuart Books of
Orders did not order the magistrates or anyone else to set prices.[108]
Third, there is no evidence that rioters had the Book of Orders or the
older regulations in mind. To take up the second point, after 1550 the
Privy Council's general orders on relief did not empower magistrates to
set prices. The attempt to set prices in 1550 had been impossible to
carry out, and it was not tried thereafter.[109] The major exception of
course was the Assize of Bread, which was still set in some towns, and
by which magistrates in effect regulated the price of bread by setting
the weight of a 4d. loaf.[110] (We still do not know how generally it was
in force in the eighteenth century, or whether it was actually revived
after 1750 along with rhetorical paternalism.) As for regulation of the
marketplace, the Book of dearth Orders in 1587 told magistrates to
order owners of grain to bring it weekly to market and sell it in small
quantities to the poor, and to accept the *going* price: 'and you [the
owners] shall not willinglie leav any parte of yor corne, so brought to
that market, vnsold yf money be offered to you fo(r) th(e) same ... after
the vsuall price of the markett there that daye'. The justices were to
attend the markets and see the orders well-observed 'and the pore people provided of necessarie corne and *that w[i]th as much favor in ye
pryces as by ernest perswasio[n] of ye justyces may be obteyned*'.[111] The difference between persuasion and coercion is not only the significant
'constitutional' difference between negotiation and the seizure of the
property of the subject: it is also precisely the difference between the

old regulations aimed at provisioning the markets, and riots which from 1756 on did sometimes lower prices by force. The Book of Orders of 1630 contained a *new threat* that government might regulate prices, but the threat was never carried out.[112]

Thus when food riots did become an established tradition after 1740, rioters did not 'appeal back to the Book of Orders' as Thompson claimed. I have seen little evidence of any such appeal or 'memory'.[113] Only rarely did mid-century rioters go to farms as officials had done under the Book of Orders, and those that did engaged in violent assaults and thefts unlike the supposed precedents.[114] Very rarely did rioters refer to the old statutes against forestalling, regrating and engrossing. They might use the words engrosser and forestaller as pejoratives for the wholesalers, but evidence has not substantiated Thompson's claim that there were 'many actions' in which 'the crowd claimed that since the authorities refused to enforce "the laws" they must enforce them for themselves'.[115] Again, one or two incidents cannot be said to typify hundreds! Rioters clearly expected magistrates to get markets supplied by curbing exports, by jawboning farmers and dealers to lower prices, or by promoting subscriptions to purchase relief supplies. So they sometimes approached magistrates to make the system work the way it worked routinely in matters of poor relief, apprenticeship, justice and patronage. One of the 1795 rioters at Brixham explained why they did not apply to government for redress: 'Government had been applied to, long enough and nothing was done for them therefore it was time they should do something for themselves to keep their families from starving.'[116] If prices were too high the obvious remedy was to lower them. That remedy went back at least to 1347 when King's Lynn rioters sold a cargo of grain 'at their own price'![117] Rather than following magisterial precedents, rioters seemed to be simply taking the most direct approach to their manifest problem of high prices, as well as avoiding outright theft, a capital felony.

One precedent did resemble mid-eighteenth-century food riots. In Tudor–Stuart dearths, rioters had blocked exports and official dearth orders had also curbed exports to prevent or pacify popular risings. It may be that some of those lessons lasted as precedents but both riots and export bans had appeared only sporadically in the century since the Restoration.[118] As the food riot tradition was 'invented' from 1740 onwards, rioters simply seized food shipments outright, while it took a laggard government three waves of riots to change course from promoting exports to stopping them in times of dearth.

Hoarding and high prices clearly provoked moral outrage, but rioters hardly needed magisterial precedents to feel legitimate. More generally

they justified their actions on the grounds that they were starving: 'We are starving alive', they cried out, or, 'It is a hard matter to starve.' The Cornish miners complained in 1795 that 'their Children are crying for Bread.'[119] Indeed there is scattered evidence of dearth-increased mortality all the way from the seventeenth to the end of the eighteenth century.[120] What particularly outraged rioters was the suspicion that they were 'starving in the midst of plenty'.[121] The right to subsist may indeed be a nearly universal and timeless claim.[122] Their occasional references to 'forestallers' and 'engrossers' were generic condemnations of 'monopolists' and profiteers, an animus that stretches from Biblical times to the present day. Moreover rioters sometimes implied that warding off starvation justified seizing food even if the vendors were not culpable. Sir G. O. Paul, a Gloucestershire magistrate, reported that 'the Cry of Want of Bread which is real … has gained allmost the whole people to the side of Plunder, they think it justifiable to seize this Vessell & sell the Corn'.[123]

Food rioters' failure to refer to old precedents is all the more striking because it contrasts with other eighteenth-century protesters' explicit reliance on legal precedents and statutes. For instance, the Statute of Artificers of 1563 (5 Eliz. I c. 4) required an apprenticeship of seven years for skilled artisans and so endowed them a 'property of skill'. That statute became 'part of the collective memory of artisans, a legitimating basis for their actions in restraint of entry' to their trade. Artisans celebrated 'the law Queen Betty made' in song in the seventeenth century and the eighteenth century. The law was even appealed to by trades that had not existed in 1563, such as the cotton weavers in 1756. Similar weapons wielded in battle included the Weavers Act of 1555 and an act of James I regulating the hatters. Workers also cited specific wage levels and customs 'during my father's memory' and practices that had 'been customary for over fifty years past', while battling employers' actions as 'contrary to law, usage and custom from time immemorial'. In 1755 Gloucestershire weavers represented by a solicitor petitioned justices to regulate wages as they had formerly done. In the 1790s Wiltshire and Gloucestershire shearmen appealed to Tudor laws against gig mills.[124] John Rule has recently explained how '"custom" was central to the culture of work in the eighteenth century' and how at the same time 'customary culture cannot be simply represented as the antithesis of "market culture"'.[125] Likewise, resistance to enclosures was often based on specific customs, precedents and charters that documented common rights.[126]

Probably the crucial issues in conflicts over labour, land use and food affected the common people differently. The 'property of skill' and common rights of pasture, turbary, estover and so on were continuously and routinely exercised.[127] Members of the trade group or village were initiated early and with memorable and solemn ceremony into the rules that underwrote their praxis. Innovations threatened permanently to undercut the whole way of life built upon those customs and rights. Hence it may be that land and labour rights entered more deeply into both material livelihood and personal and community identity than the more transient fluctuations of food prices.[128] Certainly combatants from above and below invested more lawyers' fees and spleen in social conflicts of such 'capital' importance. By contrast, rather than defending customary rights, provision politics implied an enlargement of embryonic 'entitlements' from the Poor Law's pauper relief to an expectation of emergency relief for normally autonomous artisans.

Indeed, rather than rioters deriving their legitimacy from paternalism, it seems more likely that paternalist regulations were prompted by riot. Probably riot and paternalist regulation were a political chicken and egg, emerging *pari passu* as markets and trade developed. Not only did the Tudor–Stuart Books of Orders follow riots from 1586–87 to 1629–30 but students of the Book of Orders have regularly found evidence that, in part, their authors 'were prompted by a fear of disorder ... They wished to appease "the tumult of the poor", to repress "tumultuous disorders", and to satisfy "the common poor people ... being ready to rise in tumultuous manner"'.[129] It also seems likely that the Orders' local antecedents were stimulated by popular pressure as well as humanitarianism. Wendy Thwaites has found that in eighteenth-century Oxfordshire, scarcity alone (as in 1740–41) was not enough to trigger market regulations: it typically required also the threat of riot.[130] While there was a continuing if thin tradition of humanitarian charity to the able-bodied in distress, the question is how much power and wealth it called forth. Riot made the milk of human kindness flow: riots jump-started *noblesse oblige*.[131] Officials were slow off the mark with rhetoric, regulations and relief in 1740, apparently because the older traditions had been broken by the long hiatus. When the second wave of food riots began in 1756, 'rhetorical' paternalism 'revived' with new-found urgency.

For 'paternalism' was fundamentally different from the moral claims of rioters. Paternalism did not recognise a right to food any more than a right to seize property, tear down mills, or compel lower prices.[132] Paternalism was dedicated not primarily to the survival of the poor, but to the survival of authority. For 'fear of the people commanded attention to the people's fears ... government intervened in the first instance not so much to reassure the people as to reassure itself'.[133] Riot and paternalism had antagonistic implications, not sympathetic ones, though both sides preferred to limit conflict. In this formative generation of food riots, paternalist rhetoric against forestalling, regrating and engrossing was *revived*, mostly after the rioting of 1740, and particularly after the rioting of 1756 began. Talk was cheap (it was supposed): paternalist rhetoric might prevent disorder or at least divert it away from authority. As Thompson recognised, this thunder was mostly symbolic, for prosecutions were normally carried out only against the small-fry of the market.[134] At the 1740 Bradford Quarter Sessions for the West Riding, for instance, hard on the heels of the Dewsbury riot of April, the magistrates made great stir to enforce the June proclamation against forestalling, etc., at least by enquiring into the badgers' qualifications. For a short while, informers did a thriving trade: Thomas Banks and one or two others appeared repeatedly at Quarter Sessions to prosecute badgers, who were first fined £5 (with portions to the informers). Before long the fines were reduced to a nominal 6*d*. and the informers presumably put out of business.[135] Town magistrates could ill afford to prosecute wholesale merchants and divert their communities' essential food supplies to other towns. Paternalist diatribes against merchants were more likely to come from country gentlemen surrounded by acres of corn and a docile rural populace. But such 'bad-faith' paternalism did not end rioting since it did not relieve popular hunger. That was a harsh lesson, seemingly forgotten since the days when Essex weavers had warned the king: 'words would not fill the belly nor Cloth the backe'.[136]

If riots stimulated 'paternalist' measures rather than vice versa, one can agree with Thompson that crowds probably gained some assurance from hearing their moral outrage against merchants echoed in official proclamations and public opinion. Paternalist preaching did hold out some practical hope to rioters that gentlemen might pressure farmers and middlemen to supply markets and lower prices, might organise relief supplies, and mitigate the punishment of the rioters. Hence the overlap between the crowds' moral outrage and the magistrates' 'paternalist' rhetoric created a stage on which the ambiguities of community politics could be acted out for three generations.

Conclusion

Thompson's point that the moral charge of daily bread created a political space for 'negotiation' between rulers and ruled opened up a whole field of study. Indeed, that same political space has appeared even in twentieth-century nations with well-armed authoritarian governments that purport to control prices. This liminal political space was approached from both sides: while rioters straddled the line between politics and law-breaking, officials were legitimised as they made a virtue of necessity by 'negotiating' with rioters, bending the law to send a political message by concessions or by tough sentences. We might expect popular protesters to have cloaked themselves in precedent if only as protective cover, but amidst dozens of rioters' statements, references to 'tradition' were extremely rare. Since rioters were always on the edge of the law, they could not, like artisans and commoners, look to legal precedents to protect their rights. Riot was an emergent phenomenon, incorporating hard-earned political lessons but also testing and enlarging the bounds of a protocol of riot; 'pushing the envelope', as we would say today. The rich possibilities of negotiation under that rhetorical umbrella of a 'moral economy' were to be won by experience not tradition, as we can sense from the relative crudity of the first wave of riots in 1740. The political process was interactive and adaptive; the actors were not mere puppets of an inherited culture. They were, cautiously or boisterously, innovating in practical politics rather than defending a static tradition.

However, food rioters were not simply engaged in tactical innovations. Implicit in their banner cry – 'We might as well be hanged as starved!' – was an embryonic claim to entitlement, marking out the politics of provisions as part of the social constitution. For thus did rioters make obedience conditional upon food, vowing to challenge authority even to the risk of capital punishment unless and until privilege, wealth and power ensured provisions for the people.

Notes

1. I am very grateful to Kathleen Emmett Bohstedt, James E. Cronin, John Markoff, Nick Rogers and John Stevenson for their comments on earlier versions of this chapter. The pragmatic economy is a concept I lent to Judith Ann Miller for the title of her dissertation, 'The Pragmatic Economy: Liberal Reforms and the Grain Trade in Upper Normandy, 1750–1789' (PhD, Duke University, 1987) and I am now borrowing it back.
2. E. P. Thompson, *The Making of the English Working Class* (New York: Vintage Books 1963), p. 63; and 'The moral economy of the English crowd in the eighteenth century', *Past and Present*, 50 (1971), pp. 76–136, esp. pp. 78, 79, 95, 98, 134, 136; 'Eighteenth-century English society: class struggle without class?' *Social History*, 3 (1978), pp. 154–5.
3. The demographic studies descend from Andrew Appleby, *Famine in Tudor and Stuart England* (Liverpool: Liverpool University Press, 1978): Peter Laslett,

The World We Have Lost (London: 1965); and E. A. Wrigley and R. Schofield, *The Population History of England 1541–1871* (Cambridge: Cambridge University Press, 1981), and from the comparative studies of John Post, especially *Food Shortage, Climatic Variability and Epidemic Disease in Preindustrial Europe: The Mortality Peak in the Early 1740's* (Ithaca, NY: Cornell University Press, 1985). The following outline is based upon the syntheses in R. B. Outhwaite, *Dearth, Public Policy and Social Disturbance in England, 1550–1800* (London: Macmillan 1991); John Walter and Roger Schofield, 'Famine, disease, and crisis mortality in early modem society', in their *Famine, Disease and the Social Order in Early Modern Society* (Cambridge: Cambridge University Press, 1989), pp. 1–74, and Joan Thirsk, *England's Agricultural Regions and Agrarian History, 1500–1750* (London: Macmillan 1987), and C.G.A. Clay, *Economic Expansion and Social Change*, 2 vols (Cambridge: Cambridge University Press, 1984).

4. Alan Everitt, 'The marketing of agricultural produce', in *The Agrarian History of England and Wales* (hereafter *AHEW*), vol. IV, *1500–1540*, ed. Joan Thirsk (Cambridge: Cambridge University Press, 1967).

5. Andrew Charlesworth (ed.), *An Atlas of Rural Protest in Britain 1548–1900* (London: Croom Helm, 1983), pp. 72–82.

6. Rare instances can be found of individual magistrates setting prices, but no indication that it was ever an established practice.

7. Charlesworth, *Atlas*, pp. 72–82.

8. John Walter and Keith Wrightson, 'Dearth and the social order in early modern England', *Past and Present*, 71 (1976) pp. 22–42.

9. John Walter, 'The social economy of dearth in early modern England', in Walter and Schofield, *Famine, Disease and the Social Order*, pp. 75–6. In 1976 and 1985 John Walter rendered similar judgements on the relative rarity of food riots in the period 1585–1650 (quoted in Outhwaite, *Dearth, Public Policy*, pp. 46–7). Likewise Roger Manning, *Village Revolts: Social Protest and Popular Disturbances in England 1509–1640* (Oxford: Oxford University Press, 1988) and Buchanan Sharp, *In Contempt of All Authority: Rural Artisans and Riot in the West of England, 1586–1660* (Berkeley, Cal.: University of California Press, 1980) turned up scores of enclosure riots, but few food riots.

10. R. V. Jackson, 'Growth and deceleration in English agriculture, 1660–1790', *Economic History Review* 38 (1985), pp. 333–51; and Robert C. Allen, *Enclosure and the Yeoman* (Oxford: Oxford University Press 1992).

11. Charlesworth, *Atlas*, pp. 80–2.

12. Paul Slack, *The English Poor Law 1531–1782* (London: Macmillan, 1990), pp. 29, 35, 31–2. I owe this reference to Jonathan Fowler.

13. Walter, in Walter and Schofield (eds), *Famine, Disease and the Social Order*, pp. 45, 96, 126–8, and Walter, 'Subsistence strategies, social economy, and the politics of subsistence in early modern England', in Antti Häkkinen (ed.), *Just a Sack of Potatoes? Crisis Experience in European Societies, Past and Present* (Helsinki: Suomen Historiallinen Seura, 1992), pp. 53–85. In the second paper Walter explains that the systems of formal and informal relief overlapped, but both required 'membership in a community', discretionary vetting by authorities, and thus dependency.

14. Outhwaite, *Dearth, Public Policy*, pp. 37–8; R. B. Outhwaite, 'Dearth and governmental intervention in English grain markets, 1590–1700', *Economic History Review*, 34 (1981), p. 392.

15. D. G. Barnes, *History of the English Corn Laws from 1600 to 1846* (1930; repr. New York: Augustus M. Kelley, 1961), p. xiv; Charlesworth, *Atlas*, p. 80; Outhwaite, 'Dearth and governmental intervention', pp. 395–6, 406; *idem*, Dearth, *Public Policy*, pp. 42–4; W. Thwaites, 'The corn market and economic change: Oxford in the eighteenth century', *Midland History* (1991), p. 115.

16. David Ormrod, *English Grain Exports and the Structure of Agrarian Capitalism 1700–1760* (Hull: Hull University Press, 1985), Table 5, p. 46; and Barnes, *Corn Laws*, Appendix C, p. 299; C. W. J. Granger and C. M. Elliott, 'A fresh look at wheat prices and markets in the eighteenth century', *Economic History Review*, 20 (1967), pp. 257–65; and J. A. Chartrers, 'The marketing of agricultural produce', in *AHEW*, vol. V.2, *1640–1750: Agrarian Change*, p. 460; Outhwaite, *Dearth, Public Policy* , pp. 36–8.

17. Dale Williams, 'Morals, markets, and the English crowd in 1766', *Past and Present*, 104 (1984), pp. 64–6, for the 1766 riot crisis; and Outhwaite, *Dearth, Public Policy*, pp. 36–8. Scattered riots in the 1730s, primarily in Cornwall, provoked an act of 1737 (11 Geo. II, c. 22) that punished anyone who attempted violently to hinder the transportation or export of grain with 1–3 months' imprisonment and a whipping for the first offence, and 7 years' transportation for the second offence.

18. Jeremy N. Caple, 'Provisioning, paternalism, and the moral economy', unpublished paper; Charles Tilly, 'The demographic origins of the European proletariat', in David Levine (ed.), *Proletarianization and Family History* (Orlando: Academic Press, 1984).

19. J. M. Neeson, 'The opponents of enclosure in eighteenth-century Northamptonshire', *Past and Present*, 105 (1984), pp. 114–39; P J. King, 'Gleaners, farmers, and the failure of legal sanctions in England 1780–1850', *Past and Present* 125 (1989), pp. 116–150; and E. P. Thompson, *Customs in Common* (London: Merlin Press, 1991), Ch. 3.

20. Thompson, 'Eighteenth-century society', p. 154.

21. Frequencies from my own researches in newspapers and correspondence and all available printed sources, especially: Robert F. Wearmouth, *Methodism and the Common People of the Eighteenth Century* (London: Epworth Press, 1945); Charlesworth (ed.), *Atlas*; Jeremy N. Caple, 'Popular Protest and Public Order in Eighteenth Century England: The Food Riots of 1756–7, (MA Thesis, Queen's University, Ontario, 1978); Dale E. Williams, 'English Hunger Riots in 1766' (PhD, diss., University of Wales, 1978); John Bohstedt, *Riots and Community Politics in England and Wales, 1790–1810* (Cambridge, Mass.: Harvard University Press, 1983); and Roger Wells, *Wretched Faces: Famine in Wartime England 1793–1801* (Gloucester: Alan Sutton, 1988). I count riots more conservatively than Wells, Caple and Williams, counting as one event all crowd violence that takes place in contiguous districts within the same week. Charlesworth's symbols (*Atlas*) apparently represent all the various actions of rioters, leading Ormrod erroneously to count 82 riots in 1740.

22. Thompson, 'Moral economy', p. 88.

23. S. I. Mitchell, 'Food shortages and public order in Cheshire, 1757–1812', *Transactions of Lancs and Cheshire Antiquarian Society*, 81 (1982), p. 50; cf. Martin Smith, 'Conflict and Society in Late Eighteenth Century Birmingham' (PhD, diss, Cambridge University, 1977), ch. 3.

24. The main monographs are: Robert W. Malcolmson, '1740', in Charlesworth (ed.), *Atlas*, pp. 83–5; Douglas Hay, 'Crime, Authority, and the Criminal Law' (unpub. PhD diss., University of Warwick, 1975), ch. 5; K. Lloyd Gruffydd, 'The Vale of Clwyd corn riots of 1740', in *Flintshire Historical Society Publications*, 27 (1975–6), pp. 36–42; and Joyce Ellis, 'Urban conflict and popular violence: The Guildhall riots of 1740 in Newcastle upon Tyne', *International Review of Social History*, 25 (1980), pp. 332–49.

25. William Ellis, Buckinghamshire farmer, quoted by Robert Malcolmson, in Charlesworth (ed.), *Atlas*, p. 83.

26. Overall London wheat prices for 1740 rose more than 50% above the ten-year average, and in June, July and August they peaked at 75% above that average (Post, *Food Shortage*, Tables 10, 11, pp. 117, 119;) Ormrod, *English Grain Exports*, p. 42; and on mortality and marriages cf. Post, *Food Shortage*, p. 186, and Wrigley and Schofield, *Population History*, pp. 320–8, where it is pointed out that such subsistence crises in real wages were reflected more in nuptiality and birth rates than in death rates. For six deaths in London, see *Northampton Mercury*, 3 Jan. 1740. England registered a mortality peak as pronounced as that of Scotland and France.

27. Post, *Food Shortage*, p. 187; and *Derby Mercury, Northampton Mercury, Leeds Mercury, passim*.

28. *Leeds Mercury*, 15, 22 July 1740; Outhwaite, *Dearth, Public Policy*, p. 38. For example, in April 1740 Ralph Carr of Newcastle was planning to load five ships for Holland and sundry more for other ports in southern Europe and was in regular contact with correspondents in the Low Countries, France and Lisbon (Ormrod, *English Grain Exports*, p. 42).

29. Charlesworth, *Atlas*, pp. 63–82. The previously northernmost riot was an isolated incident in Nottingham 60 miles to the south in 1701.

30. Pat Hudson, *The Genesis of Industrial Capital: A study of the West Riding Wool Textile Industry c. 1750–1850* (Cambridge: Cambridge University Press, 1986), pp. 27, 62–7.

31. *York Courant*, 6 May 1740; *Leeds Mercury*, 6 May 1740.

32. State Papers Domestic (hereafter SP) 36/53/ 101 Judge Reynold's report 19 Nov. 1740 on petitions for mercy. This account is also based on: *Leeds Mercury*, 6, 20 May, and 5 Aug. 1740; *York Courant*, 13 May and 29 July 1740; Wearmouth, *Methodism and the Common People*, p. 78.

33. Romney Sedgwick, *The House of Commons 1715–1754* (London: HMSO, 1970) vol. II, p. 184.

34. Also, 'It is the restraint, rather than the disorder, which is remarkable': Thompson, 'Moral economy', pp. 108 ('setting the price'), 112. cf. Adrian J. Randall on the food riots of 1766: 'what is surprising is not that property was seized or stolen, but that there was relatively so little gratuitous theft … unprovoked "plunder" was so infrequent … the rioters' … acceptance of the inviolability of private property' ('The Gloucestershire food riots of 1766', *Midland History*, 10 (1986), pp. 72–93. However, those riots were at least as violent as the riots of 1740.

35. Eusebius Silvester, *The Causes of the Present High Price of Corn and Grain and a State of the Abuses and Impositions practiced upon the Publik in general and the Poor in particular, by the Millers or Meal-men …* (London, 1757), pp. 13, 16.

36. R. B. Outhwaite, 'Dearth and governmental intervention', pp. 393; Christian Petersen, *Bread and the British Economy c 1770–1870* (Aldershot: Scolar Press, 1995), pp. 51–3, 57, 59; Silvester, *Causes of the Present High Price of Corn, passim*; 'By 1750...the boulting mill [had been introduced], although the extent of its adoption is unknown': Jennifer Tann, 'Corn milling', in ch. 5, of AHEW, vol. VI, *1750–1850*, ed. G. E. Mingay (Cambridge: Cambridge University Press, 1989), p. 408. For bolting mills and rioters' suspicions of their associations with exportation, engrossment and adulteration, see *Social Protest and the Politics of Provisions: Food Riots, Relief, and Repression in Britain, France, and Germany 1750–1850, and in the Twentieth Century*, John Bohstedt, Cynthia A. Bouton, Manfred Gailus and Martin Geyer (forthcoming).

37. By analogy with the interpretation of E. J. Hobsbawm, in his 'Machine breakers', [1950] in *Labouring Men* (London: Weidenfeld & Nicolson, 1964), pp. 7–9.

38. BL Add. Mss (Newcastle papers) 32693, f.311–12, Langford Collin, 4 June 1740.

39. *Leeds Mercury* 27 May, 29 July 1740; *Northampton Mercury* 2 June 1740; SP 36/50 f.454, Colchester Mayor and magistrates, 28 May 1740; SP 36/51 f.148, Colchester magistrates, 23 June 1740; and f.150 Mr Rigby of Mistley Hall nr Manningtree 24 June 1740; ASSI 31/1 Minute Book, Essex (Chelmsford) Summer 1740.

40. SP 36/50 f.418, John Creed 19 May 1740; SP 36/51 f.1, D Stanley, 1 June 1740.

41. Based on my analysis of printed sources, newspapers and correspondence; cf. Malcolmson in Charlesworth, *Atlas*, pp. 83–5.

42. SP 36/50 f.432, Wm Williamson, 24 May 1740; SP 36/51 f.86–88, Wm Price, 13 June 1740.

43. Gruffydd, 'Vale of Clwyd'; SP 36/50 f.433–4, Wm Price, Wm Myddelton, and David Foulkes 25 May 1740, f.435, David Foulkes to Sir Geo. Wynne, 25 May, and SP 36/51 f.86, Wm Price 13 June 1740, and SP 36/51 f.256, deposition of Thomas Churchill, in David Foulkes, 6 July 1740.

44. Ellis, 'Urban conflict and popular violence', pp. 340–4.

45. SP36/51 f.28, Wm Williamson 10 June 1740; *Derby Mercury* 26 June 1740; *York Courant*, 24 June 1740.

46. E. P. Thompson, 'The moral economy reviewed', in *Customs in Common* (London: Merlin, 1991), p. 323, quoting *Gloucester Journal*, 24 June 1740.

47. SP 36/51/114, Magistrates of Peterborough, 18 June 1740.

48. SP 36/52 f.158, Wm Anderson petition, Sept. 1740. He originally said he had seized corn from a house on the grounds that it had been bought in one market for sale in another (a possible confusion with regrating, one of the traditional market sins). Anderson had already been in jail for several months at the time of the autumn assizes; SP 36/53 f. 114, Petition for Mary Sillsby, c. Sept 1740.

49. BL Add Mss (Newcastle) 32693, f.278, J. Stuard May 11 1740; *Derby Mercury* 29 May 1740.

50. Yarmouth: Ormrod, *English Grain Exports*, p. 59; Colchester: J. A. Sharpe, *Crime in Early Modern England 1550–1750* (London: Longman, 1984), p. 138; I owe this reference to John Stevenson; Pembroke: SP 36/50 f.429, Jenkin Ferrior, Mayor of Pembroke 23 May 1740; Wisbech: SP 36/51/252

E. Parthericke, 5 July 1740; Wearmouth, *Methodism and the Common People*, pp. 21 and 79; Gentlemen's Magazine, X (1740) p. 355; *Northampton Mercury*, 14 July and 25 August 1740: 'the Mob's pretence was only to prevent shipping Corn, and settling the Price'.

51. SP 36/51/ 254, 268, 286 John Nuttall, 5, 7, 9 July 1740; *Derby Mercury*, 17 and 24 July 1740.

52. As they had in the 1620s and the 1690s. See Bohstedt et al., *Social Protest and the Politics of Provisions*.

53. William Salt Library, Stafford: Hand Morgan MS 31/5 Staffordshire QS Minute Book 1728–43, p. 248, and Staffordshire Record Office, QS rolls 578 f. 28; Translation 1740 Indictment of Eliz. Brooke *et al.* and depositions; the same week another small crowd seized a wagon of grain at Stone at the other end of the county; (their occupations: curriers and websters) Hand Morgan 31/15 p. 248; QS Rolls 577 f.17, Indictment of Thomas Dawson *et al.*; Other Staffordshire riot documents speak of 60 bushels of pease (taken by colliers at Cannock), and 120 bushels of oats detained; the quantities imply shipments or storehouses, not 'retail' marketplace quantities: QS rolls 578, 579 Indictments.

54. *Northampton Mercury*, 2 June 1740. The women's 'uncommon bravery and resolution' was said to be a 'matter of surprise' so perhaps women's roles in food riots was not so familiar.

55. *Derby Mercury*, 10 July 1740.

56. SP 36/51 f.260, Deposition of Rd Thomas 28 June 1740; SP 36/51 f.73, Edward Legard 13 June 1740; SP 36/51 f.263–4, Deposition of shopkeeper's wife Emme Owen 28 June 1740.

57. This statement is based on my map of riots compared with regions mapped in Thirsk, *England's Agricultural Regions*. Cf. Malcolmson, in Charlesworth, *Atlas*, p. 83.

58. In 1740, except for the districts named, there was not much imitative spread of riots through a region: the crowds came from communities, and the action and interaction took place on a local not regional basis.

59. In the Vale of Clywd, it was the London Lead Company: Gruffydd, 'The Vale of Clwyd', p. 37 n. 10; Pembroke: SP 36/51 f.101, Wm Owen 17 June 1740. It seems very likely Sir Thomas Mostyn would have supplied his colliery workers.

60. T. S. Ashton and Joseph Sykes, *The Coal Industry of the Eighteenth Century* (Manchester: Manchester University Press, 1929), pp. 128–9, speaking of 1795. The evidence for such employers' relief comes from after 1750: M. W. Flinn, *History of the British Coal Industry* (Oxford: Oxford University Press, 1984), pp. 380–6.

61. Robert W. Malcolmson, '"A set of ungovernable people": the Kingswood colliers in the eighteenth century', in *An Ungovernable People*, ed. John Brewer and John Styles (New Brunswick: Rutgers University Press, 1980), pp. 85–127.

62. See for instance: Geoffrey Holmes and Daniel Szechi, *The Age of Oligarchy: Pre-Industrial Britain 1722–1783* (London: Longman, 1993), ch. 12; John Stevenson, *Popular Disturbances in England 1700–1832*, 2nd ed (London: Longman, 1992); and Nicholas Rogers, *Whigs and Cities: Popular Politics in the Age of Walpole and Pitt* (Oxford: Oxford University Press, 1989), ch. 10.

63. SP 36/51 I-76, Wm Williamson 15 June 1740; *Northampton Mercury*, 30 June 1740.
64. SP 36/50 f.454, John Blatch, Mayor of Colchester, 28 May 1740.
65. *Derby Mercury*, 24 July 1740.
66. *Derby Mercury*, 10 and 17 July, 6 Aug. 1740.
67. *Derby Mercury*, 2 Oct. 1740; SP 36/52 f.176, Mayor Clutterbuck, 23 Sept. 1740.
68. Edward, Lord Bishop of Durham, *A Charge delivered to the Grand Jury at the Quarter Sessions held at Durham on Wednesday, the 16th of July, 1740, concerning Engrossing of Corn and Grain and the Riots that have been occasioned thereby* (Durham 1740).
69. This account is based on Ellis, 'Urban conflict and popular violence', pp. 332–49; *Gentlemen's Magazine*, X (1740), p. 355; Wearmouth, *Methodism and the Common People*, pp. 20–1; *Leeds Mercury* 8 July 1740.
70. One said they had their orders from Sir Thomas Mostyn. SP 36/51/70 Deposition of John Jones 10 June 1740, and SP 36/50 f.433–38, David Foulkes 25 May 1740 and enclosures; and SP 36/51 f.86, Wm Price 13 June 1740, enclosing deposition by John Goffe. SP 36 50 f.436, Mr John Wynne 25 May 1740; f.441, Geo Colley, 'Perkiney under a hedge' 25 May 1740. For the constituencies and Members see Sedgwick, *House of Commons, 1715–1754*, 2 vols, *passim*.
71. SP 36/51/ f.256 David Foulkes 6 July 1740 and f.65 Wm Myddleton and David Foulkes, JPs, 13 June 1740 and f.69 deposition of John Steventon, and f.89 deposition of James Dowdle; SP 36/50 f.437 George Colley 25 May 1740; SP 36/51 f.260, 264 depositions of Robert Davies, Emme Owens. A. H. Dodd (ed.), *History of Wrexham* (Wrexham: Hughes & Son, 1957), p. 79.
72. SP 36/50 f.429 Jenkin Ferrior 23 May 1740; and 36/51 f.101 Wm Owen 17 June 1740; Sedgwick, *House of Commons*, II, p. 317; and I, p. 380.
73. SP 36/50 f.432, Wm Williamson 24 May 1740 to Edward, Lord Bp of Durham, *custos rotulorum*.
74. Though eight people were killed at the populous borough of Norwich when citizens and soldiers opened fire on a crowd. *Derby Mercury* 24 July 1740.
75. This of course assumes the Namier interpretation of electoral politics, that electors got as good as they gave from their representatives.
76. For the posse, see Leon Radzinowicz, *A History of English Criminal Law and its Administration from 1750. Vol 4: Grappling for Control* (London: Stevens & Sons, 1968), pp. 106–7. The posse was used a few times between 1812 and 1839.
77. SP 36/51 I-76, Wm Williamson 15 June 1740.
78. SP 36/50 f.435, David Foulkes 25 May 1740.
79. *Gentlemen's Magazine*, X (1740), p. 355; *Northampton Mercury*, 14 July 1740.
80. *Ibid.*
81 Ellis, 'Urban conflict and popular violence', pp. 342–3.
82. Tony Hayter, *The Army and the Crowd in Mid-Georgian England* (London; Macmillan, 1978), p. 47.
83. On Porteous, see Radzinowicz, *History of English Criminal Law*, pp. 132–3.
84. North Wales: SP 36/51 f.256, David Foulkes, 6 July 1740; Durham: SP 36/51/I-76, William Williamson, 15 June 1740; Bristol: Hayter, *The Army and the Crowd*, pp. 31–2; Newcastle: Ellis, 'Urban conflict and popular violence', p. 339.

85 They were hanged for obscure reasons after sentence at the Norfolk Assizes. Norwich rioters were sentenced at the City assizes, and no other riots in Norfolk are known: *Derby Mercury*, 4 Sept. 1740

86. Transportation was the non-capital punishment of choice in the second quarter of the century, according to John Beattie, *Crime and the Courts in England 1660–1800* (Princeton, NJ: Princeton University Press, 1986), pp. 502, 507–8.

87. In addition 100 additional persons were brought before the Great Sessions (Assizes) of Flintshire for the Vale of Clywd riots (Gruffydd, p. 420) and more than 300 people were identified in connection with the Newcastle riots; of whom one-third of the earlier milder phase were brought to trial, and half of the later, more violent, phase. Besides the five men sentenced to transportation, the rest received much more lenient sentences, in part because the collieries in the area went on strike during the trials, perhaps as a caution to the judges: Ellis, 'Urban conflict and popular violence', pp. 347–8. One of the Dewsbury rioters was found to be in a state of lunacy, a rarity among rioters.

88. Professor Beattie concurs with me that this was a common pattern. (Personal communication).

89. SP 36/53 f.81, James Reynolds, Baron of the Exchequer, report 21 Oct. 1740.

90. Sheffield Central Library, Fitzwilliam MS., WWM M2, Gen. Corres., ff. 62–3, Revd Chas Zouch to Earl of Malton, 26 July 1740.

91. SP 36/51 f 252, E. Parthericke to Chas Clarke, MP and Chief Justice of the Isle of Ely, 5 July 1740.

92. SP 36/52 f.204

93 Wakefield QS Rolls, QS 1/80/2 Deposition of Benjamin ffearnley and recognisance of John Robinson, and indictments of Benjamin ffearnly, Elizabeth Robinson, and letter W. Pollard to Alan Johnson, n.d.; Indictment Book 4/29 1740–41.

94. Samples were the owners' little bags of grain representative of the quality of a large quantity. They would permit direct transactions between a farmer and an urban dealer without the grains' passing through the marketplace.

95. Thompson, 'Moral economy', p. 85; Chartres, 'Marketing', *AHEW*, pp. 471–2; Richard Perren, 'Markets and marketing', *AHEW*, VI: *1750–1850* (Cambridge: Cambridge University Press, 1989), p. 214.

96. Thompson, 'Moral economy', pp. 84–7; cf. Thwaites, 'Corn market and economic change', pp. 108–10.

97. Thompson, 'Moral economy', pp. 102–3.

98. Thompson, 'Moral economy', p. 83.

99. Carole Shammas, *The Pre-industrial Consumer in England and America* (Oxford: Oxford University Press, 1990), pp. 258–60; Silvester, *Causes of the Present High Price of Corn*; Ian Mitchell, 'The development of urban retailing 1700–1815', in Peter Clark (ed.) *The Transformation of English Provincial Towns* (London: Hutchinson 1984), pp. 259–78; Roger Scola, *Feeding the Victorian City: The Food Supply of Manchester, 1770–1870* (Manchester: Manchester University Press, 1992), chs 7, 9, 11.

100. For shops see S. Ian Mitchell, 'Urban Markets and Retail Distribution 1730–1815 with particular reference to Macclesfield, Stockport and Chester' (Oxford University D. Phil 1974), pp. 86, 113–21; Wendy

Thwaites, 'Dearth and the marketing of agricultural produce: Oxfordshire c. 1750–1800', *Agricultural History Review* 33 (1985), p. 123; Mitchell, 'Urban retailing', p. 265.

101. For working-class consumers' interdependence with small shopkeepers, see James L. Rogers II, 'Shopkeepers in Victorian Lancashire' (University of Tennessee, PhD, 1995); bakers: Mitchell, 'Urban retailing', p. 273; Petersen, *Bread*, p. 67.

102. Thompson, 'Moral economy', p. 79.

103. Wells, *Wretched Faces*, ch. 7 and *passim*.

104. PRO, H.O. 42/ 35 petition enclosed in Rev. Marker, 22 Dec. 1800. My italics. The local people complained that the buyer paid *less, not more*, than their offer.

105. Thwaites, 'Dearth and the marketing of agricultural produce', p. 122.

106. Thompson, 'Moral economy', p. 108. One must read carefully. Thompson's quotation that justices should 'sett downe a certen price upon the bushell of everye kinde of grine' comes not from the Book of Orders but from the 'Coppie of the Councells her[e] for graine delyvrd at Bodmyn the xith of May 1586', a Rawlinson ms. in the Bodleian Library. In late April and early May 1586 the Privy Council had sent letters to the Justices ordering them to see the markets supplied with corn. Is the document quoted by Thompson a reply to that letter or the Council letter itself? The Gloucestershire justices responded in 1586 or 1587 that 'according to your lettres we have sett downe several prices upon everie kinde of graine': Dom St Papers, Qn Eliz. 189: 50, quoted in E. M. Leonard, *The Early History of English Poor Relief* (1900; repr. London: Frank Cass, 1965), p. 88, n.14. That is one of the rare recorded instances of price-setting.

107. John Bohstedt, 'The moral economy and the discipline of historical context', *Journal of Social History*, 26 (Winter 1992), pp. 276–7.

108. Leonard, *Early History*, pp. 84–91; Paul Slack, 'Books of Orders: The making of English social policy, 1577–1631', *Transactions of the Royal Historical Society*, 5th series, 30 (1980), pp. 4, 13; Outhwaite, *Dearth, Public Policy*, p. 56. Thomas Gordon Barnes, *Somerset 1625–1640* (Cambridge, Mass.: Harvard University Press, 1961), ch. 7, discusses the general Book of Orders of 1631 for relief of the poor, but does not distinguish it from the Dearth Orders of September 1630, and says little about market regulation.

109. Slack, 'Books of Orders', p. 4.

110. W. Thwaites, 'The Assize of Bread in 18th-century Oxford', *Oxoniensia*, 51 (1986), p. 180; and Petersen, *Bread and the British Economy*, ch. 4.

111. Leonard, *Early History*, pp. 322, 324.

112. Slack, 'Books of Orders', p. 3. John Walter refers to 'the apparent legal uncertainty over the government's ability to dictate to holders of grain the prices at which they should sell to the poor'. John Walter, 'Social economy', p. 122.

113. Though Wendy Thwaites finds that in a popular price fixing of 1766, Oxford rioters fixed prices on groceries (butter, cheese, bacon, candles, etc.) that resembled prices set by the the Vice Chancellor in 1680. Oxford was more tightly regulated than most cities: Wendy Thwaites, 'The Marketing of Agricultural Produce in Eighteenth Century Oxford' (PhD diss., University of Birmingham, 1980), p. 480.

114. See Bohstedt *et al.*, *Social Protest and the Politics of Provisions* (forthcoming).
115. Thompson, 'Moral economy', p. 110. Thompson cited the one incident at Banbury in 1693 when rioters seized a wagon of corn, 'as it was carrying away by ingrossers, saying they were resolved to put the law in execution since the magistrates neglected it': *The Life and Times of Anthony Wood*, iii: 1682–1695 (Oxford: Clarendon Press, 1984), p. 434. Amidst dozens of rioters' statements are only one or two other such references.
116. Devon Record Office, 1262M/L52 Henry Studdy, 7 April 1801.
117. Buchanan Sharp, 'Popular protest in seventeenth-century England', in Barry Reay (ed.), *Popular Culture in Seventeenth-Century England* (London: Croom Helm, 1985), p. 281
118. Buchanan Sharp, 'Popular protest', pp. 279–80. Distressed textile workers in Worcester complained that they had applied to magistrates for relief and for a ban on exports without success: Max Beloff, *Public Order and Popular Disturbances 1660–1714* (1938; repr. London: Frank Cass, 1963), p. 61. Between 1660 and 1740, exports were banned only in 1699 and 1709.
119. Wells, *Wretched Faces*, p. 65, and Bohstedt, *Riots and Community Politics*, p. 36.
120. See, for example, Dale E. Williams, 'Were "hunger" rioters really hungry? Some demographic evidence', *Past and Present*, 71 (1976), pp. 70–5; Wells, *Wretched Faces, passim*; Walter and Schofield, 'Famine, disease, and crisis mortality', in Walter and Schofield, *Famine, Disease*, pp. 36ff.
121. PRO, H.O. 42/50, A.B. Haden, Black Country magistrate, 10 May 1800.
122. See Florence Gauthier and Guy-Robert Ikni (eds), *La Guerre du Blé au XVIIIe Siécle* (Montreuil: Editions de la Passion, 1988), pp. 23–5, and Thompson, 'Moral Economy', p. 135.
123. Quoted in Wells, *Wretched Faces*, p. 109.
124. John Rule, *The Experience of Labour in Eighteenth-century English Industry* (New York: St Martin's, 1981), pp. 95–6 p. 194; John Rule, 'The property of skill in the period of manufacture', in Patrick Joyce (ed.), *The Historical Meanings of Work* (Cambridge: Cambridge University Press, 1987), pp. 105–6; John Rule, 'Introduction', and Adrian Randall, 'The industrial moral economy of the Gloucestershire weavers in the eighteenth century', in John Rule (ed.), *British Trade Unionism 1750–1850: The Formative Years* (London: Longman 1988), pp. 8 and 34–7; Adrian Randall, *Before the Luddites: Custom, Community and Machinery in the English Woollen Industry, 1776–1809* (Cambridge: Cambridge University Press, 1991), pp. 120–30.
125. John Rule, 'Against Innovation? Custom and resistance in the workplace, 1700–1850', in Tim Harris (ed.), *Popular Culture in England, c. 1500–1850* (London: Macmillan, 1995), pp. 168–9.
126. See, for example, Keith Lindley, *Fenland Riots and the English Revolution* (London: Heinmann Educational Books 1982); J. M. Neeson, 'The opponents of enclosure', p. 122n.; J. M. Neeson, *Commoners: Common Right, Enclosure and Social Change in England, 1700–1820* (Cambridge: Cambridge University Press, 1993); Thompson, *Customs in Common*, pp. 152–9.
127. For a rich survey of this varied economy resting upon common rights to land use, see Robert W. Malcolmson, *Life and Labour in England 1700–1780* (London: Hutchinson, 1981), pp. 24–34, and Neeson, *Commoners*, ch. 2.

128. Rule, 'Against innovation', pp. 168–9, and cf. Thompson, *Customs in Common*, p. 102, referring to Bourdieu's concept of the lived habitus. Of course, a tradition of food riot could be an important ingredient in a community's political physiology.

129. Paul Slack, *Poverty and Policy in Tudor and Stuart England* (London: Longman, 1988), p. 145. Slack, 'Books of Orders', presents a combination of factors in their origins. cf. Leonard, *Early History*, p. 85.

130. Thwaites, 'Dearth and marketing', p. 124.

131. Bohstedt, *Riots and Community Politics*, pp. 66–7, 95–6. This is over simple, of course. For helpful modifications, see Susan E. Brown, '"A just and profitable commerce": moral economy and the middle classes in eighteenth-century London', *Journal of British Studies* 32 (1993), pp. 305–32. I am exploring this question much more fully in *Social Protest and the Politics of Provision*.

132. Cf. Thompson, 'Moral economy', p. 98.

133. Steven L. Kaplan, *Bread, Politics and Political Economy in the Reign of Louis XV* (The Hague: Martinus Nijhoff, 1976), p. 677.

134. Thompson, 'Moral economy', p. 96.

135. Wakefield QS rolls, 1740, July, August, October.

136. Quoted in John Walter, 'Grain riots and popular attitudes toward the law: Maldon and the crisis of 1629', in Brewer and Styles (eds), *Ungovernable People*, p. 70.

4
Moral Economy, Political Economy and Law

Douglas Hay

Moral economy was a neologism in 1971; it then entered the language of historians.[1] From that moment it began to lose some of its original sharpness of focus, and to acquire a wide range of new connotations. The power of the insight that originally generated it, and its central place in Edward Thompson's own project of recovering the ambiguities of paternalism, class and resistance, in some cases justified that expansion of meaning. The rich mix of ancient legal doctrine, customary practices, popular expectation and gentry attitudes in which mobs and magistrates negotiated the marketing of food in times of dearth had clear parallels in British labour conflicts of the period.[2] Students of other times and places have borrowed the term and wrapped it around very different social institutions in very different societies. This chapter returns to a point that was central to the original article, but that has sometimes been blurred in subsequent work: the fact that the moral economy of markets was critically, if contentiously, dependent on state law. The medieval and early-modern marketing offences of forestalling, regrating and engrossing lay at the heart of the moral economy of markets. Thompson concentrated on the popular significance of the old laws as legitimators of riot throughout the century, and on the willingness of government at mid-century, and many gentlemen and country magistrates for decades after, to express their conviction that middlemen in food did indeed enhance prices, and hence effective dearth, through the practices stigmatised by the ancient status. In their eyes, in those of the mob, and (the evidence suggests) in those of a substantial body of 'middling' opinion, this traditional view of markets and of human greed in times of dearth was self-evident.[3] The analysis of the political economists, that a wholly free market could not, over a harvest year, do other than wisely ration supplies, seemed to many such traditionalists a wholly speculative exercise that denied their own knowledge of the happy and opportunistic responses of millers and farmers and wholesalers to apprehended harvest failures.[4]

Yet in an important sense both political economy and traditional moralities might be irrelevant to the issue if the law found them so to be. For the marketing offences were, after all, created by law. The ancient statutes were repeatedly cited by magistrates in charges at sessions in London and in the country throughout the first half of the century. Forestallers and other such offenders, it was said, 'render the Poor less able to support their families' (Middlesex, 1718); they were 'Pernicious Sorts of People; who Plot and Conspire together to Advance unreasonably, or without any Real, Just Occasion the Price of Victuals, to the great Oppression, and Breeding of Murmuring and Discontent, especially amongst the lower and meaner Sort of People' (Middlesex, 1725). They were held to enhance prices to the 'common Prejudice of all Buyers' (Barnsley, 1741), and the offenders were esteemed by law 'great Offenders' (Guildford, 1745). A charge repeatedly used in Norwich in the early 1750s grouped the marketing offences with usury, monopoly, deceits and 'Cozinage in Weights and measures by which in a more particular manner the poor & needy are oppressed & ruined for the emolument of some few of the most Worthless of Mankind'. In September 1767, the citizens of the city were again alerted from the bench to 'that cruel hardship on the poor Usury Forestalling Monopoly & the like'.[5]

In both case law and statute the ancient laws were reconsidered, and briefly renewed in the later eighteenth century. New statutes in other parts of the common law world enacted new penalties and enforcement mechanisms against these offences, and a significant body of opinion in Parliament, local government and the courts upheld its policy in England. Moreover, the law itself was cast overtly in the rhetoric of moral imperative. The moral economy was explicitly, resonantly, embedded in the texts of English law and given expression in the deliberate utterances of the high court judges at the end of the eighteenth century. The attack on moral economy thus was also an attack on legal doctrine, and its destruction required the remaking of that doctrine. A reading of the social significance of the marketing laws, of their meaning and their rationales, therefore is ultimately, and crucially, dependent on the views of the legislature and even more of the judges of the Court of King's Bench when they came to consider, alter or uphold the law. In this chapter I give an account of some of the debates in the second half of the century and the critical role of legal

discourse, deliberation and decision in ultimately ratifying the doctrines of political in place of moral economy. What follows is an
attempt to reconstruct some of the range of opinion among legislators,
lawyers and the judges up to great dearths at the end of the century.
From the first of these, in 1795, an extraordinary conflict began
between the Court of King's Bench and the government, a conflict that
was resolved only after the death of Lord Kenyon, the Chief Justice, in
1802. In that conflict the law and politics of the new political economy
achieved a decisive victory.[6] Kenyon supported what looks very like the
classic version of moral economy, in Thompson's original sense.
Why he did so, and why he was so derided for his stand, can in part
be explained by looking at how the law was discussed in the
preceding decades.

Attitudes in Parliament and the City

The dearths in the 1750s, accompanied by widespread food riots,
prompted Parliament to consider the laws against forestallers, regrators
and engrossers, although no legislation resulted. There were similar initiatives in later years (as there had been earlier), often prompted by
petitions.[7] In 1764 a Commons committee explicitly blamed forestallers
for raising the price of beef.[8] In 1765 members of the public called for
forestallers of Smithfield to be prosecuted 'with utmost severity' and a
summary of the entire statute and case law was published 'in order to
point out the defects in the law, as it now stands', apparently to
encourage legislation.[9] The following year another Commons committee investigating high prices reported evidence of corn jobbers in
London engaged in what amounted to regrating.[10] There were pressures to extend the scope of the law in ensuing decades and the result
was a series of contradictory initiatives in Parliament, the product of
different vested interests but also of profound disagreements about the
nature of markets and their proper regulation.

One persistent concern affecting the debate throughout the later
eighteenth century was the practices of cattle jobbers in provincial and
London markets. Perhaps more visible than corn merchants, they
aroused passions among farmers as well as consumers and provided a
recurrent source of support for enforcement or re-enactment of marketing laws because conflicts between wholesale and retail butchers also
often turned on the old offences. A petition to the Commons earlier in
the century had estimated that prices of veal were raised by a third
in one day by regrators, that other offenders sold tainted meat to

the poor, and that theft of cattle and sheep, and killing them in the
fields, was thereby encouraged.[11]

Now, in May 1766, in response to petitions from Westminster and
Spitalfields decrying the 'iniquitous practices of jobbers, forestallers,
and engrossers', a committee of the Commons reported evidence that
jobbers in Smithfield were indeed committing those offences and
greatly raising prices. A bill to 'explain, amend, and enforce' the existing laws against engrossers and forestallers of cattle and other provisions was prepared and given its first reading, but not enacted.[12]
The widespread use of the old statutes after the harvest failure of that
year, and the government's eventual proclamation of the offences,
showed that important constituencies believed the ancient statutes to
be salutary and necessary.[13]

A 1766 pamphlet did argue that larger traders believed the laws were
bad law, and that the 'principal factors' ignored them.[14] But it was only
in the aftermath of the dearth and riots of 1766 that traditional support for the penal laws encountered robust criticism in Parliament,
as opponents of the marketing laws sought to repeal the statutes and
undermine their enforcement in the courts. They agreed with the traditionalists on the gravity of great harvest dearth, the threat to public
order posed by extremely serious and widespread food riots, but, ten
years before Smith's classic account of the corn trade was published in
The Wealth of Nations, they gave a similar analysis, couched in the
terms of the infant discipline of political economy, in favour of repeal.

In 1767 they dominated a new committee of the House of Commons
which reported 'That the several Laws relating to Badgers, Engrossers,
Forestallers, and Regraters, by preventing the Circulation of, and free
Trade in, Corn and other Provisions, have been the Means of raising
the Price thereof in many Parts of this Kingdom.' In April leave was
given to bring in a bill, and thirteen members, including Edmund
Burke, were instructed to prepare it.[15] The Common Council of London
also heard evidence from corn factors and others from November 1767
to March 1768 that the increase in the price of wheat and other provisions could be attributed to a great increase in the number of horses,
a small and poor crop, to rioters pulling down mills and to the engrossing of farms: to everything but the actions of middlemen. They were
clear that those who bought corn in one market for sale in another
were 'useful and necessary'.[16]

Over the winter, however, petitions arrived before Parliament from
'Gentlemen, Graziers, and others, Feeders of Cattle' in Somerset and
Dorset, and the Somerset justices and grand jurors, complaining of the

'monopoly' of cattle jobbers in terms very similar to the London petitions of 1766. The result was the same: in February 1768 a committee of the Commons again resolved that such illegal practices were the cause of high prices and that the penal laws were ineffectual and must be strengthened. A Somerset JP, Sir Abraham Elton, recommended in testimony that persons so accused should be bound to answer at sessions, with a presumption of guilt; the onus should be on them to establish their innocence.[17]

In the end no legislation was forthcoming, either from the 1767 committee charged to prepare a bill to repeal the old laws, or the 1768 committee considering the causes of high prices. The eventual decline of prices, and evident disagreement in Parliament, appears to have caused the issue to be dropped. It was revived by the dearth of 1772 which, although not comparable to that of 1766–67, was serious enough to revive fears of the possible consequences. Again, agitation against jobbers in Smithfield, who also forestalled that market by buying at Islington and other places, led to proposals for a stiffening of the old laws.[18] Burke and others clearly decided that they must instead be given their final quietus. In March 1772 the resolutions of 1767 against the old laws were read in the Commons and leave was again given for a bill to be brought in to repeal them. Three of the nineteen members of the committee had been on the committee of 1767; one of them was Burke.[19] The bill was given first reading on 6 May, Burke reported from the committee of the whole on 14 May and carried the bill back and forth between the two houses, and by 9 June it had passed both with a few amendments, and received Royal Assent.[20]

An Act for repealing several laws therein mentioned against Badgers, Engrossers, Forestallers, and Regrators, and for indemnifying Persons against Prosecutions for Offences committed against the said Acts (12 George III c. 71) explicitly asserted that the laws had discouraged the growth and increased the price of corn, meal, flour, cattle and other victuals, harmed the 'labouring and manufacturing Poor of this Kingdom', and were especially dangerous to the provisioning of London and Westminster. In addition to repealing all or part of six of the ancient statutes, the *Act* voided all current as well as future prosecutions on them.[21] Although we do not have a record of debates on the bill, the concurrent debate on a bill to regulate imports and exports saw a full defence of modern marketing practices: 'storing of corn must not be discouraged, nor the middle man; for if they were, great towns could never be regularly supplied, but must be in perpetual danger of famine', said Thomas Pownall. Burke 'explained, with that distinction of which he is master, both the effect of supply and trade'.[22] His central role is clear, as is his full commitment to the theoretical assumptions behind it.[23] Adam Smith is reported to have told Burke 'after they had conversed on the subject of political economy, that he was the only man, who, without communication, thought on these topics exactly as he did'.[24] Burke and Smith probably thought the battle against the old law was won in 1772. Not only the legislature had been finally won over; so too had the courts.

The Attitude of the Courts before the 1790s

The Chief Justice of King's Bench, Lord Mansfield, had invoked the doctrines of political economy on a number of occasions since his appointment in 1756. Later claims that he was an initiator of the 1772 Act are therefore not implausible.[25] In the extraordinary trial in 1800 of Samuel Waddington, his counsel repeated this claim, pointing out that a prosecution was actually before the Chief Justice in 1772, and that Mansfield's 'understanding and feelings revolted so much at the judgment which ... he was obliged to pronounce', that he delayed judgment until the Act was passed, voiding all prosecutions. The story appears substantially correct.[26] In all, only five marketing cases appear in Mansfield's notebooks over the period 1756–72, and only one, in 1770, two years before the repeal, resulted in a conviction.[27]

There therefore appears to have been a strong convergence in 1772 in understanding between the political economists in Parliament, notably Burke, and the Chief Justice of the King's Bench. This should not surprise us. It is not necessary to examine Mansfield's connections with his fellow Scots who were the inventors of political economy (although far too little is known about those connections). It is sufficiently clear that in a great many other instances Mansfield enunciated from the bench the same strictures that Adam Smith published on ancient English statutes which contradicted market forces. Moreover, Mansfield often used the same policy reasoning, in judgments that anticipated the *Wealth of Nations* by many years.[28] His views on forestalling, regrating and engrossing are very likely to have closely resembled those of Smith and of Burke, and the anecdote told in court in 1801, although part of a trial argument and mistaken in detail, is probably accurate in substance.

In these circumstances, it seems likely that few if any in Parliament anticipated in 1772 that criminal sanctions would again be endorsed by the high judiciary and, since Mansfield was on the bench for another sixteen years and dominated his fellow judges, that belief remained undisturbed.[29] Lord Mansfield apparently heard no case after 1772. A consequence, however, was that the *exact* state of the law became uncertain and open to interpretation and invocation in contradictory ways. For any traditionalist country gentlemen turning to his justicing manual usually found, no matter which edition of which author he possessed, both before and after the repeal of 1772, the unequivocal statement that forestalling, regrating and engrossing were offences at common law, quite apart from the statutes, and therefore still punishable by (unlimited) fine and imprisonment after their abolition.[30] This opinion was based on two of the leading authorities on the common law of crimes: Sir Edward Coke, and Serjeant William Hawkins. Justices' manuals frequently quoted Hawkins, the leading writer on the criminal law, who described the marketing crimes as 'high' offences, 'extremely oppressive to the poorer sort' and 'just cause of complaint to the richest'.[31] The great Coke, a revered authority, was even better: 'A Forestaller is called by my Lord *Coke, Pauperum Depressor & totius Communitatis & Patriae publicus inimicus* (a Depressor of the Poor, and a publick Enemy of the whole Community and to his Country), and therefore is punishable at Common Law.'[32] The point was reiterated in all authoritative summaries of the law and forms of indictment were provided for magistrates concerned to punish the common law offences.[33] Blackstone accepted the policy reasoning behind all three offences; as late as the twelfth edition of the *Commentaries*, edited by Edward Christian, Professor of English Law at Cambridge, the wisdom of the common law offences is accepted without comment.[34] In short, not only the legal validity but also the moral censure of the old law had scarcely been weakened; indeed it was reiterated in the sources most often consulted by magistrates. Moreover, many statutes that provided penalties for marketing offences, some of them amounting to forestalling, regrating and engrossing, remained in the statute book after 1772 and became part of the argument: prosecutions under them were termed either vexatious, or lawful and salutory, depending on the speaker.[35]

In some legal texts more likely to be consulted by lawyers than by magistrates, there also appeared explicit contemporary comments on the policy of the law. Bacon's *Abridgement* has a passage in the 1778 edition that does not appear in the 1762 one:

Perhaps in this Country there is not a Statute more beneficial for the Poor, and, in Fact, for the People in general, nor a Law to which so little Attention is paid, or the Execution whereof is so shamefully neglected. The constant Practice of the Salesmen of Cattle in *Smithfield* Market, sufficiently justifies the severest Censures on this Subject.[36]

The argument on the other side also appears in some of the professional literature. Daines Barrington argued in the 1760s that the laws should be repealed, as their effect could only be to raise prices, praised the Act of 1772 in his later editions, and suggested that the ancient law, while perhaps once relevant, was now an absurd archaism.[37]

There was thus both authority and continuing policy arguments among legal writers in support of criminal proceedings even after 1772. But the Chief Justice of England was hostile to the idea and he probably had wide support at the bar.[38] Moreover, without a modern precedent in King's Bench, it was unclear just what evidence would be required to constitute proof of such a crime in England. The expectation among lawyers in the 1770s and 1780s probably was that Mansfield would require proof of intent to raise prices and of actual harm to the public, rather than just proof of the particular proscribed acts of repeated and profitable buying and selling in the same market, or buying before the market, or acquiring very large quantities for resale. And the expectation undoubtedly grew that actual harm was either not susceptible of proof, or, indeed, that the new economic science showed conclusively that unsupervised markets and even repeated sales in them were beneficial to the public rather than the reverse. The expectation must have been that the court would direct verdicts accordingly. Of course, it was possible for other prosecutions to be taking place before lesser benches who perhaps held a more traditional view of the law.

Local Enforcement and Parliamentary Opinion

Attitudes to the marketing offences in the wider community must have been greatly shaped by local practice and belief. In the decade before the repeal of 1772, prosecutions took place both in King's Bench and at provincial quarter and borough sessions. No survey of all local prosecutions has yet been done and many are unrecoverable, but some examples show the range of activity. In 1764 there were several Middlesex prosecutions, brought in King's Bench, against forestallers of Smithfield.[39] A systematic search in Staffordshire court records of 1742–1802, where a riotous population was increasingly dependent on purchase in markets, shows that there were prosecutions at Quarter

Sessions or Assizes in 1762 (four for engrossing), 1766 (one for engrossing), 1795 (five for regrating, one for forestalling), 1800 (one engrossing, one forestalling, three regrating.)[40] There was thus a total of 16 over a period of 60 years, confined to the 1760s and the end of the century.[41] In Northamptonshire, where a local poet had prayed in 1764,

Pity our Woes, let Justice draw her Sword,
Dilate th'Engrosser's Heart, and save us, LORD!
Or send a *West* Wind, as in *Egypt*'s Land,
And sweep these Locusts from our fertile Strand

there were prosecutions at Quarter Sessions for forestalling the cattle fair in 1766 and at least two other marketing prosecutions in 1767, one of which was removed to King's Bench on *certiorari*, and two cow dealers from the county were prosecuted in King's Bench the following year for regrating. Then in 1796 there was another for engrossing wheat.[42] In Oxford City and county, there was a constant trickle of prosecutions from the 1680s to the 1720s, one or two or more a year, in many years but not in all. After a hiatus, prosecutions are recorded again from 1757 to 1767, marking the dearths at the beginning and end of that decade in particular, and encouraged by the mayor and justices. There was again a gap, until 1795/6, when J. S. Girdler prosecuted a regrator of wheat, and 1800/1, when presentment juries and a City committee brought other regrating charges.[43] In the Court Leet of Manchester the prosecutions in the second half of the century were also concentrated in the 1760s and 1790s, although there was also one in 1785 for regrating.[44]

These limited soundings show that in the four provincial jurisdictions, at least at Quarter Sessions and Assizes, there does appear to be an almost complete hiatus in prosecutions following 1772. Nor are there any reported leading cases in King's Bench in the crisis years 1782, 1783 and 1787, when Mansfield was still Chief Justice. It is clear, none the less, that many gentlemen, besides the minority of lawyers already quoted, continued to believe in the offences and to refer to them. And at the local level, local market law (distinct from statute or common law, but informed by both) probably helped keep alive the idea that forestalling, regrating and engrossing were crimes. Some local markets had statutory monopolies requiring that specified foodstuffs be sold in the market, and making it clear that selling by sample in or near a market with intent to evade tolls was fraud, a point emphasised by Lord Kenyon in 1790.[45] These two kinds of case almost certainly kept alive a belief in the criminality of marketing offences at the local level because the common law offences helped to secure tolls, and because the term 'forestalling' was probably used for both the common law offence and some of those against market statutes.[46] The case in Manchester Court Leet in 1785 may be such an instance. Such regulation continued well into the nineteenth century; thus the Clerk in Uttoxeter (Staffs.) regulated the weights and measures but also tried to prevent forestalling.[47] The Oxford market committee advertised in 1808 that it would prosecute forestallers, regrators and engrossers 'to the utmost rigour of the law', citing both common law and the Oxford market statutes. They repeated the warning in 1824.[48]

Even in Parliament repeal of the statutes had never commanded total assent in the decades after 1772. Part of the reason was the continuing controversy in the London meat markets. The division of interest between jobbers and wholesale 'carcass' butchers on the one hand, and retail 'cutting' butchers on that other, continued to inspire efforts to make forestalling, regrating and engrossing of cattle and sheep a criminal offence until the end of the century.[49] In the summer of 1786, the Court of Common Council appointed a committee to consider the causes of high prices and in August it received resolutions from a meeting of master butchers who objected to regrating 'jobbers', but especially to the 'monopolising' carcass butchers who bought cattle and sheep before they got to Smithfield, avoiding tolls and keeping the market thin. By September the Committee of Privileges agreed to a number of 'suggestions' for an elaborate regulation of Smithfield, among them proposals to prevent what amounted to forestalling, regrating and engrossing. They were particularly concerned about sales made at Islington, Mile End and Knightsbridge, and declared that 'the laws against forestalling should be revived in order to check and if possible put a stop to these very injurious pratices. The penalties against such nefarious conduct should be considerable and levied upon either buyer or seller by summary process before two magistrates.' Tickets would certify bona fide sellers; forging them should be a capital offence. In November the committee considering high prices reported and endorsed these recommendations to the Court. Apparently some prosecutions for regrating were under way under a statute that had survived the 1772 repeal, but the City wanted to go farther and obtain new criminal legislation.[50]

In May 1787 a divided corporation voted to apply to Parliament for restoration 'to a proper extent' of the laws repealed in 1772 as a partial solution to prevailing high prices of meat and other provisions. There was public support for such measures, but Burke's wit was deployed to 'prevent the dry bones of those gibbeted laws from being again clothed with flesh'.[51] His jokes about overfed aldermen's fears for their dinners, followed by a paean to the virtues of free commerce (in slaves, among other things), won over the House. Lemesurier, the London alderman who moved that the petition be considered by a committee, argued rather feebly that there was no real comparison between the commerce of provisions and that of other articles; he reminded the House that there were laws against forestallers and regrators still in force and that they had been passed in popular reigns; his only wish was to have a bill as the basis for further discussion. Newnham, also a merchant alderman, seconded the motion, accepted that 'the repeal of them generally was a wise measure', but that moderate regulations were necessary, as the clear evidence of forestalling Smithfield showed. Only Alderman Sir Watkin Lewes defended the Common Council's investigation and objected to the levity that Burke engendered to defeat the petition. On the other hand, Robert Vyner, a crustily independent country gentleman, declared that 'the landed interest was not to be wantonly sacrificed to the capricious speculations of the Common Council of London'. The petition was 'an affront to the House'.[52]

The retail butchers again petitioned Pitt in 1795 to deal with forestalling and regrating by the carcass butchers, but he refused to act against such 'a very useful set of people'.[53] In the same year Burke reiterated the crucial importance of the wholly free market in foodstuffs during the dearth of 1795 in his savage attack on what he considered the pernicious idea of public granaries: 'The moment that government appears at market, all the principles of market will be subverted.' One should:

resist the very first idea, speculative or practical, that it is within the competence of government, taken as government, or even of the rich, as rich, to supply to the poor, those necessaries which it has pleased the Divine Providence for a while to with-hold from them. We, the people, ought to be made sensible, that it is not in breaking the laws of commerce, which are the laws of nature, and consequently the laws of God, that we are to place our hope of softening the Divine displeasure to remove any calamity under which we suffer, or which hangs over us.[54]

A few Members of Parliament muttered about 'jobbers in corn' and the inadequacy of Pitt's solutions to the crisis (such as changes in the assize of bread), but there was no attempt to restore the legislation repealed in 1772.[55] Probably many in Parliament followed Thomas Pownall, who published his view that there was forestalling, that there was a near-monopoly in wheat, that prices were artificially raised, but that in spite of 'a pretty general opinion' in favour of restoring the old criminal laws, that could be no answer. The laws had been repealed in 1772 because they were evaded, and obsolete. If they were re-enacted, they would be equally useless. (His own solution was public granaries.)[56]

The last eighteenth-century attempt to restore the old statute law took place the following year. The retail butchers petitioned the Commons, complaining that some of the legislation that had not been repealed in 1772 was none the less being ignored and that jobbers and carcass butchers were greatly enhancing prices by engrossing and forestalling the market: the 'sordid Arts of monopolizers', the 'Hand of Avarice', was ruining the retail trade. It was referred to a committee headed by Mainwaring, which reported in detail the retailers' evidence about the perfidious practices of jobbers and carcass butchers, said to have increased after the 1772 repeal. The committee prepared resolutions for regulating the wholesale trade; its general conclusion was that forestalling and regrating had greatly increased the price of meat, especially in recent years, and that legislation was needed to allow for summary convictions.[57] Mainwaring introduced a bill in the following session, in March 1797, determined to end the 'enormous sums' dishonestly earned by resaling jobbers, regraters in Smithfield and carcass butchers who forestalled that market. Mainwaring and Alderman Combe, who also spoke in support, were sensitive to the arguments of political economy: the former 'subscribed to that doctrine in a general way', but distinguished 'artifices' which might starve honest labourers, whose labour underpinned national prosperity. The bill, after its first and second reading, was supported by a petition of Somerset farmers, amended in committee and in committee of the whole, but then given the three months hoist.[58] Burke, who had been horrified by the whole initiative, a decade after that of 1787, lived just long enough to see the bill defeated by a vote of 39 to 7.[59]

By the time of the dearth of 1800, the worst of the century, abstaining from legal interference with the markets, including what were now acknowledged to be widespread practices of resale and buying outside the market, was the position of Pitt, of Portland (the Home Secretary), of Grenville (who argued that 'the best way would be to leave the grain to find its own value'), of Richmond, and also of the leaders of the opposition, Fox and his nephew, the third Lord Holland, who supported Pitt's approach to the dearth. That was not the opinion of all Members of Parliament or even the government: Lord Liverpool,

President of the Board of Trade, argued that Smith's principles were theoretical extravagances.[60] Nor was the Common Council of London of one mind, as the attempts at legislation in the 1780s and 1790s show. But the free market was the credo of those who controlled majorities in the House of Commons.[61]

However, outside Parliament, in the provinces, prosecutions began again in the higher courts (quarter sessions, assizes, King's Bench) in 1795. In Staffordshire, the grand jury apparently considered (but rejected) instituting public prosecutions of forestallers and engrossers two years earlier, in 1793. But in July 1795 the Birmingham High Bailiff announced that all forestallers, and those who sold to them, would be prosecuted and Oxford City Council instructed the city solicitor to prosecute all offenders dealing in corn, grain or flour, and offered a 20 guinea reward.[62] The spate of prosecutions which began in many counties in 1795, and became even more numerous in 1800, were in part stimulated by the activities of a number of traditionalist country gentlemen, including Joseph Girdler of Maidenhead, Kent, who offered rewards for convictions of forestallers, regrators and engrossers in the provincial papers. He spread the gospel through letters and handbills even more widely from the beginning of 1796, with some success: he was threatened with death as a result. He credited to his efforts a number of successful prosecutions and also a lawsuit, instigated in Common Pleas by the City of London, in which the plaintiff got a verdict and damages for regrating.[63] But Girdler's activities, and those of others who suspected that prices were being enhanced by resales, by forestalling markets, and by very large purchases by dealers, depended on the activities of the Chief Justice, Lord Kenyon, and his fellow judges.

The Crisis of 1795

In 1795 Kenyon announced on the summer assize circuit that forestalling was still indictable at common law, a reaffirmation of what was undoubtedly to be found in Coke and Hawkins, but a significant statement because it gave notice that any hostility against the doctrine in King's Bench under Mansfield was now replaced by a different attitude.[64] His charge to the grand jury in his own county of Shropshire was reprinted in many provincial newspapers:

> Gentlemen, since I have been in this place, a report has been handed to me, without any foundation I sincerely hope, that a set of private individuals are plundering at the expence of public

happiness, by endeavouring in this county, to purchase the grain now growing upon the soil! – For the sake of common humanity, I trust it is untrue: Gentlemen, you ought to be the champions against this hydra-headed monster. It is your duty, as Justices, to see justice done to the country! In your respective districts, as watchmen, be on your guard.

He warned that anyone convicted before him would feel 'the full vengeance of the law ... Neither purse, nor person, shall prevent it.'[65] The grand jury in Shrewsbury immediately resolved that they would use all their powers against such illegal contracts and would punish all nefarious practices against open markets.[66]

In Staffordshire, the first prosecutions since 1766 took place at Translation and Michaelmas quarter sessions, following an order of the magistrates that the Clerk of the Peace prosecute at the public expense.[67] In Wolverhampton the constables took several regrators to court, and this pattern of public enforcement is found in other counties.[68] Even before Kenyon's intervention, as we have seen, local authorities were supporting public prosecutions of offenders to emphasise (in a system of private prosecution) their deep concern. Now the Birmingham High Bailiff was assisted by an association of 'many respectable Inhabitants' who advertised repeatedly that they would pay for prosecutions and appoint detectives in the markets, in order to end 'these enormous abuses' and 'shameful practices'; they promised to publish the names of offenders and to reward citizens informing against such 'pests of society'.[69] Similar initiatives took place in other parts of the country.

However, the dearth of 1795–96 also generated, as we have seen, highly authoritative lay opinions on the futility of such measures, notably Burke's attack on any interference with market forces. In the spring of 1796 rising prices again resulted in local government prosecutions, but Parliament and Pitt, having explicitly rejected the notion of restoring some statute law on the marketing offences a decade before, did so again in 1797.[70] By 1800 even some traditionalists were beginning to wonder whether the old doctrine was defensible. In April 1796 a wealthy Bedfordshire farmer, Thomas Battams, had pleaded guilty at Buckingham sessions to regrating 14 quarters of oats at a profit of 6*d.* the quarter. The Chairman, the Marquis of Buckingham, had had Battams watched in order to get the evidence to convict him, and the prosecution was by a county subscription. At the sessions, Buckingham warmly denounced the crime, and a very large bench of justices sentenced Battams to 14 days in gaol and a fine of £200. Some of the press commented that the law 'throws a man entirely on the mercy of the Justices' and that 'no respectability of character can screen the offender from severe punishment.'[71] At the time, Buckingham thought the consequence was a salutary fall in prices and had no doubts about the value of the prosecution. But by 1800 he noted 'as I have frequently been obliged to argue with some whose opinions have great weight with me, and who doubted not only the policy, but the law of our proceedings in that case, I have paused upon one or two opportunities of making similar examples'. To settle those doubts, he wrote to Lord Kenyon for reassurance that the offence was indeed punishable at common law.[72]

In short, if the common law was to continue to be put into effect, Kenyon and his brother judges needed to do two things: establish a modern authoritative precedent by a judgment after full argument by counsel and encourage prosecutions through the most public discussion of the grounds of that judgment. By the time Buckingham wrote, as corn prices mounted to vertiginous heights, Kenyon and several of the other eleven common law judges had been busy for some months working to those ends. The result was a spectacular case (and another almost as notorious) that crystallised the legal, moral, political and economic issues during extended and widely reported hearings in 1800 and 1801.

Waddington, Rusby, Lord Kenyon and Lord Ellenborough

The case against Samuel Waddington, a London merchant who had recently entered the hop trade in Kent and Worcester, was brought in January 1800 by the London brewers and hop factors.[73] They resented his intrusion into their markets and his encouragement to the growers to bid up prices. For the judges of King's Bench, who personally took the affidavits, it was an ideal test case. Waddington had announced his intention in Kent of moving the market up by his purchases; act and intent were both likely to be made out in testimony. Moreover, he was a Jacobin sympathiser, an evident illustration of the traditionalists' belief that such radicals wished to bring ruin on the nation. He was prosecuted on a criminal information, a form of proceeding (involving many hearings in King's Bench) that gave the judges many opportunities to comment on the traditional law. Another marketing case, against the London corn factor John Rusby, for regrating and engrossing, was due also to come before King's Bench, but not so soon.

At London sessions and on the Lent assizes in the spring of 1800, the common law judges charged their juries on the evils of forestalling and their criminality at common law, in spite of the fact that *Waddington* and *Rusby* had not been heard. Meanwhile, Waddington openly urged the Worcester hop-growers to hold out for higher prices, entered into futures contracts and promptly had another cirminal information exhibited against him. At the hearing in King's Bench, Kenyon, in allowing the charge to proceed, made some withering remarks on the irrelevance of Adam Smith's theories on famine to the real world in which speculators thrived at the expense of the consumer. In July Rusby was convicted in London, and Waddington in Worcester (to the cheers of the public) and also in London, where the Kent charge had been removed for trial.

Technical law did not figure greatly in these trials: both sides were hampered by the fact that the precedents were old and often unclear. It was really Adam Smith who was on trial. Waddington's counsel, the leading barrister Edward Law, cited Smith's 'luminous' book and lectured the bench and jury on price theory; Thomas Erskine, Waddington's eminent counsel, ignored political economy, drew attention to the crisis of dearth afflicting England, quoted Lord Coke, appealed to all the traditional beliefs surrounding the moral economy, and won a verdict from the trial jury.

He did so in part because he had the ear of Kenyon (they corresponded about the case privately, before final judgment), and because Kenyon, a religious man of evangelical persuasion, and a judge who sincerely felt that the law must sustain the rights of the poor as well as the wealthy, was profoundly convinced of the immorality as well as illegality of the marketing offences. He was convinced that the poor were suffering unnecessarily because of the actions of middlemen. He read the exposition of the corn trade in *The Wealth of Nations* before he gave judgment and he was not convinced. His private notes are clear.[74] Mark Lane 'regulates the whole kingdom'; the invisible hand might regulate the whole market but marketing offences 'may hurt the inhabitants of a particular place'. To Smith's argument that 'those who may be hindred from supplying themselves on that market day, may supply themselves as cheap on another', he retorted 'What are they [to] do in the mean time? Eat they must.' And he noted that even Burke admitted that fraud could infect the corn market. His statements in court fully reflected these views, even if he did not condescend to debate political economy in any detail.

There is some evidence that King George III approved of Kenyon's handling of forestallers. Certainly a great many correspondents of the chief justice wrote to say that they approved of his Christian and moral stand against profiteers. Clearly a strand of evangelical opinion supported the old law, as did more traditional country gentlemen, and probably a number of military officers who had experience of regulating markets on campaigns. Men like these, and Kenyon and some of the other common law judges, such as Mr Justice Grose, were traditionalists whose arguments were couched in moral rhetoric: the description 'moral economy' is entirely apt for their outlook on markets threatened by dearth. To Kenyon, Burke must have seemed not only mistaken and hard-hearted, but also blasphemous, when he wrote (in words widely reprinted in 1800) of 'the laws of commerce, which are the laws of nature, and consequently the laws of God'. The Chief Justice knew a different truth: 'Our [common] law, thank God, is the same with the divine.'[75]

By November the final arguments (on motions for arrest of judgment, and a new trial) were being made in Waddington's case, before final judgment. But meanwhile the consequences of Rusby's conviction were alarming the government and a great many others.

Part of Kenyon's rationale for upholding the marketing offences, both in 1795 and in 1800, had been the practical usefulness of prosecutions for forestalling, regrating and engrossing. Like country gentlemen for centuries past, he knew that the promise of such a prosecution was often enough to stop a riot. In 1795, he believed, his endorsement of the old laws had helped prevent virtual insurrection in the Midlands. But the logic of this venerable assessment of crowd behaviour was cast into serious doubt in September 1800 in the wake of Rusby's conviction. Kenyon had virtually instructed the jury to convict, and had conjured up for them the vision of a rich man monopolising provisions at every road into London. On 15 September a mob began throwing mud at the mealmen in the corn market; a riot ensured, and by midnight the mob had gone to Rusby's house and gutted it.

In November the court of King's Bench heard the final arguments in Rusby's case (on a motion in arrest of judgment). Law described the awful consequences if the common-law offence of regrating was sustained: the starvation of London. He also raised an important new point. There appeared to be no decided cases on regrating before the statue of Edward VI, and it had been repealed in 1772. Kenyon granted the rule: there would be further argument in the case. But many in the courtroom were undoubtedly thinking of some of the other consequences of stigmatising middlemen, especially the danger to public order. It was felt that the judges had given enormous encouragement to the mob. People had papered inflammatory handbills on the Monument, sung ballads in the streets in honour of the Chief Justice, painted walls with slogans, 'No hoarders – no grinders of the poor – Lord Kenyon, and down with the mealmen.'[76] Members of the government privately deplored the zeal of the Lord Chief Justice. Some talked of impeachment.

Kenyon and his brothers did not initially draw back. Waddington was sentenced in Hilary term, in two hearings in January and February 1801 (although all his appeals were over by November) for the Worcester and Kent offences. He had already been in prison for many weeks; he was now sentenced to a further four months' imprisonment and a fine of £1000. The language of moral condemnation in which the sentences were cast was unequivocal. The crime was 'merciless', the work of an avaricious man at the expense of the poor. The fact that Waddington was a Jacobin, and that he had also published several pamphlets during the trial attacking the judges, doubtless influenced the sentence, and was certainly the reason they delayed final judgment for two months, to give him time to reflect in prison on his misdeeds.

Kenyon now had his precedent. (Indeed, he had announced it as a precedent to grand juries on assize immediately after the first trial verdicts.) But the implications of the old offences for the supply of London markets were clearly in the minds of many, including some on the bench. The final arguments in Rusby's case came before King's Bench on 31 January, and three of the judges now felt that the indictment was defective in not showing an intent to raise the market, and probably that the offence of regrating had not antedated the statute of Edward VI. Kenyon disagreed. But the division of opinion was the beginning of the end for Kenyon's desired broad precedent. In the event, no judgment or sentence was ever passed on Rusby: the prosecution was absolutely discharged a few years later. A few other cases that had been progressing through the labyrinthine procedures of King's Bench resulted in acquittals in 1801, or were dropped.[77] The common law had triumphed through its ambiguity. A Jacobin engrosser had been publicly and severely punished, the justice of the law's interference with commerce had been vindicated. But with the sudden discovery by the judges that regrating no longer existed as an offence, the pressing practical danger to the London markets had been adroitly avoided. Lord Holland, who attributed Kenyon's hostility to middlemen to ignorance, concluded that, in the end, the Lord Chief Justice rather ignobly capitulated to the Ministry.[78] It seems more likely that when he died in 1802, Kenyon, if not his brothers on the bench, still believed that he was right to enforce the marketing laws and probably was hopeful that the new precedent in *Waddington* would still curb evils of forestalling and engrossing, if not regrating, for the future.

Kenyon was not to know that his successor as Chief Justice was to be Edward Law, now Lord Ellenborough, who as Waddington's counsel had lectured Kenyon on the wisdom of the market and the improving writings of Adam Smith.[79] Ellenborough displayed his ideological commitment to Smithian economics in a number of ways,[80] but he also had the immediate policy argument that he had urged unsuccessfully against Lord Kenyon the preceding year.

This was that enforcement of the marketing laws was dangerous to the state in a way that Kenyon had not foreseen, and that the alleged benefit, pacification of the mob, was non-existent and in any case unnecessary. The dangers were two. If the laws were enforced, the middlemen upon whom the supply of large urban markets, especially London, depended, could not trade and the supply of food would be greatly disrupted, with all the dangers of riot that that entailed for the early-modern state. The second danger lay in the fact that Kenyon's analysis of the mood of the people was wrong: far from reassuring them that the authorities were acting, denunciations of middlemen from the bench now *encouraged* the mob to riot. Rusby's house had been destroyed shortly after he had been declared a social parasite by one of Lord Kenyon's juries. The most serious riots in the capital in a century took place a week after Waddington's second conviction before Kenyon. More fundamentally, by 1802 the balance of persuasion and coercion in the maintenance of public order had changed in England, during the very months when Waddington and Rusby were being prosecuted. There had been a massive reinforcement of military power in England, as Pitt constructed barracks and thousands of troops were poured into the Midlands and other parts of the country.

In short, Kenyon's theory of social pacification through invocation of the law was rapidly becoming irrelevant, at least in terms of marketing. As one highly respected contemporary put it, 'doctrines of most serious tendency had been propagated from the bench, the bar, the hustings, and the press, directly, although unintentionally, countenancing the popular passions and prejudices' which incited the mob to acts of violence. 'What has saved us lately, from conflagrations and massacres, but the country happening to be in a state of armed preparation?'[81] Kenyon and his brothers had blundered into inflaming the mob. Denouncing forestallers from the throne or the bench had always been a calculated risk, and the purpose, calming anxiety about the markets in order to prevent riot, was now becoming irrelevant as Britain became an armed camp.

Ellenborough, it was clear, would be a Chief Justice difficult to convince that the marketing offences still stood at common law. At the time of Rusby and Waddington's cases, at least seven other marketing prosecutions were under way in King's Bench. But, as the price crisis eased, most were dropped, resulted in acquittals before juries, or were found insufficient in law. One, the prosecution of a Carmarthen miller for engrossing very large quantities of grain, was due to go before a jury in March 1802 but Kenyon was ill (he died in April). The case never came to trial. Once Ellenborough was on the bench, it was evidently realised that no convictions could be had, or would stand re-examination, in King's Bench. In 1804 Rusby, who had been held to a recognisance until the disputed point of law on whether regrating was still an offence had been determined, was given a final and free discharge.

Conclusion

The eighteenth-century history of the marketing laws is a reminder that the moral economy was in large measure a matter of law: law not only in the sense of a broad legitimator, but in a highly instrumental sense. Unless judges and magistrates believed that criminal offences were being committed, and allowed cases to be prosecuted to conviction, the moral economy could be no more than a set of assumptions about markets and morals. The highest cirminal court discouraged such prosecutions under Mansfield after 1756 and also appeared to have discouraged successful prosecutions in lower courts. This was so especially after 1772, and until Mansfield's death and the appointment of Kenyon in 1788. It is possible that the discrepancy between the unwillingness to enforce the law, and the continuing belief in the reasonableness of the law, made food riot much more likely. Magistrates sitting alone may have been unwilling to commit offenders for trial, and magistrates sitting in quarter sessions may have been unwilling to encourage juries to convict, if it was well-known that Mansfield was likely to grant relief to the accused. Local justices of the peace had no taste for having cases removed on *certiorari* into King's Bench, which was not uncommon, or for having their actions attacked through a criminal information, which was uncommon but very uncomfortable when it happened.[82] Both those avenues might have been pursued by those prosecuted under the old statutes or the common law when Mansfield was Chief Justice.

At the same time, however, the law in the wider, quasi-constitutional sense remained a powerful supporter of the traditional view of markets. Coke was a powerful name to conjure with, and he had denounced offenders against the marketing laws as a public enemy and traitor. Hawkins and Burn, the bibles of county and borough magistrates, reiterated that the offences were still offences under common law. In short, the most widespread genteel lay legal culture in the country sustained the idea of a moral economy, one that protected rather than depressed the poor (in Coke's words), one that ensured the security of the state and the welfare of the weakest members of the community. This conflict of local law with that in Westminster Hall, and of the common law with the intentions of the parliamentary leaders after 1772, created in the second half of the eighteenth century a sphere of legal ambiguity. It contained and required that atmosphere of accomodations between mob, magistracy and government that sustained the practices and beliefs we now call the moral economy. It barely outlived the century.

Notes

1. E. P. Thompson, 'The moral economy of the English crowd in the eighteenth century', *Past and Present*, 50 (February 1971), pp. 76–136. He recapitulated the argument with new evidence and a consideration of the ensuing debate, in 'The moral economy reviewed', *Customs in Common* (London: Merlin, 1991), pp. 259–351. There was truly ancient law on the matter: the Athenian constitution provided special officers of the state to detect and punish engrossers, and those who made more than the legal profit on corn. The death penalty probably did not apply, but a member of the Atheninan Council in a speech in 386 BC demanded punishment for men making such 'illicit gain': 'pity those of our citizens who perished by their villainy, and the traders against whom they have combined': 'Against the Corndealers', ch. 22 in *Lysias*, trans. W. R. M. Lamb, Loeb Classical Library (Cambridge, Mass., 1960); Aristotle, *The Athenian Constitution*, trans. P. J. Rhodes (Harmondsworth: Penguin, 1984), s.51. I owe these references to Professor Virginia Hunter.
2. An extended example is Adrian Randall, *Before the Luddites: Custom, Community and Machinery in the English Woollen Industry 1776–1809* (Cambridge: Cambridge University Press, 1991); see also A. Randall, 'The industrial moral economy of the Gloucestershire weavers in the 18th century', in John Rule (ed.), *British Trade Unionism 1750–1850: The Formative Years* (London: Longman, 1988), and Douglas Hay and Nicholas Rogers, *Eighteenth-Century English Society: Shuttles and Swords* (Oxford: Oxford University Press, 1997), ch. 6.
3. Recent studies that include consideration of the role of middling groups in the moral economy include those by Steven Poole, Simon Renton and Wendy Thwaites in Adrian Randall and Andrew Charlesworth (eds), *Markets,*

Market Culture and Popular Protest in Eighteenth-Century Britain and Ireland (Liverpool: Liverpool University Press, 1996), and Susan Brown, '"A just and profitable commerce": moral economy and the middle classes in eighteenth-century London', *Journal of British Studies*, XXXII (1993), pp. 305–32.

4. The classic account is Adam Smith, *An Inquiry into the Nature and Causes of the Wealth of Nations*, ed. W. B. Todd (2 vols, Oxford: Clarendon Press 1976), i, pp. 524 ff., 'Digression concerning the Corn Trade and Corn Laws' (IV. v.b).

5. These examples and others are reprinted in *Charges to the Grand Jury 1689–1803*, ed. Georges Lamoine, Camden Society, 4th ser., XXXXIII (London: Royal Historical Society, 1992), pp. 73, 105, 126, 188, 203, 218, 235, 297, 313, 323, 360, 369, 373, 378, 382.

6. I summarise below the marketing cases at the end of the century (principally *R. v. Waddington*, *R. v. Rusby*), but for a fuller account see D. Hay, 'The state and the market in 1800: Lord Kenyon and Mr Waddington', *Past and Present*, 162 (February 1999), pp. 101–62. Some passages in that article also appear here.

7. *Commons Journals* (hereafter *CJ*), 2 Feb. 1757. For an earlier petition of 1733, see below.

8. *CJ*, vol. 29, pp. 797, 949, 982, 983, 1046–7 (8 Feb. to 11 April 1764).

9. For example, petitions from Newcastle under Lyme and Stafford, *CJ*, vol. 27, pp. 639–40, 656 (21 Dec. 1756, 18 Jan. 1757); Anon. *A Letter to the House of Commons; in which is set forth the Nature of Certain Abuses Relative to the Articles of Provisions, Both with Respect to Men and Horses; together with their Remedies* (1765), pp. 5–10; Stephen Browne, *The Laws against Ingrossing, Forestalling, Regrating, and Monopolozing ... Compiled by Desire of a Great Personage, for the Use of the Magistrates in Town and Country* (London, 1765), title page.

10. *CJ*, vol. 30, pp. 762–71, 781, 783, 788, 800, 812, 819 (25 April to 13 May 1766).

11. *The Case of the Inhabitants of the Cities of London and Westminister, and the suburbs thereof, as also of the Inhabitants of the Adjacent Counties; relating to the Oppression they lye under by means of the Forestallers, Engrossers, and Jobbers of Cattle, and Flesh-Provisions brought to the several Markets; Humbly Offer'd to the Honourable House of Commons* (n.d., 1 p.), Lincoln's Inn, Miscell. Pamphlets 103, f.380; *CJ*, vol. 22, p. 265 (2 March 1733). There was also a petition concerning forestalling of corn the following year (2, 27 March 1734).

12. *CJ*, vol. 30, pp. 714, 751, 787–8, 1 May 1766, Sir George Yonge reporting from a committee appointed 10 April. The bill does not appear to survive, and I have found no further references to it: Sheila Lambert, *House of Commons Sessional Papers of the Eighteenth Century: Introduction and List* (Wilmington, Del.: Scholarly Resources, 1975–6), ii, p. 29. It may have been a product of the conflicts between wholesale and retail butchers, well-established by the beginning of the century, that is discussed below. The importance of that controversy is understated in Brown, '"A just and profitable commerce"', but she makes the important point that expectations of civic paternalism were probably stronger in the intimate setting of the City than in the rest of London.

13. For the incidence of prosecutions, see below. The King's Proclamation of 10 September 1766 began by referring to the 'several good statutes... against Forestallers, Regrators, and Ingrossers, who are thereby declared open oppressors of the poor, and enemies of their country', which it then detailed, and then charged all judges, justices and legal officers to put the acts into effect and to prosecute offenders: William Illingworth, *An Inquiry into the Laws, Antient and Modern, Respecting Forestalling, Regrating, and Ingrossing* (London, 1800), pp. 271–7. One other interesting aspect of the government's response was the defence given by Lord Camden, the Lord Chancellor, for the government's use of the prerogative to suspend exportation of grain during the crisis. The government subsequently brought in indemnifying legislation, but at first seemed reluctant to admit that the prerogative in itself was not sufficient to justify the suspension of the statute. This was seized on by the opposition as an echo of Stuart tyranny, and their delight was unbounded when Camden defended it as 'forty days' tyranny at most', since, as Chief Justice of Common Pleas, he had been notoriously critical of the previous administration's abuse of power in the proceedings against Wilkes, and especially of the actions of Lord Mansfield: see D. Hay, 'Contempt by scandalizing the court: a history of the first hundred years', *Osgoode Hall Law Journal*, 25 (1987), pp. 431–84. But Camden's defence, subsequently developed at some length, was that 'the maxim *salus populi suprema lex* was never more applicable', an argument for intervention in markets in spite of any law to the contrary (*Parliamentary History*, vol. 18, p. 812). Mansfield, who opposed Camden on virtually every other political issue, apparently opposed him on the issue of the sanctity of markets also: see below.

14. Anon, *Reflections on the Present High Price of Provisions, and the Complaints and Disturbances Arising Therefrom* (London, 1766), 37, cited in Thompson, 'Moral economy', p. 96 nn. 63, 64.

15. *CJ*, vol. 31, pp. 275, 291 (3, 8 April 1767). I have not traced any further proceedings.

16. Corporation of London Record Office, Misc. Mss 117.4; Misc. Mss 171.8.

17. *CJ*, vol. 31, pp. 587, 603, 610, 618, 626; 8, 11, 15, 18, 22 Feb. 1768, when the report was recommitted to the committee.

18. The press reported that a bill was ready to be laid before Parliament next sessions for new regulations for the London markets, including a requirement that every farmer and grazier residing within 100 miles should be obliged (with some exceptions) to attend the sale of his own cattle in London markets: *Westminster Journal*, 4–11 Jan. 1772. I owe this reference to Dr Ruth Paley.

19. *CJ*, vol. 33, 13 March, pp. 590, 591. The others were Cornwall and Gilbert.

20. *CJ*, vol. 33, 6 May p. 732, 7 May p. 736, 13 May p. 754, 14 May p. 759, 20 May p. 774, 3 June pp. 945, 953, 9 June p. 957. See also *The Proceedings at Large in the Cause of The King v. Waddington, For Purchasing Hops, in Kent. Also the Pleadings, &c. when the defendant was called upon for Judgment upon the Verdict at Worcester* (London: E. Rider, 1801), p. 63.

21. The statutes were 3 & 4 Ed. VI c. 21 (1549, butter and cheese); 5 & 6 Ed. VI c. 14 (1551, regrators, forestallers, engrossers); 2 & 3 Ph. & M c. 3 (1555, cattle); 5 Eliz. I c. 12 (1562, corn badgers and cattle drovers); 15 Chas. II c. 8 (1663, butchers); 6 Ann. c. 34 (in part; continuing laws re Smithfield).

22. *Parl. History*, vol. 17, cols 477, 479, 14 April, 1772. In 1776 Pownall proposed the establishment of university lectureships in political economy:
Dictionary of National Biography. See also his intervention in the debate in
1795, below.

23. Erskine, prosecuting Rusby in 1800, repeated as well-known the fact that
Burke took the lead in the 1772 repeal; *The Times*, 5 July 1800, and below,
n. 59. Alderman Thomas Harley, MP, wine-merchant and brother of the
Earl of Oxford, was also closely involved. He had been head of a committee
of Common Council that had investigated high prices in November 1767
and exonerated middlemen (above, in text); City of London Record Office,
Misc. Mss 117.4 (10c, 5b).

24. Robert Bisset, *Life of Burke*, 2nd edn (London, 1800), vol. 2, p. 429, who
attributed their agreement to both having read Aristotle.

25. Mansfield appears to have supported the old laws to some extent in 1758
(see n. 38, below), but in 1787, when the City of London petitioned
Parliament for a revival of the laws against the marketing offences,
Alderman Townshend retorted in the House of Commons that they had
been repealed 'on the recommendation of the present Chief Justice of the
Court of King's Bench', 4 May 1787, *Debates and Proceedings of the House of
Commons during the Fourth Session of the Sixteenth Parliament*, iii (1787),
p. 127; *Parliamentary History*, xxvi [15 May 1786–8 February 1788] (1816),
col. 1168. (I owe this reference to Joanna Innes.) On the 1787 bill, see below.

26. *Proceedings*, p. 63. A special verdict was found before Mansfield against an
engrosser a week before the Commons gave leave for the repealing bill of
1772 to be brought in; the Chief Justice never gave judgment upon it. Law
named one Cullum as the accused, but perhaps meant Capel. (Law also
noted that Cullum had been attacked by the London mob in 1800, presumably in the riot of December 1800; see below.) Cullum and Capel came
before Mansfield in London. John Cullum's first prosecutor in 1770 was
non-suited on a qui tam proceeding: Mansfield MSS, 471 nb 32, 21 June
1770, Woodrich, q.t.v. Cullum, in James Oldham, *The Mansfield Manuscripts
and the Growth of English Law in the Eighteenth Century* (Chapel Hill, NC:
University of North Carolina Press, 1992), vol. 2, p. 984. Cullum (identified
as a butter factor) was then indicted in King's Bench in early 1772 on two
more counts of engrossing, to which he pleaded not guilty, but on which
he does not seem to have been tried (PRO, KB 15/26 Hilary 1772 pp. 35–6).
Henry Capel, cheesemonger, was acquitted on one charge of forestalling
butter, but the jury found a special verdict on another of engrossing;
Mansfield appears never to have given judgment upon it (Mansfield MSS,
474 nb 124, 130, 4, 5 March 1772 in Oldham, vol. 2, pp. 988–9; PRO, KB
15/26 pp. 31–2). During the preparation of the bill, the House instructed
the committee to prepare a clause (enacted as clause II) voiding prosecutions that had not yet come to judgment: *CJ*, xxxiii, p. 736 (7 May 1772).

27. The others cited in Mansfield's notebooks, in addition to Woolrich q.t.v.
Cullum in 1770 and the two cases of *R. v. Capel* in 1772 (above) were
R. v. Heron (1758) for forestalling butter at Sunderland (County Durham),
and a successful prosecution (Woolkick q.t.v. Cook, 1770) of a London
butcher for selling live fat cattle, in effect a regrating, and criminal under
15 Chas. II c. 8 (Mansfield notebooks, 450 nb 223, 469 nb 200, 471 nb 32,

474 nb 124, 474 nb 130, in Oldham, vol. 2, pp. 940, 978). In early 1772 there were also four prosecutions against two other London butter factors, John Chandler and Edward Folly, that apparently did not get to trial before the statute was enacted: PRO, KB 15/26 Hilary George III pp. 29–30, 33–4.

28. I develop the argument elsewhere. See also Oldham, vol. 1, pp. 685 ff.; vol. 2, pp. 932–4.

29. In 1800 Kenyon remarked, 'the Acts of Parliament ... were in my opinion in an evil hour, without consideration enough, repealed; yet, thank God, the power which repealed it was not informed of, or did not intend to repeal those provisions made by the Common Law'. The former seems the more likely. Another reason may be the fact that wholesale abolition of a common law criminal offence was probably unprecedented in the eighteenth century. The quotation is from the judgment in *Rusby*, as given in J. S. Girdler, *Observations on the Pernicious Consequences of Forestalling, Regrating, and Ingrossing, with a List of the Statutes, etc.* (London: Baldwin & Son, 1800) pp. 255–6; a shorter version of 96 pp. was also published in 1800 under almost the same title.

30. For example, W. Nelson, *The Office and Authority of a Justice of Peace* (editions of 1721, 1736, 1745); Theodore Barlow, *The Justice of the Peace* (1745 edition); Edward Barry, *The Present Practice of a Justice of the Peace* (London, 1790), vol. 2, p. 175. See also virtually all the editions of Richard Burn, *The Justice of the Peace and Parish Officer*, e.g., 12th edn, 1772, vol. 2, pp. 194–5, which cites the common law from Hawkins and Coke, but follows with much longer section on the statute 5 & 6 Ed. VI c. 14 and (briefly) a few others. The statute of Edward VI continued to be cited after the repeal of 1772 for its definitions of the offences. Burn was by far the most common reference for justices in the second half of the century.

31. See, for example, Thomas Walter Williams, *The Whole Law Relative to the Duty and Office of a Justice of the Peace* (London, 1793–5), vol. 2, p. 566, quoting William Hawkins. *A Treatise of the Pleas of the Crown* (London, 1716), ch. 80, s.2. The 1795 edition of Hawkins contains the same passage.

32. W. Nelson, *The Office and Authority of a Justice of Peace* (London, 1745), vol. 1, p. 404, and subsequent editions, quoting Coke, *Institutes*, iii, pp. 195–6. Coke in fact was quoting from a statute of Edward I.

33. See, for example, Williams (1793), ii, pp. 567–8.

34. William Blackstone, *Commentaries on the Laws of England*, Book IV, ch. 12.

35. See the debates of 1786 and 1796, below, for examples. For a summary, see *Abstract of the Statutes respecting Forestallers, Regrators, and Ingrossers* (A. Straban, 1800), Lincoln's Inn Mss, Trials 217. Examples of statutes sometimes cited include 3 & 4 Edward VI c. 19 and 15 Charles II c. 8 ('No person shall buy any oxen, steers, runts, kine, heifer, or calves, but in open market, nor shall sell the same again alive in the same market, on penalty of double the value'; 'butchers must not buy any fat cattle (or sheep) and sell the same again alive, on pain of forfeiture of the cattle or sheep sold'); 31 George II c. 40 s. 11 ('no salesman or factor, employed to buy or sell cattle by commission, shall ... on his own account ... buy any cattle at any place while they shall be on the road to London for sale'). The final repealing statute, 7 & 8 Victoria c. 24, which ended the common law offence, also repealed these and all or part of 37 other statutes.

36. Matthew Bacon, *A New Abridgement of the Law*, 2nd edn, 1762, 4th edn,
     1778, vol. 2, p. 574, final note *a*. A note to this note mentions the repeal-
     ing statute, enacted before the revision went to press. The quoted passage
     also appears in a pirated 5th Irish edition of 1786, but disappeared from the
     5th edn (London, 1798, ed. Henry Gwillim). Bacon and the other standard
     abridgements (Viner, 1791; Comyns, 1792) all restated the criminality of
     the offences at common law.
37   *Observations on the More Ancient Statutes* (2nd edn, 1766), pp. 171–2. He
     explained in the 3rd edition (1769, p. 189) that they might have appeared
     less absurd in the distant past, because want of communication might
     make forestalling a local market possible. He hailed their repeal in the 4th
     edition (1775, p. 213, note *t*).
38. Of course, related crimes, such as conspiracies to raise prices, were another
     matter. See, for example, Mansfield's comments shortly after he became
     Chief Justice in *R. v. Norris et al.* (1758), 2 Keny. 300, a conspiracy to raise
     the price of salt:

> if any agreement was made to fix the price of salt, or any other necessary
> of life (which salt emphatically was), by people dealing in that commod-
> ity, the court would be glad to lay hold of an opportunity, *from what
> quarter soever the complaint came*, to shew their sense of the crime... He
> mentioned an indictment, upon one of the last home-circuits, against
> the bakers of the town of *Farnham*, for such an agreement.

     This is the report taken down by Kenyon, then a law-student, and
     published in his posthumous *Reports*; emphasis in original.
39. Charles Parsons and John Grainger, both of Kensington, Thomas
     Bartholomew, St George Hanover Square, and John Edus, St James, all
     butchers. Parsons was convicted of forestalling a bullock coming to
     Smithfield, imprisoned in King's Bench prison for two months, and fined
     £14, the value of the bullock. Bartholomew demurred and had judgment
     for want of joinder in demurrer; I have not been able to trace the outcome.
     PRO, KB 1/16/2 Hilary 1765 pt 2; KB 15/25 Trinity 4 George III, Hilary and
     Trinity 5 George III, pp. 18, 19, 34, 61. Grainger and Parsons were both
     prosecuted by William Payne, carpenter, an active informer: see Joanna
     Innes, 'William Payne of Bell Yard, Carpenter c. 1718–1782: The Life and
     Times of a London Informing Constable' (unpublished).
40. PRO, Assi 5/82 Summer 1762 and Staffs. Record Office (hereafter SRO),
     Q/SR (Tr 62; Assi 5/86, Summer 1766; Q/SR Tr, Mich 95; Q/Sr Ea, Mich
     1800. In Epiphany 1767 a recognisance to answer (James Gough) was
     apparently discharged without a prosecution; Q/S Pr2.
41. The actual number may be slightly higher, since such prosecutions were
     particularly likely to be undertaken in market towns, and Walsall had its
     own active borough sessions, of which the records do not survive. On the
     other hand, the surviving records for other separate jurisdictions (Lichfield,
     Tamworth, Newcastle, Stafford) do not reveal any prosecutions of market-
     ing offences. In the period before the repealing statute of 1772, such prose-
     cutions could be laid either on indictment or as quitam proceedings at
     quarter sessions: see Mansfield's cases, above, some of which came to him
     on *certiorari*, and the Northamptonshire cases, below.

42. *Northampton Mercury*, 22 October 1764; Northamptonshire Record Office (hereafter NRO), Q/S Grand Files Mich 1766, informations of Robert Williams of St Mary le Bone, Middlesex, butcher, against Daniel Harris late of Grays Inn Lane, Holbourn, cowkeeper (15 cows), Samuel Roads late of Hackney, cowkeeper (19 cows), and Robert Fryer late of parish of St John, Hampstead, cowkeeper and grazier (16 cows), all at Kingsthorpe, Northants.; NRO, QS Order Book 1754–1782, pp. 285, 287, Robert Fryer, Robert Hall. NRO, Q/S Grand Files Mich 1796 presentment of Daniel Abbot for engross-ing 50 quarters of wheat, intent to sell again. The qui tam proceedings begun by Williams, concerning cows valued at £532, would have given him half that amount, if he was successful. PRO, KB 29/427 Mich 8 George III, 5, 11, Robert Hall and Procter, forestalling 15 cows, St Sepulchre fair.

43. W. Thwaites, 'The Marketing of Agricultural Produce in Eighteenth-Century Oxfordshire' (University of Birmingham PhD thesis, 1980), pp. 382–97 and 432–50; W. Thwaites, 'The corn market and economic change: Oxford in the eighteenth century', *Midland History*, XVI (1991), pp. 112–17. Thwaites notes that although the pattern of enforcement appears largely to be dearth-related, quarter sessions records and other sources may considerably under-state enforcement levels, especially of less formal kinds. On Girdler, see below.

44. *The Court Leet Records of the Manor of Manchester*, ed. J. P. Earwaker (Manchester, 1888/9), vol. 8, p. 254. Other prosecutions of the three mar-keting offences (among other market-related offences) took place in 1759 (7 forestallers), 1763 (4 forestallers), 1764 (1 forestaller), 1766 (2 forestallers), 1797 (two regrators): vol. 8, pp. 38, 79, 87, 103; vol. 9, p. 124.

45. *Moseley* v. *Pierson* (1790), 4 Term. Rep. 104 at 107; followed in *Tewksbury Corp.* v. *Bricknell* (1809), 2 Taunt. 120. For the Oxford market legislation, see Thwaites, 'Marketing', pp. 118 ff.

46. Thwaites,. 'The corn market and economic change', p. 118.

47. William Pitt, *A Topographical History of Staffordshire* (Newcastle under Lyme, 1817), p. 206.

48. *Jackson's Oxford Journal*, 28 May 1808; Oxford City Archives, D.3.11 (26), Papers of the Market Committee 1774–1823. I am very grateful to Dr Thwaites for making this material available to me, and for bringing to my attention the significance of local market statute law and regulation. See also W. Thwaites, 'Oxford food riots: a community and its markets', in Randall and Charlesworth (eds), *Markets, Market Culture and Popular Protest*.

49. Above; in 1726 the Butcher's Company also prosecuted those who were not freemen, accusing such hawkers of forestalling. Philip E. Jones, *The Butchers of London* (1976), pp. 101–3; Arthur Pearce, *History of the Butchers' Company* (1929), pp. 112, 160–1. See also A. B. Robertson, 'The Smithfield cattle market', *East London Papers*, vol. 4 (1961), pp. 80–7.

50. Corporation of London Record Office, C/2OI, *Report of the Committee of the Court of Common-Counsil of the City of London appointed on the 16th day of July 1786 to consider of the Causes of the High Prices of Provisions and Reported to the Court on the 16th day of November 1786*; Misc. Mss 118.2; Misc. Mss 353.2, 1 Aug. 1786; Misc. Mss 85.12. The report was published in December: *The Times*, 12 and 15 Dec. 1786. The statute being used was probably 3 & 4 Edward VI c. 19, finally repealed by 7 & 8 Victoria c. 24.

51. *CJ*, vol. 42, p. 780; *Parl. Debates*, vol. 12, pp. 127–32, 16 May 1787; *Parl. History*, vol. 26, pp. 1167–71, 16 May 1787; Girdler, *Observations*, 163, note; *The Times*, 5, 21, 31 May, 21 Oct. 1787. On 12 July 1786 *The Times* had noted that in spite of fine weather, 'every species of provisions, animal and vegetable, are monopolized and forestalled for the purpose of keeping up the price'. See also 16 July, 15 Aug., 11 Oct. 1786.
52. *CJ*, vol. 42, p. 720; *Parl. History*, vol. 26, p. 1167, and *Parl. Debates*, vol. 12, pp. 127–32, 4 and 16 May 1787; *History of Parliament*, Nathaniel Newnham, James Townshend, Paul LeMesurier, Robert Vyner.
53. Girdler, *Observations*, pp. 327–8. The carcass butchers had apparently succeeded to the primacy in London politics formerly held by the retailers: Jones, p. 103.
54. E. Burke, *Thoughts and Details on Scarcity, Originally Presented to the Right Hon. William Pitt, in the Month of November, 1795* (London, 1800), p. 32; see also Clive Emsley, *British Society and the French Wars 1793–1815* (London: Macmillan 1979), pp. 43 ff.
55. Edmund Lechmere, a barrister and MP for Worcester, speaking in the debate on high prices of corn. Girdler was in correspondence with Lechmere, pressing him to seek legislation, but he was not re-elected in 1796: *Aris's Birmingham Gazette*, 9 Nov. 1795; Girdler, *Observations*, p. 211; *Parliamentary History*, vol. 32 (1795–97), pp. 236–7 (3 Nov. 1795); R.G. Thorne, *The History of Parliament: The House of Commons, 1790–1820* (London: Sacker & Warburg, 1986), vol. 4, p. 398.
56. 'Governor' Thomas Pownall, *Considerations on the Scarcity and High Prices of Bread Corn and Bread at the Market...* (Cambridge, 1795), pp. 50–5. Originally published in the *Cambridge Chronicle*, these remarks appeared at the end of September.
57. *CJ*, vol. 51, pp. 551–2, 572, 636–40, 4, 13, 29 April 1796; Lambert edition, vol. 99, pp. 313–26.
58. *Parl. History*, vol. 33, cols 29–31, 6 March 1797; *CJ*, vol. 52, pp. 370–1, 528, 574, 585, 592, 625, 647, 652, 660, 672, 685, entries for 6 March, 2, 15, 17, 19, 31 May, 9, 13, 16, 22, 29 June 1797; Lambert edition, vol. 103, pp. 267–74, 277–85, 287–94; Girdler, pp. 160–3, 326.
59. Burke wrote Arthur Young in May 1797:

> I am extreamly sorry that any one in the House of Commons should be found so ignorant and unadvised, as to wish to revive the senseless, barbarous and, in fact, wicked regulations made against the free trade in matter of provision, which the good sense of late Parliaments had removed. I am the more concerned at the measure as I was myself the person who moved the repeal of the absurd code of Statutes, against the most useful of all trades, under the invidious Names of forstalling regrating: But however I console myself on this point by considering that it is not the only breach by which barbarism is entering upon us. It is indeed but a poor consolation and one taken meerly from the balance of misfortunes.

> *The Correspondence of Edmund Burke*, vol. 9, ed. R.B. McDowell and John A. Woods (Cambridge: Cambridge University Press 1970), pp. 361–2.
60. See Hay, 'The state and the market'.
61. It was also the opinion of Jacobins: see below.

62. The 1793 resolution followed the assizes, which were held before Kenyon and Grose, the two judges most active in Waddington's case. SRO, Q/SB Michaelmas 1793/175 (resolution, struck through); *Aris's Birmingham Gazette* 6 July 1795; *Oxford Council Acts 1752–1801*, ed. M. G. Hobson (Oxford: M. G. Hobson, 1962), p. 233, 8 July 1795. (This was two weeks before Kenyon sat there at the summer assizes noted below.)
63. Girdler, *Observations*, pp. 209–15, 288, 295–7.
64. For Kenyon's reasons, see below.
65. *Berrow's Worcester Journal*, 13 Aug. 1795. Quoted Girdler, *Observations*, p. 298, who misdates it 1796. The offence of purchasing growing grain was considered a species of forestalling, according to a statement of Coke's quoted in most justices' manuals. On the timing of Kenyon's decision to emphasise the common law, see below.
66. 4 Aug., reported in *Shrewsbury Chronicle*, 7 Aug. 1795.
67. When Thomas Smallwood wrote 12 Sept. 1795 to report a farmer, Robert Glover, for buying 300 strike of barley, John Sparrow, JP, alluded to the repeal of the statutes against forestalling, and suggested that only if Glover sold again in a distant market would it be an offence: he asked the clerk to give Smallwood a fuller answer: SRO, Q/SB Michaelmas 1795 pt 1.
68. SRO, Q/SB Michaelmas 1795 [recommendation that John Salt be appointed clerk of Wolverhampton market]. Reeves, Povey, Welch, Ward were all fined 1s. and costs at Staffs. sessions on promising not to offend again; Welch (who had regrated lamb) was also imprisoned for 4 days: *Aris's Birmingham Gazette* 12 Oct. 1795.
69. *Aris's Birmingham Gazette* 7, 14, 28 Sept., 12 Oct. 1795.
70. For example, the City of Winchester offered 20 guineas reward for information leading to convictions; *Hampshire Chronicle*, 23 April 1796. I have not made a systematic search of the local press. On 1797 see above.
71. *Northampton Mercury*, 23 April 1796; *Berrow's Worcester Journal*, 28 April 1796; *Shrewsbury Chronicle*, 29 April 1796. Girdler, *Observations*, p. 215, later noted that a similar prosecution in Oxfordshire resulted in only a 5s. fine.
72. Nugent Buckingham to Lord Kenyon, 8 July 1800, Kenyon MSS, Box 23; George T. Kenyon, *The Life of Lloyd, First Lord Kenyon* (London, 1873), pp. 374–6; Girdler, *Observations*, pp. 214, 296. Buckingham was probably referring to William Wyndham Grenville, Baron Grenville, his younger brother, who was a convinced follower of Adam Smith: see above.
73. The following account is based on a much fuller examination of the cases in Hay, 'The state and the market', where complete references are supplied.
74. Lincoln's Inn Library, Dampier MSS, L.P.B. 339a. This bundle of papers once belonged to Sir Soulden Lawrence, a puisne judge of King's Bench when Waddington and Rusby were tried; he took some of the depositions in the case. But the memoranda are apparently Kenyon's notes: the passages cited below are all in Kenyon's hand. I wish to thank the Honourable Treasurer and Benchers of Lincoln's Inn for permission to use and quote from these papers.
75. Burke quoted above; Kenyon from *Proceedings*, p. 5, after arguments on the motion for arrest of judgment in the Worcester prosecution of Waddington.
76. Kenyon, *Life of Lloyd, Lord Kenyon*, p. 372.
77. Hay, 'The state and the market.'
78. Henry Richard, Lord Holland, *Memoirs of the Whig Party During My Time*, i (London, 1852), pp. 167–9.

79. Of which his father, Dr Edmund Law, Master of Peterhouse at mid-century, had not heard: 'Last week I called a meeting of the heads, who heartily concurred in endeavouring to break a combination of ingrossers and forestallers that had almost ruined our market', 20 Jan. 1756, BL, Add Mss 32862 f.163. For Oxford University's active market regulation see Thwaites in Randall and Charlesworth (eds), *Markets, Market Culture and Popular Protest*.
80. As I show elsewhere.
81. Gilbert Blane, *Inquiry into the causes and remedies of the late and present scarcity* (1800).
82. Hay, *Crown Side Cases in the Court of King's Bench* (forthcoming, Staffs. Hist. Soc.).

5
Food Riots Revisited: Popular Protest and Moral Economy in Nineteenth-Century India[1]

David Arnold

Since it first appeared in 1971, E. P. Thompson's 'moral economy' article has been a seminal influence on the writing of modern Indian history. In the early 1970s India's historiography was greatly in need of fresh ideas and inspiration, and the concept of a moral economy, in company with the broad and imaginative sweep of English and European social history as practised by Hobsbawm, Hill, Rudé and others, drew a warm response from a new generation of South Asia scholars. There was at the time much dissatisfaction with the limitations of the old colonial historiography and with its nationalist rivals. There was impatience with the stifling economism ('the crass economic reductionism', to steal a phrase of vintage Thompson) of many Marxist as well as non-Marxist historians, whose work left little room for 'complexities of motive, behaviour, and function'.[2] At a time when the insurrectionary Naxalite movement was grabbing the headlines and state repression was reaching a peak in the mid-1970s with Mrs Gandhi's 'Emergency', it was not surprising that historians of India should seek a history more in keeping with current needs and the people's past. To boldly talk of 'popular politics', to see 'crowds' where previously only 'mobs' had rampaged, to posit logic and order in place of 'blind eruptions' and 'involuntary spasms', to make the poor the subject of history and allow them a voice: this was a much-needed breath of historiographical fresh air. Thompson may have written with eighteenth-century England in mind, but his work had a welcome resonance for the history of modern India. His attacks on 'vulgar economic determinism' and the arbitrary division between economic 'base' and cultural 'superstructure', his emphasis upon class as experience and the value of examining riots and other 'untypical' episodes for the light they might throw upon 'the norms of tranquil years', his insistence that historians seek out new sources for the study of the poor:[3] these views and injunctions did not go unheeded in India. Indeed, they appear in retrospect almost to have constituted a manifesto for the kinds of social history that have emerged and flourished in India since the mid-1970s.

At the time India was often compared unfavourably with China. It was well-known that China had a long history of peasant rebellion, culminating in the Communist take-over of 1949. India's peasants, by contrast, were seen to be passive and inert, divided by caste and religion, disposed to fatalism, and incapable of more than an occasional, fleeting (and invariably futile) uprising.[4] One of the first tasks of the new historiography was to try to recover the history of popular revolt in India and rescue it from archival obscurity and scholarly neglect, to piece together its aims, its actors, its antinomies. This project has had a considerable impact on how Indian history is viewed and there now exists an extensive literature documenting the 'history from below'. But it has also brought a reaction: a surfeit of riots and revolts has bred a healthy hunger for the history of more 'normal' times. More problematically, it has also fed doubts about the historian's ability to understand and represent the mentality of the subaltern subject.[5] But it is surely worth – two decades on – going back to the moral economy argument as advanced by Thompson in 1971 to ask whether it still has insights to offer into the history of popular protest in modern India.

The Market Nexus

Food riots deservedly formed a central theme in Thompson's *Past and Present* article, and though subsequent discussion of the moral economy has ranged widely over rural, urban and even industrial society, it is worth returning to a consideration of the significance of this most emblematic form of protest and collective action.[6] As short-lived, localised events, food riots seem ideally suited for close scrutiny. They, or more precisely the marketplaces in which they occurred, constituted well–defined arenas within which many of the fundamental social, economic and political issues of the day were fought out, as if in gladiatorial combat. They represented moments of crisis (alike in terms of subsistence and order) and forced to the fore attitudes and values that in more 'normal' times remained concealed. Food riots were sufficiently dramatic to command the attention of literate observers, sufficiently menacing or destructive to involve the magistracy, the police and the courts, and so, conveniently for us, they have left extensive

historical traces. Partly for these reasons, and partly too because food riots were a widely distributed as well as distinctive form of popular action, they invite comparison between one society and another. The food riot is hardly likely to have been disseminated from France and England to India, Iran or China (unlike trade unionism at a later date) but, it is pertinent to ask, was the nature and function of the food riot essentially the same in the many different countries in which it occurred? Is there a shared sense of the moral economy of the poor, or did the form and content of the food riot differ significantly from place to place? Are certain forms of social action common to all societies at a comparable stage in their economic and social evolution, or do different societies remain for ever attached to their separate identities?

Before we turn to the nature of food riots in India, they need to be placed in a wider context. Recent scholarship on South Asia has been highly critical of the view once shared by writers as diverse as Moreland and Marx that the economy of rural India before the advent of British rule was a crudely pre-capitalist one, based on 'self-sufficient' villages and the exchange of goods and services through the local *jajmani* system. The strength of indigenous, pre-colonial capitalism is now seen in, among other things, the nature of agrarian property rights, the scale and sophistication of commercial activity, and Indian participation in the trading world of the Indian Ocean.[7] Some areas (such as lower Bengal and the Kaveri delta in the south-east) had been highly commercialised for centuries; some of the rice they produced entered wider networks of continental and oceanic trade.[8] In general, though, the costly and laborious nature of overland transportation, the relatively low value of cereal grains (compared with such items of trade as cotton textiles, indigo and opium), and the tendency for each locality to rely on its own food staples severely restricted grain movements. In many inland areas, except perhaps in times of exceptional dearth and profitability, the grain trade tended to be 'fitful and fragmented'.[9] The slow movement of grain by cart and pack bullock meant that, when the rains failed, many people went hungry or were forced to rely upon private stores accumulated in years of relative plenty.

British rule brought significant changes to the movement and marketing of grain. In south India there was a long period of depressed grain prices between the 1820s and 1850s, caused, it has been argued, by increased production coupled with a heavy state revenue demand which forced large quantities of grain onto the market. The result was a severe glut and low prices in the bazaars.[10] Only after about 1850 did this situation change, with improved transport and communications (railway construction dates from the 1850s and more especially the 1870s) and with the growth of urban centres and export markets. Cultivators who formerly produced largely for their own needs or for local markets were increasingly drawn into cash-crop production.[11] A series of droughts and crop failures in India between the 1860s and 1900s helped stimulate large-scale grain movements, but this traffic was at first slow to develop despite the apparent incentive of high prices and the state's policy of *laissez-faire*.[12]

Given the immense size of India, the enormous variations of climate, soil and vegetation, and even the great variety of regional food crops and dietary preferences, an integrated grain market was difficult to achieve. None the less, regional price levels were becoming more closely linked as the century drew to a close and the Famine Commission of 1898 noted a 'very marked tendency to equalization of prices throughout India ... due to the extension of railways and to the opening up of large tracts of country formerly provided with inadequate means of communication'.[13] The food riots of the nineteenth century thus need to be understood against the background of an increasingly, but still imperfectly, integrated grain market, and an expanding trade, especially by rail. A sudden surge in local prices and the export of grain from a district already fearful for its livelihood helped precipitate many an Indian food riot.

It is clear that food riots occurred in nineteenth-century India in considerable numbers. They were probably present in earlier times though we have, as yet, little detailed evidence for them, and they continued sporadically up to the 1940s and beyond. But, for reasons this chapter will try to explain, they seem to have been especially widespread in a century of famine and free trade. It would seem that no province of India was entirely unaffected by food riots, but equally (for reasons that require investigation) they were more common in certain regions and at certain times than others. In my own research I have come across numerous references to food riots in south India, particularly in 1823 (Madras city), 1833 (Madras and North Arcot), 1855 (Bellary and Madurai), 1858 (Thanjavur), 1866 (in Madras city, adjoining villages and Krishna district), 1876 (in several districts including Tiruchirapalli, South Arcot, Kurnool and Bellary), 1889 (Thanjavur), 1891 (Kurnool), in 1897 (Godavari), and in 1918, by way of a grand finale, in almost every district in the Madras Presidency.[14] There were also major outbreaks of food riots elsewhere – in the North-Western Provinces in 1837–38 and in Orissa in 1865–66 – but this chapter will concentrate mainly upon the Madras Presidency in south India, the area for which I have most information.

Food Riots in South India

The story of India's food riots begins with urban markets. As elsewhere the market in India was, as Thompson reminds us,[15] a social nexus, not just an economic arena. It was a favourable site for the collective articulation of subsistence demands by the poor, perhaps all the more so in a largely illiterate society, where rumour, verbal communication and the visible signs of anger and distress took the place elsewhere occupied by handbills and newspapers. In colonial society the volatility of the market (both the physical arena and the broader processes of commercial transaction) had always to be watched. Thus, among the duties assigned to the newly-formed police Special Branch in 1888 was that of observing and reporting on any 'indication of distress or anticipation of famine, scarcity of food, or water for man or beast'.[16] In general, though, insurrection was not seen to be a threat likely to arise from food riots in India, unlike their counterparts in eighteenth-century England and France. India's food riots were more generally seen as a temporary disturbance rather than a serious challenge to colonial control. It was not untypical for the Commissioner of Police in Madras to remark in the wake of food riots in the city in September 1866 that 'Grain disturbances are of a peculiar and evanescent character, and the riots of the 7th [September] were not of a nature to rouse very grave apprehensions'.[17] The only major exception to this view was the widespread rioting and looting of 1918, which came at a time of nationalist unrest, economic discontent and growing labour militancy. Far from seeking to overthrow authority, one of the objectives of popular protest in towns and cities like Madras was to invite official intervention and support against the grain traders. In the countryside and in small town bazaars, by contrast, there were seldom any officials to appeal to. Perhaps it was as much because of its conspicuous officialdom as its large grain bazaars and the size of its food-buying classes that Madras was the site of several major grain riots in 1823, 1833, 1866 and 1918.

In India it is more accurate to speak of grain than of food riots, for it was the high prices and scarcity of certain grain staples – rice (or paddy), wheat and various millets like *ragi* and *cholam* – that fuelled tension in the marketplace. Occasionally, cloth and other goods were also looted.[18] Flour (*atta*) and the varieties of Indian bread (*roti*) did not figure in the Indian riots, as these were largely domestic commodities: there were no millers or bakers to attack.

The sequence of urban unrest was usually as follows. Because agriculture in most parts of India was so heavily dependent upon adequate and timely rainfall during the monsoons, their failure quickly led to anxiety over the season's grain harvest and more immediately the price of grain in the bazaars. In south India, the failure of the south-west monsoon in July was likely to lead to unrest in the interior districts of the Madras Presidency in August and September. But more commonly it was the failure of the north-east monsoon in the eastern coastal districts in October which brought high prices and food riots in its wake. Thus almost all the food riots in the Madras Presidency occurred between early August and late December. The failure of the monsoon led to a rapidly growing sense of alarm among the rural population, whose subsistence was obviously at stake, but it also produced almost immediate despair in the urban bazaars. Traders began to raise their prices in the hope of profiting from an anticipated scarcity,or denied credit to poor customers. Prices doubled or trebled in a matter of weeks, and the price of millet, normally the cheap food grain of the poor, began to rise to the level of rice, thus putting further pressure on low-income groups. In Bellary district in the interior of Madras, the price of *cholam* rose from 1.82 rupees per maund (a maund is roughly 82 lb) in July 1876 to 1.91 in August, 2.45 in September, 3.92 in October and 5.63 in November: a threefold rise in five months. In coastal Nellore between July 1876 and January 1877 the price of rice rose from Rs2.67 per maund to 5.71 (a twofold increase) while that of *cholam*, the staple of the rural and urban poor, leapt from Rs1.59 per maund in July to Rs5 the following January, a threefold increase.[19] Even district averages give a poor indication of how steeply grain prices could rise in such uncertain times. Moreover, from fear of being looted or in the hope of realising higher profits later, traders closed up their shops and so left consumers with no means of buying the grain they needed. Those most rapidly affected were town labourers and artisans with small, fixed incomes, whose purchasing power rapidly shrank as prices rose, or who found themselves unable to buy grain at all. These included boatmen, fishermen, weavers, porters (or 'coolies'), day labourers, *syces* (grooms) and domestic servants.

These developments can best be illustrated by a brief account of events in 1866 in Madras, often still referred to as a 'town' but in actuality already a city of half-a-million people. The disturbances began on the evening of Thursday 6 September (in Madras much of the purchasing of food took place in the cool of the evening), following two days in which grain prices had risen sharply. Large crowds gathered listlessly at rice stalls in several parts of the city, including Black Town (where the largest grain depots and markets were located), Triplicane and Chintadripet. Eventually, after some hours, the traders closed their shops for fear of being looted. The 'invariable result', according to the Police Commissioner, Major C. S. Hearn, was that 'the mass of daily buyers, disappointed of their food, collect[ed] into angry crowds'. They included women and children, but also, according to the police, 'paupers and evil disposed persons'. When eventually a few traders were persuaded to open their shops, there was rush and, in the ensuing 'confusion and panic', 'some of the dregs of the mob' were able to 'help themselves'.[20] Little violence was reported, but that evening ten of the seventy rice shops in Rasapah Chetty Street in Black Town and twelve of the twenty-five in Royapetta bazaar were looted. Those at Triplicane were threatened by a crowd of about a hundred boatmen (from the nearby beaches) on the morning of 7 September, and there was further looting that day in Choolai bazaar to the north-west. The disturbances spread not only from one grain market to another within the city, but also between 7 and 18 September affected outlying towns and villages in Chingleput, North Arcot and Nellore, and as far away as Krishna district, 200 miles to the north.[21] In Madras itself 160 shops and 21 houses were looted. Despite the large numbers of people said to have been involved, few arrests followed, partly because the police were overwhelmed by the size of the crowds and also, it was suspected, because many of them sympathised with the rioters. Furthermore, 'Grain and articles of food were not of course subsequently identifiable, and the multiplicity of cases rendered it difficult to prosecute close inquiries.' Of the 359 sentenced for their part in the city riots, 211 were labourers, 37 coachmen and grooms, 25 domestic servants, and 35 shopkeepers and traders. In terms of caste or community, 134 were identified as Pariahs and 39 as Vanniyars (a labouring caste), along with 34 Muslims, and 51 others from low castes.[22]

The impact of sudden price rises in the bazaars can also be illustrated by events in the Madras Presidency in 1876. In May of that year a rupee bought 28 seers (or about 14 lb) of *ragi* or *cholam* in Kurnool district; by September it would buy only 20 seers and by the end of October barely 10. Rice, too, doubled in price over the same period, from 15 seers per rupee to 7. In neighbouring Cuddapah the quantity of *ragi* exchanged for a rupee dropped from 13.5 seers on 1 October to 8 a fortnight later, and traders were said to be making six times their usual profit on a sack of grain.[23] The result was a series of urban and small-town disturbances, or, where the intervention of the authorities was more effective than in Madras city in 1866, threatened disturbances. These occurred in many parts of the Madras Presidency between September 1876 and January 1877, particularly in the interior districts where the drought was most acute. But they also affected towns like Cuddalore in South Arcot, where there was a grain riot on Christmas Day 1876, triggered by a steep rise in grain rates in sympathy with price movements elsewhere rather than due to local shortages.[24] At least twenty such incidents were reported in the press, and it is likely that there were actually many more. In 1876–77, as to a lesser extent in 1866 and some earlier episodes, urban food riots spilled over into neighbouring bazaars or merged into rural looting. Grain carts and barges moving grain by river and canal were major targets for attack. By the 1870s railway yards, where grain was temporarily stored before being moved elsewhere, were also threatened or besieged (as at Coimbatore in October 1876).[25] Partly because of the pre-emptive deployment of police and troops, many potential incidents failed to develop beyond the stage of rumour, unrest and threatening crowds, but often it needed only a minor incident to spark a riot. In Madras city looting began on 16 October 1876 when a few young men ran through the bazaars shouting 'loot, loot'.[26]

In their outward form at least, many of these nineteenth-century food riots in India appear similar to those found in eighteenth-century England. But Thompson has insisted that the most important feature of such episodes was not the sacking of granaries and markets but the fact of 'setting the price'.[27] In India, however, a dividing line between food riots and looting is not easy to discern. There are certainly some indications of an explicit 'moral economy' element in the crowd's actions, but evidence of 'price-fixing by riot' is relatively rare. Perhaps this reflects the inadequacy of the Indian source materials or a different kind of crowd culture and a want of the self-discipline that Thompson and others have detected elsewhere. It was more common for the poor to vent their anger at the prices demanded by traders (or their refusal to sell) by looting grain and other commodities, sometimes discarding their plunder shortly afterwards. The evidence for a 'moral economy' is to be found rather more in nature of the appeals for intervention which crowds addressed to any government servants they could persuade to listen to their demands.

In the towns of coastal Orissa, between the Madras Presidency and Bengal, traders usually supplied grain on credit to their customers, but in October 1865, with the failure of the year's rains, they refused to make any further loans and shut up their shops. The immediate response of labourers and artisans was to appeal to government officials, begging them to intervene to fix prices at affordable or customary levels. At Cuttack in October 1865, Sir Cecil Beadon, the Lieutenant-Governor of Bengal, was besieged by crowds calling on him to 'cheapen rice' and 'fix a rate'.[28] He refused, regarding price-fixing as akin to robbery, but in this and many similar instances this was evidently one of the principal objectives of crowd action, and it was often only when officials declined to enforce price controls that looting followed. In the town of Vellore in North Arcot district in 1833 four sepoys of the 13th Regiment of Native Infantry were so enraged to find traders selling rice at 4.5 seers to the rupee that they dragged several of them to the office of the local *kotwal* (Indian police chief) and demanded that he tell them to sell at the former rate of 5 seers to the rupee. When the *kotwal* explained that he was not permitted to fix prices, the sepoys were furious, a crowd gathered and looting began.[29]

Managing Markets

As these examples suggest, market relations in nineteenth-century India were complicated by an official policy of non-intervention in the grain trade. In the early 1800s the colonial administration abandoned its previous policy of involvement in the pricing, marketing and movement of grain during famines and acute shortages. Obedient to the dictates of Adam Smith and classical political economy (which had a profound effect on policy-making and administrative practice in nineteenth-century India), it switched to a position of strict non-intervention in the grain trade even in times of high prices and dearth. The government argued, in the spirit of *The Wealth of Nations* (and often indeed its very letter), that any inference in the movement and sale of grain would adversely affect private initiative and so intensify food shortages. Thus the Madras Board of Revenue declared in November 1806:

> Whenever the officers of Government, influenced by a humane desire of obviating the inconveniences of scarcity, imprudently direct that private grain be sold in the public market at a fixed price, or injudiciously send grain themselves into the market for that purpose, they either prevent dealers from bringing their grain thither, which sometimes increases the dangers of a famine, or they encourage the people to consume it so fast, as must necessarily, in the end produce such a calamity. The unrestrained freedom of the grain market, is at the same time the best preventive of famines and the best palliative of dearth.[30]

Dearth and threatened disturbances in Nellore district in 1811 encouraged the provincial Board of Revenue to make a similar declaration, observing that although 'the fears of famine, or the impatience of the people under a temporary inconvenience frequently urge them to commit outrages', officials should not succumb to popular pressure or in any way meddle with market prices. The temporary rise in prices, 'although productive of some trifling temporary inconvenience,' the Board noted, 'is as salutary and as necessary for the public safety as putting the crew of a ship on short allowance when a scarcity of water or provisions may be expected'.[31]

There were inconsistencies in the policy of the government and the conduct of its local officers, however. Adam Smith was heartily endorsed but he was not all-powerful. In 1833, for instance, faced with a serious famine in the northern districts of the Madras Presidency, the provincial government removed all import duties on grain and urged district collectors to *persuade* grain merchants to reduce their prices 'whenever they had reason to believe that the merchants were withholding grain from the market, in hopes of exorbitant profits'. The collectors were not, however, to use any coercion, merely to 'endeavour to effect the objects of Government by personal influence'.[32] In practice, many local magistrates and subordinate officials were swayed by humanitarian concern for the poor (or by their own antipathy to 'grasping' traders) to respond to the crowd's anguished and insistent demands.

One of the precipitating factors in a grain riot in Madras in December 1823 was the apparent determination of the city's European police establishment (in ignorance or defiance of official policy) to impose fixed prices on grain traders. On the evening of 22 December a crowd, consisting largely of 'boat people' and 'pariahs', surrounded a police officer as he was passing a *godown* (warehouse), asking that rice be sold to them at a fixed rate. Perhaps simply in order to free himself from the attentions of the crowd, he promised that this would be done the following day at 8 o'clock, and that if it was not they were entitled to do whatever they liked. As soon as they heard this the crowd broke down the doors of Condiah Chetti's *godown* on the beach and had virtually cleaned it out by the time a detachment of sepoys arrived. The next day, the officer, Gasgoine, was unrepentant and told Condiah Chetti it was his fault for not doing what he was told by selling grain at approved prices. The Chetti claimed to have lost Rs25 000 worth of grain in this and similar episodes, and petitioned the government to compensate him for his losses.[33]

Even without apparent official sanction, the urban and rural poor were often firm in their conviction that grain traders were exploiting them mercilessly in times of hardship and deserved to be punished or forced to sell at acceptable rates. One official reported from Bellary in September 1876 that:

The feeling against merchants is very bitter in some parts. It is a common thing to be told by the poor that the sowcars [traders] are cheating them, by which they mean that they pretend to have no grain and are reluctant to sell even when they cannot deny that they have it. The poor ryots [peasants] consider that, as they have helped to enrich the sowcar, the latter should not fail them in their time of need, and that Government should step in and prohibit sowcars from selling at more than what they call a fair rate of profit. The opinion that sowcars should not make the ryots' distress their own opportunity is, I believe, the opinion of all native officials as well.[34]

Other sources confirmed that the poor saw 'the grain-dealers, and their great accumulation of corn, as the real authors of the distresses that oppress them',[35] and also that rumours of government approval for the looting of recalcitrant traders were 'the more readily believed because they fall in with the general idea of what is proper and probable'.[36] Thus the crowd's 'legitimizing notion' sprang both from its own sense of outrage at the traders' selfish behaviour and the apparent approval bestowed by officials. Possibly it came, too, from the fact that pre-British regimes – such as the Mughals and Marathas – had intervened in times of dearth to prohibit the export of grain and regulate prices; but how effectively they did so, even in urban areas, is open to question.[37] Moreover, by the 1860s and 1870s the days of independent prices were long gone as far as south India was concerned, and I have not come across any appeals by the public to the policies of former rulers, only to customary prices and the needs and morality of the current market situation.

Given a policy of official non-intervention, did grain riots work as a form of popular protest? Thompson has argued that in eighteenth-century England they were both 'rational and effective',[38] and in India, too, they had some measure of success. Quite apart from such grain as was actually carried off by the rioters and might be consumed by them, the effect of such demonstrations was often to force traders to lower their prices or to implicate policemen and subordinate officials in their demands. 'The main cause of reduced rates', commented the Commissioner of Police for Madras in the wake of the riot of September 1866, 'was undoubtedly fear of the mob'.[39] But riots also had a contrary effect on the markets and the supply of grain. They could convince traders that it was unsafe and unprofitable to continue trading openly and that they would do better to keep their remaining stocks concealed in locked *godowns*, or that it would be foolish to move grain through countryside lest it be plundered *en route*. Looting, officialdom repeatedly warned, led to a contraction of supply and a sharpening of the crisis, and hence one of the main reasons for intervention by the police and military lay not so much in the often idle hope of catching looters red-handed as in restoring confidence to panicky traders.[40]

However, there was a further aspect to state policy. One of the principal outcomes of the Indian Famine Commission of 1878–80 was the creation of a Famine Code. This represented 'the first serious attempt [in India] to systematize the prediction of famine, and to set down steps to ameliorate its impact before its onset'.[41] But the Famine Code was a half-way house: the Government of India was not prepared to institute a system of permanent poor relief on the lines of the New Poor Law in England, but neither was it willing to depart from the general principle of non-intervention in the grain trade. And yet, at the same time, it felt morally and politically obliged to accept responsibility for saving its subjects from starvation in times of famine. The Famine Code has been seen by some commentators as being relatively successful in meeting its limited objective: saving lives while prudently holding down state expenditure.[42] It would be unrealistic to argue that food riots and other forms of popular action in themselves forced the government to introduce the codes in the first place: the sheer scale of famine mortality and the disruption of agriculture and state revenue were surely more influential. But it could be said that by setting in place a system whereby the state could respond promptly to the first indicators of incipient distress – such as rising grain prices and soaring crime levels[43] – and by providing relief works for the employment and feeding of the destitute poor, the Famine Code removed some of the need for food riots and so provided one reason for their eventual decline. It should, however, be noted that food riots lived on in India for a generation or two after the Famine Code was introduced. One reason for this was that the introduction of relief measures was held up by administrative hesitancy and delay; another that, as in south India in 1918, the authorities felt that, despite high prices, genuine famine conditions did not exist and so the Famine Code could not be implemented. A further possibility is that feelings of antagonism towards merchants and traders in times of high prices and shortages were so intense that food riots would have happened regardless of whether the government chose to intervene or not.

The Unfolding Crisis

Although the form and function of India's food riots were recognisably similar to those Thompson describes for eighteenth-century England, was their context significantly different? As Michael Adas has remarked in cautioning against James C. Scott's application of the moral economy concept to rural south-east Asia, 'a pattern identified in one society and historical period may not be transferable, at least without major modifications, to others that are fundamentally different'.[44]

In India food riots and the expression of moral economy ideas most commonly belonged within an evolving famine situation. The sequence did not run from food riot to insurrection, as it threatened to do in England and France in the eighteenth and early nineteenth centuries, but from food riot to famine. The 'calamity' of riot, as Thompson has described it, real though it was in the short term, was rapidly engulfed by the far greater catastrophe of mass starvation.[45] This was not invariably so. The food riots of 1918 in south India occurred without accompanying famine, though the prospect of one must have seemed real enough to many of the rural and urban poor at the time. Wartime shortages and transport difficulties, rapid inflation, and the profiteering of grain traders and speculators produced a powerful mood of public anger.[46] But the food riots of 1823, 1833, 1866 and 1876 in the Madras Presidency, like those in Orissa in 1865, fit clearly into an unfolding sequence of dearth and famine and within the harsh chronology determined by the monsoon rains. As already indicated, food riots in the Madras Presidency almost invariably occurred between August and late December, the period of the expected arrival and evident failure of the two monsoons. Once famine had become an inescapable reality, food riots petered out. Thus they were not a self-contained phenomenon, but rather marked a critical threshold, the moment when anxiety about the monsoon and the coming agricultural season erupted into anger and alarm at the imminent prospect of hunger.

As food riots died away, other forms of action took over in which the element of moral economy and protest was not always so evident. This was particularly so in the countryside. Among the most conspicuous result was an outbreak of 'famine crime'. To an extent unparalleled in more recent episodes of dearth and hunger in South Asia (perhaps because state intervention has become more predictable or the forces of 'law and order' more effective), the onset of famine was characterised by massive crime waves.[47] This commonly took the form of thefts of grain by hungry labourers and peasants. Here the immediate search for food to eat was evident, but a sense of anger at those who hoarded grain and denied the hungry still sometimes surfaced. In Orissa an increase in the number of thefts was observed as early as April 1865 along with the first signs of distress, but the bulk of reported crimes occurred later in the year after the failure of the monsoon. This included arson, said to originate in 'a feeling of discontent at, and disposition to resent, the fact that those who held stores of grain withheld it from sale and raised their prices'.[48] It was followed by a huge increase in the incidence of dacoity (technically robbery by five or more people), sometimes designated the 'special famine crime'.[49] In Orissa these raids were accompanied with relatively little violence. Ten to twenty men (dacoity, unlike food rioting, was almost entirely confined to men) surrounded the house of a trader or wealthy landlord, sometimes bound and assaulted the inmates, then carried off as much grain as they could. In one case of night-time raid in Balasore district, the attackers found a quantity of cooked rice in a house and sat down to eat it before collecting and making off with the rest of their plunder.[50] 'Hunger and want', it was officially acknowledged, 'appear to have been the motives to crime'.[51] Many of those known to be involved were labourers with little or no land of their own and normally dependent upon grain payments which had abruptly stopped with the failure of the monsoon. In Balasore more dacoities were reported for the first four months of 1866 than in the whole of the previous three years.[52]

Similarly in the first seven months of 1876, before famine struck, there were few dacoities in the Madras Presidency. In the interior district of Kurnool nine were reported up to the end of August but, with the onset of famine, 114 more occurred in the last four months of the year. In Madurai, where the famine arrived later, there were seven dacoities up to the end of October 1876; but then, as drought and famine intensified, 38 more in November and December. In 1877 dacoity was rife in the first six months of the year, with between 100 and 150 cases a month reported in the twelve main famine districts. In July and August, as the famine entered the second cycle of failed monsoons, even that rate doubled, and not until the arrival of rains in September and October did dacoity drop to, and by December fall below, the levels at which the year had opened. In 1875, 229 dacoities had been reported in the Madras Presidency: in 1877, with famine at its peak of intensity, there were 1695. Again, as in Orissa in 1866, these dacoities were often barely distinguishable from looting in the bazaars, with the perpetrators said to be 'hungry people not ordinarily criminal'. Unable to beg, buy or borrow grain, the poor returned, under cover of darkness, to loot the houses and granaries of wealthy peasants and traders. But unlike daytime protesters, nocturnal looters seized whatever they could, their intentionality announced by the baskets they brought with them to carry off the grain. Other forms of crime also proliferated: pilfering and petty theft, cattle theft and housebreaking.[53]

It was not infrequently claimed by the colonial authorities that the poor committed many of these crimes purely in order to be arrested and sent to jail, knowing that there they were guaranteed food at a time of extreme scarcity outside.[54] The validity of this claim might be doubted, if only because it was in the nature of colonial rhetoric to exaggerate the attractions and minimise the horrors of Indian prison life. Such an argument also denied the real element of anger and protest evident in many acts of looting and rioting, and implied that Indians were simply too lazy to look for work or seek to obtain food by honest means. But the claim, so often made, cannot be entirely dismissed and may perhaps indicate the sheer desperation felt by many of the poor with the onset of acute dearth and hunger.

In order to survive the rural poor also turned to other survival strategies and expedients which took them further away from the marketplace and popular protest and drove them in on their own dwindling economic and social resources. The unfolding crisis was increasingly internalised: inside the home and within the disintegrating family. Fewer meals were eaten; the amount of food at each meal shrank. Aged, female and infirm members of the household probably bore more than their share of this domestic rationing. Famine foods – roots, leaves and berries – took the place of conventional foodstuffs. Men migrated in search of work; women and children drifted to relief works and towns in search of food.[55] The poor did not take the loss of their slender livelihoods passively, as Amartya Sen's 'entitlement thesis' too readily implies, nor was their response simply fatalistic.[56] One of the strengths of the moral economy argument as it was pioneered by E. P. Thompson (and subsequently taken up by James Scott in a very different context) was precisely that it identified and gave emphasis to the determination of the poor actively to defend their subsistence needs. It would be deeply regrettable if the historiography of hunger were now to substitute for ideas of popular protest and a moral economy a legalistic and economistic notion of 'entitlements', lose sight of popular consciousness, and abandon the social historian's hard-fought struggle to recover subaltern attitudes and experience. The savage paradox of famine was not that the poor were resigned to their fate or believed themselves rendered powerless by the loss of their 'entitlements', but that many of the expedients and survival strategies they actively employed in their struggle to survive led in the end only to death and despair. Villages were deserted; epidemics of cholera, dysentery and malaria weakened and killed the already stricken poor. Mortality passed the 100 000 mark and climbed into the millions: an estimated 1.3 million dead in Orissa in 1865–66, 3.5 million in the Madras Presidency in 1876–78, 1.3 million more in the North-Western Provinces in 1877–78.[57] Within months of the onset of famine there was little left in the countryside to riot about or to rob, and scarcely enough individual energy or collective will to do much about any lingering sense of injustice.

Paternalism and Dearth

What do food riots and other expressions of a moral economy in India tell us about the place of the poor within the wider social and political order? An important part of Thompson's argument (even more clearly as presented in *Customs in Common*) is the role of paternalism as a counterpoise to popular protest. Does this, too, have its parallels in colonial India?

This discussion has already touched upon the attitudes of the colonial officials and the ambivalence of their position: on the one hand formally committed to a policy of non-interference in the grain trade, on the other swayed by an antipathy to the traders and a concern for 'law and order', and moved by the distress of the poor who appealed for their intervention. But food riots brought to the fore not only contradictory relations between the Indian poor and British officialdom, but also a third element in the moral economy equation: the Indian elites.

In the countryside the first appeal of the needy was logically to wealthier peasant proprietors and, where they were present, to leading landholders or zamindars. These were the rural masters, the 'lords' for whom the lower castes laboured and who were expected, in return, to reward them with grain and occasional gifts. To describe this relationship as one of reciprocity is to carry its mutuality too far, but traditionally there were obligations as well as benefits on both sides. If the landholders could not in times of drought and dearth provide work, they might at least give out doles of grain, and in view of their need to maintain a force of field labourers for the future, it was in their material interest to respond positively to such demands.

Rural India had, too, a notion of the duty (*dharma*) of rulers or rural magnates to act benevolently towards their subjects and dependents in times of need. To be the *annadata*, the provider for the poor in times of need, enhanced the prestige and authority of the zamindar or raja; it was also enjoined by custom.[58] In practice, of course, the landlords' bounty had its limits, particularly when tested by the extremity of famine, rather than mere seasonal dearth, and especially when, under colonial rule, many of the old elites had been replaced by new zamindars, outsiders recognising no ties of custom and no paternalistic obligations. Moreover, the advent of a rail-borne grain trade in India from the mid-nineteenth century, and the expansion of the cashcrop economy, further eroded local interdependence and subsistence. Grain, increasingly commoditised, was becoming too valuable and too marketable an item for those who had it to store it as security against a poor harvest or to give it away to crowds of hungry labourers and tenants. Considerations of social prestige might make members of the rural elite feel that their present status and future authority required them to act in a lordly manner by distributing alms, but they could not always afford to do so. In mid-nineteenth-century Orissa, zamindars were said to keep large stores of grain, their 'respectability' being 'measured by the amount of *dhan* [paddy] in their *golahs* [granaries]'. With the onset of famine in 1866 some old zamindari families provided food for their dependents as far as they could but many of the newcomers from Bengal, who had recently bought estates in Orissa, felt no such obligation.[59]

Zamindars were not the only Indians for whom dearth was a testing time. While the hegemony of the old landed elites was in decline, other elements of Indian society were bidding for authority in the colonial marketplace. Destitution, coupled with the more urgent spur of food riots and looting, induced merchants and others – from maharajas and temple trustees to merchants and 'native gentlemen' of the urban middle classes – to offer free or below-market-price grain or cooked food to the poor. Typical instances of this are to be found in the famines of the late 1870s in Madras, Mysore and the North-Western Provinces.[60] Charity served many masters. For the merchant classes it met an obvious need in reducing hostile pressure from officials as well as the public. Better to forgo a little profit than to be pilloried and plundered. For princes like the Maharaja of Gwalior, who gave Rs1000 for the famine poor at Varanasi in 1877–78, beneficence was directed as much towards keeping in the good books of the British as assuaging hunger among the poor. For the urban middle classes, there was a social and cultural imperative to keep alive Indian traditions of charity and paternalism rather than allowing everything to be collapsed into the domain of colonial authority. Indian charity and philanthropy, though it might never be on a sufficiently large and secular scale to satisfy the British, was one way of keeping alive a vernacular idiom of power, a moral economy operative between Indian elites and subordinate classes, albeit within an encompassing colonial order.

The British were well aware of the financial and social importance of private and religious charity. The last thing they wanted to do was to usurp this and make the poor and needy dependent on the state instead. In 1807 Thomas Munro, Principal Collector of the Ceded Districts in Madras, in advocating non-intervention with respect to the grain trade, remarked that 'The natives of India are probably as charitable as those of any other country and the poor may be left to their care with more safety than to that of any public institution.'[61] Other administrators took a similar view and claimed that because of the extent of Indian philanthropy there was no need for a poor law in India.[62] And yet in many colonial accounts of the famines of the late nineteenth century, Indian charity and agency is cast in a more censorious light. Officials complained that zamindars and merchants were doing too little to help the needy and that charity had to be looked for elsewhere, including public subscriptions from Britain (as in the 1876–78 Madras famine). In a manner that flattered themselves and reaffirmed the contrast habitually drawn between Indian sloth and European energy, the British saw their rule, their charity, their agency, as alone guaranteeing the subsistence needs of the Indian people. They complained that Indians, when they were moved to act at all, provided the wrong kind of relief: for instance, by directing their charity to indolent (if indigent) Brahmins while low-caste or untouchable labourers went hungry, by giving grain or cooked food gratis instead of in exchange for work as the Victorian fear of dependent pauperism demanded, or by failing to keep proper order among the crowds at relief depots (feeding some twice and others not at all, allowing disease and disorder, running riot where the situation required discipline and sanitary order).[63]

It was not just, then, that Indian philanthropy and paternalism were collapsing and, with them, the vestiges of an old moral economy. They were being actively pushed aside by colonial disdain and yet still struggled to find a place for themselves. The marketplace and the economic and social relations that surrounded it thus remained an important, indeed exemplary, site for two contending and contrasting hegemonic orders.

Conclusion

Many similarities can be drawn between food riots in nineteenth-century India and those of eighteenth-century England, and enough evidence of a moral economy exists for that term to be of critical value in seeking to analyse and assess the motives, values and actions of the urban and rural poor, Indian elites and the colonial state. But what is particularly striking about India's food riots (and it suggests both parallels and contrasts with the European experience) is their transitional nature. In a great many cases they mark a painful moment of transition from a precarious subsistence to a certain famine: as such they were a widespread but essentially short-lived phenomenon, rapidly overtaken by the greater calamity of mass hunger and death.

Food riots were transitional in a second sense, too. Although we as yet know little about food riots in India before 1800, and although some undoubtedly occurred after 1918, they appear to have been particularly common during the nineteenth century. This was a period in which the Indian economy was undergoing significant changes, especially as the rail-borne grain trade expanded, and when state policy (contrary to popular expectations) favoured *laissez-faire*, the free movement of grain and unregulated commodity prices. By the late nineteenth and early twentieth centuries, although *laissez-faire* had not been abandoned (in some respects it lingered on until the Second World War), state policy had been forced to move towards greater responsibility for providing relief works and, in effect, to intervene at a relatively early stage in the famine sequence. In this way food riots lost some of their former utility. Moreover, after 1918 new forms of mass mobilisation, from trade unions to nationalist and sectarian organisations, were beginning to provide alternative channels for popular action even when the price or limited availability of food was an issue. Perhaps, too, food riots were transitional in the further sense that the grain trade by the early twentieth century was becoming more efficient in distributing foodstuffs within India; although when this system broke down, as it did in 1918 and more severely in 1943 in Bengal, the consequences could still be utterly catastrophic for the Indian people.

Notes

1. I am grateful to comments made on an earlier draft of this paper by participants at the 'Moral Economy' conference at Birmingham on 31 March–2 April 1992, and the stimulus of their discussion. Thanks, too, to Pramit Chaudhuri, David Hardiman and Sanjay Sharma for their valuable suggestions.
2. E. P. Thompson, 'The moral economy of the English crowd in the eighteenth century', *Past and Present*, 50 (1971), p. 78.
3. E. P. Thompson, 'Folklore, anthropology, and social history', *Indian Historical Review*, 3, 2 (1977), pp. 247–66.
4. Barrington Moore, *Social Origins of Dictatorship and Democracy* (Boston: Beacon Press 1966); but cf. Kathleen Gough, 'Indian peasant uprisings', *Bulletin of Concerned Asian Scholars*, 8, 3 (1976), pp. 2–18.
5. Especially Ranajit Guha (ed.), *Subaltern Studies*, 6 vols (Delhi: Oxford University Press 1982–9); Ananda A. Yang (ed.), *Crime and Criminality in British India* (Tucson, 1985), pp. 1–25; but cf. Douglas Haynes and Gyan Prakash (eds), *Contesting Power: Resistance and Everyday Social Relations in South Asia* (Delhi: Oxford University Press, 1991) for an attempt to move the debate away from riot and rebellion to resistance in everyday life, and for critical reviews of the 'Subaltern Studies' project, see Rosalind O'Hanlon, 'Recovering the subject: Subaltern Studies and histories of resistance in colonial South Asia', *Modern Asian Studies*, 22, 1 (1988), pp. 189–224; Jim Masselos, 'The dis/appearance of subalterns: A reading of a decade of Subaltern Studies', *South Asia*, 14, 1 (1992), pp. 105–25. Several leading Indian historians have been influenced by Thompson and his writings, in particular Ranajit Guha, Dipesh Chakrabarty, Sumit Sarkar and Ramachandra Guha.
6. Thompson was not, of course, the only historian to comment on food riots and their significance, but his moral economy argument gave them fresh meaning: cf. R. B. Rose, '18th-century price-riots, the French Revolution and the Jacobin Maximum', *International Review of Social History*, 4, 3 (1959), pp. 432–45; *idem*, 'Eighteenth-century price riots and public policy in England', ibid., 6, 2 (1961), pp. 277–92; Louise A. Tilly, 'The food riot as a form of political conflict in France', *Journal of Interdisciplinary History*, 2, 1 (1971), pp. 23–57.
7. Frank Perlin, 'Proto-industrialization and pre-colonial South Asia', *Past and Present*, 98 (1983), pp. 30–95; D. A. Washbrook, 'Progress and problems: South Asian economic and social history, c.1720–1860' *Modern Asian Studies*, 22, 1 (1988), pp. 57–96. On *jajmani*, see C. J. Fuller, 'Misconceiving the grain heap: A critique of the concept of the Indian jajmani system', in J. Parry and M. Bloch (eds), *Money and the Morality of Exchange* (Cambridge: Cambridge University Press, 1989), pp. 33–63; Simon Commander, 'The jajmani system in North India: An examination of its logic and status across two centuries', *Modern Asian Studies*, 17, 2 (1983), pp. 283–311.
8. K. N. Chaudhuri, *Trade and Civilisation in the Indian Ocean: An Economic History from the Rise of Islam to 1750* (Cambridge: Cambridge University Press, 1985), pp. 29, 193.
9. C. A. Bayly, *Rulers, Townsmen and Bazaars: North Indian Society in the Age of British Expansion, 1770–1870* (Cambridge: Cambridge University Press 1983), pp. 153–4. Cf. Tom G. Kessinger, 'North India', in Dharma Kumar and Meghnad Desai (eds), *The Cambridge Economic History of India. Volume 2,*

c. 1757–c. 1970 (Cambridge: Cambridge University Press 1983), pp. 248–62; S. Bhattacharya, 'Eastern India', ibid., pp. 280–1; Rajat Datta, 'Merchants and peasants: A study of the structure of local trade in grain in late eighteenth century Bengal', *Indian Economic and Social History Review*, 23, 4 (1986), pp. 379–402.

10. Arun Bandopadhyay, *The Agrarian Economy of Tamilnadu, 1820–1855* (Calcutta: K. P. Bagchi & Co. 1992), pp. 156–63; see also A. Sarada Raju, *Economic Conditions in the Madras Presidency, 1800–1850* (Madras, 1941), pp. 226–40.

11. Michelle B. McAlpin, 'Railroads, prices, and peasant rationality: India, 1860–1900', *Journal of Economic History*, 34, 3 (1974), pp. 662–84; idem 'Price movements and fluctuations in economic activity (1860–1947)', in Kumar and Desai (eds), *Cambridge Economic History*, 2, pp. 884–8; I. D. Derbyshire, 'Economic change and the railways in north India, 1860–1914', *Modern Asian Studies*, 21, 3 (1987), pp. 521–45.

12. For example, in Madras in 1866: R. A. Dalyell, *Memorandum on the Madras Famine of 1866* (Madras, 1867), pp. 107–8, 155–6.

13. *Report of the Indian Famine Commission, 1898* (Simla, 1898), p. 359; cf. Jean Drèze, 'Famine prevention in India', in Jean Drèze and Amartya Sen, *The Political Economy of Hunger: Volume 2, Famine Prevention* (Oxford: Clarendon Press, 1990), p. 22.

14. For 1918, see David Arnold, 'Looting, grain riots and government policy in south India, 1918', *Past and Present*, 84 (1979), pp. 115–45; N. Ram, 'An independent press and anti-hunger strategies: The Indian experience', in Jean Drèze and Amartya Sen (eds), *The Political Economy of Hunger: Volume I, Entitlement and Well-being* (Oxford: Clarendon Press, 1990), pp. 160–9.

15. Thompson, 'Folklore', p. 253; Thompson, 'Moral economy revisited', in E. P. Thompson, *Customs in Common* (London: Merlin, 1991), p. 259.

16. Government Order 210–211 A, Madras Judicial Proceedings (hereafter MJP), 26 January 1888, India Office Library London (IOL).

17. C. S. Hearn to Secretary, Government of Madras, 17 November 1866, MJP, 319, 30 January 1867, IOL.

18. Ibid.

19. *A Statistical Atlas of the Madras Presidency* (Madras, 1949), pp. 309, 439.

20. Hearn to Secretary, Madras, 10 September 1866, MJP, 193, 21 September 1866, IOL.

21. Inspector-General of Police, to Secretary, Government of Madras, 17 September 1866, MJP, 224, 24 September 1866; Joint Magistrate, North Arcot, to District Magistrate, Vellore, 18 and 20 September 1866, MJP, 3–5, 1 October 1866; Joint Magistrate, to District Magistrate, Krishna, 13 October 1866, MJP, 38, 3 November 1866, IOL.

22. Hearn to Secretary, Madras, 17 November 1866, MJP, 319, 30 January 1867, IOL. At Vellore in August 1833 fishermen and soldiers were said to be the instigators of the food riots, backed by a huge crowd (estimated at 7000 to 15 000) of all classes, mainly the poor and vagrants: Madras Board of Revenue Proceedings (hereafter MBRP), 7 November 1833, IOL. At the town of Madurai in November 1855 the looters were chiefly of the weaver caste: District Magistrate, Madurai, to Chief Secretary, Madras, 26 November 1855, MJP, 6, 11 December 1855, IOL.

23. C. Benson, *An Account of the Kurnool District* (Madras, 1889), p. 34; Government of Madras, *Review of the Madras Famine, 1876–1878* (Madras, 1879), pp. 10, 15.

24. W. Francis, *Madras District Gazetteers: South Arcot* (Madras, 1906), p. 182.

25. Madras Times, 30 October 1876, 24 November 1876, 30 November 1876. For similar episodes in north India in the 1830s, see Sanjay Sharma, 'The 1837–38 famine in U.P.: Some dimensions of popular action', forthcoming in *Indian Economic and Social History Review*.

26. David Arnold, 'Famine in peasant consciousness and peasant action: Madras 1876–8', in Guha, *Subaltern Studies*, vol. III (Delhi: Oxford University Press, 1984), pp. 86–9.

27. Thompson, 'Moral economy', p. 108.

28. *Report of the Commissioners appointed to enquire into the Famine in Bengal and Orissa in 1866* (Calcutta, 1867), p. 57; Sir Cecil Beadon, *Minute by Lieutenant-Governor of Bengal of Famine in Bengal and Orissa* (Calcutta, 1867), appendix, p. 3.

29. MBRP, 7 November 1833, IOL. It is important to the understanding of this episode that before the 1890s Indian soldiers were not fed in common messes but were given an allowance (*batta*) with which to buy their own food: in times of rapidly rising prices they were therefore as vulnerable as any other group on a low fixed wage.

30. MBRP, December 1806, cited in S. Ambirajan, *Classical Political Economy and British Policy in India* (Cambridge: Cambridge University Press, 1978), p. 66.

31. Secretary, Board of Revenue, Madras, to Collector, Nellore, 30 December 1811, Board's Collections, F/4/383, IOL: the directions were reissued in 1864: MBRP, 1349, 4 March 1864, Tamil Nadu Archives, Madras.

32. Dalyell, *Memorandum on the Madras Famine of 1866*, pp. 32–3.

33. Petition of Condiah Chetti to Governor of Madras, 27 December 1823, Madras Public Proceedings, 19 March 1824, IOL. There were similar complaints of police attempts at price-fixing or complicity in the food riots in Madras in 1866: Hearn to Secretary, Madras, 17 November 1866, MJP, 319, 30 January 1867, IOL.

34. C. J. Crosthwaite, Sub-Collector, to Collector, Bellary, 21 September 1876, MBRP, 2486, 2 October 1876, IOL.

35. *Madras Times*, 10 November 1876.

36. Memorandum of John Strachey, Collector, Moradabad, North-Western Provinces, February 1861, in Beadon, *Minute*, appendix, p. 32.

37. David C. Curley, 'Fair grain markets and Moghul famine policy in late eighteenth-century Bengal', *Calcutta Historical Journal*, 2, 1 (1977), pp. 1–26; David Hardiman, 'The peasant experience of usury: Western India in the nineteenth century', unpublished paper, Princeton, April 1991, p. 44; cf. Sharma, '1837–38 famine in U.P.'

38. Thompson, 'Moral economy revisited', p. 302.

39. Hearn to Secretary, 17 November 1866, MJP, 319, 30 January 1867, IOL; cf. Francis, *South Arcot*, p. 182.

40. Government of Madras, *Review of the Madras Famine, 1876–1878*, p. 15.

41. L. Brennan, 'The development of the Indian famine codes: Personalities, politics, and policies', in Bruce Curry and Graeme Hugo (eds), *Famine as a Geographical Phenomenon* (Dordrecht, 1984), p. 91. This is not to say that

relief measures had previously been absent, but that they were generally small scale and erratic. For relief in earlier Madras famines, see Dalyell, *Memorandum on the Madras Famine of 1866*, pp. 23, 34–9.

42. Drèze, 'Famine prevention', pp. 26, 32. For the debates behind government policy on famine relief, see Ambirajan, *Classical Political Economy*, pp. 80–100. For an example of the code in operation, see R. W. Carlyle, 'Famine administration in a Bengal district, 1896–7', *Economic Journal*, X (1900), pp. 421–30.

43. The Madras code indicated that a rise of 40 per cent above normal in the price of the common (or 'second sort') of rice and 50 per cent in dry grains (like *ragi* and *cholam*) should be taken as a sign of severe scarcity: *Famine Code, Madras Presidency* (Madras, 1884), p. 7.

44. Michael Adas, '"Moral economy" or "contest state"?: Elite demands and the origins of peasant protest in Southeast Asia', *Journal of Social History*, 13, 4 (1980), p. 540.

45 Thompson, 'Moral economy', pp. 120, 122, 126. Thompson makes it clear that in England the issue was dearth and not famine: ibid., pp. 86, 88, 90, 126. For the disappearance of famine in England by the eighteenth century, see John Walter and Roger Schofield, 'Famine, disease and crisis mortality in early modern society', in John Walter and Roger Schofield (eds), *Famine, Disease and the Social Order in Early Modern Society* (Cambridge: Cambridge University Press, 1989), pp. 1–73.

46. Arnold, 'Looting'.

47. This was also an urban phenomenon, despite reports of the remarkable 'self-denial and resignation' shown by the starving poor. 'In this town', wrote the Madras Police Commissioner in December 1877:

> during all the distress there has been no augmentation of crime beyond what was to be expected from increased population [of famine immigrants], nor the slightest appearance of violence or combination for criminal purposes. Gangs of unemployed empty-bellied men, women, and children, have wandered through the streets for days, in vain search of work, but they never seem to have thought of looting a grain shop.

> None the less a second wave of looting had been threatened in July 1877 and the military was put on standby in anticipation. No fewer than 3125 people were tried in 1877 for petty grain thefts, mainly from the beach where grain was being unloaded: Colonel W. S. Drever to Additional Secretary, Madras, *Review of the Madras Famine, 1876–1878*, appendix G, pp. 240, 244.

48. T. E. Ravenshaw, Commissioner, Cuttack, to Secretary, Bengal, 2 May 1866, in Beadon, *Minute*, appendix, p. 117.

49. *Madras Police Administration Report, 1877* (Madras, 1878), p. 1.

50. Report of District Superintendent of Police, Balasore, in Beadon, *Minute*, appendix, p. 123.

51. Ravenshaw to Secretary, Bengal, 2 May 1866, ibid., p. 117.

52. Ibid.

53. *Madras Police Administration Report, 1876* (Madras, 1877), pp. 2–3, 19, 23; *Madras Police Administration Report, 1877*, pp. 1, 19; appendix A, p. 1;

146 *Moral Economy and Popular Protest*

David Arnold, 'Dacoity and rural crime in Madras, 1860–1940', *Journal of Peasant Studies*, VI (1979), pp. 145–9. For a similar pattern in northern India, see Sharma, '1837–38 famine in U.P.'

54. William Robert Cornish, *On the Nature of the Food of the Inhabitants of the Madras Presidency* (Madras, 1863), p. 26; C. E. R. Girdlestone, *Report on Past Famines in the North-Western Provinces* (Allahabad, 1868), p. 56.
55. On famine migration, see Girdlestone, *Report on Past Famines*, p. 3; R. Baird Smith, *Report on the Famine of 1860–61 in the North-Western Provinces* (London, 1861), section I, pp. 20–4, section II, pp. 5–6; Frederick Henvey, *A Narrative of the Drought and Famine which Prevailed in the North-West Provinces during the Years 1868, 1869, and Beginning of 1870* (Allahabad, 1871), pp. 44–5, 81.
56. Amartya Sen, *Poverty and Famines: An Essay on Entitlement and Deprivation* (Oxford: Clarendon Press 1981); Paul R. Greenough, *Prosperity and Misery in Modern Bengal: The Famine of 1943–1944* (New York: Oxford University Press, 1982). Thompson's probing critique of Greenough's 'holistic anthropology' ('Moral economy reviewed', pp. 345–7) makes further comment on his work unnecessary here. There has been some modification of Sen's original 'entitlement thesis' in his more recent collaborative work with Jean Drèze: Jean Drèze and Amartya Sen, *Hunger and Public Action* (Oxford: Clarendon Press 1989), pp. 20–31. But from the viewpoint of a social historian there remains a basic failure to take popular ideas and actions seriously.
57. For famine mortality, see Roland Lardinois, 'Une conjuncture de crise demographique en India du sud au XIXe siècle: La famine de 1876–1878', *Population*, 2 (1982), pp. 371–404; A. K. Sen, 'Famine mortality: A study of the Bengal famine of 1943', in E. J. Hobsbawm *et al.* (eds), *Peasants in History: Essays in Honour of Daniel Thorner* (Calcutta: Oxford University Press, 1980), pp. 194–220; Tim Dyson, 'On the demography of South Asian famines: Part I', *Population Studies*, 45 (1991), pp. 5–25.
58. Greenough, *Prosperity and Misery*, pp. 46–7.
59. Ravenshaw to Secretary, Bengal, 2 May 1866, in Beaton *Minute*, appendix, p. 119: cf. Sharma, '1837–38 famine in U.P.'; A. P. MacDonnell, *Report on the Food-grain Supply and Statistical Review of the Relief Operations in the Distressed Districts of Behar and Bengal during the Famine of 1873–74* (Calcutta, 1876), p. 15.
60. *Madras Times*, 26 October 1876 (for subsidised rice sales in Madras); W. S. Whiteside, Collector, North Arcot, to Secretary, Board of Revenue, Madras, 7 November 1876, MBRP, 11 November 1876, IOL (for feeding by zamindars); Charles A. Elliott, *Report on the History of the Mysore Famine of 1876–78* (Calcutta, 1878), pp. 30, 55; *Report on the Scarcity and Relief Operations in the North-West Provinces and Oudh during the Years 1877–78 and 1879* (Allahabad, 1880), p. 76.
61. Munro to Board of Revenue, Madras, 19 February 1807, Board's Collections, F/4/206:4612, IOL.
62. A. Appadorai, *Economic Conditions in Southern India (100–1500 A.D.)* (Madras; 1936), II, pp. 734–5.
63. Elliott, *Mysore Famine*, pp. 78–9; Sir Richard Temple, 'Minute', 31 October 1874 (on the famine in Bengal), pp. 68–9, V/27/830/35, IOL.

6
Moral Economy, Political Economy and the American Bourgeois Revolution

Edward Countryman

What most historians produce during their writing careers has a short life. The better books may survive in paperback, particularly if they enter the undergraduate curriculum. Articles are interred decently in the depths of research libraries. But once in a while historians do develop concepts that keep their vitality. The American frontier, Italian civic republicanism, the 'rise' of the English gentry: these are three such; so is Edward Thompson's notion of a 'moral economy', now twenty years old.[1]

Thompson's critics and his less subtle imitators notwithstanding, the original essay in *Past and Present* made no attempt to posit an abstract, reified notion of '*the* moral economy', independent of place, time and situation. It set its subject in England, during the eighteenth century. It dealt with the kinds of people who got involved with popular uprisings to set the prices and control the supplies of foodstuffs during times of shortage. Among these there would be a trader who was exporting goods or raising prices, a crowd that intervened by direct action or by its threat, and magistrates who might take either side.

Thompson offered no comparisons. He made no general statements about 'pre-industrial' or 'traditional' or '*ancien régime*' social relations.[2] He simply sought to show that 'the food riot in eighteenth-century England was a highly complex form of direct popular action, disciplined, and with clear objectives'.[3] Yet both this volume and books and articles in many other places demonstrate that scholars have found the essay useful far outside the framework of eighteenth-century England, even outside the discipline of history itself.[4]

The Enduring Power of an English Idea

One of the major uses has been for understanding Britain's mainland North American colonies during the time when they became the United States. Consider the record of market relationships in early New York City.

In 1648, when the city was still Nieuw Amsterdam, its Dutch governor Pieter Stuyvesant established a controlled market and fair. After the English conquest in 1676, Governor Thomas Dongan renewed 'the benefit of ye Markett'. Forestalling (buying goods that were on their way to market), regrating (buying in the market to sell again) and engrossing (contracting for an entire crop while it was still growing) were offences in England, at both common and statute law. But whether English law applied outside the realm was an open question.[5] So in 1684 the city council defined them as offences again, under a by-law of its own. In 1741 New York forbade exporting wheat because 'the poor, both in town and country, were distressed'. In 1742 the whole set of market regulations was renewed. In 1748 another embargo was sought when 'great and Unusual Exportation to foreign markets' made provisions 'most oppressive dear, to the great oppression of all degrees of people, but more especially to the industrious poor.' In 1763 the 'leading citizens' agreed 'that...the regulation of the public Markets respecting the Price of Provisions hath ever been esteemed a Matter of great Importance to the Inhabitants and worth the Attention of the Public'. Until well into the nineteenth century the city fathers published an assize of bread.[6] Here, fully choreographed, is the role that early New York's rulers took in market relations.

The marks of other feet are visible as well. During the winter of 1753–54 New York's merchants agreed that they would refuse to accept half-pennies any longer at the traditional rate. These were the coins most likely to find their way into a poor person's pocket and from there to change hands for firewood or bread or salt. The result was a 'popular cry that the Merchants did it, with a design to sharp [the coins] away.' Processions took to the streets, led by a drummer, the marchers bearing clubs and stones.[7]

It was not a price riot, merely the threat of one. In England the threat by itself was often enough. This time in New York it did not work. The authorities backed the merchants, the new exchange rate became official, and that was as close as New Yorkers got before the Revolution to what ordinary English people were doing regularly throughout the century.[8] But the Boston merchant Andrew Belcher experienced real market riots in 1709 and again in 1713 when word got out that he was planning to sell his grain at buoyant prices in the West Indies, rather than for less at home. Both times, the town select-men tried to dissuade him. When they failed, 'his ships were attacked and his warehouses emptied by an angry crowd.'[9]

Any Tory paternalist in England might have done the same as New York's magistrates usually did or as Boston's selectmen tried to do about Belcher. Any English merchant might have done the same as Belcher himself. Any English crowd might have threatened riot or actually rioted. There is no surprise in finding people doing in the city of New York or the town of Boston, Massachusetts, as they might have done in the city of York or the borough of Boston, Lincolnshire. White colonials were the first to assert that they were as English as anyone 'at home'.[10]

But even colonial Americans were not as English as they liked to think. During the late eighteenth century they ceased to be English at all. The interest of their story is twofold. First, it tells how people adapted the ideas and practices that the modern phrase 'moral economy' connotes to distinctively American social conditions. Second, it tells what happened to those ideas and practices during a historical event that eighteenth-century England did not undergo: a revolution.

England's Eighteenth-Century America

Morality aside, early mainland America was a curious mixture.[11] In the Chesapeake Tidewater and the Carolina lowlands it was colonial in the strict sense. These places' populations, their social institutions, and their economic lives were fundamentally different from anything in Britain. Virginia was two-fifths black and South Carolina's slave majority made it 'more like a negro country'.[12] Slavery subordinated all these places' black people to all whites in a way that no real English man or woman knew. Economically, the primary task of the southern colonies was to produce staple crops – tobacco, rice, naval stores, and indigo – under conditions that no free person would have toler-ated for long. This, too, was without English parallel. Such towns as they developed were also 'colonial'. They did little more than funnel raw or semi-processed staples in one direction and finished metropoli-tan goods in the other.[13] Plantation masters liked to fancy themselves as English country gentlemen, and they did their best to act the part. George Washington even had the wooden beams of Mount Vernon bevelled to look like the blocks of stone from which an English manor house might have been built. But the conditions of his life made him no more a genuine English gentleman than his slaves were genuine English peasants or those bevelled beams were genuine stone.[14]

North of the Chesapeake the resemblance between colonies and metropolis was deeper.[15] Philadelphia was still a lower-level trading centre at mid-century, but it had artisan and merchant groups that were developing their own institutions and that served the local economy first.[16] British working people did not find these places strange; Tom Paine's easy entry into the world of Philadelphia artisans in 1774 provides evidence. An American of the same sort could feel just as comfortable in England: witness the young Benjamin Franklin's sojourn as a printer in London.[17]

For a black American the difference between north and south made little difference. Slavery set the terms of race relations in Boston and Philadelphia as much as in Williamsburg and Charles Town. The north had no plantations. But its black people were not mere ornaments, kept to show off a person's wealth. They formed perhaps one-fifth of the population of eighteenth-century New York City and they did much of the city's worst work. They laboured on the farms of the Hudson Valley, Long Island, New Jersey and Pennsylvania as well.[18]

South or north, slaves were not wholly without power. Relations with their white oppressors, like the relations of English rioters with their 'betters', could be a matter of negotiation. By the mid-nineteenth century some slave societies had developed powerful customs that effectively negated the official law of slavery. None the less, slaves were not in a position for any kind of quasi-legitimate collective action.[19]

However, free people, or servants who could expect to be free in time, formed the vast northern majority. They, not slaves, did most of the north's productive work. Some of what they produced was for export to the great Atlantic market: New England's dried fish, the middle provinces' wheat, the ships that made up a full third of the British merchant fleet by 1770, the crude iron that represented one-seventh of the world total the same year. But none of these was a staple, produced for virtually exclusive sale to a distant market. Fish, wheat and iron all required finishing before they were shipped, in a way that tobacco or rice did not. A good proportion of these and other goods were for local exchange and use, not for transatlantic sale. The issue is how colonials exchanged what they needed and used.

There is a fondly-held popular image of the independent early American, owing nothing to another soul and completely remote from commerce. No northern farmer or artisan approached that image in reality. Rural New England was perhaps least involved in large-scale trade. But even its most insular villages formed local trading networks. People understood who owed what to whom, and they recorded their debts in monetary terms. But a local debt might persist for years without interest. It would probably be paid off in kind or labour, not cash. When these people dealt with outsiders, profit did count. That was how they earned money in order to buy from outside. But they dealt with 'neighbours' and with 'strangers' under different rules.[20] Within the community, mutuality and reciprocity were paramount, or so, at least, people expected.[21]

The northern colonial situation was not absolutely identical to Thompson's England. Part of the difference was juridical. England comprised one realm and its counties possessed no real autonomy. But each American province was separate and none acknowledged any higher authority below the Crown itself. New York could close its economy when provisions became 'most oppressive dear': Boston could not argue, however much it might need New York wheat. Another part of the difference was the urban–rural balance. There was no American London, so swollen in numbers and so politically sensitive that the government had to regard its provisioning as an absolute necessity. Part of the difference was the balance of classes. Americans knew poverty, and as the eighteenth century progressed their knowledge increased. But outside the cities, whites rarely faced the permanently miserable situation of an English day labourer.[22] Part of the difference was simple productive capacity in relation to population. New England's thin soil and harsh climate made it unable to feed itself as early as 1700; but from New York southwards there was no danger of a natural crisis of subsistence.[23]

In England the 'grain nexus' was absolutely central in binding communities together. The terms on which grain, flour and bread ought to be exchanged counted among Americans too. But these were not the only material goods whose misuse or maldistribution could lead to direct action. For all these reasons, most historians of early America prefer the adjective 'corporate' to Thompson's word 'moral'. What people threatened or did was often much the same. The actual reasons why they threatened or acted might not be.[24]

The colonial economy and the English economy did share a tension between the demands of small communities and the demands of a large-scale long-distance market. On both sides of the ocean small communities still carried a special moral legitimacy that even men in high authority often recognised. On both sides, the large market was on its way to enduring triumph: but, in the American case at least, the transition was riddled with ambiguity.

Return for a moment to the Boston riots of 1709 and 1713. People broke open Andrew Belcher's warehouses and kept his ships from sailing. They did it because they believed that he was turning food they needed into a mere commodity, for sale to the distant West Indies. They were right, but more than avarice was at stake.

In a better world, the Caribbean islands might have produced their own necessities. Before the European invasion they had done that well enough. But now the fields of Barbados or Antigua produced little more than sugar. The grain Belcher was shipping was his means of paying for sugar to sell again, perhaps refined as molasses. A Bostonian who worked in a distillery where molasses became rum might gain from the transactions Belcher was setting in motion, even if he joined in the riots. So might another who made a pair of shoes for the first, and still another who worked in a shipyard or rope-walk. The cordwainer might make cruder shoes for slave use as well, and a Boston vessel might easily enter the African slave trade. An enslaved African whose life was paid for with Boston rum, who made the middle passage in a Boston ship and who wore foot-pinching Massachusetts shoes when not barefoot, would not gain from these transactions at all. But the grain Belcher shipped became a necessity again when it arrived in the islands, this time for the slaves themselves, assuming that they wanted to survive. Two incompatible visions of how, in whose interests, on what scale, and at what price the economic world might best be organised were in fundamental conflict. That was the heart of the issue. It was also at the heart of the transformation of the thirteen colonies into one republic.

The Revolution in America

The events that turned the colonies into the United States have always been known as the American Revolution. It has long seemed in popular and even scholarly imagery that this revolution was different from any other. Where in this tepid little dispute about taxes and tea were the crowds, the passion, the anger and the radical social transformations that would alter France so profoundly after 1789? Where among the likes of Washington, Jefferson and John Adams was there room for someone cut from the same cloth as Cromwell or Robespierre?

During the late twentieth century historians have spent enormous effort recovering what actually was revolutionary about the American

Revolution. We now see that the Revolution profoundly altered American life on at least two levels. One was political society: how people dealt with one another in the public arena. The other was political consciousness: how they made sense of their relationships of power and obligation. We are beginning to see that these political and ideological changes were bound up with the emergence of the United States as a self-transforming bourgeois country.[25]

This complex revolution worked itself out through the making and unmaking of three great coalitions. The first resisted the British between 1765 and 1775. The second waged war and won independence between 1775 and 1783. The third made and ratified the Federal Constitution, creating the United States in its present political form. Running through the whole period was an extended struggle over politics, property and society. During the Revolution the small-community corporate model fused with the highest questions of revolutionary politics. At the Revolution's end, however, the builders of the republic made a deliberate and successful effort to untangle the two and to strip the corporate model of its power to direct the course of trade.

The initial issue was quite simple. Parliament claimed the power to tax the colonies directly, without recourse to the colonial assemblies. Establishing that claim would have meant the effective end of the assemblies as quasi-parliamentary institutions. It would have undermined seriously the colonial elites, who used those assemblies to run their own societies. That the elites responded strongly is hardly surprising. They passed resolutions and wrote pamphlets that demolished Parliament's rationale. They invoked the whole history and ideology of British liberty in order to frame the issue in the most stirring possible terms.

Words were not enough, however. The colonial rulers needed determined, massive support. They found it first in the three great port towns, Boston, New York and Philadelphia. From the Stamp Act in 1765 to the Boston Tea Party in 1773, urban crowds gave power to the American position. They made the Stamp Act unenforceable by forcing every stamp distributor save Georgia's to resign his post. They sacked British officials' houses and offices and destroyed their moveable property. Crowds harassed meddling customs officials, often by defacing their dwellings with 'Hillsborough Paint'. Named in honour of the secretary of state for colonial affairs, Lord Hillsborough, this consisted of the contents of their privies. Colonials brawled with British soldiers in streets and in taverns. Twice during the late winter of 1770 Bostonians walked in huge political funeral processions.

The first, in February, was for eleven-year-old Christopher Sneider. A panic-stricken customs man named Ebenezer Richardson had shot the boy when he fired into a crowd outside Richardson's house. The second, in March, was for the five victims of the 'Boston Massacre' in which British soldiers guarding the Customs House opened fire on a protesting crowd.[26]

Nothing these crowds did is understandable in terms of the great imperial issues alone. Nor can it be understood just in terms of the high level political language in which the colonial elite wrote its resolutions and pamphlets. Great issues and political language alike were of importance. But local matters and popular traditions did count. The intertwined themes of communities protecting themselves against the outside and of lesser people protecting themselves against their betters ran through the protests.

Consider in detail just one instance: the killing that took place outside the Customs House on King Street in Boston on the cold night of 5 March 1770. The story is simple. Three years earlier the town had been made the headquarters of a separate American customs service. The customs men worked on percentage. The laws were full of technicalities that allowed ready seizures and protected a customs man against prosecution if his case failed. Both in Boston and elsewhere customs officials made themselves extremely unpopular. Five regiments of regular soldiers were sent to Boston in 1768, primarily to protect the customs headquarters. The detachment on duty on the night of the massacre found itself taunted and harassed by a hostile, snowball-throwing crowd. Frightened, and believing their captain had given the order, the soldiers opened fire. When they were tried for murder their lawyer was the Boston radical John Adams, who argued that the soldiers had believed they were under orders. His argument worked and the soldiers were acquitted.[27]

There were plenty of reasons for the hostility that Boston civilians showed the troops. Before the regiments came, the town had never had a garrison. However, New Englanders and redcoats did know each other well from experience in the colonial wars. They did not like each other at all. Not the least reason was the clash between New Englanders' communal traditions, which colonial militiamen carried into active duty, and British military ways. To colonials, the class-bound highly-disciplined troops represented all that was wrong with England. To the troops the colonials were slovenly cowards with no sense of what warfare required.[28]

When the troops came to Boston in 1768 they pitched their tents on the town common. They took over public buildings, including a manufactory set up to provide employment in a harsh time. The troops paraded on Sunday mornings, at hours calculated nicely to disrupt Puritan services. They put up guard posts where sentries challenged every civilian. One post was on Boston Neck, the narrow spit that connected the then peninsular town to the mainland. Any of these grievances would have been enough to make any Bostonian angry.

Still more was at stake for some of the town's people. In 1770 working people in all three major port towns were defending their right to employment in a time of economic distress. For artisans in Philadelphia and New York the colonial policy of not importing British goods in protest against the Townshend Acts was a 'great benefit', not a burden.[29] New York City working men brawled with soldiers for a whole week in January. There, as in Boston, British troops amounted to an occupying force and the troops made themselves just as unpleasant. But the prime issue was off-duty soldiers taking part-time work that New York civilians needed. All that distinguished this 'Battle of Golden Hill' from what happened in Boston was that no New Yorkers died.[30]

The events that led to the Boston Massacre began just after Christopher Sneider's funeral. Patrick Walker, a soldier from the Twenty-Ninth Regiment of Foot, approached a rope-walk seeking work. One of the ropemakers offered him a job cleaning 'my shithouse'. While the insulted soldier fetched his mates, other ropeworkers gathered, and a brawl ensued. Officers from the regiment and Boston political leaders joined forces to break the fight up, but the tension remained. It was the Twenty-Ninth that had guard duty on the night of 5 March. Some of the same men, from both sides, were in King Street when the snowballs and then the bullets flew. One ropemaker was among the five who died. The others were a half-Indian half-African sailor, a ship's mate, a journeyman leathermaker and an apprentice ivory turner.

Work was not the only issue, of course. The master craftsmen and journeymen and apprentices and labourers and seamen who converged on King Street were not engaged in outright, self-conscious class struggle. On the contrary, the rioters were part of a large coalition that brought colonials of many sorts together in a common programme of resistance. But they knew that some of their 'betters' who wrote stirring words about liberty also cheerfully mingled with British officers, employed off-duty soldiers at cheap rates, and sought military contracts. The rioters joined the coalition on the basis of their firm belief that the community's own members came first.

Virtually any popular rising of the period makes sense best if we look at it this way. The imperial issue was central. The politics of resistance was based on bringing Americans of different sorts together in a common front, not on setting them at one another. But without understanding how the culture of English class relations applied in the American context we cannot understand the movement. The American 'corporate' popular ethos and the English 'moral economy' were not too far removed from each other, even before the War of Independence taught the Americans about real shortage and hunger.

Moral Economy, National Economy

The years of war, from 1775 to 1783, were a time of genuine and general economic crisis. The American, British and eventually French armies and navies all needed to provision themselves. Meanwhile the Revolution was trying to pay for itself by printing paper money. The result was that both continental and state currencies were inflating as early as 1776. By the end of the decade the inflation was catastrophic and Congress finally resolved it by a drastic devaluation in 1780. This conjuncture of distress and inflation amounted to America's first national economic crisis. Within the crisis, an American national economy was emerging where none had been before.

This was also the time when the Americans got closest to their English cousins in terms of the issues that Thompson has described. Between 1775 and 1779 there were more than thirty outright price riots in the northern states. The subject was not only bread; people broke into storehouses and they stopped loaded wagons over 'West Indies goods', tea, coffee, sugar, salt and unspecified items. No more than in England itself were these mindless outbursts. American price rioters negotiated with merchants. They offered what they regarded as just prices. They staged public rituals, as when Bostonians carted 'monopolizers' out of town in 1777, passing the town gallows on the way. What these people did demonstrates that, however seldom their colonial forebears had actually resorted to a price riot, the traditions that told them when rioting was legitimate had remained alive.

The difference was that in America it was happening in the midst of a revolution. In Barbara Clark Smith's words, 'these riots offer a new and decidedly popular angle of vision on Americans' movement for independence from Great Britain and for liberty at home'.[31] The Revolution gave rioting a new legitimation by identifying it directly with the American cause. As early as 1774 the first Continental Congress defined patriotism on the premises that 'a patriot did not import, consume, nor raise prices on goods or produce on hand'.[32] The popular committees that took power between 1774 and 1776 made it their business to enforce controls on prices and on supplies: a hoarder or price-raiser could always be accused of trying to aid the British. When inflation and shortage reached their worst, in 1779, popular committees reappeared from Pennsylvania to New England with the specific goal of getting the economy under control. They imposed embargoes, set prices and hunted out hidden supplies. Doggerel poets published lines like 'extortioners and tories, which of them is the worst? One brings a fair story, the other a blunderbuss.'[33]

Not all of the explicitly political content that price rioting acquired during the Revolution was new. During the decade of imperial strife New Englanders, in particular, harked back to the 1640s. Parents named newborn sons Oliver, in honour of Cromwell, and conjured up the figure of Cornet Joyce, the captor of Charles. A costumed 'Joyce, Jr.', actually led the largest uprising of all during the crisis of the late 1770s.[34]

In the revolutionary conjuncture, however, the small community model also fitted almost perfectly with the 'civic humanist' political ideology that the elite leaders of the revolutionary movement were using to make sense of their own situation. Civic humanism was derived from the ancient world via Renaissance Italy. It was filtered into the minds of literate colonials via James Harrington and the writers of the eighteenth-century 'country' or 'commonwealth' tradition. Its beliefs about the good political society had a great deal in common with corporatism's beliefs about the good working economic community. Both respected the particularity of a time, a place and a situation. Both turned on the reciprocal, negotiated interplay of rulers and ruled. Both valued disciplined self-assertion, whether by the citizen-soldier that civic humanism idealised or by the price-setting crowd that corporatism legitimised. Both turned on the assumption that a single public good could be defined and realised in practice. Both assumed that this recognisable public good ought to be paramount in relation to any private good of individuals.

The Continental Congress brought together these two traditions, one popular and one elite, as early as its anti-British 'Association' of 1774. Their fusion became part of the terms on which Americans resisted Britain. Five of the original state constitutions (South Carolina, North Carolina, Maryland, Pennsylvania and Vermont) empowered the government to close the state's economy in time of crisis. Local needs came first, a position that any food rioter would have understood. Any paternalistic gentleman in England or colonial America would have understood it too. During the crisis of 1778–80, when inflation and actual shortage sent the market for foodstuffs and other necessities mad, all the northern states acted on the same basis, whether their constitutions allowed it or no. Where they did not, riots broke out.[35] Meanwhile popular writers were complaining of how men who 'but a little while ago seemed ready to sacrifice their all to the shrine of liberty' were now 'by the vile practice of extortion' making 'extravagant demands for what they have to sell'.[36]

This joining of small-community economics with the language and imagery of civic republican liberty was short-lived. Even as it flourished during the wartime crisis, the absolute need to supply the army was rendering corporatism unpatriotic. Supplying the army, in turn, was leading to the creation of an American national economy where none had been before. In the long run the imperatives of that economy would render the small-community model anachronistic as well. A decade later the Federal Constitution brought the fusion to a legal end. Henceforth Congress alone would regulate commerce among the states, within the largest common market the world had seen to that point. The states themselves would have no power to interfere in obligations of contract. The American version of the English 'moral economy' had been central in driving the revolutionary movement; but the Revolution's final settlement killed it, at least for the purpose of legitimating pre-capitalist terms of exchange.

Good Small Communities and White Supremacy

Corporatism's economic legitimacy in late-colonial America was linked directly to the uneven bundle of traditional British 'liberties' that the colonials set out to protect against the British government's imperial policies. Its demise was linked just as directly to the undifferentiated bourgeois 'liberty' that was extolled in the Declaration of Independence and whose 'blessings' the federal Constitution was written to 'secure'. If the reality of those blessings had in fact been experienced equally by every member of early national American society, the sacrifice of the one for the sake of the other would without doubt have been well justified.[37]

A great deal of the bitter complexity of subsequent American history would also have been avoided. One specific 'liberty' in the old sense did survive all the changes of the revolutionary period: that of some persons to hold others as slaves. Under the old order the contradiction was not, perhaps, apparent. The 'liberty' of holding slaves went with one set of social conditions; the 'liberty' of political representation went with another; the 'liberty' of local economic self-control went with a third. Under the new order, however, the contradiction glared. Ultimately its resolution could not be avoided. Even when slavery finally ended, a malign shadow from the uneven liberties and the small community peculiarities of America's beginning continued to be cast. In the mid-nineteenth century the code phrase 'state's rights' meant the legitimacy of slavery itself, justified by southern usage whatever the outside world might say. In the mid-twentieth, it meant the legitimacy of white supremacy, and, if the white community wanted it, of lynching, justified on the same ground. The line from a crowd that could close out the world and set its town's own prices to one that could close out the world and hang a black man because he had looked the wrong way at a white woman is not pleasant to trace; but in American history it runs straight.

Despite the Constitution, crowd uprisings of the old price-setting sort did take place occasionally in the nineteenth-century north. New York City's grain riots of 1837 and its kosher meat riots of 1898 provide well-studied examples.[38] But it was in the south during the Civil War that the fullest post-independence examples appear. This era began the south's own bourgeois revolution, although admittedly one forced upon it from outside. There, as in the north during the late 1770s, a combination of military necessity, inflation and absolute material shortage created real suffering. There, as in the earlier north, suffering's victims called it 'oppression' and 'extortion'. And in cities and towns across the South – Augusta, Columbus, Savannah, Atlanta, Milledgeville, Mobile, Raleigh, Petersburg, Salisbury and, most notably, the capital city of Richmond – citizens turned to violence to procure the goods that the market denied them.[39]

Like their northern counterparts during the struggle against England, these people explained the way they were protecting their own small communities with the concept of freedom. In the larger sense of the struggle against their Yankee foes, white southerners invoked the same idea. Confederate soldiers actually did sing 'Battle Cry of Freedom' as they marched off to die in their hundreds of thousands for the sake of the slave regime.[40] But if 'freedom' was involved, it was in the oldest possible sense one that the capitalist north had long since abandoned. As Drew Gilpin Faust comments, 'slavery depended not only on the restriction of the market in labour power. It rested as well on an ideology of paternalistic obligation and authority fundamentally at odds with the notion of a *laissez-faire* world.'[41]

The power of corporatist or moral economy ideas in early North America demonstrates how complete was the transfer of English ways to the distant colonies. That their fullest American expression came during the Revolutionary War in the north and during the Civil War in the south demonstrates how much these ideas clashed with the ways and the needs of the bourgeois society that the United States became. Born during the first war, bourgeois America triumphed over its great domestic enemy during the second. During both wars the American ideology of community self-control provided a powerful countervailing force, just as it did for Thompson's people during the triumph of bourgeois social relations in late eighteenth-century England. That in the end community self-control became inextricably bound up with the equally American ideology of racial supremacy provides an instance in which history indeed did repeat itself, not as farce, but in the most tragic of terms.

Notes

1. E. P. Thompson, 'The moral economy of the English crowd in the eighteenth century', *Past and Present*, 50 (1971), reprinted in Thompson, *Customs in Common* (London: Merlin, 1991), pp. 185–258. All citations are to the *Customs in Common* printing.
2. The most obvious comparison is with the French notion of *taxation populaire*, already developed at some length by Albert Soboul and George Rudé. See Soboul, *Les Sans-Culottes Parisiens en L'An II: Mouvement Populaire et Gouvernement Révolutionnaire, 2 Juin, 1793–9 Thermidor, An II* (Paris; 1962) and Rudé, *The Crowd in History, 1730–1848* (New York: John Wiley, 1964).
3. Thompson, 'Moral economy', p. 188.
4. It should be noted that Thompson began the work that led to the essay with collaboration and comparison in mind and that he has dealt at length with non-English applications of the concept. See 'The moral economy reviewed', in *Customs in Common*, pp. 259–351.
5. The applicability of English law to the American provinces would, of course, be the defining issue in the revolutionary crisis of 1765–76. By then Parliament was asserting its sovereign authority over all British subjects everywhere. But in the seventeenth century it was not yet making such claims and there is good reason to regard the congealing overseas empire as a composite state rather than a unitary one. See H. G. Koenigsberger, 'Composite states, representative institutions and the American Revolution', *Historical Research*, LXII (1989), pp. 135–53.
6. Laws and Ordinances of New Netherland cited in Isaac Newton Phelps Stokes, *The Iconography of Manhattan Island, 1550–1812* (6 vols, New York: R. H. Dodd, 1915–28), IV, pp. 113–14; entries for 1683 and 1684, ibid.,

pp. 327, 961; entries for 1741 and 1742, ibid., pp. 571 ff.; entry for 1748, ibid., IV, p. 613; entry for 1763, ibid., IV, p. 737.

7. *The New York Gazette* (J. Parker and W. Weyman), 3 (18 December 1753); 14 (21 January 1754), cited in Stokes, *Iconography*, IV, pp. 645–8.

8. See Thompson, 'Moral economy', p. 239. For the failure of the threat in New York, see Paul A. Gilje, *The Road to Mobocracy: Popular Disorder in New York City, 1763–1834* (Chapel Hill: University of North Carolina Press, 1987), pp. 13–14.

9. Gary B. Nash, 'Social change and the growth of pre-revolutionary urban radicalism', in Alfred F. Young (ed.), *The American Revolution: Explorations in the History of American Radicalism* (Dekalb: Northern Illinois University Press, 1976), pp. 11–12.

10. The literature on how Americans imitated English cultural models is now enormous. For some instances see: David Grayson Allen, *In English Ways: The Movement of Societies and the Transferal of English Local Law and Custom to Massachusetts Bay in the Seventeenth Century* (Chapel Hill: University of North Carolina Press, 1981); Bernard Bailyn, *Voyagers to the WEST Passage in the Peopling of America on the Eve of the Revolution* (New York: Alfred A. Knopf, 1986); David Hackett Fischer, *Albion's Seed: Four British Folkways in America* (Oxford: Oxford University Press, 1989); Eric Foner, *Tom Paine and Revolutionary America* (New York: Oxford University Press, 1976); Jack P. Greene, 'Political mimesis: a consideration of the historical and cultural roots of legislative behaviour in the British colonies in the eighteenth century', *American Historical Review*, LXXV (1969–70), pp. 337–67 and 'Search for identity: an interpretation of the meaning of selected patterns of social response in eighteenth-century America', *Journal of Social History*, III (1969–1970), pp. 189–221; Rhys Isaac, *The Transformation of Virginia, 1740–1790* (Chapel Hill: University of North Carolina Press, 1982); Margaret Jacob and James Jacob (eds), *The Origins of Anglo-American Radicalism* (London: Allen & Unwin, 1984); Gary B. Nash, *The Urban Crucible: Social Change, Political Consciousness, and the Origins of the American Revolution* (Cambridge, Mass.: Harvard University Press, 1979). For one instance that bears directly on the emergence of capitalist social relations in the colonial and revolutionary periods, see Edward Countryman, 'The uses of capital in revolutionary America: the case of the New York loyalist merchants', *William and Mary Quarterly*, 3rd ser., XLIX (1992), pp. 3–28.

11. See: Alice Hanson Jones, *Wealth of a Nation to Be: The American Colonies on the Eve of the Revolution* (New York: Columbia University Press, 1980), and *American Colonial Wealth: Documents and Methods*, 3 vols (New York: Arno Press, 1977); John J. McCusker and Russell Menard, *The Economy of British America, 1607–1789* (Chapel Hill: University of North Carolina Press, 1985); Jack P. Greene and J. R. Pole (eds), *Colonial British America: Essays in the New History of the Early Modern Era* (Baltimore, MD: Johns Hopkins University Press, 1984), and Ronald Hoffman *et al.* (eds), *The Economy of Early America: The Revolutionary Period, 1763–1790* (Charlottesville: University Press of Virginia, 1988).

12. Allen Kulikoff, *Tobacco and Slaves: The Development of Southern Cultures in the Chesapeake, 1680–1800* (Chapel Hill: University of North Carolina Press,

1986); Peter H. Wood, *Black Majority: Negroes in Colonial South Carolina from 1670 through the Stono Rebellion* (New York: Alfred A. Knopf, 1974).

13. Jacob M. Price, 'Economic function and the growth of American port towns', *Perspectives in American History*, VIII (1974). But see also Carville Earle and Ronald Hoffman, 'Urban development in the eighteenth-century South', *Perspectives in American History*, X (1976), pp. 7–78, which argues that towns of a non-colonial sort began to develop in the northern Chesapeake interior as a result of the emergence of wheat cultivation, as opposed to tobacco.

14. For explorations of the British and not-British world of Virginia tobacco planters, see: Isaac, *The Transformation of Virginia*; T. H. Breen, *Tobacco Culture: The Mentality of the Great Tidewater Planters on the Eve of the Revolution* (Princeton, NJ: Princeton University Press, 1985); Kenneth A. Lockridge, *The Diary, and Life, of William Byrd II of Virginia, 1674–1744* (Chapel Hill: University of North Carolina Press, 1987); Jack P. Greene (ed.), *The Diary of Colonel Landon Carter of Sabine Hall, 1752–1778* (2 vols, Charlottesville: University Press of Virginia, 1965); and Paul G. E. Clemens, *The Atlantic Economy and Colonial Maryland's Eastern Shore: From Tobacco to Grain* (Ithaca, NY: Cornell University Press, 1980).

15. I draw this point from theorists of dependency and underdevelopment. For Samir Amin, New England (meaning the North) 'from the start...was special, and not shaped by the metropolis as a dependency'. See his *Unequal Development: An Essay on the Social Formations of Peripheral Capitalism*, trans. Brian Pearce (Hassocks; Harvester, 1976), 365. For André Gunder Frank a colonial lumpen bourgeoisie leads to post-colonial lumpen development. But the bourgeoisie of the northern colonies was not lumpen at all; it was the real thing: *Dependent Accumulation and Underdevelopment* (London: Macmillan, 1978), p. 61. Immanuel Wallerstein agrees: 'the northern colonists came to be competitors of English producers' with the result that 'the English made a conscious effort' to stifle 'incipient industrial production'. See his *The Modern World-System: Mercantilism and the Consolidation of the European World-Economy, 1600–1750* (New York: Academic Press, 1980), p. 238.

16. See Price, 'Economic function and the growth of American port towns', pp. 143, 152–3, and Nash, *The Urban Crucible*. This is not intended to contradict my recent assertion that a major transformation took place in urban economic life during the revolutionary period: see Countryman, 'The uses of capital in revolutionary America'. The argument there is that even in New York City colonial economic life was distinctly colonial and distinctly pre-capitalist. The Revolution created the political conditions that favoured bourgeois development as opposed to colonial backwardness and dependency. The issue is one of balance, not one of absolute contradiction. The emphasis here is on the undeniable point that even in the colonial period the northern ports were autochthonous in a way that a southern or Caribbean or Latin American port never was.

17. For Paine, see Foner, *Tom Paine*. For Franklin see Esmond Wright, *Franklin of Philadelphia* (Cambridge, Mass.: Harvard University Press, 1986). The important work of Marcus Rediker carries the connection further. See Rediker, *Between the Devil and the Deep Blue Sea: Merchant Seamen, Pirates, and the Anglo-American Maritime World, 1700–1750* (New York: Cambridge University Press, 1987).

18. See Shane White, *Somewhat More Independent: The End of Slavery in New York City, 1770–1810* (Athens, GA: The University of Georgia Press, 1991) and Gary B. Nash, *Forging Freedom: The Formation of Philadelphia's Black Community, 1720–1840* (Cambridge, Mass.: Harvard University Press, 1988).
19. I draw these points from: Rhys Isaac, *The Transformation of Virginia*; Charles Joyner, *Down by the Riverside: A South Carolina Slave Community* (Urbana: University of Illinois Press, 1985); and White, *Somewhat More Independent*.
20. See Bruce H. Mann, *Neighbors and Strangers: Law and Community in Early Connecticut* (Chapel Hill: University of North Carolina Press, 1987).
21. The classic studies are: Michael Merrill, 'Cash is good to eat: self-sufficiency and exchange in the rural economy of the United States', *Radical History Review*, III (1977), pp. 42–71; James A. Henretta, 'Families and farms: *Mentalité* in pre-industrial America', *William and Mary Quarterly*, 3rd ser., XXXV (1978), pp. 3–32; and Christopher Clark, 'The household economy, market exchange and the rise of capitalism in the Connecticut Valley, 1800–1860', *Journal of Social History*, XIII (1979), pp. 169–89. One of the best synthetic statements is Fred Anderson, *A People's Army: Massachusetts Soldiers and Society in the Seven Years' War* (Chapel Hill: University of North Carolina Press, 1984), ch. 2. See also Thomas S. Wermuth, 'To market! To market!: Yeoman farmers, merchant capitalists and the development of capitalism in the Hudson River Valley, Ulster County, 1760–1830', (PhD diss., State University of New York, Binghamton, 1991), which uses the account books of Ulster County, New York, merchants to establish precisely such local networks.
22. Consider the difference between the situation of a tenant farmer in England and in New York's Hudson Valley. In the former, tenancy represented rural prosperity. From the point of view of a day labourer the tenant might well be the villain of the piece. In the latter, tenancy was the bottom of the white social scale. Not all New York landlords were oppressive and not all tenants rebelled: but tenants figured prominently during a full century of New York rural unrest. See Alfred F. Young, *The Democratic-Republicans of New York: The Origins, 1763–1797* (Chapel Hill: University of North Carolina Press, 1967). The assertions in this paragraph are not intended to contradict the important findings of Gary B. Nash and his graduate students at the University of California, Los Angeles. See: Nash, *The Urban Crucible*; Sharon V. Salinger, *To Serve Well and Faithfully: Labor and Indentured Servants in Pennsylvania, 1682–1800* (New York: Cambridge University Press, 1987); Billy G. Smith, *The "Lower Sort": Philadelphia's Laboring People, 1750–1800* (Ithaca, NY: Cornell University Press, 1990.)
23. On this count is it significant that Boston experienced actual grain rioting and price-setting during the colonial period whereas New York City and Philadelphia did not. For New England as a food-deficit region, see David Klingaman, 'Food surpluses and deficits in the American colonies, 1768–1772', *Journal of Economic History*, XXXI (1971).
24. See, for instance, Foner, *Tom Paine*, and Gilje, *The Road to Mobocracy*.
25. For a synthesis of current research and thinking see Edward Countryman, *The American Revolution* (New York: Hill & Wang, 1985). For the Revolution's social character see: Allen Kulikoff, 'The transition to capitalism in rural America', *William and Mary Quarterly*, 3rd ser., XLVI (1989), pp. 120–44, and 'Was the American Revolution a bourgeois revolution?', paper presented

at the conference '"The Transforming Hand of Revolution": Reconsidering the American Revolution as a Social Movement' (Washington, DC, 1989); James A. Henretta, 'The transition to capitalism in America', in Henretta *et al.* (eds), *The Transformation of Early American History: Society, Authority, and Ideology* (New York: Alfred A. Knopf, 1991); and Countryman, 'The uses of capital in revolutionary America'. Gordon S. Wood's new *The Radicalism of the American Revolution* (New York: Alfred A. Knopf, 1992), has it both ways, arguing simultaneously that the Revolution was historically unique and that it was 'one of the greatest revolutions the world has known, a momentous upheaval that not only fundamentally altered the character of American society but decisively affected the course of subsequent history' (p. 5).

26. This composite paragraph is drawn from: Nash, *The Urban Crucible*; Dirk Hoerder, *Crowd Action in Revolutionary Massachusetts, 1765–1780* (New York: Academic Press, 1977); Pauline Maier, *From Resistance to Revolution: Colonial Radicals and the Development of American Opposition to Britain, 1765–1776* (New York: Alfred A. Knopf, 1977); and E. Countryman, *A People in Revolution* (Baltimore: Johns Hopkins University Press, 1981).

27. For the fullest discussion, see Hoerder, *Crowd Action in Revolutionary Massachusetts*.

28. See Fred Anderson, *A People's Army: Massachusetts Soldiers and Society in the Seven Years War* (Chapel Hill: University of North Carolina Press, 1984).

29. 'To the Free and Loyal Inhabitants of the City and Colony of New York' (Broadside, New York: n.p., Evans no. 11588); 'To the *Tradesmen, Farmers* and other *inhabitants* of the City and County of Philadelphia' (Broadside, Philadelphia 24 September 1770, Evans no. 11892); 'To the Free and Patriotic Inhabitants' (Broadside, Philadelphia n.p., 1770, Evans no. 11882).

30. See Countryman, *A People in Revolution*, pp. 63–6.

31. Barbara Clark Smith, 'Price riots and the American Revolution', *William and Mary Quarterly*, forthcoming. Smith's article, based on her Yale PhD thesis (1983), reached me during preparation of this chapter. It supersedes all previous work on the subject of American price rioting and although it is not published at the time of this writing it is impossible not to draw upon it. I am deliberately avoiding making a summary of all Smith's points, particularly her important discussion of the marked presence of women in the American riots.

32. Ibid., p. 11.

33. In addition to Clark Smith, 'Price riots', this paragraph is drawn from: Foner, *Tom Paine*; Steven Rosswurm, *Arms, Country, and Class: The Philadelphia Militia and the 'Lower Sort' During the American Revolution* (New Brunswick, NJ: Rutgers University Press, 1987); Countryman, *A People in Revolution* and '"To Secure the Blessings of Liberty": language, the revolution, and American capitalism', in Alfred F. Young (ed.), *Beyond the American Revolution: Further Explorations in the History of American Radicalism* (Dekalb, Illinois: Northern Illinois University Press, forthcoming).

34. Alfred F. Young, 'English plebeian culture and eighteenth-century American radicalism', in Jacob and Jacob, *The Origins of Anglo-American Radicalism*, pp. 185–212.

35. At this point I recognise explicitly my debt to Clark Smith, 'Price riots and the American revolution'.

36. 'An Address to the People on the Subject of Monopoly and Extortion', in Nathanael Low, *Astronomical Diary or Almanack for 1778* (Boston, Mass.: J. Gill, 1777).

37. See Edward Countryman, '"To secure the blessings of liberty"'.

38. See Herbert G. Gutman, *Work, Culture and Society in Industrializing America: Essays in American Working Class and Social History* (New York: Knopf, 1976), pp. 59–62. The difference between these risings and those of the colonial and mid-revolutionary periods is that Americans in authority now conceded no legitimacy to them.

39. Drew Gilpin Faust, *The Creation of Confederate Nationalism: Ideology and Identity in the Civil War South* (Baton Rouge: Louisiana State University Press, 1988), p. 52.

40. James M. McPherson, *Battle Cry of Freedom: The Civil War Era* (New York: Oxford University Press, 1988), p. vi.

41. Ibid., p. 57.

7
Industrial Disputes, Wage Bargaining and the Moral Economy

John Rule

Edward Thompson has remarked that if he did, 'father the term "moral economy" upon current academic discourse', then while he does not disown it, 'it has come of age' and he is no longer answerable for its actions. He is, however, happier with some of the paths along which the 'moral economy' has been led away from the straight and narrow of the food market than others. He is less happy, for example, that it should be extended to the expectations of the poor from the Old Poor Law, than with the contextually more specific adoption of it by Adrian Randall to assist understanding of the industrial dispute of 1756 between the Gloucestershire woollen weavers and their employers, the clothiers.[1]

Away from the food market, the concept has perhaps been borrowed more often by historians of industrial conflict than by those of any other form of confrontation or popular expectation. Possibly led by the persuasive vocabulary built around 'custom' and 'tradition', a 'moral economy of labour' for the eighteenth century has been commonly asserted. Widely generalised and seriously underspecified, its value has been diminished by those who ask it to explain too completely the complex forms and episodes of eighteenth-century industrial conflict and the types of consciousness and *mentalités* which underlay them. The 'moral economy' has much to offer, but on its own it falls short of wholly explaining industrial disputes, which we now know to have been much closer to food riots in incidence than was believed twenty years ago. For many urban artisans who never came within hearing distance of a food riot, disputes with employers were an occasional fact of life.[2]

In reviewing my book on eighteenth-century industrial labour, Lawrence Stone wrote that it had demonstrated 'a commonly shared

166

sense of a moral economy of the proletariat with recognised rights and freedoms'. In fact I used the phrase 'moral economy' only once and that was in a specific reference to the food-rioting proclivities of some industrial communities. Richard Price has written of eighteenth-century social conflict that it typically occurred at:

> the point at which the logic of capitalism threatened to breach customary standard traditions and relationships. Price riots and struggles over rationalised use of land were the characteristic forms of this clash between the innovations of market forces and the assertion of a 'moral economy' of reciprocal obligations and responsibilities. The same pattern dominated the more purely industrial relations of production. But here efforts to resist the depredations of *laissez-faire* could be legitimated by the presence of a tradition of legal protection and regulation of the conditions of production and the operation of the labour market.[3]

Two points cause unease here. How does bringing industrial relations under the umbrella of the 'moral economy' actually contribute to their understanding? If the phrase had not already been given currency by Edward Thompson's famous article on the food market, would historians of industrial conflict have had to invent it? The second problem is whether, even if the 'moral economy' can embrace many episodes of industrial conflict, do these episodes, in terms of frequency and reach, 'dominate' the disputes between labour and capital in the eighteenth century? Certainly some eighteenth-century disputes involved workers' attempts to preserve or restore what Price calls 'a prior political economy' which regulated and arbitrated the balance of power between groups in the labour market.[4] This balance could be as much a matter of holding advantage as of resisting disadvantage. At moments when the balance swung hard against labour, then naturally its struggle assumes a moral dimension. Labour's disadvantage after all is a matter of un- or underemployment, hunger or worse, let alone those matters we now rate highly such as 'pride', 'status' and 'independence'. Capital's profits, on the other hand, were hardly seriously affected simply by any short-term disadvantage in the labour market. Struggles of this kind were often long lasting, fought to the point of desperation and involved entire occupational communities, yet it is by no means clear that they were more numerous than actions to increase wages. Of the industrial disputes counted by Dobson, 62 per cent of the 103 between 1790 and 1799 took place in the three years 1791–3 when the economy was doing well. Indeed, this surge was of similar size to the well-known one when a boom year followed the repeal of the Combination Acts in 1824.[5] John Bohstedt has even argued that collective labour action was 'predominantly offensive rather than defensive'.[6] I am not sure that one can be as certain. A large number of instances which he considers 'offensive' were directed at securing wage increases to keep up with prices, especially in the 1790s. In so far as these actions sought to preserve a customary standard of living, rather than to advance to a new level of comfort, then they could as well be considered 'defensive'. Furthermore, workers were often represented by their employers as seeking advances when they were in fact taking advantage of better times in the labour market to restore wage levels which had been earlier reduced.

However, even if their proportion of the total number of disputes is unknowable, it seems clear to me that labour actions of the kind which Adam Smith called offensive were a regular feature of rural, and to a greater extent of urban, industrial relations; so much so that I do not find it as anachronistic as some have suggested to write about 'industrial relations' and 'collective bargaining' in an eighteenth-century context. I think Marx saw this too, in respect of the way in which some skilled workers sold their labour power, and do not see how some passages in the 'Period of Manufactures' section of *Capital* can be read otherwise.[7]

Until recently, historians had seriously underestimated the occurrence of industrial disputes in the eighteenth century. Where they once talked of dozens, they now must accept hundreds. Robert Malcolmson's social history is perhaps the first general survey to recognise this: 'It appears however, that industrial conflicts were much more widespread than has sometimes been allowed.' Even so, Malcolmson is still content to place such disputes largely within a traditional, paternalist framework of popular rights: 'of the right to a basic subsistence; of the right to have their interests considered and taken account of by the established authorities; of the right to resist the "arbitrary will" of employers.'[8]

However, we also need to consider the 'aggressive' strike and the use of collective strength to improve conditions or advance wages, rather than to resist the impositions of employers. Even within a group of workers with well-established traditions of organised labour protest and of food rioting, both offensive and defensive forms of industrial action can be found. Adrian Randall remarks of the long-organised cloth-dressers that their industrial actions were very effective in times of good trade, even in keeping real wages up in the inflationary 1790s, and describes their use of the strike up to then as 'an effective offensive weapon'. However, after 1800, as a result of the attempted introduction of cloth dressing machinery, 'strike action was instituted more as a reaction to worsening conditions than as an aggressive weapon of improvement'.[9] Other groups could show a similar history. The calico-printers were so assured of their collective strength when they moved from London to Lancashire in 1783 that their employers called them 'gentlemen journeymen' and complained of their ability to gain 'most extravagant wages'. Although the journeymen lost a strike in a trade slump, they were able to make effective use of the rolling strike during the upswing of 1788/90. This success intensified the employers' search for cheaper methods of printing, either using cheap female labour or machinery. By the early nineteenth century the journeymen were desperately petitioning for a statutory regulation of apprenticeship in the trade. Here too a shift from offensive to defensive trade unionism brought with it an increased use of the language of the moral economy.[10]

The applicability of the 'moral economy' to industrial relations could be endlessly discussed in general terms, but there is, as Edward Thompson has recognised, a considerable danger of its losing its focus.[11] This study will proceed by examining three specific industrial disputes in and around Exeter. To some extent a case could perhaps be made for seeing each as an expression of the 'moral economy' of skilled labourers, but the differences in labour consciousness and purpose which they reveal suggests that we must go rather further than that if we wish to understand more fully relations of production and employment in eighteenth-century manufacturing. Exeter, it might be remarked, was the last outpost of the classic food riot in England.[12]

The Shipwrights in 1766

At Topsham, the point of the salt-water reach on the Exe, ship-building on a small scale took place, utilising some of the Scandinavian and Baltic imports which came through the port. In 1766, a year of high prices, the master shipwrights of the port were attempting to force wage-cuts and deteriorating conditions of work on their journeymen. This attempt led to an agreement among some of the latter not to accept work from any master on the new worsened terms. Eleven of them signed a remarkably formal document to this effect. They bound, under default of 'twenty pounds of lawful British money', not only themselves but their 'Heirs, Ex[ecut]ors and Administrators and Assignees' to an agreement which was to last 'for so long a time as any three of us shall be living and capable of working and labouring as a Journeyman Shipwright'.[13]

Two grievances were clearly set out in the preamble: reduction of wages and lengthening of hours, while a third – curtailing of beer allowances – appeared later. The formal legal appearance of the document reinforced a language redolent with phrases of 'rights' and 'privileges' confirmed by timeless custom and observance. The masters were seeking to deprive the journeymen of their 'Ancient Rights and Privledges [sic]' by reducing wages which had been 'from time immemorially paid' and by imposing 'new burthens' in lengthening the working day beyond what had been 'usual and customary for Journeymen Shipwrights to work and labour'. The journeymen bound themselves to accept no work for less than the 'full sum' of 2s. 6d. a day, 'being the usual and accustomed wages'. Nor would they accept any less than 'the usual allowance' of liquor. So far as hours were concerned they would work no longer than 6 a.m. to 6.15 p.m. in the summer, with half an hour for breakfast and an hour for dinner. In the winter months (November to 1 March) the same hours applied except that the dinner break was shortened by fifteen minutes. (As the agreement was drawn up in December, when the masters would have had little scope to extend the day, it may well have been the meal breaks which were at issue.)

Why were some master-shipwrights seeking to lower wages in 1766? That was, after all, a year in which resistance might have been expected. In their preamble, the journeymen claimed that the reduction would bring them to 'the greatest distress' and render them 'totally unable to provide for themselves and families'. On their 'usual' wages, which probably averaged out at 12s. 6d. to 15s. a week, they would have been well enough off at most times, but 1766 was a year of exceptionally high food prices. Wheat prices had been rising steadily since 1762 when the Exeter price had been 29s. 11d. the Winchester quarter. By 1765 it had reached 40s. $\frac{1}{2}d.$, then leapt to 50s. $2\frac{3}{4}d.$ in 1766. The price was then at a level it had last reached in 1756, when the City's first recorded eighteenth-century food riot had taken place. Not surprisingly food riots again broke out in Exeter and its district in 1766. One incident took place at Topsham, where the shipwrights lived and worked, only a matter of weeks before the agreement was signed. A corn cargo was seized and sold at low prices by a crowd who had marched out from Exeter. Wage cuts were being attempted at a time when even level earnings would have meant a substantial fall in living standards. The employers were probably seeking advantage from a slackening in the labour market after the ending of the Seven Years War. Small scale ship-building on the Exe was not directly affected, but the shipwright establishment at Plymouth Naval Dockyard was being reduced from its peak in 1763 when it had reached more than 600, and there can have been no shortage of skilled men in south Devon.[14]

There is no difficulty in fitting the skilled-worker consciousness revealed in the Agreement into well-established models which stress defensive and, more specifically, reactive attitudes. It is 'labour consciousness' of a sort, for its perception of a separation of interest is clear, but its theme is betrayal: the breaking by the masters of the time-honoured customs of the trade. The document seems exceptional in its form rather than in the mentality it reveals. Edward Thompson has remarked that the language of 'duties', 'obligations', 'reciprocity' and even of 'rights' is mostly that of historians. Written examples of that discourse are for evident reasons more found in industrial disputes than in those over food prices. As Robert Malcolmson has pointed out, it is in the nature of an industrial dispute that, if it lasted for a number of weeks, then both sides have to organise their resources, and clear signs of conscious organisation begin to appear among the workers, even when there is no clear evidence that they had a form of trade unionism before the dispute.[15]

The Woolsorters in 1787

Twenty years later a well-documented dispute in Exeter between the journeymen woolsorters and their employers reveals a form of labour consciousness which seems not to have been reactive to employer action or defensive in any more general sense. At the beginning of February 1787, a master woolstapler was approached by one of the three journeymen woolsorters in his employ. Times, he was told, were so hard that the journeymen could not support their families on their wage of 9s. a week and, unless it was increased to 10s. 6d., they would leave his service at the end of the week. This they accordingly did on the next Saturday when their demand was refused. At the beginning of the following week the four journeymen employed by another wool-stapler came into his counting house, asked for a rise to 10s. 6d. and, when refused, left immediately. The same evening seven journeymen quit the service of a third employer. The three masters straightaway laid information of illegal combination against the fourteen journeymen, who, they said, were members of a club and had 'entered into

Combination with others for the purpose of raising their wages'. Warrants were issued, and within twenty-four hours ten of the fourteen had been taken to either the Southgate gaol or the Bridewell and committed for one month by the summary jurisdiction of the magistrates under the 1727 statute prohibiting combinations of woollen workers.[16]

Within a week they were freed. They had solicited their employers to intercede and this had been done under the condition that the journeymen publish an apology recognising the illegality of their action, as 'a warning to others of the same business' and that they return to work at the old wages until mid-summer. The whole dispute, then, lasted only a week and seemed to involve only fourteen journeymen. However, because depositions were taken and survive along with other documents, it is possible to understand the background to the event in unusual detail. The woolsorters were indeed members of a 'club'. They were among the forty members of the 'Union Society', their name for the Exeter branch of the Woolstaplers Society which had been established in London two years earlier in 1785, and had 478 members over England.[17] (The woolsorters at times called themselves 'journeymen woolstaplers'.) The formation of the national club may well have been a formalisation of previously looser tramping arrangements, for this was the purpose for which funds were claimed to have been formed. Certainly the establishment of a national union seems to have given a measure of confidence to the Exeter men, for one boasted to a reluctant joiner that he had better stick to his present employer, for the Union could 'prevent his being employed in this city, or in any part of the kingdom by sending letters to all the Towns in England where the woolsorting business is carried on'. It seems, however, most likely that the City's forty members had been meeting in the Blue Boar's Head Tavern for some years before the establishment of the national society, for not only is it clear that they had long controlled entry to the trade, but they had also won wage increases since 1764, when they had been paid 6s. a week plus a shilling for taking home wool to cut off the pitch marks. In 1765 they increased this to 7s. basic plus the shilling, followed by 8s. (plus the shilling) in 1768/9 and to a basic 9s. in 1770 for work carried out on their employers' premises, being no longer required to earn the last shilling by taking work home. This steady increase of wages was quite against the trend for the City's workers, who, the weavers in particular, had been suffering falling wages from the middle of the eighteenth century. It had been 'won' by the journeymen, for the leading employer referred to the men as having 'advanced their wages' in 1765 and stated that in 1768 the men 'were dissatisfied and rose their wages' and in 1770 'again advanced their wages'.

The printed regulations issued in 1785 did not initiate the woolsorters' control over apprenticeship which was the basis of their exceptional wage bargaining success. According to one society member, it existed 'for the purpose of regulating the trade'. No member would work for any master who 'shall take an apprentice or journeyman contrary to their will, or secret rules'. In particular, they intended to keep out woolcombers, who in many cases worked for the same employers, and whose knowledge of raw wool would have been a basis for easy adaption to a trade where wages were comparable, but where hours were considerably shorter. The structure of the trade was that a population of around fifty journeymen were divided among perhaps eight or nine employers on whose premises they worked, performing an essential role in the preparatory stages of the serge manufacture. Were they in the real sense skilled? They do not seem to have had any rhetoric of skill or 'mystery', but the ability to judge, select and match different wools was certainly one which needed experience and knowledge. In pointing out that in Gloucester women were employed as sorters at only 4s. a week, one of the employers does not seem to have been denying the required abilities, but emphasising that the work was 'easy' in the sense of requiring no wage-compensation for hard physical labour.

For some time before the events of February 1787, the journeymen had been preparing to make a wage demand for 10s. 6d. a week, an increase of almost 20 per cent. A woolsorter who did not join the Society deposed that he had been pressured to do so for two months before the turn-out, but had refused, 'apprehending the true meaning of [?] association was to form some plan against the interest of their masters' and that 'they probably would raise their wages or refuse to work on some frivolous pretence'. The forty members paid 1d. a week 'towards the support of the travelling labourers, only in the same trade', but were in fact building up a strike fund which they judged, at the beginning of 1787 when it had reached £8, to be sufficient 'for maintaining the turn outs'. At 40d. (3s. 4d.) a week it would have taken almost a year to raise this sum, assuming there had been no calls upon it for tramping or other expenses. It would seem that the journeymen had been building up their strike fund from the founding of the national society in 1785.

One sorter, trying to persuade a colleague to support the 'turn-out', responded, when asked how he would live, that 'the Club would engage to pay him 10s. 6d. for this week', and that he 'would have wages from the Club until he was again employed'. Clearly £8 would not have supported a full turn-out of 40 men for very long and, with nice touch of irony, the journeymen had nicknamed their fund 'the loaves and fishes'! In fact, the Union Club was neither intending to bring out all its members at one time, nor expecting to have to stay out for long. Professor W. G. Hoskins, in a brief account of the dispute, notes that only 'about a dozen' sorters struck (in fact, it was precisely fourteen) and asserts on this basis that 'Most apparently refused to come out on strike' and labels the fourteen 'militant'.[18] This is a misreading of the documents. The turn-outs were intended to follow the strategy of the 'rolling strike' which was well known in several trades by the late eighteenth century. Only three shops were intended to turn out at the beginning, with support coming from those remaining at work: 'This informant having heard several shops had turned out on account of the Club asked ... what shop was to turn out next, to which he replied it is not as yet determined by them, meaning as he understood by the Club.'[19]

The strategy also involved the choice of moment: 'if they persevered a fortnight ... the Masters would be obliged to comply with their Demands, and that now was the time to turn out and get their price'. The arrested men had stated to the justices that they had thought the 'large stocks of wool on hand *would insure* them their demand'. In their retrospective assessment of the course of events, the employers also referred to them as taking place in February last, 'when the Masters had great quantities of wool on their hands to be sorted'.

The journeymen had been confident of success: they had the funds, the support and the moment. They must have had some among their number with memories of the masters' giving in to wage demands on earlier occasions. They seem to have been taken totally by surprise when their employers resorted so promptly to the law (which, indeed, they could have done when faced by the earlier demands). Why did they do so in 1787? As we shall see, their later inclination was to agree to pay almost as much as the men demanded. Among the requests for legal opinion, depositions, notices and other papers which make up the documentation, there is no expression of hostility or even bitterness from either side. It seems that the employers were concerned with the appearance of what they considered a tighter and deeper form of union among their employees. This is suggested by their insertion of an advertisement into the same issue of the *Exeter Flying Post* which carried the journeymen's apology, offering constant employment to any journeymen woolsorters, 'provided they do not belong to or are members of any Combination, Society or Club'.[20] A month after the dispute they issued a sheet of printed resolutions. They had met, they said, because of 'some *recent* combinations among their workmen' (their stress), and were unanimously agreed that 'Combinations among Labourers may be very prejudicial to them and also to the Masters'. They instanced a fine of 5*s*. imposed for violation of Union by-law as an example of an illegal act, as well as their 'very reprehensible conduct' in unlawfully directing woolsorters to leave the service of a master who took an apprentice 'prohibited in their System of Club-Laws.' This long-standing point of contention was emphasised in their specific assertion of the right to bind someone who had served his time as a woolcomber. If faced by combination in future, then the employers pledged themselves to mutual assistance.

At this meeting they also bound themselves not to pay more than the one wage of 9*s*. a week, but that was evidently not their major concern for among the papers is a letter from the leading employer seeking legal opinion on securing a regulation of wages from the City's justices at the next sessions. They intended to offer at the court a wage of 10*s*. a week throughout the year, without any increase in hours. They wanted the regulation 'in order to prevent the like Combinations of the Journeymen Woolsorters in future'. Legal opinion was that a rate could be set under the powers of 5 Eliz. I extended by 1 James c. 6. and that the application could hope for success if someone experienced in the trade testified 'that the price of labour has increased near fifty per cent within these twenty years without sufficient cause'.[21]

It is to be noted that in this dispute the wish for wage-fixing under 5 Eliz. I came from the employers. A motion for a wage table for the woolsorters was put at the mid-April Sessions, the employers' counsel arguing that such a regulation was needed 'to preserve the peace and commerce of the nation'. The discussion was adjourned until 30 April and then again until 19 May, but no record of its implementation exists, although the city was still following the practice of fixing weavers' rates, setting one of 7*s*. in 1791.[22]

How can the consciousness of the journeymen woolsorters best be described? The masters had not been attempting to reduce wages, increase hours or otherwise worsen the conditions of employment. Indeed, in the cited utterances of the striking journeymen there is no note of recrimination against either employers in general or any particular employer. It seems evident that we cannot place the consciousness evidenced in 1787 alongside that of the journeymen shipwrights in 1766 for it was neither defensive nor reactive. One of the striking journeymen had asserted that 'sooner than work for 9s. a week he would go home to the work house', while others had complained that 'times were hard'. Was the action, then, aimed at increasing wages in the face of a rising cost of living? If so, then it was not a short-term response to a recent price-rise. The turn-outs began early in 1787 whereas the price of wheat in Exeter in 1786 had been at 42s. 6d. the quarter, the lowest of the decade, lower than the 44s. 10¼d. of 1770 when the sorters had secured their last advance. Real wages seem to have suffered a little from 1780 to 1782 for wheat had been at its lowest in a thirty-year period in 1778 and 1779 and had then risen by a third to 1780, further increasing over the two following years to a peak of 52s. 10¾d. in 1782, higher even than in the food riot year of 1766. From that peak prices came slowly, but steadily, down until 1786. Had the journeymen received the extra 1s. 6d. in 1787, then it would seemed a genuine increase in their standard of living.[23]

Adam Smith accepted the disposition of workmen to 'combine in order to raise...the wages of labour'. In his account he begins by describing *defensive* combinations, but continues: 'workmen... sometimes...without any provocation...combine of their own accord to raise the price of their labour. Their usual pretences are, sometimes the high price of provisions; sometimes the great profit which their masters make by their work.' The generally pessimistic tone of this passage in *The Wealth of Nations* is qualified to some extent elsewhere in that work:

> Half-a-dozen woolcombers, perhaps, are necessary to keep a thousand spinners and weavers at work. By combining not to take apprentices they can not only engross the employment, but reduce the whole manufacture into a sort of slavery to themselves and raise the price of their labour much above what is due to the nature of their work.[24]

The local irony of 1787 is that there existed a tightly organised group of journeymen who occupied a strategic position in the chain of serge production prior even to that of the woolcombers, whom they particularly excluded from their trade and whose conditions of employment they bettered. There seems little doubt that this was achieved through 'Union' (the word preferred locally to 'Society'). How can we describe the woolsorters' form of labour consciousness, for it was clearly that, other than as 'a trade union consciousness'? Indeed, in Adam Smith's usage it must be defined as an *offensive* trade union consciousness.

Weavers and Combers in 1726

Events in Exeter, Taunton, Tiverton and other towns engaged in the serge manufacture which came to a head in early 1726 (late 1725 Old Style) are much better known, even if a failure to separate them adequately from events in the woollen cloth districts of the west country has produced a degree of misunderstanding. Failing to note that the petitions since 1707, as well as the evidence collected by the Commons committee which led to the Act of 1726 prohibiting combinations among woollen workers and containing the important wage-fixing clause, came from Devonshire and the adjacent parts of Somerset, Cole and Filson wrote of ephemeral combinations of 'country weavers' which were 'unlike' the local trade clubs of artisans and accordingly unable to maintain a continuous existence: that is, less like proper trade unions.[25] They were wrong. The organisation of weavers and combers in these serge towns *was* based on well-established trade clubs, and the evidence for continuous existence is indisputable. In 1707 the weavers at Taunton were reported to have a club with 'a common Seal, tipstaff and Colours, which they displayed at Pleasure and meet as often as they think fit, at their Club-house, being an Inn at Taunton'. At Tiverton the combers were organised at least as early as 1700. Petitions to Parliament reveal that by 1717 clubs of weavers and combers were an established matter of concern at Exeter, Taunton, Tiverton and Bradninch, and their activities produced the Proclamation of 1718 against 'unlawful Clubs, Combinations etc' (later 'lawless') among combers and weavers, who:

> illegally presumed to use a Common Seal, and to act as Bodies Corporate, by making and unlawfully conspiring to execute certain Byelaws or Orders, whereby they pretend to determine who had a right to the Trade, what and how many Apprentices and Journeymen each man should keep at once, together with the prices of all their Manufactures, and the manner and materials of which they should be wrought.

Journeymen who were out of work because their masters had refused their demands were supported by the clubs. Riots had occurred with cloths being cut from looms, houses broken into and prisoners set free. Although the Proclamation refers to the problem as existing 'in several parts of the Kingdom', it especially picks out Devon and Somerset. Petitions to Parliament in 1726 from Exeter, Tiverton, Bristol and

Taunton repeat the allegations of 1717. That from Taunton describes the clubs as having existed 'for some years past' and, significantly, as having 'assumed a power to raise their wages'. That from Exeter states that both wool combers and weavers had 'refused to work'.[26]

In fact, although there was a grievance over masters paying in truck,[27] the events of 1725/6 in the south-west were not really defensive or reactive: they were an attempt at employing both union and crowd action to advance wages. The basic approach was to make a wage demand and, if it were refused, to turn-out, no weaver or comber taking the places of those who thus struck. Workers who accepted work on the old terms were intimidated: one at Taunton was 'carried upon a Coolstaff' because he fetched 'Mr Myner's work contrary to the orders of the Club'. Indeed, over the last months of of 1725 and the early ones of 1726 crowd theatre was much in evidence in the streets of Exeter and the other serge towns. At Crediton a mob, headed by a 'Captain', threatened masters who refused to advance wages and paraded the town carrying aloft a piece of serge cut from the loom of one of the refusing masters. At Callington a master-weaver was coolstaffed, and others threatened with the same. At Taunton the town clerk, attempting to read the riot act, was treated to the ritual indignity of having his wig removed and dirt put upon his head. One employer at Exeter agreed to increase his weavers' wages although, he insisted, they had been willing to continue working at the old rates, but 'the Club threatened if they did so to pull them out of the house, and coolstaff them.'[28]

'Pull them out of the house': the phrase is significant. The weaving of serges was not organised under a putting-out system. The master weavers employed journeymen on their premises, but there was nevertheless little prospect for most journeymen of becoming masters themselves. The employment structure, in other words, more resembled that of, say, the London tailoring trade than that of the proto-industrial rural textile manufactures. Merchant capital in the Exeter district, except at Tiverton, kept aloof from the manufacturing processes. The master weavers were best described as prosperous upper-middling men. They were organised at Exeter into the Company of Weavers, Fullers and Shearmen, incorporated in 1490, which still managed to exercise a considerable degree of control over the serge manufacture throughout the eighteenth century. The master-weavers became a hereditary caste for the capital requirements of the manufacture were high enough to freeze mobility, but not so high as to define the master-weavers in the same terms as the 'gentlemen clothiers' of Gloucestershire. Indeed, 'clothier' was not a label in common use in the serge districts because of the separation of merchant and manufacturing capital. When we read of rioting journeymen coolstaffing a master, we know we are in a different world of industrial and social relations from those which characterised the woollen broadcloth districts. It is hard to imagine the great clothiers of the western counties, men who some-times did not even know the number of weavers to whom their wool was put out, being the subjects of such an *overt* infliction of indignity, although they might well have received letters like those sent to the master-weavers which threatened to 'burn their houses, kill their horses, and cut down and deface their orchards'.[29]

Clearly the number involved, and the crowd at Taunton was said to have numbered about a thousand, is the most evident difference between the incidents of 1725/6 and the disputes of the shipwrights in 1766 and the woolsorters in 1787. But we should not blind ourselves to similarities. As in the case of the woolsorters, turn-outs were to take place when wage demands were refused and those who turned out were to be supported from the funds of a union which pre-existed the dispute. Timing was also deliberate: 'they generally begin in the Spring, when there is the greatest demand for goods, and most plenty of work'. There was no talk of *defending* ancient rights and privileges against attack from employers, although the legitimacy conveying power of ensigns, flags and seals strongly suggest a degree of continuity with guild traditions. The petition from the weavers of Wiltshire and Somerset of 1718 in which they described themselves as 'poor' and 'distressed' and complained of an 'oppressive combination' of clothiers cutting wages by lengthening the warping bar 'contrary to law, usage and custom from time immemorial' and by imposing 'illegal and arbitrary' deductions from wages, seems not to have been echoed from the serge districts at this period.[30] Possibly we should think of an over-lapping of forms of consciousness, but something which could be described as 'trade-union consciousness' is clearly there.

There is, however, evidence which helps explain why the woollen workers of the Exeter district were so especially riotous in the winter of 1725/6. This is provided by the series of wheat prices available for the city:

Shillings per Winchester Quarter

1721	29s. 4¼d.
1722	30s. 8¼d.
1723	29s. ½d.
1724	34s. 6¾d.
1725	41s. ½d.

In fact the movement of cereal prices over 1725 shows the sort of abrupt increase over the year (38 per cent above the average for 1721–23) which later in the century would have precipitated food riots in the area. Food riots do not, however, seem to have occurred in the Exeter district until 1756. Thereafter they regularly did so, and, as Dr Swift has shown, persisted as a form of protest until those of 1854 provided the last English example of the genre.[31] Not surprisingly, John Bohstedt finds woollen workers 'the most prominent group' in the Devon food riots of 1790 to 1810. He notes their 'militant tradition', but also the decline of the industry. He concludes that their participation in food riots after 1790 represented:

> industrialization run backwards, that is a shift from associational to communal collective action. Strikes gave way to food riots as Devon's woollen industry unravelled. A formerly-powerful organised labour force could no longer stave off industrial disaster, but their militant tradition undoubtedly contributed leaders, experience, and pride to the communal food riots of 1795 and 1801.[32]

There is quality in the insight, but if there is a watershed in the consciousness of the weavers and combers from offensive to reactionary, it took place long before the food riots of the 1790s. By the middle of the eighteenth century the great days of the serge manufacture were over. Hoskins suggests that weavers' wages, then around 9s. a week, had fallen to 8s. by 1787 and 7s. in 1791; this last level had actually been fixed at Quarter Sessions and renewed up to 1800. In fact, despite brief interludes of relative recovery, the labour market never again so advantaged workers as it had done in the first quarter of the eighteenth century.[33] Food riots took place in the serge districts in 1756, 1766 and 1773. There is no suggestion of a watershed around 1790. The more surprising aspect is the absence of defensive industrial action on the part of weavers during their long wage decline.

Presumably the statutory prohibition of combinations of woollen workers had some short-term effect, for no industrial riots were recorded in 1727, although cereal prices then were extraordinarily high and well above those even of 1725. Disputes did not end in other serge towns, but in terms of Adam Smith's distinction they did become defensive. Those which have been recorded do seem to have been in reaction to employer action. Woolcombers at Tiverton in 1720 rioted against the use of ready-combed Irish yarn, and in 1738 marched with the weavers there as a protest against merchants who did not 'give a price for goods whereby a poor man can live'. One *dealer* was 'horsed on a staff' in this incident. The Tiverton combers struck against the use of Irish wool again in 1749, this time battling with the town's weavers who were waiting to work on it, the latter coolstaffing one of their own number who sympathised with the combers and refused to weave the Irish yarn.[34] (In fact, weaver reaction to Irish yarn was not entirely predictable. It was not simply a matter of reverting to self-interest after their combined actions of the 1720s. At Cullompton in 1787 it was said that a 'combination of weavers' was still preventing its use. This was, however, an outlying centre, and it is possible that the income of weaving households there depended upon the spinning earnings of the women, whereas very little spinning was done in Exeter itself.)[35] Unease among Taunton's weavers in 1764 was said to have been occasioned by the intent of a combination of employers to cut wages.[36] Perhaps the explanation lies in the persistence at Exeter of the old 'corporate' economy. The manufacture continued to be controlled by the Company of Weavers, Fullers and Shearmen. The Company, although taking on 'foreigners' from time to time, generally gave work only to properly apprenticed journeymen. This was in marked contrast not only to the more rural weaving centres, but also to Taunton where even by 1700 barely half of 3500 weavers had been properly apprenticed. After mid-century, when women were increasingly working at the loom elsewhere, the continuance of apprenticeship regulation at Exeter was one of the factors which meant that the decline of the serge manufacture there was accompanied by a very gradual decline in wages, controlled by the continuance of wage-assessment at sessions.[37]

Conclusion

The evidence from these three cases suggests that industrial disputes in the eighteenth century were complex phenomena, neither entirely within or without the reach of the 'moral economy'. Closer investigation of the combination histories of more groups would help. When a group of journeymen was on the defensive, it was most likely to invoke notions of the 'community of the trade' as a vertical consciousness group within which men and masters respected their reciprocal obligations. 'We are social creatures, and cannot live without each other; and why should you destroy community?' was the question addressed to their employers by the journeymen woolcombers of Norwich during a dispute in 1752.[38] As I have suggested elsewhere, the harmony of this form of 'community' was capable of renewal if temporarily broken by dispute, or broken perhaps by, as the Wiltshire weavers termed them in 1739, 'unmasterlike masters'. The poem entered in a silk-weavers' rate book after the bitter Spitalfields dispute of 1773 expressed a similar sentiment:

> May *upright* masters still augment their treasure,
> And journeymen pursue their work with pleasure.[39]

Journeymen cabinet makers issued a book of prices in 1788, below which they were not prepared to accept work. They denied they were dictating new terms to their employers, stating rather that they were seeking to 'conciliate mutual regard – to be treated as men possessing an ingenious art'.[40]

It is sometimes useful to refer, as Maxine Berg has done, to the 'moral community' of the skilled trades, the basis of their 'corporate, collectivist and solidarist idiom'.[41] But there is a fuller sense of 'occupational community'. Dr Berg remarks on a 'striking difference' between the cultural and community basis of the urban journeymen trades and rural or family-based manufacture:

> The custom and community which impinged upon the work unit of domestic industry, particularly on the women, was one which moved in quite different directions, out to a plebeian culture based on community ties between families and neighbours, not on the ties established between workers in a journeymen's association.[42]

Here, where 'community' refers to more than a trade, whose members may well not live in immediate proximity, but to a place where occupation is reinforced by locality and hence by family, kinship and neighbourhood relations, the 'moral economy' as a *holistic* device comes into its own. Adrian Randall's work on the industrial strife of 1765–66 and the food riots of 1766 in the Gloucestershire woollen districts confirms the existence of a 'community of shared values and expectations' incorporating beliefs and attitudes inexplicable by purely economic considerations underlying *both* forms of protest. He has shown, among several convincing links, that the tradition of protest 'extended out from industrial conflicts to embrace in particular food marketing and the price of provisions'. A history of 'active self-defence' already characterised the woollen communities when they faced the threat of machinery in the 1790s.[43]

Dr Randall asserts his 'industrial moral economy', not only against the 'compartmental' approach to protest, but also against Rodney Dobson's precocious stress on skilled workers' perception of labour as a commodity which could be bargained with, and his suggestion of this as a step towards a more 'modern' system of industrial relations. Among the groups of London artisans, tailors, compositors, hatters and others which Dobson mostly studied, one can sense an arena of interaction within which employers and workers to some extent perceived their roles and the moves which were open to them. Possibly even Dobson's suggestion of 'conflict resolution', based upon mutual recognition of bargaining strength, is applicable to some eighteenth-century industrial situations.[44] The dividing lines can be thin: the 'closed shop' is recognisably part of the language which surrounds wage bargaining, while 'apprenticeship regulation' invokes the corporate image of the artisan's traditional economy.

Both 'moral' and '*laissez-faire*' models of the economy embrace the recognition of labour *markets* and accordingly of wage *bargaining* in some form. What the 'moral economy' rejects is the *free* labour market, in which contracting is individual and in which labour is a commodity to be bought at the lowest price offered. Traditional labour markets were both segmented and regulated, and in them labour and capital were expected to bargain within accepted customary parameters. Different markets involved different forms of bargaining. 'Bargain' was itself part of the language of labour in some industries. It was the usual way of describing wage agreements in both Cornish mining and on the coalfields.[45] Dr Jaffe has shown that, on the north-eastern coalfield, by the early nineteenth century the collective bargaining around the annual 'bond' had combined with everyday bargaining over local situations at the different coalfields to create within working-class culture 'a fundamental acceptance of the utility of the market'.[46] There may well have been a degree of such acceptance by the beginning of the eighteenth century. Levine and Wrightson describe the pitmen as belonging by then to an 'antagonistic industrial culture', manifested as much in 'constant minor friction' arising from the 'unquiet nature of day to day industrial relations' as from the annual bond, although it was an attempt to change the date of the latter to the disadvantage of the pitmen which led to the major confrontation of 1765. Coal owners complained in 1713 that when food prices rose, the pitman 'accordingly set a value upon his Labour and all this goes out of the coalowner's pocket'.[47] Randall and Charlesworth consider the pitmen's 'undoubted industrial muscle' was effective enough in the preservation of living standards to make food riots among them rare, despite their industrial and community cohesion.[48]

Perhaps, as is suggested in my application of Adam Smith's sense of offensive combination in two of my selected case studies which indicated long and careful preparation before embarking on strikes, choosing the moment of maximum advantage[49] and the employment of deliberate strategies in industrial action, my conclusion is a qualified one: there is evidence enough of what can be fairly described as 'trade union consciousness' among eighteenth-century journeymen in a number of trades, yet I doubt whether any group had jumped with both feet into a 'system of industrial relations'. The language of times of confidence and labour-advantage did not persist when times changed.

Notes

1. E. P. Thompson, *Customs in Common* (London: Merlin, 1991), pp. 351, 338–59.
2. See C. R. Dobson, *Masters and Journeymen. A Prehistory of Industrial Relations 1717–1800* (London: Croom Helm, 1980), and John Rule, *The Experience of Labour in Eighteenth-Century Industry* (London: Croom Helm, 1981).
3. Lawrence Stone in *New York Review of Books*, XXXI, 5 (29, March 1984), p. 46; R. Price, *Labour in British Society* (London: Croom Helm, 1986), p. 29.
4. Ibid., p. 31.
5. Dobson, *Masters and Journeymen*, pp. 154–70.
6. J. Bohstedt, *Riots and Community Politics in England and Wales, 1790–1810* (Cambridge, Mass.: Harvard University Press, 1983), pp. 214–15.
7. Adam Smith, *Wealth of Nations* (1776, ed. E. Cannon, 1904; paperback edition, London: Methuen, 1961), I, pp. 74–5; see the discussion in Rule, *The Experience of Labour*, p. 147. See also Rule, 'The property of skill in the period of manufacture', in P. Joyce (ed.), *The Historical Meanings of Work* (Cambridge: Cambridge University Press), pp. 99–100.
8. R. W. Malcolmson, *Life and Labour in England 1700–1780* (London: Hutchinson, 1981), pp. 113, 126.
9. A. J. Randall, *Before the Luddites. Custom, Community and Machinery in the English Woollen Industry, 1776–1809* (Cambridge: Cambridge University Press, 1991), pp. 146–7.
10. *Facts and Observations, to prove the Impolicy and dangerous Tendency of the Bill now before Parliament, For limiting the number of Apprentices, and other restrictions in the Calico Printing Business. Together with a Concise History of the Combination of the Journeymen* (Manchester, 1807); M. Berg, *The Age of Manufactures 1700–1820* (London: Fontana, 1985), pp. 76, 84, 172, 279.
11. Thompson, *Customs in Common*, p. 338.
12. R. Swift, 'Food riots in mid-Victorian Exeter, 1847–67', *Southern History*, II (1980), pp. 101–28.
13. The only evidence on this dispute is a single document in the Devon County Record Office, 146 B/add 21.
14. The Exeter grain price series, here converted into *s. d.*, is in B. R. Mitchell and P. Deane, *Abstract of British Historical Statistics* (Cambridge: Cambridge University Press, 1962), pp. 486–7; W. G. Hoskins, *Industry, Trade and People in Exeter 1688–1800* (Exeter: Exeter University Press, 1968), p. 138; G. and

F. L. Harris (eds), *The Making of a Cornish Town. Torpoint and Neighbourhood through Two Hundred Years* (Exeter: Exeter University Press, 1976), p. 22.

15. Thompson, *Customs in Common*, p. 350; R. W. Malcolmson, 'Workers' combinations in eighteenth-century England', in M. and J. Jacob (eds), *The Origins of Anglo-American Radicalism* (London: Allen & Unwin, 1984), p. 154.
16. My account of this dispute is based on the bundle of documents relating to it in the Devon County Record Office: Misc Legal Papers Box 64.
17. The membership ticket of the Amicable Society of Woolstaplers is Plate II in Thompson, *Customs in Common*. The particular one reproduced came from Kidderminster.
18. Hoskins, *Exeter*, pp. 54, 60–1.
19. Devon Record Office Misc. Legal Papers, Box 64, Deposition of John Wood.
20. *Exeter Flying Post*, 22 Feb. 1787.
21. 5 Elizabeth I c. 14, usually known as the Statute of Artificers of 1563, had two main features: the requirement of serving a seven-year apprenticeship to trades and the empowering of magistrates to fix wages at Quarter Sessions. The first of these was repealled in 1814 and the second in 1813. 1 James I, c. 6 had been passed in 1603 to reinforce the wage-fixing power.
22. *Exeter Flying Post*, 18 April, 19 May 1787.
23. Mitchell and Deane, *Abstract*, pp. 486–7.
24. Adam Smith, *Wealth of Nations*, I, pp. 74–5, 141.
25. G. D. H. Cole and A. W. Filson (eds), *British Working Class Movements. Select Documents 1789–1875* (London: Macmillan, 1965), pp. 82–3, 86–8.
26. *Journals of the House of Commons*, XV, p. 312 (26 Feb. 1707); XVIII, pp. 715, 1717; XX, p. 598–9 (3 Mar. 1725); p. 602 (7 Mar. 1725); p. 627 (19 Mar. 1725); p. 647 (31 Mar. 1726).
27. *Journals of the House of Commons*, XX, p. 627.
28. Ibid., XX, p. 647.
29. For the Gentlemen Clothiers of the west of England broadcloth districts see: E. A. L. Moir, 'The gentlemen clothiers: a study of the organisation of the Gloucestershire cloth industry 1750–1835', in H. P. R. Finberg (ed.), *Gloucestershire Studies* (Leicester: Leicester University Press, 1957).
30. *Journals of the House of Commons*, XX, p. 627; PRO, SP 35/14 f. 132.
31. Mitchell and Deane, *Abstract*, pp. 486–7; No earlier riot is noted in A. Charlesworth (ed.), *An Atlas of Rural Protest in Britain, 1548–1900* (London: Croom Helm, 1983); Swift, 'Food riots in mid-Victorian Exeter'.
32. Bohstedt, *Riots and Community Politics*, p. 46. For a valuable critique of Bohstedt's important work see: A. Charlesworth, 'From the moral economy of Devon to the political economy of Manchester 1790–1812', *Social History*, 18, 2 (1993).
33. Hoskins, *Exeter*, p. 56.
34. M. Dunsford, *Historical Memoirs of Tiverton* (1790), pp. 226, 228, 230.
35. Hoskins, *Exeter*, p. 56.
36. *Exeter Mercury*, 11 May 1764.
37. Hoskins, *Exeter*, pp. 50–3.
38. Quoted in Malcolmson, 'Workers' combinations', p. 149.
39 See Rule, *Experience of Labour*, p. 209.
40. Preface to London cabinet makers' Book of Prices, 1788, Modern Records Centre, University of Warwick.

41. Berg, *Age of Manufactures*, p. 159.
42. Ibid., pp. 160–1.
43. See Adrian Randall, 'The industrial moral economy of the Gloucestershire weavers in the eighteenth century', in J. Rule (ed.), *British Trade Unionism 1750–1850, The Formative Years* (London: Longman, 1988), pp. 29–51, and Randall, *Before the Luddites*, p. 49.
44. Dobson, *Masters and Journeymen*, ch. 10.
45. For bargaining in the Cornish mines see J. G. Rule, 'Attitudes towards trade unionism and Chartism among the Cornish miners: A 'Configuration of Quietism'?', in *Tijdschrift voor Sociable Geschiedenis*, XVIII, no. 2/3 (July 1992), pp. 248–62.
46. The argument is pushed with great insistence and at some length in J. A. Jaffe, *The Struggle for Market Power. Industrial Relations in the British Coal Industry, 1800–1840* (Cambridge: Cambridge University Press, 1991).
47. D. Levine and K. Wrightson, *The Making of an Industrial Society, Whickham 1560–1765* (Oxford: Oxford University Press, 1991), pp. 392–4, 409–26.
48. A. Charlesworth and A. J. Randall, 'Morals, markets and the English crowd in 1766', *Past and Present*, 114, (1987), p. 204.
49. For examples of such strategies by weavers, woolsorters, printers, coopers fellmongers, shipyard workers and silk-ribbon weavers see Rule, *Experience of Labour*, pp. 178–9.

8

The Moral Economy as an Argument and as a Fight

James C. Scott

'The moral economy of the English crowd in the eighteenth century' is one of a handful of articles which actually merits a birthday celebration after twenty years. Unlike the vast majority of its peers which sank without a trace to a richly deserved obscurity, Edward Thompson's article has grown to a handsome and fertile maturity, spawning hundreds of offspring who may never have heard of their patriarch. It also follows, of course, that the better part of these offspring, if they were in fact brought to his notice, would be disowned as unrecognisable mutations.

As one instance of this motley progeny, I should probably begin by specifying what my own relationship to the article is. In 1973 and 1974, I was minding my own business at the Maison des Sciences de l'Homme in Paris, trying to understand the wellsprings of two major rebellions in Burma and Vietnam during the 1930s. I had written the first draft of a book manuscript on the subject and had two tentative titles: 'The Political Economy of the Subsistence Ethic: Peasant Rebellions in Southeast Asia' or 'Exploitation: A Victim's Perspective' (same subtitle). Although I was by no means completely innocent of E. P. Thompson's work, being a great admirer of *The Making of the English Working Class*, in which the phrase, 'the old paternalist moral economy' – first? – appeared, I had not yet read 'The moral economy of the English crowd in the eighteenth century'. The major theoretical and conceptual influences on my manuscript at that point came from Marc Bloch, A.V. Chayanov (the great Russian agronomist), game theory, and Richard Cobb's *The Police and the People: French Popular Protest 1789–1820*. Cobb's book, particularly Part Two, titled 'Popular Attitudes and the Politics of Dearth' with its analysis of *le droit à la subsistance* and of the claims and action of the *menu peuple* to enforce these rights, bears a family resemblance to the argument of

'The moral economy of the English crowd'. The enactment of the Jacobin Maximum, in fact, looks very much like an attempt to embody in positive law many of the 'price-setting' measures found in the 'eroded body of Statute law' ('The moral economy', p. 83) to which the English crowd appealed. Early in the process of revisions, I read Thompson's original article. It was enormously important in that it both clinched and extended the (much less elegant) argument I had been making with respect to south-east Asian peasants. Above all, it captured the sense of right and entitlement that suffused pre-capitalist practices and that alone could account for the sense of justified outrage and indignation so plainly evident in the rebellions I was examining. There were, to be sure significant differences in what I was explaining and what E. P. Thompson was explaining. (I specify the most important of those differences below.) Nevertheless, the term 'moral economy' seemed quite apt, and I appropriated it forthwith for my new title: *The Moral Economy of the Peasant: Rebellion and Subsistence in Southeast Asia* (1976).

This move turned out to be intellectually appropriate but strategically disastrous. If I had covered one flank with the arsenal of a famous British historian, I inadvertently exposed another flank to those of my American colleagues working diligently to reduce the study of politics to a few deductive principles on the order of neo-classical economics. For them, most of politics can be understood as the interaction effects of individual actors striving to maximise their expected 'profit' or 'utility' or 'power'. They generally call themselves 'public choice' or 'rational choice' theorists. Within four years, one of them (Samuel Popkin) flattered me by writing an entire book attacking my argument (E. P. Thompson will appreciate such instincts). It was modestly titled *The Rational Peasant: The Political Economy of Rural Society in Vietnam* (1980) *as if* I had been writing about weepy, irrational, altruistic, sentimental peasants. Seizing on the seeming pedagogic potential of a debate over distinct models of human action, many social scientists assigned both books to their students and watched the feathers fly. The result, aside from selling more books, was to generate a considerable secondary debate evaluating both positions and rarely, alas, returning to the original article we are both celebrating and re-examining here.

Lest my readers grow apprehensive, I hasten to assure them that the last thing I intend here is to provide a partisan account of 'The Adventures of "Moral Economy" in North American Social Science and in South-east Asia'.

I can be perhaps more provocative by setting myself three specific and limited tasks. First, it might be helpful to explain briefly how the problems I addressed in *The Moral Economy of the Peasant* differed from Thompson's objectives. The second task is to shift the focus slightly from 'riot' and 'the threat of riot', which represent the means of popular enforcement for Thompson's eighteenth-century crowd, to the social sanctions which operate at the community level to reinforce the claims of the poor to some measure of social insurance from their better-off neighbours. Although such activities seldom make headlines, they constitute a vital realm of collective political action that has yet to be adequately mapped and understood. 'Everyday forms of peasant resistance' in this sense also represent the elementary building blocks (in the Durkheimian sense) of political life upon which more elaborate forms – for example, the riot – are typically based. Here I want to make the case for the analysis of the micro-politics of class relations (a field that Thompson has also pioneered in, among others, *Whigs and Hunters*, and 'The crime of anonymity'), a politics which often stops short of fully-fledged public acts. Finally I want to emphasise the constant argument between classes over the 'moral economy' and the rights and obligations of the various classes towards one another that follow from this assumption. This debate over the meaning of 'paternalism' is, of course, intimately connected with the above- and below-ground struggle over material appropriation. The public dialogue, however, frequently provides the poor with rhetorical advantages that derive from the very history of hegemonic claims by their opponents. It is perhaps not so surprising that the poor are likely to do better in the debate than they do when the grain is divided.

Subsistence and Social Insurance

The argument of *The Moral Economy of the Peasant* began with a key material fact about most peasant households in colonial Burma and Vietnam: namely that they lived perilously close to the subsistence minimum. I found Tawney's metaphor characterising the position of the rural population in China as 'that of a man standing permanently up to the neck in water, so that even a ripple might drown him' useful for much of south-east Asia as well.[1] The search for a secure subsistence explained, I argued, many otherwise anomalous and apparently unrelated technical, social and moral arrangements in peasant society. To condense mightily, I argued that cultivation practices such as the sowing of many seed varieties, the preference for planting several fields with varying soils and micro-climates, and the avoidance of non-edible cash crops when they conflict with subsistence cultivation reflected a rational aversion to risk by peasants who were less concerned with maximising their crop than with avoiding a disaster. Given a choice, in other words, many peasant households would forgo profitable but risky strategies when, and if, they had a more reliable – if less profitable – alternative. The same subsistence concerns could be detected behind village customs that periodically redistributed cultivation rights, made small provisions for the maintenance of widows, orphans and dependants of conscripts, and for the social pressures impelling richer peasants to be more charitable, to take on more dependants, to be lenient about land rents in hard times, to sponsor more lavish celebrations, to help out temporarily indigent neighbours and relatives, and to give more to local shrines and temples. Personal dependency, in the form of patron-client links, represented a characteristic, if onerous, solution to the fear of hunger, not to mention physical protection. It is all too easy, and a serious mistake as well, to romanticise these social values and practices. They are not radically egalitarian. Rather, they imply only that all villagers are entitled to a *living* out of the resources of the community, and that living is often attained at the cost of a loss of status and autonomy. They work, moreover, in large measure through the abrasive force of gossip, envy and the knowledge that the abandoned poor are likely to be a real and present danger to the better-off villagers.

The importance of subsistence security to the rural poor in late nineteenth- and early twentieth-century Burma and Vietnam led me to re-examine indigenous concepts of 'exploitation'. Whether it was a question of the taxes collected by the state or the rents in grain and cash collected by the landowners, the absolute amount appropriated mattered less than what was left. Those claims on peasant resources that were adjustable, or varied according to the peasant family's crop yields and capacity to pay, were, other things equal, more tolerable (not necessarily *just*) than claims which were fixed and invariable and which thereby were more likely to aggravate a subsistence crisis. With this perspective, which I tried to demonstrate was in keeping with folk understandings, the colonial history of commercialisation and state-making could be re-examined in terms of how it exacerbated or eased the basic existential dilemma of the peasant household. Forms of tenancy, for example, could be compared in terms of the degree of subsistence security they offered rather than the average income they afforded. Descending levels of subsistence security in tenancy patterns (from share-cropping tenancy with leniency in bad years, to rigid share tenancy, to fixed cash rents) were feared in proportion to the risk they carried *despite* the fact that the average income of the riskier forms might be higher. And, of course, the smallholder feared losing his land and becoming a tenant while the tenant feared losing his tenancy and becoming a landless labourer (especially one hired by the hour or day rather than by the year). While the average income loss might be negligible from one step down to the next, the decline in subsistence security was potentially threatening. Actual shifts in land tenure in colonial Burma and Vietnam tended to follow this step-wise progression, exposing the peasantry to increasingly more devastating subsistence risks. As south-east Asia was more thoroughly integrated into the world economy, these shifts became more collective and hence politically more explosive, as could be seen in the aftermath of the 1907 world credit crisis and, most notably, the 'crash' of 1930.

A parallel analysis of the claim of the greatest landlord of them all, the colonial state, can specify those forms of taxation which were more or less deadly. The pre-colonial state, in addition to conscription and corvée, collected a host of taxes in specie and kind that were potentially deadly. If they were far less deadly in practice than in theory, this was due to the fact that the ambitions of kingly courts far exceeded their grasp. Their subjects often fled to the hills or the open frontier, their intelligence was limited, their 'bureaucracy' was porous to say the least, and their sanctions against the population, while draconian, were sporadic. It was a state with powerful thumbs but no fingers.

The colonial state, by contrast, gradually pinned down its subjects with nets of finer and finer official weave: cadastral surveys, population rolls, land tenure records, identity cards, court records, and so on. Even with the same fiscal system, the colonial state would have been able to impose itself with greater rigour than its predecessor. The amount – or percentage – of a peasant household's income that a fiscal claim might represent, while important in its own right, was often a less reliable guide to its political impact than the timing, inflexibility and nature of its collection. Thus a land tax at least varied with the size of the landholding even if it did not vary with the crop yield. A head tax, on the other hand, was typically a fixed cash claim that remained constant no matter whether the 'head' being taxed was rich or poor, an infant or a producer, and no matter how well the crops had fared. Here the fiscal logic of the colonial state ran directly counter to the subsistence logic of the peasant household. The head tax, though it might represent a small amount of total revenue, was the 'darling' of collectors of revenue for its yield was predictable and steady year in and year out.[2] For the peasantry, the colonial head tax was the worst possible levy; in a bad year it might mean the difference between starvation and survival. The only rival of the head tax in arousing dread and anger was the salt tax inasmuch as it raised the price of a popular commodity essential for preserving food and for preparing the fermented condiments (*nuoc-mam* in Vietnam, *ngapi* in Burma) that were staples in the local diets.

Under colonial rule, then, both the land tenure system and the fiscal system posed increasing threats to the subsistence security of the poorer rural populace. Of the two, the fiscal system, and particularly the head tax, was politically more volatile. Land tenure, as always, produced regional disparities and conflicting interests. The circumstances of large landowners, smallholders, labourers, tenants, rice planters, rubber growers and others led them in divergent directions and, occasionally, into conflict with one another. Opposition to the head tax, on the other hand (especially during an economic crisis like the Great Depression), produced nearly unanimous and militant opposition. Broadly considered, the threat to subsistence security emanated from many quarters including the closing of the frontier, the growth of colonial bureaucracy and military power in the countryside, the restrictions on the use of forests and wasteland, new disparities in landownership, cash cropping of non-edibles and commercial debt, among others. The colonial fiscal system was the flashpoint, however, largely because the French and British authorities insisted on pressing their claims in the midst of the economic calamity and because the forms it took were so deeply resented.

For social facts to become politically mobilising, they must be seen to be due to human (and hence reversible) action *and* they must affect many people in roughly comparable ways. Demographic pressure, the closing of the frontier, and – to a lesser degree – price movements struck the rural population hard, but were seen as largely impersonal and beyond the realm of political action. The claims of landowners and moneylenders were, in contrast, personal, but affected different classes of farmers, tenants and labourers quite unevenly and at different times. The head taxes of the state, however, were the logical issue around which collective indignation centred. They were collected by human agents at a time of great distress; they were collected from everyone; and they were collected simultaneously.

From Material Needs to Moral Entitlements

Thus far, a reader might reasonably conclude that the argument is entirely materialist and, for that matter, mechanical. Were we to leave it at that, these historical actors would be not much more than robots whose politics was directly 'wired' to their stomachs. This is precisely the one-dimensional view against which so much of Edward Thompson's scholarship – and wit – have been directed. This one-dimensional view comes in two quite different forms, I believe. The first is the bare-bones materialism I have just described. The second is an equally bare-bones emotionalism, perhaps most graphically captured not by Gustave Le Bon but rather by Zola:

> He had centuries of fear and submission behind him, his shoulders had become hardened to blows, his soul so crushed that he did not recognize his own degradation. You could beat him and starve him and rob him of everything, year in, year out, before he would abandon his caution and stupidity, his mind filled with all sorts of muddled ideas which he could not properly understand; and this went on until a culmination of injustice and suffering flung him at his master's throat like some infuriated domestic animal who had been subjected to too many thrashings.[3]

In this version, the 'wiring' is not quite the same but it most certainly does not pass through the 'reasoning' part of the brain.

If we concentrate our attention exclusively on the Saya San Rebellion in Burma and the Nghe-An/Ha-Tinh Soviets in Vietnam in 1930, it is clear that popular conceptions analogous to a 'moral economy' are animating the crowds. Petitions and appeals point to the injustice of collecting the usual taxes in a time of such economic hardship when the very survival of the taxpayers hung in the balance. (In Annam, the crisis was compounded by a series of crop failures in the region of the rebellion.) Although observers in Saigon, Hanoi and Hue might characterise the rebellion as a 'jacquerie', those closer to the scene remarked on the 'lawlike' and orderly confiscation of food supplies from the rich and officials and its meticulous distribution to the needy. As the French Inspector of Political Affairs in Ha Tinh emphasised:

> Small bands have instructions to hold wealthy people for ransom ... in a way that I would not call pillaging. It is not a question of acts of piracy accompanied by violence ... They thus look for stocks of paddy which excite the envy of people in need, which are then taken in an orderly fashion (*correctement*) and distributed.[4]

Popular wrath more than once proved fatal to those rare rebels who attempted to keep the food for themselves. Local officials, who were the custodians of communal paddy stores, delivered them up for distribution under threat of beating or execution. The poor, pleading hunger, at first asked to have the *capitation* reduced or postponed; next, they threatened the notables who insisted on payment and, when all else failed, sacked the tax office and burned the records. In Burma, the rebellion itself began on 22 December 1930, nine days before the collection of the head tax and just *one* day after the cultivators of Tharrawaddy (in the Irrawaddy Delta) had had their petition for a reduction or postponement of the tax refused by the acting governor.

If the appeals to a moral economy are much abbreviated and schematic in these two cases as compared with the eighteenth-century English crowd, the difference is surely due to the cultural and social distance between the petitioners and the colonial state. The opposing parties were, literally and figuratively, not speaking the same language. The Burmese and Vietnamese rural cultivators knew from long and bitter experience that their claims for tax relief in a crisis rarely gained a hearing and, if they did, were even more rarely conceded. The dialogue between Thompson's English crowd and the authorities who, even if their interests conflicted, at least shared the same language of paternalism, was unthinkable in Burma or Vietnam. Appeals to the customary responsibilities of the authorities in time of dearth simply made little sense in the colonial context, whether that context were south-east Asia or Ireland. Since the colonial authorities could not be summoned to observe their duties, they must be overthrown. Saya San, the Buddhist monk and would-be saviour king who led the Burmese rebellion, *did* in fact make explicit appeals to a tradition of reducing taxes when the people were hard-pressed. The appeals, however, referred not to English common law but rather to the pre-colonial millenarian tradition of a conquering Buddhist monarch who would end hardship and bring justice to his people.

The Micro-Politics of 'Moral Economy' in the Village

Thompson is surely correct when he points to the threat of riot as the trump card of the crowd, the card that gained them at least a reluctant hearing. The price-setting riot is, however, by definition, an urban – or at the very least a market – phenomenon. If we wish to explain village-level 'moral economy' practices and expectations, we cannot rely on the riot in the same fashion. By village-level moral economy practices, I mean any of a large variety of customs which precluded certain market outcomes in the interest of assuring the subsistence of the poor. These might include communal practices such as giving the poor a plot to cultivate from common land, surveying and dividing grain stores in the community after a crop failure, communal support in kind, cash, or labour for the indigent or disabled, and so on. More commonly, such practices were not formally communal but represented prevailing norms about how the 'honourable' rich peasant or landowner ought to conduct himself *vis-à-vis* his poorer neighbours and kinsmen. Such norms might include taking on more tenants and labourers than strict economic logic might dictate, providing loans to needy villagers and being liberal about the terms of repayment, sponsoring lavish feasts and celebrations at which the poor are fed, lowering land rents in a bad year, making gifts to the destitute and ill, or other such actions. It should be emphasised that these were normative ideas promoted with varying enthusiasm by different villagers rather than iron-clad rules applied in a administrative fashion. They thus represented a politico-ethical resource available to poor villagers in transmuting their needs into moral claims.

The question is: how are these practices sustained as more than the self-interested and pious wishes of the poor if the threat of riot is not invoked? On narrow material grounds, of course, the least well-off of a community have a vital – in the literal sense of that word – interest in maintaining these customs. It is not, however, immediately obvious why better-off villagers would give lip service to these claims, let alone act on them. Why would the wealthy in the village not prefer to keep their resources and relish the spectacle of the village poor reduced to a Hobbesian struggle among themselves to survive, thereby improving the bargaining position of the rich over wages, rents and services? Of course, it is undeniable that village elites have, in fact, taken advantage of subsistence crises to grab land and reduce wages. What is noteworthy, however, is that in much of village south-east Asia they have been unable or unwilling to take *complete* advantage of their strategic control over scarce land and capital to impose draconian terms.[5]

Two years of fieldwork in a rice-growing Malaysian village, which I shall call Sedaka, exposed me to much of the micro-politics of the moral economy. As this was a period (1978–80) of mechanisation, shifting tenure relations and commercialisation, there was a constant tension and debate about the reciprocal obligations of poor and wealthy villagers, with the rich attempting to renounce many practices they now found too costly. That they did not entirely succeed was due to the various pressures and stratagems brought to bear by poorer villagers.

Understanding this micro-politics has little to do with riot, though it has a great deal to do with 'threat', providing we take an extremely broad view of what counts as a threat. It requires that we grasp the shape of a shadowy form of collective action that works quietly but powerfully to bring about certain ends. It reminds us just how much of the political life of subordinate groups lies between public defiance and quiescence. It implies, in fact, that the goal of the peasantry is generally to stay out of the archives and newspapers and to conduct instead low-profile campaigns to which their political skills and resources are best suited. The micro-politics of the moral economy in Sedaka as described below is, to be sure, particular to its place and time. I attempt, however, to point to themes that might find echoes elsewhere.

Perhaps the most important resource of ordinary villagers might be called 'the politics of reputation'. Villagers can, if they have the weight of 'public opinion' behind them, damage or destroy the reputation of anyone in the village through character assassination, gossip, nicknames, innuendo and symbolic gestures. One of the richest landowners in the village was called 'Haji Kadir' to his face and 'Pak Ceti' behind his back. His public name recognised his pilgrimage to Mecca while his off-stage nickname removed the honorific 'Haji' and added 'Ceti', a reference to the infamous money-lending caste of South India, and thus to the suspect means by which he acquired the land he now owns. Rhymes are chanted offstage about his legendary cheapness: for example, how he has built the narrowest bunds in his paddy fields (almost impossible to balance on during the wet season) so he can plant one extra row of paddy; how he charges the neighbours for fallen coconuts that others always give away; how he gave the smallest contribution of all to the funeral expenses of his neighbour and harvest labourer. Like most gossip, the attack on Haji Kadir's reputation is always a commentary on the violation of norms of conduct. Such stories would not damage his reputation unless others agreed that such behaviour were blameworthy. Much of the gossip and character assassination relevant to class relations in Sedaka are an appeal by the poor to norms of tenancy, generosity, charity, employment and feasts that were taken for granted before double cropping. This gossip is not disinterested; it is a partisan claim against the rich. In this respect, the use of gossip is a kind of 'democratic voice' where power and possible retaliation make open acts of disrespect risky.

Yet why should the wealthy in the village care whether they have a good reputation or not? It is not only in Dickens' novels that one meets characters who are willing to exchange their good names for profits and interest. What is the cost of a bad name?

There are material as well as non-material costs to a bad name. Before turning to them, however, I want to explain how the non-material costs of a bad name are far from trivial. Most of these costs come in the form of subtle and not-so-subtle shunning and social boycotts. A very unpopular rich person will be passed on the village path without a greeting, as if he were invisible. His neighbours will be 'seen' to whisper about him behind his back.[6] In extreme cases the treatment will extend to his family. Villagers will be 'busy' when he gives a feast. They will either not invite him to their feasts at all or else invite him so late that he often cannot come. They will not speak to him at public gatherings. The final humiliation, the *coup de grâce* as it were, is not to come to his wake; a prospect of *social* death that is truly terrifying. It is a very rare and brave villager, however rich and ambitious, who is willing completely to ignore the opprobrium of most of his neighbours. The daily toll of slights and cold shoulders to oneself and one's family would be all but intolerable.

Notice that the effectiveness of social ostracism depends on the existence of a face-to-face community and on a reasonable degree of agreement in enforcing the sanctions.[7] The more permanent and immobile the face-to-face community, the more telling its social censure. It is for this reason, I believe, that the wealthiest families – often at the point when a new generation inherits land – tend in time to move to larger towns and the provincial capital. Not only do they wish to escape the material claims of neighbours and relatives, but they find it impossible to treat with impunity the public disdain that a purely market-oriented conduct would bring.

The importance of relative unanimity alerts us to the fact the pressure of social sanctions are at least as important *among* the less-well-off as *between* the less-well-off and the wealthy. Such unity, if it is ever achieved, is rarely achieved without a great deal of social friction. Any stratified society, after all, presents constant temptations to members of the underclass to break ranks and improve their situation at the expense of their fellows. If they resist this temptation it is likely to be due, in large part, to the threat of being shunned.[8]

The tenants and labourers of Sedaka generally observe a few rules that prevent them from benefiting at one another's expense. They will, for example, not offer a landowner a higher rent in order to get a tenancy another villager now occupies; women's transplanting groups (*derau*) will not offer to replace another village group or to work for less than the established rate; individuals will not take a job that 'belongs' by custom to another. When they are asked why they refrain, say, from outbidding another villager for a tenancy, they reply in terms that capture both the shame and guilt it would entail. They say: 'That would go against social opinion [*pandang masyarakat*].' 'I would feel embarrassed before my friends.' 'Our friends wouldn't agree to it; it wouldn't be seemly to scramble like that.' 'You can't cut [*potong*] your friends.' 'You wouldn't be respected.' 'He would be accursed [*jahanam*].' 'Someone who steals land like that would be despised [*denki*].' It is also abundantly clear that such vital matters can easily escalate beyond mere 'words' and social censure. As one poor man said: 'He [the displaced tenant] would be angry, he would go look for his machete [*cari golok*].'

One sure way of finding how strongly a particular custom is adhered to is to observe what happens when it is violated. The following case is the only instance I encountered of one tenant taking land from another in Sedaka. Until 1975, both Rokiah and Samat rented adjacent paddy fields from the same outside landowner: 4 *relong* (one *relong* = 0.7 acre) were rented to Rokiah and a single *relong* to Samat. On the strength of the fact that his mother-in-law had once owned all this land, Samat went to see the landlord before the 1975 irrigated season began and, by offering M$20 more in rent, persuaded him to transfer one additional *relong* from Rokiah to him. Since that day, no one in Rokiah's family has spoken to anyone in Samat's family. Although they belong to the same political party and Samat's store is the favoured one for party members, neither Rokiah nor anyone in her family has set foot in the store since then. In fact, some villagers claim, although Rokiah denies it, that she has been responsible for an informal boycott of Samat's store by others, which may explain why it failed in 1981. When Rokiah's daughter was married in 1980, Samat and his father Tok Mahmuud told me that they were the only two families in the village who had not been invited.

Two poor men in the village are the butt of gossip as being toadies (*tukang suruh*, *hamba*) of the rich landowners in the village. As one might expect, these two are precisely the men praised as 'good' (one of the explicit features of the 'good' worker according to the landlords was that they were not given to slandering their employers behind their backs!), 'loyal', 'honest' workers by the landowners in question. The stories told about them by the poorer villagers, however, are a standing warning of how not to behave if you want the respect of your peers.

Less-well-off villagers have other means of promoting a unity of perspective than 'talk'. They have a range of material sanctions they can bring to bear on their fellows: they can refuse to exchange labour

with them; they can deny them entry into the small rotating credit
groups the poor establish; they can deny them information about wage
work; and, in the final analysis, they have their machetes. But the striking fact about the relative unity which the poor do achieve is the
extent to which it is brought about by a powerful and unrelenting
social pressure.[9]

The influence that the poorer villagers can bring to bear on the
wealthy is hardly confined to 'the politics of reputation'. A wealthy
family in the village with a bad name is in danger of finding its property and, in extreme situations, its physical well-being in jeopardy.
Inasmuch as I have devoted much space to such activities elsewhere,
here I wish only to examine the pattern of paddy thefts in the village.[10]
The purpose is to relate those thefts to 'the moral economy' at the village level and to emphasise the degree to which such theft is, in this
case, quite precisely targeted and dependent on a high degree of solidarity among the village poor.

Thefts of paddy are quite common in Sedaka. Here we are not talking
about the petty thefts of grain by threshers who fill their pockets and
shirts with grain before leaving the field or who leave half-threshed
grain beside the threshing tubs for their relatives to glean, although
these 'thefts' are common. Instead, we are talking of whole gunnysacks
of paddy (roughly 130 lb apiece) spirited away from the fields at night
during the harvest. During the rain-fed season of 1979–80, I kept close
track of such reported thefts in the village; they amounted to 14 sacks.
While this represented considerably less than 1 per cent of the total
village harvest, it represents a significant addition to the food supply of
the poorest families in the village who, all agree, take the grain.

Such theft, in and of itself, is unremarkable. Three considerations,
however, led me to believe that this was not merely the random pilfering of the poor. The first is statistical. Of the ten landowners who lost
paddy, all but one were among the first, and hence most resented,
farmers in Sedaka to use the combine harvesters.[11] The second reason
relates to a declining tradition of Islamic charity. It was customary in
the past for the larger farmers to make gifts of paddy (typically) after the
harvest was concluded and to call such gifts *zakat peribadi* (private tithes).
The practice, now fairly rare, was especially widespread shortly after
the beginning of double-cropping when labour was short and served to
ensure that the labourer would thresh for the same farmer in subsequent
harvests. Labourers, naturally, came to see the gift as an anticipated
part of the wage itself. In this context, it is indicative that I twice heard
poor men refer smilingly to paddy thefts (*curian padi*) as 'a private tithe

that one takes for oneself' (*zakat padi angkat sindiri*). The thefts in question may represent a kind of forcible poor tax that replaces the wages
and gifts they no longer receive. At the very least, the description indicates that such thefts are understood quite differently by the village
poor. A final straw in the wind is that no such thefts from the field
have ever been reported to the police. Thefts of paddy from houses,
on the other hand, were reported, and one villager has spent time in
prison for just such thefts. When I asked why thefts from the fields
have never been reported, the wealthy victims of the thefts indicated
that they were afraid of provoking retaliation in the form of more
theft, arson, or even murder (*takut mampus*). One large farmer actually
saw a sack being carried from a neighbour's field, realised who the thief
was, and yet did not intervene to stop it or to report it to the police or
his neighbour. He explained that the thief had seen him too and, if he
reported it, the thief would know he was the informer and steal his
paddy next. For a handful of the more daring village poor, it would
appear that something of a small balance of terror has been struck that
permits such (social?) pilfering to continue.[12]

I have deliberately concentrated on the more banal and daily aspects
of class relations in Sedaka. Other, more dramatic alternatives, were
available. When, in 1976, combine harvesters began to make serious
inroads into the wages of poor villagers, the entire region experienced
a rash of machine-breaking and sabotage reminiscent of the 1830s in
England. The provincial authorities called it 'vandalism' and 'theft',
but it was clear that there was a fairly generalised nocturnal campaign
to prevent the use of combines. Batteries were removed from the
machines and thrown into irrigation ditches; carburettors and other
vital parts such as distributors and air filters were smashed; sand and
mud were introduced into the gas tanks; various objects (stones, wire,
nails) were used to jam the augers; coconut trees were felled across the
combine's path; and at least two machines were destroyed by arson.
Two aspects of this resistance deserve emphasis. First, it was clear that
the goal of the saboteurs was never simple theft, for nothing was actually stolen. Second, all of the sabotage was carried out at night by individuals or small groups acting anonymously. They were, furthermore,
shielded by their fellow villagers who, even if they knew who was
involved, claimed total ignorance when the police came to investigate.
As a result, no prosecutions were ever made. The practice of always
posting a night watchman to guard combines dated from this period.

The achievements of this 'everyday resistance' are modest. It almost
certainly retarded the full adoption of combines by several seasons,

but it did not prevent combine harvesting. If the larger landowners hire a few more labourers than they strictly require, provide a bit more Islamic charity, and let out some land to tenants that they might otherwise farm themselves, this is surely due in some measure to the social pressure of the poor. Where the pressure alone fails, the poor manage simply to appropriate some of their grain needs. Possibly, although it would be hard to tell, the poor may have been spared further inroads into their subsistence security due to the resistance, modest though it may be, that they have thus far demonstrated.

The Sedaka poor pose a 'threat' to the reputation, property, conduct and physical well-being of the wealthy. That threat is not, for reasons too elaborate to detail here, a threat of 'riot' but a much more modest and localised threat. It requires a relatively high level of 'mutuality' to be at all successful. That mutuality takes at least two forms. It depends on a shared opinion about the obligations of the wealthy with respect to feasting, employment, loans, charity, mechanisation, tenancy and honour which allows them to deploy quite well co-ordinated politics of reputation via gossip, nicknames and shunning. It also rests on a willingness not to break ranks to curry favour among the rich and, at the very least, to avoid giving evidence against one another. At most, it sustains the widespread nocturnal attacks on the threshing machines.

The term 'mutuality' is misunderstood if it is taken to mean a pattern of sanctions and social relations that is frictionless. The fact is that solidarity among the village poor and, in other settings, in the village as a whole, is only achieved at the cost of some considerable social conflict. Although such solidarity is underwritten by a consensus about social conduct, there is always the temptation to evade this consensus to gain a tenancy, a job, or some other benefit. If these temptations are by and large resisted, it is also because, in the final analysis, there are sanctions of gossip, material costs and even physical harm that can be brought to bear. Thus we have something of a paradox. Social conflict of a particular kind is typically *the condition* of social solidarity (among the poor *vis-à-vis* the rich in a village or of the village *vis-à-vis* outside authorities). The existence of a great deal of social tension, back-biting and even violence within a group, far from being prima-facie evidence of a lack of solidarity, *may* actually be the social machinery by which its solidarity relative to a social antagonist is created and sustained.

I suspect finally that such homely activities, as a sub-species of collective action in its own right, represent the micro-foundations of larger acts that *do* figure in the archives and newspapers. As Thompson has noted in 'The moral economy' (1971, p. 119), 'In truth, the food riot did not require a high degree or organization. It required a consensus of support in the community, and an inherited pattern of action with its own objectives and restraints.'

It is not so much that little organisation is required but rather that, in this instance, the organisation is embedded in a pattern of pre-existing practices of resistance. Here we need look no further than the ubiquitous Malay feast for a model of co-ordination without formal organisation or hierarchy. The feast and its variations have been so often repeated that virtually anyone arriving knows just what has to be done and at what tasks their labour is required: peeling onions, collecting firewood, setting out the bowls, etc. Like a repertory company that has played Hamlet hundreds of times, anyone can recognise the role that needs to be filled and step in.[13] The understandings and practices that constitute the basis of such homely forms of resistance are, I believe, the enabling conditions of larger political acts, such as riots, that appear to come 'out of nowhere'. Political authorities, it is worth nothing, often make the same mistake, assuming that any crowd assembled in opposition to them must have been mustered by agitators or organisers whose seizure, they believe, will dissolve the seditious gathering. To make such assumptions is, at least among the peasant societies with which I am familiar, to miss forms of co-ordination that suffuse daily practice.

The Logic of Local Paternalism

The poor and wealthy in Sedaka are not only having a fight, albeit a low profile fight; they are also having an argument. By drawing on my fieldwork there I hope to elaborate a bit on the micro-foundations of paternalist rhetoric and to suggest why those most disadvantaged by the imposition of capitalist relations of production often have, paradoxically, something of rhetorical advantage.

In order to grasp the contours of this argument, some understanding of what has happened to agrarian class relations over the past decades, and particularly since the introduction of large combines, is helpful. The Kedah rice plain was, at the turn of the century, a frontier. A combination of bureaucratic influence, money-lending and force conspired to foster a highly inegalitarian land-tenure pattern. For substantial farmers, the key production problem was the timely and reliable mobilisation of a labour force for the major operations of transplanting, reaping and threshing. The constraints of a rain-fed production schedule produced striking peaks of labour demand which, even with the use of migrant labour from Kelantan and Thailand, required readily available local help in the inevitable rush to get the paddy planted and harvested. In the three or four years between the beginning of double-cropping and the introduction of combine harvesters, the problem of labour supply actually became more severe. Under these circumstances a set of social practices developed which was intended to tie labourers and desirable tenants to landowners.[14] These practices included frequent feast-giving by the wealthy, loans and advance wages, Islamic charity, a 'bonus' sack of paddy after the harvest to most labourers, reduced rents for tenants after a crop failure or illness, and – by no means trivial – social recognition and respect shown to poorer villagers.

These practices, to be sure, were underwritten by the material interests of the larger landowners competing for scarce labour and wary of the other 'weapons of the weak'. What is notable for our purposes, however, is the extent to which these practices were given a moral, 'euphemised' form that, in public at least, went unchallenged. Landowners described the bonus of paddy they gave as *zakat peribadi* (personal Islamic charity), their loans and advances as *sedekah* (alms) or *bantuan* (assistance/help), their lenience about rents after a bad year as *hati besar* (big-heartedness), and so on. I do not mean to imply that the village poor necessarily accepted these self-descriptions by the well-to-do. In fact, while large farmers regarded the sack of paddy given to labourers after the harvest as a 'gift' or a 'favour' (that is, as discretionary), it is clear that the labourers themselves came to regard it as part of their wage to which they were entitled as a matter of right. But in the public sphere of village class relations (what I would call the 'public transcript') it was rarely in the interest of the poor to challenge openly the euphemisms used by the wealthy to characterise these practices. In the realm of public discourse, a language of paternalism and beneficence held sway.

This public discourse is a double manipulation, as Edward Thompson has recognised in another context:

> And the deference was often without the least illusion; it could be seen from below as being one part necessary self-preservation, one part calculated extraction of whatever could be extracted. Seen in this way, the poor imposed upon the rich some of the duties and functions of paternalism just as much as deference was in turn imposed upon them.[15]

I can ground this important insight in a particular example from Sedaka, in which it was possible to 'peek' backstage. Hamzah, a poor labourer, knows that his frequent employer, Haji Kadir, is in a position to provide him with, say, work or a loan against future wages. He also knows that Haji Kadir and others like him have typically described such actions as 'help' (*tolong*) or 'assistance' (*bantuan*). Hamzah then *uses* this knowledge to pursue his concrete ends; he approaches Haji Kadir using all the appropriate linguistic forms of deference and politeness, asking for *bantuan* or *tolong*. In other words, he appeals to the self-interested description that Haji Kadir would give to his own acts to place them in the most favourable light. In the safety of friends, Hamzah complains bitterly about Haji Kadir, but he is careful not to let his anger spoil his chance of extracting a favour. When, for example, I ask him why he did not complain when Haji Kadir shortchanged him on his wages recently, he replied: 'Poor people can't complain; when I'm sick or need work, I may have to ask him again'; and 'I am angry in my heart.' If Hamzah's public performance succeeds, he not only achieves his immediate objective of a loan or a job, but he contributes willy-nilly to the public legitimacy of the principles to which he will strategically appeal.[16]

From one perspective, what the wealthy did was to transmute a portion of their disproportionate economic means into forms of status, prestige and social control by means of acts which they *passed off* as voluntary acts of generosity or charity. It is significant that they achieve this amalgam of public prestige and social control *only* by claiming that they 'socialise' the profits of their property by putting it to public good. The social control they achieve was, of course, again covertible into labour services and hence again into material wealth. As a public, on-stage social discourse, this process was uncontested.

Double-cropping, mechanisation and growing state power have, in the meantime, made possible a massive shift in production relations. Large farmers and landowners have dismissed tenants, replaced wage workers with machinery, raised rents and introduced leasehold tenancy which older tenants cannot afford. The shift in the balance of economic power has also enabled them to curtail a host of social practices that were part and parcel of earlier production relations such as Islamic charity, loans and advance wages, lavish feasts, and even daily forms of social respect accorded the poor.

While the new agrarian order has provided larger landowners with great practical advantages in improving their bargaining position *vis-à-vis* tenants and labourers, it has left them almost bereft of an ideological discourse by which they can justify their new behaviour. No Adam Smith or David Ricardo has appeared who would clothe the actions of the wealthy farmers in the mantle of justice or, at least, inevitable economic law. The ideological struggle in Sedaka thus takes place almost entirely *within* the normative framework of the older agrarian system. The struggle is, in other words, within what most observers would call an existing hegemony. Small-holders, petty tenants and landless labourers are continually using the values and rationale of that earlier – and still hegemonic – social order to press their claims and to disparage the claims of the rich. Ideologically speaking, the large landowners find themselves hoisted on their own petards. The poor make abundant use of the values of help, charity and assistance that richer villagers have typically used to describe their own behaviour. They stigmatise the rich as hard hearted and stingy, thereby turning the values of generosity and liberality against those who once justified their property and privilege in just such terms. They insist, albeit in vain, on their right to employment and to tenancies, which the large landowners once claimed to bestow upon them out of a sense of helpfulness. In each respect, the claims of the poor derive their normative force and strategic value from the fact that lip service is still being paid to them by the locally dominant elite.

It is paradoxical, but perhaps not all that rare, for those who are marginalised by an economic transformation to have rhetorical advantages that seem to far outstrip their practical power. The revolutionary character of capitalism (and of capitalists) is such that they are continually uprooting the expectations and practices of earlier relations of production. Malay landowners want, naturally, to realise as much profit as possible from their land, now that double-cropping and mechanisation are available. But they have not yet absorbed a *laissez-faire* view of the world in which a straightforward appeal to the laws of supply and demand would satisfy them or their interlocutors. They are obliged, instead, to make creative use of the nooks and crannies of the older agrarian discourse to justify themselves. Thus they have developed a nearly Victorian view of the 'deserving poor' (very few indeed) and the 'undeserving poor' (almost all the village poor) that allows them to maintain that they are, in principle, charitable and generous, while avoiding much in the way of actual charity. They are thus unable to claim openly that it is on pure market grounds that they are transferring land from one long-standing tenant to a competitor (often a stranger) who can pay a higher rent. Instead they will claim (often in complete bad faith) that they have bad debts or medical bills that 'force' them to take back the land. Alternatively, they will take back a tenancy, claiming that it is for a needy son (this move is justifiable in the older scheme of things) and, after one season, rent it out to an out-sider or Chinese paying premium rents. Examples could be multiplied. The point is that the landed elite lack a worldview, a language of dis-course, which would legitimise the practical advantages they now rush to enjoy. They must make do with a rickety bricolage of elements which they have inherited from the paternalist moral economy in which they grew up. Nor is it merely a question of needing a language that would justify their new behaviour in the eyes of the poor: no such language exists. Rather, they need a language that will legitimise their actions to themselves. They are, collectively, like Dickens' Mr Wegg (*Our Mutual Friend*), in 'that very numerous class of imposters, who are quite as determined to keep up appearances to themselves as to their neighbours.' Most dominant ideologies, I suspect, are like this. They are less important for convincing subordinate groups of the truth and jus-tice of the social order in which they live than as 'just so stories' whose purpose is to instil unity, conviction and a sense of larger purpose among the elites themselves. On this view, the function of a ruling ide-ology is not primarily to convince underlings that the social order is fair, or, failing that, inevitable. It seldom succeeds in this because the implicit promises of that hegemony are typically contradicted in crucial ways by the lived experience of subordinate classes. The capital (no pun intended) thing that a ruling ideology does often accomplish, however, is to induce a kind of self-hypnosis that allows ruling groups to go about their daily and often socially unpleasant business of profit and rule with a certain confidence that they are nobly accomplishing God's will or natural law. If piety and progress can be conjoined, so much the better.

There is frequently, however, a temporal gap between the brusque advances of capitalist production relations and the ideological work designed to euphemise and naturalise them. It is especially in this tem-poral gap, when economic practice is at variance with received values, that subordinate groups frequently have the rhetorical resources and sense of justice that foster indignation and resistance.

Notes

1. I did not realise at the time that Tawney had taken this metaphor, without attribution, from Hippolyte Taine.
2. Head taxes were a staple of all pre-colonial revenue systems as well. The dif-ference was that techniques of evasion meant that a substantial proportion of the rural population escaped the tax rolls altogether (on the order of 20%), there were fairly routine mechanisms for reducing or suspending the tax after a crop failure, and, in any event, the means of collecting the tax against stiff resistance and flight were quite limited.

3. Emile Zola, *La Terre*, trans. Douglas Parmée, (Harmondsworth: Penguin, 1980), p. 91.

4. Weekly Report to the Inspector of Political Affairs at Thanh Hoa from Inspector Lagreze, 20 April 1931.

5. The evidence for this is more than anecdotal. Akimi Fujimoto examined four paddy-growing villages, each in a different area of Malaysia, to determine whether rent levels, land prices, the amount of land rented out, and the wages and volume of agricultural labour could be explained entirely by neo-classical assumptions of maximising net return. He concluded, in each case, that actual practice did not coincide with these assumptions and that 'noneconomic' income-sharing assumptions were necessary to explain 'sub-optimizing' outcomes. A good many landowners did, in fact, take on more tenants, charge lower rents and hire more labourers at higher wages than was compatible with maximising their net return: 'Land Tenure, Rice Production, and Income Sharing among Malay Peasants: A Study of Four Villages', PhD thesis, Flinders University, Australia, 1980. For Java, see Martin Ravallion and Lorraine Dearden, 'The distributional outcomes of a "moral economy"', mimeo, Department of Economics, Research School of Pacific Studies, The Australian National University, no date.

6. In Andalusia, one form of social aggression is for villagers to cup their hands openly, whispering to one another and pointing at their intended victim, as he passes by. He knows they are publicly gossiping about him, but he hears nothing explicit. Deployed repeatedly and widely, such gossiping has been known to drive people out of the village or even to suicide.

7. See Donald Black, 'Social control as a dependent variable', in Donald Black (ed.), *Toward a General Theory of Social Control*, vol. I (Orlando: Academic Press, 1984), pp. 1– 36, for a review of the literature and its findings.

8. One of the best empirical studies of social pressure promoting solidarity and egalitarianism among agricultural labourers remains Juan Martinez-Alier, *Labourers and Landowners in Southern Spain*, St Antony's College, Oxford, Publications No. 4 (London: Allen & Unwin, 1971).

9. The nearly fatal shortcoming of this social pressure is that it is largely con-fined to the village: that is, to the face-to-face community where it is most powerful. Villagers will not compete with one another for tenancies or wage labour, but such competition with outsiders does take place, although it is frowned upon. When combine harvesters were first introduced into the village, thereby eliminating many harvesting and threshing jobs, one labour gang (*derau*) of women transplanters decided to deny transplanting services to the landowners who had first rented the combines. Rather than openly refusing to transplant, they simply postponed the work, claiming that they were too busy with other fields. The anxious landowners approached the three other transplanting gangs in the village but all refused to replace their neighbours. The landowners eventually broke the boycott by hiring gangs from elsewhere. At the same time, the boycotting women were seeking transplanting work in other villages. At least one of the jobs they accepted was being boycotted by local residents although *derau* members claim they didn't know that the time they accepted the work. Thus, if we take a supra-village view, transplanters who were enforcing local boycotts were, by accept-ing work elsewhere, almost certainly breaking each other's local strikes.

Whenever, as is typically the case, the labour market is larger than the unit of peasant solidarity, the effectiveness of class action is fatally compromised.

10. *Weapons of the Weak: Everyday Forms of Peasant Resistance* (New Haven, Conn.: Yale University Press, 1985), pp. 241–303.

11. The exception may be one that proves the rule. He is Samat (see above), who is disliked for having outbid another villager for a tenancy.

12. A related 'attack' on property fitting this pattern is the murder of livestock under certain circumstances. Many of the wealthy, and virtually none of the poor, keep livestock: goats, steers and water buffalo. Occasionally the animals, which the poor believe should be tethered, break into paddy fields and nursery beds of seedlings, trampling and grazing. When this happens, the animal is often killed. The 'moral economy' aspect of such slaughter is apparent in how the poor justify it: 'His meat was eating my vegetables!' (The poor eat meat only at feasts and it is virtually part of the definition of being wealthy in this context that one can eat meat without being invited to a feast.) I know of only one water buffalo killed in this fashion (after repeated transgressions) but the killing of chickens that are discovered in a poor family's compound pecking at grain through the small holes in a gunnysack is quite common. In all these cases, the animal is never taken and eaten; it is left for the owner to discover, at the site of the transgression. No 'crimes' of this kind have ever been reported to the police.

13. See in this context the fine article by William M. Reddy. 'The textile trade and the language of the crowd in Rouen 1725–1871', *Past and Present*, 74 (February 1977), pp. 62–89. Reddy argues that it was precisely the *lack* of organisation in crowd behaviour that was enabling, and that the crowd came to value and use spontaneity in the knowledge that it was the most effective and least costly means of protest. The cultural understandings were so well developed that any just grievance could, he claims, bring together a crowd without any planning or organisation, let alone formal leadership.

14. A single family could ordinarily manage more than 15 *relong* (4.5 hectares) by itself, even with hired labour. Thus landowners with more land were generally obliged to rent it out to tenants.

15. E. P. Thompson, 'Eighteenth-century English society: class struggle without class', *Social History* 3, 2 (May 1978), p. 163.

16. Compare this with the following quote from a southern black sharecropper:

> I've joked with white people in a nice way. I've had to play dumb sometimes – I knowed not to go too far and let them know what I knowed, because they'd taken exception of it too quick. I had to humble down and play shut-mouthed in many cases to get along, I've done it all – they didn't know what it was all about, it's just a plain fact... And I could go to 'em a heap of times for a favor and get it... They'd give you a good name if you was obedient to 'em, acted nice when you met 'em and didn't question 'em 'bout what they said they had against you. You begin to cry about your rights and the mistreatin' of you and they'd murder you.

Theodore Rosengarten, *All God's Dangers: The Life of Nate Shaw* (New York: Knopf, 1974), p. 545.

9
The Moral Economy of the English Countryside

Roger Wells

Introduction

In his 'Moral economy reviewed', Edward Thompson expressed excitement at the concept's trajectory across two decades of intense interdisciplinary scholarship, but was cautious over indiscriminate applications: if 'moral economy values ... on their own, make a moral economy then we will be turning up moral economies everywhere'. When the moral economy was 'extended to other contexts ... it must be redefined' to preserve its critical 'focus'. This test was not passed by Keith Snell, the historian of English agrarian labour, who argued a case for a countryside moral economy. Snell's model included traditional live-in farm service, which facilitated initial work-experience for the young of both sexes, mature labourers' rights to 'fair wages', their families' entitlements to reasonable consumption patterns and 'fashion and leisure pursuits'. Finally, and quite crucially, Snell's moral-economic model also embraced the right to poor-relief for those in genuine need of public assistance at times during their lives. These inclusions comprised a hotchpotch and earned a stern rebuke for lack of clarity from Thompson. In his estimation, Snell's brief, imaginative, but unsystematic attempt to identify a countryside moral economy did not satisfy the exacting redefinitional exercise.[1] Snell's principal error, Thompson argued, was the removal of '"values" or "moral attitudes" out of the context of a *particular historical formation*'.[2]

The present chapter evaluates the case for the identification of an English countryside moral economy through examining the country's premier cornlands[3] between 1760 and the late 1830s. Developments over these years constitute a particular historical formation. The agricultural revolution of this period constituted a transformation of

209

agrarian economy and society[4] with the exposure of entire rural communities to rapid socio-economic change, driven by a very marked intensification of agrarian capitalism in unison with a demographic explosion. However, this time scale must be divided into two very distinct periods. For agrarian capital at least, the years to 1815 witnessed accelerating prosperity. The end of the French wars proved a watershed. Thereafter, the agrarian economy fell into prolonged depression. These contrasting periods are critical but they do not compromise Thompson's insistence on a particular historical formation. Rural communities' accommodation of change germinated a distinct rural variant of moral economy, ensuring that all retained a legitimate place with a right to at least a basic standard of living. In essence this countryside model functioned to reconcile the conflicting interests of capital and labour, during both the decades of prosperity and the years of depression, to ensure a rough socio-economic equilibrium.

The main analytical component of this chapter explores multifarious social protest in conscious imitation of Thompson's pioneering work on the 'food riot'. Indeed, those disturbances are relevant here, though of lesser consequence than the demonstrably rural revolts, the East Anglian 'Bread or Blood' protests of 1816, the broader 'Captain Swing' quasi-insurrection of 1830, and the less spectacular reaction to the New Poor Law's implementation in 1835–36. Rural workers' recurrent attempts to adopt trade-unionist tactics also figure, as does protest against parliamentary enclosure and discontent over Old Poor Law administration. These also reveal pronounced recourse to covert forms of action, ranging from 'malicious' minor damage to property, to animal-maiming and especially incendiarism. As an analytical tool to explore changing popular perceptions and ideologies, this reconstruction of a rural moral-economic model goes further than Professor Tilly's inadequate conceptualisation of 'contentious gatherings' and their shifting 'repertoires' across time,[5] embracing additional phenomena, notably 'social crime', threatening letters and popular ballads. More orthodox contemporary commentary also has a relevance, especially the many critiques of the development of agrarian capitalism, not least the perceptions and prejudices of that quintessential Englishman, William Cobbett.

Agrarian Capitalism and Cornland Historical Formation

The key components of the intensification of agrarian capitalism are the continued trend towards larger and consolidated estates, enclosure under parliamentary Acts and enclosure by agreement. All three facilitated a marked increase in larger farms at the expense of smaller farms, a phenomenon accelerated by the 'engrossing of farms'. The extinction of common rights by both enclosure mechanisms is already well known, though the clandestine 'incroachments made by the Plow on the Greenways & communable Places' also reduced access to land for people able to supplement incomes from a range of occupations, from tradesmen to labourers.[6] The decline of smallholders, family farmers and classic dual-occupationists must not be exaggerated as the latter two categories revealed a pronounced tenacity, but heavy capital investment underpinned marked rises in agricultural productivity while increased market orientation of profit-maximising farmers came to dominate most rural communities economically. Here, opportunities to get a toehold on the land were reduced quite drastically.

Although historians have traced a direct relationship between parliamentary enclosure and proletarianisation,[7] the principal engine was demographic growth. The decline in other sources of demand for labour, including that of women and children, derived from cornland de-industrialisation, notably textiles. There were few compensations.[8] Farmers' demand for labour therefore became paramount and the main source of agrarian labour's exposure to free-market forces. Workers' dependency on the market for employment was paralleled by their dependency on it as consumers, for food, fuel, clothing and housing. The shopocracy expanded to become ubiquitous, exposing rural workers to volatile food prices before 1817. Similarly, demographic growth exerted enormous pressure on rural housing stocks; rents rose inexorably.

From the mid-eighteenth century, intensifying corn production maintained a rough equilibrium of the supply and demand for adult male farmworkers. Signs of supply outstripping demand in the 1780s[9] were localised and proved ephemeral owing to unprecedented wartime mobilisation after 1792–93. This postponed the impending crisis until 1814–15. Historians disagree over the issue of agrarian labour shortages during the war.[10] Enlistment had a disproportionate impact on the age and gender structure of the labour supply between 1793 and 1815 through a dramatic reduction in the numbers of older youths and younger men at the peak of their physical powers. A sufficiency of them (at least during seasonal peaks in demand) was secured only through the substitution of piece rates for day or weekly wages demanded by workers exploiting the effects of mobilisation.[11] The wartime availability of piece-work encouraged localised migration by younger married men and youthful bachelors.[12]

This migration and its causes had several knock-on effects. First, it stimulated a marked diminution in customary annual live-in service for boys and more especially youths. Fathers profited where they were assisted by their boys in piece-work,[13] and youths seized the opportunity to earn more by breaking free from traditional service. Second, it reversed the trend against the employment in agriculture of women and younger children.[14] Labour shortages principally affected harvesting and were reflected in rises in family harvest earnings, and by the marked wartime growth in migrant Irish harvest labour, particularly in the underpopulated reclaimed fenlands.[15] The underemployment of agricultural labourers and their families was not a problem between 1793 and 1815.

Rural service industries' fortunes generally reflected those of agrarian capitalism. The latter's wartime prosperity boosted demand for all manner of products. Farmers invested heavily in farm buildings, implements and haulage equipment. The marked growth in their domestic consumption from 1750[16] accelerated during the war years, ostentatiously symbolising their unprecedented wealth. Additional competition for skilled men derived from a range of peculiarly wartime economic stimulants. This buoyancy also enabled many village tradesmen to invest some of their new-found wealth in buying up and converting existing property, and by speculative erection of more buildings, for rental to farmworkers.[17]

Historians are in rough agreement that farmworkers' real wages and family incomes declined between 1760 and 1790. By the outbreak of war in 1793 they barely secured a basic subsistence. Service-sector journeymen's wages are unknown, but customary income disparities between them and their farmworking neighbours widened as their earnings more than equalled fierce wartime inflation. In stark contrast, farmers held their labourers' real wages down, in spite of work by the piece: not one knowledgeable commentator believed they kept up with living costs. Family men, notably those with large numbers of small children, and older workers, whose waning strength rendered them ineligible for piece-work outside harvesting, were particularly disadvantaged. The ultimate proof came from rocketing poor-law expenditure.[18]

Orthodox accounts of the depression focus on its impact on agrarian capital, with reductions of arable acreages and marginal lands going out of cultivation. Attention has been paid to bankruptcies among farmers, which were not confined to the smaller category, and to the incapacity of landowners to maintain inflated wartime rents, compounded by difficulties in replacing tenants. But what is often overlooked is that the depression affected virtually everybody in entire communities, including the service sector, whose wartime prosperity collapsed as spectacularly as that of the majority of farmers.

Reductions in arable acreages *and* less-intensive cereal cultivation caused demand for landworkers to plummet.[19] Simultaneously, the labour supply was vastly inflated by demobilisation and fuelled further by the not unrelated sharp upturn in the birth rate. Contemporaneous conceptualisation of 'surplus labourers' was one result, reinforced by calculations of their precise numbers on a parochial basis. Under- and unemployed farmworkers became chronic problems. Parish followed parish in adopting defensive measures. Migrants and their families, so welcomed in wartime, were unceremoniously expelled through settlement law, while vestries demanded that farmers employ only legally-settled workers and their families.[20]

Settlement considerations pre-empted substantial recreation of live-in service.[21] Instead farmers more generally discriminated against the regular employment of workers except men with young children, a tactic dictated by poor-relief cost considerations, though even these men remained vulnerable to further reductions. Reducing labour costs was not restricted to casualisation. After 1815, cereal farmers made further large cuts through the use of threshing machines which decimated residual winter-season work, and they reduced harvesting costs by exploiting migrant Irish labour, a seasonal supply bloated further by migrants from English communities, including urban and rural craftsmen.[22] Farmworking families' harvesting earnings were reduced, thereby compromising the customary source of the clearance of debts to village shopkeepers, shoemakers and cottage landlords.

The scale of local artisan participation in the harvest during the depression, and its extension beyond harvesting, were unprecedented and reflected the simultaneous casualisation of the rural skilled labour force by their employers. The supply was further inflated by demographic pressures, as many labourers turned their hands to traditional crafts despite the overcrowding of these callings, as rudimentary competence in carpentering, tailoring and shoemaking was not difficult to acquire.[23] The result was typified by Oundle, Northamptonshire, where it was reported in the 1820s: 'many mechanics ... are great incumbrances, such as carpenters, masons, tailors, and shoemakers ... there is such a redundancy of them, that they keep increasing yearly.'[24]

Craftsmen, including most journeymen and many of their masters, also saw their incomes fall, often drastically as farmers relentlessly forced down prices and then delayed payment. The depression also hit tradesmen dependent on a plebeian clientele.[25] Many small masters' businesses collapsed; they were reduced to labouring.[26] Again, the few compensatory openings were available only to a minority. Those with financial reserves, or capacity to organise partnerships, speculated in the buoyant plebeian housing market by conversions of old dilapidated larger buildings into tenements or through running up new jerry-built cottages.[27]

Other developments, notably those associated with new technologies, also impacted adversely on rural service industries. In their initial diffusion from the early 1790s, most threshing machines were built by ingenious 'local blacksmiths, millwrights and carpenters who copied the machines within their limited experience'.[28] By the 1820s, specialist manufacturers were established in many market towns, pioneering an agricultural engineering industry, with capabilities beyond those of most village craftsmen. Advanced engineering transformed urban-based iron-founding. They accelerated the mass production of all manner of things, among them wrought-iron gates and fencing, buckets and a multitude of household fittings. Traditional countryside skills and crafts in the timber industry were also compromised by machine sawing and through the mass production of a whole range of items including machine-planed wood of 'various thicknesses for doors and windows', available from impressively mechanised substantial saw-mills.[29]

New technologies also had an impact on other broadly-diffused rural industries, especially paper and flour-milling.[30] The adverse effects of new technologies extended far beyond the ranks of agricultural labourers and served to deepen the depression. Few economic interests in any cornland community escaped, though the worst effects impacted on labour. Not only did their living standards collapse through reduced earnings: as under- and unemployment generated degrees of redundancy, an economically-driven crisis transmuted itself into a seemingly chronic social crisis.

Compensation principally derived from the massive extension of poor-law operations, initially almost exclusively directed towards agricultural labourers from 1792–93. After 1815 poor-relief was extended to numbers of service-industry workers. However, historical appreciations of both the causes and, more especially, the nature of that expansion are oversimplistic. If the poor law became embedded in a demonstrably countryside variant of moral economy, its reconstitution necessitates a more sophisticated appreciation of the complexities of the process and the nature of the system's expansion.

Customary interpretation of the key initial extension persists in its association with Speenhamland allowances in aid of wages tied to agricultural labourers' family size and oscillations in the cost of living. I have argued elsewhere that the latter element in individual claimants' allowances predicated on the price of bread was an almost immediate casualty of both the huge costs involved and government policies during the famines of 1794–96 and 1799–1801.[31] The most common payments were *static* and paid with respect to the number *and* ages of children in individual families. These criteria were regularly changed and usually covered only slack seasons. The 'scales' drawn up after 1801 almost invariably relate to these static payments. Many parish wartime accounts reveal rising poor-law expenditure, not solely owing to child allowances but also to 'casual' payments to help meet the costs of clothing, shoes, fuel and cottage rentals. Some parishes built or purchased cheap houses in line with their long-established responsibility to house at least family men unable to lodge, the option available to unmarried workers of both sexes.[32]

Historical explanations of the origins of regular allowances in aid, and (by inference) of enhanced resort to casual payments, customarily focus almost exclusively on the larger farmers' interests and their supposed political dominance of the vestries. In this projected wartime scenario, the farmers forced the subsidisation of their wages bill by non-employing ratepayers.[33] It was, even at this stage, less one-sided. If wage supplementation had been impossible, farmers would either have been compelled to pay different wage rates dependent on employees' family size and, even more ludicrously, differential piece rates, or discriminate against hiring fathers with numerous young children. That would have cut a shrinking labour supply, while the entire cost of supporting such men fell on public funds, to which farmers made the largest contributions. But these were not the only considerations. Tenant farmers were also engaged in a burgeoning battle with their landlords, who drove rentals upwards. Landlords invariably held that wages were a matter between tenants and their employees, but entered poor-rate levels into the account when rent rises were implemented. Moreover, tithes were assessed to the poor rate and incumbents still in receipt of tithes contributed to relief costs.[34]

The innovative post-1793 factor was enhanced dependency on public assistance. As the special problem of poorly-paid employed men with large families intensified after 1815, existing methods of relief were maintained and further measures focused on the new difficulties of under- and unemployment. To soak up these categories, parish followed parish in make-work schemes, including the Roundsman system, over the winters. But imposing labourers on employers proved problematic, notably for small farmers who depended on their own offspring and had little need for extra labour. But compromises were found. It was common for family farmers to count sons who worked against their quotas of labourers.[35] Alternatively, attempts were made to engage the surplus by auctioning to the highest bidder. Other initiatives included employment on the roads, financed from the highway rate, and related work on parish-hired sand, stone and gravel pits. Some parishes also rented untenanted farms, a practice legitimated by the Sturges Bourne Acts of 1818–19.[36]

Localised wartime difficulties in finding work for children and youths of both sexes now assumed much graver proportions. Parishes offered a variety of premiums, but problems with adolescents endured, as did those with securing work for adult unmarried males. A high proportion ended up in parish work, with boys' first work experience often commencing on the roads at the age of eleven.[37] To control these categories, who became demoralised, truculent and increasingly insubordinate, and remove them from their overcrowded parental homes, some places accommodated all of them in workhouses.[38] Existing inmates, often elderly, were foisted on those tenanting parish houses or paid to live with other residents. But this comprised one component, most notable in open parishes, of an acute housing crisis. Rents maintained their upward spiral and cottage landlords insisted that vestries underwrite plebeian tenancies and directly hire additional cottages into which they packed more and more families.[39]

Regular and casual payments were extended to journeymen in the rural service industries. Goudhurst recipients of allowances in aid of wages included bricklayers, brickmakers, sawyers, shoemakers and a journeyman miller. And they are much more broadly recorded being put to work on parish schemes for the unemployed, including the roads. Even several thatchers, unambiguous rural labour aristocrats, were engaged on a parish gravel pit at East Grinstead. Elsewhere, Roundsman systems were introduced for 'all Tradespeople applying for work'.[40]

The sheer complexity of the problem precluded any simple exploitation of circumstances by bigger farmers after the war. Many parishes attempted to stem the returning tides of legally-removed workers, including tradesmen, by paying every form of relief to non-residents. Some successes followed, notably but not exclusively with those living in towns. In 1826 West Grinstead was making payments to 64 non-resident couples and for 187 *eligible* children between them. Preserving these people in employ by subsidies was much better than their return home to neither work nor accommodation. Where this occurred, it represented the subsidisation of employers in entirely different communities.[41]

When viewed at the level of the individual parish, the poor-law theatre reveals considerable reciprocity between various interest groups. In many villages, cottages were owned by quite a broad section of inhabitants who benefited from rent subsidies.[42] Tradesmen profited in further ways: parish contracts to supply shoes went to cobblers, while the 'grocer and draper' supplied cloth and ready-made clothing, and the fuel-merchant wood and coal. Carpenters provided pauper coffins and, along with bricklayers, plasterers and roofers, repaired publicly-owned buildings. It was quite common for loans and gifts to be made to struggling self-employed artisans and petty entrepreneurs. Better to incur expenditure in supplying replacement tools, and even raw materials (including bricks for bricklayers, and leather for shoemakers) and extend this calculated munificence to hucksters with capital to purchase wholesale stocks, replace a knackered horse and finance cart repairs, than have these people go out of business and into perhaps chronic dependency. Even endangered small farmers looked for succour, and some received it in the form of rent-free parish fields while others were actually preserved through periodic receipt of poor-law payments.[43] Where parishes hired farms, landed proprietors joined the beneficiaries.

Perimeters of reciprocity did not end here. Given the scale of pauperism, economies of scale could be achieved by payments in kind. Parochial contracts, notably for flour and bread, were identified by the Poor Law Commissioners as obtained nepotistically and executed fraudulently.[44] But the fact that contracts also served to ease parochial liquidity by delayed payment puts a different construction on both nepotists and their higher prices: the latter represented low levels of interest. Payments in kind had the additional advantage of reducing claimants' propensity to misapply cash benefits.[45]

Such devices, whatever their parochial *political* importance, could not by themselves, however, contain escalating poor-law expenditure which dovetailed with low prices for rural products to undermine the equilibrium of agrarian capitalism. If prices were beyond vestry control, relief costs could be directly addressed. Economy drives were facilitated by the Sturges Bourne Acts, which allowed the creation of select vestries and were widely adopted. The Acts' provision of plural voting rights increased bigger ratepayers' control over parochial policies and their day-to-day implementation, thus facilitating initiatives, notably by utilitarian converts. At Midhurst, Robert Weale, 'invariably called to the Chair', celebrated his authority by levelling artisans in difficulties with farmworkers: bricklayers and carpenters who earned higher wages during the summer were then put to parochial employ over the winter, interrogated, subjected to calculations, and 'allowed to earn so much money as will make their earnings for the year average the same as the agricultural labourer or any other Pauper'.[46]

The legislation also legitimated the employment of salaried officials, especially assistant-overseers, who cut expenditure much more drastically than the costs of their salaries through the closest investigation of every claimant's precise circumstances. Most were failed farmers and tradesmen from other communities and were therefore 'strangers' in popular perception and parlance.[47] As outsiders – in stark contrast to traditional overseers – they allegedly 'felt no sympathy for' claimants' 'condition', were 'callous to the ties of nature', and 'paid with so much the greater cheerfulness as he makes fewer calls on the purses of his employers' by 'browbeating the Applicants for relief'.[48] They adopted strategies aimed to deter claimants, often coupled with a cruel combination of humiliation and punishment, especially the notorious substitution of human for horse-power, and wheelbarrows for carts. Road and quarry workers, including boys and sometimes women, are repeatedly encountered physically hauling heavy loads across considerable distances. Relief was withdrawn for all manner of 'offences' ranging from answering back to inadequate performance of allotted tasks and petty delinquencies by claimants' children. Select vestries usually upheld this exercise of power by the assistants and introduced additional sanctions. Not surprisingly, the assistants generated considerable hostility, but they also cut costs.[49]

Although the magistracy achieved a contemporary notoriety for overruling such parsimonious decisions, the 1819 Act required two rather than the customary single justice to hear appeals. Many magistrates were influenced by utilitarian tracts.[50] Such Petty Sessional minutes which record the grounds as well as the rulings at these tribunals reveal that vestries could expect magisterial support for both parsimonious policies and punitive decisions.[51] They upheld making relief for the elderly who owned their own homes conditional upon them assigning their properties to the parish on their deaths. The justices also sustained reinvocations of disused Poor Law stipulations, notably that relatives able to maintain claimants should do so even if this meant selling real estate.[52]

From around 1820 significant sectors of an entire generation of agricultural labourers had spent their teens partly in parish employ, and by

1830 they too were the fathers of another generation for whom prospects were equally sour. Many had tarnished reputations, or worse. In the early 1830s, assistant overseer Bourne of Cranbrook identified three categories of claimants 'to whom adminstering Relief is very trying and painful'. First 'We have ... some Married Men of worthless and grossly bad habits, who none will employ in the Winter season, and at any other time when there are a surplus of Labourers ... a heavy Burden on the Parish 6 or 7 Months out of twelve.' The second grouping comprised 'young fellows whose Characters forbid them servitude', who spent much of their time in workhouse accommodation. Bourne's third category were winter-season inmates, young women who spent the summers as whores working the fairs, and 'such is there destitute condition that humanity compels us to comply with there request' [for a roof over their heads].[53]

Resort to prostitution was not new, though its inflated scale and seasonal regularity symbolised the social degradation inflicted by the depression. Fallen women mirrored much more generalised downward social mobility, as did bankrupted smaller farmers, failed tradesmen of all hues and rural artisans reduced to farm and parish labouring, with their proud tradition of independency a visual casualty. Now they were being embraced by a dependency culture already imposed on farmworkers. But Bourne's concept of the dictates of 'humanity' was equally symbolic of protection under the law for those at greatest risk. In so doing, it revealed a capacity for reciprocity which helped to reconcile opposing interests, including conflicts between capitalists, and between capital and labour. It succeeded to degrees in crudely shoring up the socio-economic equilibrium, but ironically the costs aggravated the crisis of agrarian capitalism which appeared to threaten its survival. Those involved in cost-cutting in the 1820s reflected the determination of its authors to preserve advanced agrarian capitalism itself.

The Ideology of Agrarian Capitalism's Critics

Cobbett was one particularly strident critic in a long tradition of hostility to the socio-economic transformation of cornland communities. Recurrent eighteenth-century dearths unleashed contemporary anger. That accompanying the 1766–67 dearth focused on the engrossing of farms as a prime cause. Estate owners who amalgamated existing farms for rental to substantial tenants enhanced the significance of capital, employed not simply to increase productivity but also to finance withholding of foodstocks to drive up prices. This implicated farmers in moral-economic fractures, and put them on a par with exploitive merchant wholesalers, food manufacturers and retailers.[54] These critiques endured and were articulated during the more serious wartime famines. One irascible MP, Lechmere, told the Commons in March 1796 that:

> the scarcity … proceeded from the consolidation of farms, and an enormous monopoly among the great and opulent farmers, mealmen and flour dealers … The scarcity … mere bugbear, held forth to the people, under which the opulent farmers contrived to keep up a crass and scandalous monopoly.[55]

However, the impact of engrossing and enclosure on rural communities themselves was of equal concern. Contemporaries believed they diminished demand for labour and reduced the numbers of farmers, pushing the displaced into labouring ranks. Customary socio-economic structures enabling upward social mobility on the part of labourers were compromised, preventing them from initially renting a very small farm. Victims left the countryside for the towns and preventing rural 'depopulation' comprised 'the most powerful argument' for smaller farms' retention. These mid-century complaints were also repeated during the French wars.[56] Enclosure, combined with rocketing poor rates, served to generate proposals for allotments for them. The most famous convert was enclosure's most voluble advocate, Arthur Young. Allotment campaigners' repeated parliamentary failures proved that the farmers had convinced their landlords of the paramountcy of an unambiguous agrarian proletariat.[57]

If Cobbett was a somewhat belated convert to the anti-enclosure cause, he was the principal early nineteenth-century contributor to it, railing against the poor's inability to obtain all manner of things from wastes and commons, the erosion of workers' cottage gardens, the decline in cottagers' bread-baking and their consequent dependency on the shopocracy. Substantial farmers, the beneficiaries of enclosure and engrossing, also bore the brunt of criticism for putting profits before social responsibilities, notably over their use of threshing machines and employment of migrant Irish harvest labour. Cobbett's initial defence of threshing machines in 1816 was a transparent attempt to evade threatened prosecution at the instance of government ministers alarmed at his journalism. He subsequently abandoned this stance, and other radical writers were equally condemnatory of their owners. Irish harvesters not only brought reaping rates down, but also reduced the time to complete the operation, thus injecting two factors which cut indigenous workers' family earnings, carrying 'away the *cream* from the English labourers' milk pan' in Cobbett's metaphor which reflected the erosion of this annual source of cash to repay the latter's debts. These views were echoed by the Tory press which condemned Irish 'usurpation' of English 'rights' and farmers who, 'to save a few pounds', refused to employ their own neighbours.[58]

Many commentators condemned rural labourers' dependency on allowances before 1815, the loss of 'laudable pride' and its cancerous impact on industrial relations. Resistance to overtime derived from commensurate deductions from wage supplements. But such critics veered into support for Malthus and joined the hostile ranks of the old poor law's utilitarian opponents. Others became appalled at the effects of select vestries and their make-work schemes. The former were denounced as 'a Junto who are judges in their own cause'.[59] A Cambridge print lamented the 'broken ... spirits' of parish road and quarry workers 'constantly repining at their hard condition', who regarded 'their employers as taskmasters' while 'the ties of attachment to the land of their birth become gradually torn asunder'. Cobbett lambasted all this, but he also tellingly claimed that: 'The Poor Law ... is the greatest law that ever was passed, springing as it does, out of the law of nature; founded, as it is, in the very principle of civil society; sanctioned ... by ages upon ages of experience.'

However, if Cobbett defended poor relief as a right, he condemned virtually every major facet of intensified agrarian capitalism, embraced in this archetypal passage from his *Political Register* in May 1821: he asserted that 'To enumerate the moral evils of the rise of large farms would require the pages of very large volume', a threat in itself. He continued:

> There ought to be ranks and degrees in husbandry as well as in trade and in all the other classes and callings which make up a community. The greatest farmer ought to approach nearly to a gentleman, and the least to nearly a labourer ... Instead of an agricultural population connected, the highest to the lowest, by links almost imperceptible, and having interests and feelings in common, we now have a few *masters* and a great number of slaves, each having an interest directly opposed to the other.[60]

Countryside Moral Economy

I have outlined the principal elements of a particular historical formation. The conservative critique serves as a base to identify potential components of a rural moral economy, but there were tensions within that critique and these suggest that it was by no means inevitable that all the points advanced were reflected in popular perceptions, attitudes and actions, which together constitute the evidence for the reconstitution of a countryside moral-economic *mentalité*. The rest of this chapter is devoted to evidential analysis, including the wide range of social protest mentioned in the introduction, to identify which features of the conservative critique became wholly or in part embraced in this countryside moral economy and which did not. Some results are surprising.

Live-in Service and Settlement

Cobbett extolled the virtues of live-in annual service for adolescents and unmarried young people of both sexes, principally on the grounds of its critical training function. But he also claimed that it reinforced social cohesion between farmers and their employees, while providing a wherewithal for savings for financing a home on marriage and, for the most industrious and conscientious couples, savings adequate to take a small farm. Cobbett, in common with other defenders, painted far too rosy a picture, ignoring the fact that many farmers and their wives exercised tyrannical powers in their households, requiring long hours and the perfect execution of allotted tasks and restricting leisure activities. Those who failed to satisfy could be taken before a magistrate whose sanctions included terminating contracts, reducing the sum agreed for the year, imposing fines and even prison terms. Lasses were vulnerable to sexual advances from farmers and their sons. Older youths of both sexes resented limitations on their freedoms.[61] During the wars they seized the enhanced piece and day wage rates on offer: as early as 1793 the Essex Bench denounced the resultant 'great nuisance' of servants not completing their contracted year. Farmer Field of Rumboldwick recalled that 'young men ... would not do anything but task work', and neither they nor older bachelors 'would ... abide in the farmhouse for 2s 6d or 3s a week ... and board' when the money element could be earned by the day: Field insisted that 'it was they ... who broke through that'. Others asserted that employers' social aspirations rose with their prosperity, making them quite happy to lose the responsibility for truculent youths living in their houses. Whatever the degrees of mutuality, the result was the same.[62] Although the system certainly survived when it did not create new settlements for the individuals involved, there is no evidence of any popular demand for its restoration, an absence which reflects deep hostility from workers and by most farmers. It was a discredited tradition. Dr Snell's suggestion that annual service constituted a component of rural moral economy, through its training function and because it was a common criterion for establishing settlement, *and* therefore entitlement to poor relief, cannot be sustained. In fact, live-in service was ultimately irrelevant to gaining a settlement as children automatically took their father's. *Adult* farmworkers prized settlement certificates, but these were issued to facilitate migration to obtain work. This was very different, and certification evaporated after the changes to settlement law in 1795.[63]

The Land

Dr Neeson has proved that parliamentary enclosure generated more riotous and enduring protest than historians have believed. However, her arguments do not significantly revise what in aggregate impressed Edward Thompson as the 'fatalism of the cottagers'.[64] This *relative* passivity in the face of land privatisation *and* the engrossing of farms owed something to the compensatory operations of the poor law, [65] the costs of which were easily met from promoters' inflated profits. Did enclosure's radical reduction of the numbers of small farmers, destruction of the economic equilibrium of dual-occupationists and the capacity of cottagers to exploit common rights to preserve themselves, transmutate into a countryside moral economy? An identical question must be asked of the impact of the more universal engrossing of farms, whether in conjunction with enclosure or not, which undermined the traditional structures of rural communities with their 'almost imperceptible ranks and degrees' so superbly identified by Cobbett. Ultimately it is not just the fatalism of the cottagers, but the apparent fatalism of *all* the victims of enclosure and engrossing – in short, the loss of access to land – which is at issue.

However powerful the ideological opposition to enclosure, the fact that many were statutorily underpinned legitimised the mobilisation of the state's coercive powers, at times deployed with a combination of subtlety and cunning perhaps unique to the English ruling class, at least in England.[66] Recurrent victory for agrarian capital at the moment of enclosure also implies that militant tactics against the continued engrossing of farms was never likely to succeed, in stark contrast to Irish experiences. In England, prolonged and partially successful militant and overt opposition occurred only in extraordinary locations, notably where rights over extensive commons belonged to numerous *menu peuple* domiciled in several distinct adjacent communities.[67] All enclosures generated enduring bitterness. Workers from parishes both in the process of enclosure and for which Acts had been recently passed were prominent in the East Anglian rising of 1816.[68] Although Hobsbawm and Rudé have famously found that recently enclosed villages were more prone to participate in the Swing explosion,[69] a close reading of their text reveals a caution against overemphasis of this linkage, [70] to which must be added our flawed knowledge of 'Swing parishes'.[71] Neeson's splendid study concludes that the scale even of rioting will never be known, and it is a great pity that her exploration of the duration of covert expressions of hostility, principally in Northamptonshire, does not embrace Swing in 1830. Dr Bushaway identified holidays and their 'far from deferential' customs, spawning 'ritual demonstration of strength by the labouring poor', facilitating symbolic expressions of antipathy to enclosure for decades after the event.[72]

However, these latter-day celebrations have all the residual features of earlier festivities when the world was turned upside down. Neeson's text is littered with quotes from John Clare's poems in which he extols, amongst so much more, the virtues of access to the multiple fruits of the wastes, the right to leisure through unimpeded roaming and the degree of social harmony obtaining. Enclosure terminated access, restricted cross-country strolling and severed social harmony, corroding traditional relationships as social class emerged. Fences, closed footpaths and 'no trespassing' notices were realities, not merely symbols 'of freedom bade goodbye'. Clare articulated the obliteration of what W. G. Hoskins later conceptualised as the 'satisfying economy'. The 'dissatisfied', in the main, comprised enclosure's promoters. They were already wealthy: why should they even want more, let alone seize it to the manifest deprivation of others? Clare reserved his greatest scorn for the 'middling yeomen' who emerged essentially enriched with modest but profitable apportionments of 30–70 acres, the 'little tyrants' who conspired with the 'philistines'. Parallel messages are central to the lyrics of much popular song, and confirm the accuracy of Clare's perceptions of loss.[73]

If contemporary fears of depopulation through the wider engrossing of farms were not realised (though it stimulated limited migration and emigration), it served to generate frustration as 'Farmers sons' were prevented from marrying and were 'forced to live at Home with their Fathers'.[74] The cumulative impact of this situation in the mid-1760s can only have intensified as engrossing continued apace and accelerated with post-1793 prosperity. In the depression, regions with high small-farm densities witnessed numerous untenanted farms, but this also emphasises that the victims of bankruptcies were not restricted to the farmers themselves but included their sons without the capital needed to take tenancies, with the resultant end of many farming families. Bankrupted owner-occupiers and impoverished landowners sold farms, and among the purchasers were urban-based speculators and prosperous bourgeois more concerned with the social advantages of landowning, notably game-licence qualifications.[75]

There are too many reports of small farmers, and their sons, joining the bloated ranks of the rural proletariat to ignore.[76] Their traumas and frustrations paralleled those of disfranchised commoners. But this powerful socio-economic phenomenon did not generate anything remotely approximate to its Irish equivalent. I have encountered only one specific classic expression in England of threats relating to taking 'a farm over another man's head', made by an alleged arsonist.[77] Unsatisfied aspirations for land proprietorship must have generated strains among those whose youthful assumptions turned on inheriting common rights, family tenancies or farms, perhaps represented by the 'grumblings' detected by Neeson over enclosure.[78] Threatening letters and arson were deployed against those responsible for wartime encroachments in Ashdown Forest, but this was a peculiar locality.[79] If 'grumblings' manifested themselves elsewhere in feuding at village levels, they went unrecorded and are not directly represented in the copious documentation of Swing. One witness detected the 'revenge of the expropriated smallholders' in protesters' actions at North Curry, in Somerset.[80] Just one activist is documented, though in bar-room advocacy of incendiarism, specifically castigating a man with ' "a larger farm than would employ three farmers" '. One major landowner, Sir Timothy Shelley, of Warnham, West Sussex, received an anonymous missive, containing, among other sentiments, a challenge to consult the New Testament to see 'if that sanctions any such monopoly' of land. However, Warnham hosted a nucleus of radicals. The principal concerns of small farmers engaged in Swing protests were rent levels, and especially tithe exactions. In one exasperated exchange at Goudhurst after farmers rejected higher wages, their labourers rhetorically demanded the land, but this crowd was led by Cobbettites.[81]

Popular demand for access to land eludes the early history of allotments. If they were utterly irrelevant to the aspirations of those imbued with ideologies pertaining to family-farming, or smallholding, ostensibly they offered compensation to the lesser losers from enclosure and more obvious benefits to rural proletarians. Labourers were happy to cultivate pieces of waste land and plots carved out from the commons so long as they were rent free and the gardeners retained their autonomy. However, those who lost such access did not insist on its restoration even during Swing. The extensive evidence reveals no specific demands for allotments, and their provision as part of a typical parochial package *negotiated* by Swing is known to have occurred only at Amport in Hampshire.[82]

The principal rider to this trajectory over attitudes to access to land concerns squatting, an understudied aspect of cornland history. Some comprised stable communities, among them that of Stelling on the Downs, north of Folkestone (which probably dated from the sixteenth century). Here the central feature, much of it extra-parochial, was the Minnis, a huge common, originally heath and still partly wooded in 1800, extending into two neighbouring parishes. The 'barren soil' and flint-choked 'infertile red earth' never attracted normal Downland intensive capital investment, but it hosted 'a strange little squatters' settlement' domiciled in disparate 'houses and cottages'. The 'inhabitants' had 'inclosed' such 'fields and orchards' as they could and were 'as wild as the country they live in': most supplemented their incomes by farm labouring in adjacent typically 'close' Downland parishes. Significant districts with poor soils, among them the heaths of West Surrey and East Berkshire, remained well into the nineteenth-century, and smaller pockets of wasteland were to be found in many cornland locations.[83] Although they were targeted by enclosers, and owners also adopted other means of privatisation, many endured. Considerable populations remained domiciled in a 'vast number of ... small cottages', some of which were legitimated 'by the grant of the lord' of the manor, but others were simply run up by interloping newcomers. Manorial rights were often ambiguous, and when contested 'remained a subject of constant dispute'. As late as 1877 'the quasi-inhabitants of the manor' embracing Limpsfield Common near Godstone 'believed ... they had rights over the waste', and, on being fined yet again, announced that 'they would cut the gorse and would do it again and sell it where they liked'.[84]

Godstone 'commoners' tenacity reflects the fact that where such communities lasted, circumstance facilitated the invention of rights of access by those whose future depended on their survival. The duration of amorphous forms of protest over the losses of commoners through parliamentary enclosure and other processes, its embracing in forms of festival and popular lyrics, and its articulation by the likes of Cobbett, in fact testify to the fatalism identified by Thompson. The sense of outrage possibly accounts for its transmutation into nineteenth-century urban and industrial communities, its appearance in Spencean ideologies and its most potent expression in the enthusiasm for the Chartist Land Plan, which also attracted countryside subscribers. But there were other political influences at work here.[85] The loss of access to land, which it must be stressed affected many more strata of countryside communities than labourers and 'commoners', was not convincingly embraced by a rural moral economy, although it found expression when customary rights were being defended against attack. Once these defences failed there were few subsequent opportunities for their re-enaction, in stark contrast to the reaffirmations of moral-economic ideology facilitated by recurrent subsistence crises.

Food Supplies and Prices

The dependency of most countryside workers for food on village retail outlets and their counterparts in nearby market towns exposed them to volatile prices before 1816–17. They too should have developed that 'highly sensitive consumer consciousness' which Thompson originally identified as central to food rioters during recurrent dearths. However, he argued that 'conflict *between the countryside and the town* was mediated by the price of bread', implying that rural workers, and presumably especially agricultural labourers, identified with a geographically and economically defined countryside interest.[86] An impressive corpus of studies emphasises that food rioting was principally experienced in urban locations and/or in industrialising districts.[87] This *apparent* specificity has encouraged one particularly obstinate critic, D. E. Williams, to challenge Thompson's entire concept of moral economy, while an historical geographer suggests that mapping its incidence may proffer a solution to this problematic.[88] I adhere to my original diagnosis of evidential problems precluding such an authoritative methodological strategy,[89] but the sources for rural workers' beliefs in the central ideological tenets of Thompson's identification warrant examination as a contribution to this debate and because they are important in their own right.

Precise identification of rural workers' faces in the food-protesting crowd is difficult, but further evidential snippets emerge. The 1756–57 crisis saw an invasion of Lewes by people from 'several neighbouring parishes', seizures of corn from seaport and inland granaries and from carts progressing along High Wealden roads. The extensive disturbances in 1766 were not confined to clothing districts. Villagers in the agrarian hinterland of St Albans also intended to set prices in the city on fair day, while the similarly-motivated labourers who invaded Maidenhead about the same time were probably farmworkers.[90]

The evidence for the wartime famines, especially 1794–96 and 1799–1801, is more substantial. Modest market towns were the scenes of recurrent mobilisations and the sources identify farmworkers in several of them over a wide area, including Cambridge, Blandford, Lewes and Romney. At Chichester and New Alresford, agricultural labourers named withholding farmers. Disturbances at Guildford and Midhurst in September 1800 were orchestrated by paper-makers from various villages and, if their systematic proceedings reflect their trade union network, it is unlikely that their farmworking neighbours disapproved of their intervention. These years also reveal the subjection of rural shopkeepers, and bakers on itinerant rounds in the countryside, to *taxation populaire*, together with several *apparently* isolated purely rural stoppages of food shipments on the roads. The particularly fierce blockading of much of the cornlands, at the village level, against the continued passage of cereals to the centres of consumption during the midsummer 1795 hyper-crisis must have included farm labourers. *Taxation populaire* featured during the East Anglian rising of 1816 and elsewhere in the cornlands during this dearth, a fitting finale to the 'long eighteenth-century'.[91]

Once the 1795 crisis failed to end with the new harvest, Richard Harrison of Woolverton, Northamptonshire, feared in October that, if corn prices were not lowered within realistic reach of farmworkers' wages, risings would commence, during which they would 'help themselves, may perhaps, set fire to…Barns & Rickyards…thro' the whole kingdom'. Anonymous arson threats communicated to farmers and others in the countryside, including millers, articulated moral-economic precepts, exemplified by a letter received at Odiham in Hampshire: 'We know Every Stack of Corn about this Country and Every Barn that have Corn concealed…the poore in Every place is willing to tell us the Farmers that ask the most Money and Likewise the Millers that Bid the most.' These threats were not empty, as a Sussex farmer discovered in November 1799 when £500 worth of corn was incinerated after he 'stupidly said', once prices again surged strongly upwards, 'that he would not thrash until wheat was £40 the load'. Threats, often accompanied sooner or later by arson, were widely experienced: by the spring of 1800 they extended to all 'the most opulent' farmers in East Anglian locations. The scale achieved by incendiaries, 'displeased with the price of Grain' and motivated to 'lower Prices', stimulated no less than three major insurance companies to publicise that they, 'who cannot have offended', were the real victims. Anonymous notes also legitimated theft from breakers of the moral code by their self-perceived victims. Miller Nottage, wrote an Essex worker, 'is a damn Rogue...you sink [lower prices] for we have rob your Mill seavel Times and we will rob it again'.[92] All of this evidence power-fully underwrites the case that Thompson's moral economy was not geographically specific, but comprised a universal ideology. In the countryside, where the capacity to mobilise was restricted by protest-ers' vulnerability, resort to arson to address infringements of the moral code, together with punishment of offenders by theft, proved portentous.

This evidence conclusively proves that all rural workers subscribed to Thompson's moral-economic ideology over problems with the food supply, unacceptably high prices and manipulative marketing prac-tices. Many historians have correctly identified a marked decline in food rioting after the war, partly attributable to the stabilisation of supplies and, with them, prices. Relatively moderate price rises coin-cided with Swing, but the sole known cornland food riot occurred in Lincolnshire where one village baker's products were subjected to *taxation populaire*.[93]

Wages

E. F. Genovese detected a change in popular economic perceptions with wage levels replacing prices of basic consumer goods as the key element in proletarian living standards from the late eighteenth cen-tury.[94] Farmworkers certainly comprehended the basic laws of supply and demand.[95] Collective action on the wages front accompanied the first wartime inflationary decade. In November 1792, when day and weekly wages were traditionally reduced for the winter season, and with food prices rising, the 'labouring men' of Alfriston 'formed...a club' to 'compel' their employers to supply wheat at five shillings the bushel and 'to augment their wages'. At Funtingdon on 11 November 1794, a crowd of agricultural labourers 'assembled in a riotous manner, stopped several farmers waggons on the road...committed divers other outrages, with intent to *oblige* their employers to raise their wages'. Four 'ringleaders' were arrested for conspiracy to increase wages to a daily 2s. Similar attempts to force wage increases occurred in Kent. In East Anglia, after a strike led by Isaac Seer, the 'first known farmwork-ers' leader' in 1793, a much more ambitious movement centred on Norfolk commenced in 1795. Here activists emphasised their disap-proval of vestries selling subsidised flour to labourers, 'thereby rendering him an object of a parish rate...an indecent insult', and insisted that 'The Labourer is worthy of his Hire'. Nothing more was heard after the initial meetings, though simultaneous strike preparations by 'Farmers Servants & other work-people in Hertfordshire' were reported.[96]

The 1799–1801 famine saw renewed attempts. Early in 1800 Dorking was repeatedly besieged by large groups of labourers 'declaring that they would not work, while bread was at such a price, unless their wages were raised again ... They declare they cannot keep their families from starving'. Parts of Berkshire and Essex saw parallel mobilisations, though both were vigorously suppressed, and agricultural workers from Kent again found themselves before the courts for identical offences. There is limited evidence of localised increases of regular wages by farmers in response to pressure from their men in 1795–96 and again in 1799.[97] No doubt further successes accrued throughout the war years with respect to harvest wages, the moment when individual employers were vulnerable to collective action as the need to reap expeditiously negated resort to the law. Inflated harvest earnings, however important for domestic budgets, were a palliative when regular wage rates were held down. Outside harvesting, resort to industrial action exposed agricultural labourers to considerable dangers, and failed.

Some rural artisans, among them Kentish biscuit-makers and Hampshire millers, and cornland town journeymen, including Brighton shoemakers and tailors, were also prosecuted under the new Combination Acts.[98] This evidence suggests that systematic study of the sources might reveal greater cornland use of these statutes than suggested by historical orthodoxies.[99] However, it is unlikely that a revised picture would seriously challenge the contrasts drawn by contemporaries between artisans able to win wage increases more than adequate to accommodate inflated living costs and 'husbandmen' who were not. Strikes by journeymen in market towns remained frequent and collective pressure exerted by their countryside counterparts included Kent carpenters, Sussex building crafts, blacksmiths and wheelwrights, and Cambridgeshire 'carpenters, bricklayers, blacksmiths etc', action repeated in places around 1811 when living costs soared again. Workers in declining cornland industries, among them those in East Anglian textiles and Surrey hosiery, adopted imitative initiatives. Their more stable industrial neighbours, especially paper-makers and millwrights, won wage increases. The capacity of non-agricultural workers to secure ample wages was determined not simply by market forces but by resort to industrial action or its threat.[100]

The depression's impact on the labour market reduced rural skilled workers to a rough par with farm labourers. Raising wages through industrial action was implausible,[101] and it is significant that, in some instances where harvesters tried to collectively pressurise farmers, abundant labour supplies encouraged the latter's recourse to the courts.[102] On the other hand, arson followed harvest wage disputes.[103]

Farmworkers' growing dependency on regular wage supplementation was revealed in protesters' changing objectives, neatly symbolised by the angry groups which converged on Lewes in 1801. The Buxted column intended to set food prices in orthodox style, but the others aimed to lobby Petty Sessions. Although the Framfield contingent had threatened to strike, they joined their Chiddingly and East Hoathly counterparts in demanding increased allowances in aid of wages, and the Bench responded positively with appropriate orders circulated to overseers in every parish. Militant action to force improved allowances became more common, exemplified by the 'riotous' assemblage confronting Cocking overseers in December 1794, insisting on 'an Increase in their weekly pay over and beyond' vestry stipulations.[104] Such foci reflected farmworkers' acceptance that inadequate wages were compensated by regular and casual statutory relief.

Employment

Farmworkers had always distinguished the better from the poorer among local employers and continued to do so, notwithstanding the new post-war issues of under- and unemployment and poor-law benefits.[105] Local opinion certainly operated, not necessarily effectively, and no doubt rural terrorism, threatened and real, concentrated farmers' minds, but circumstances precluded other forms of action to force the niggardly to expand their workforces.

Cornland working-class attitudes to the availability of work were revealed in two principal features after 1815, namely the expanding use of threshing machines and the employment of migrant Irish labour. The East Anglian rising of 1816 displayed several objectives, but the strongest was an end to the machine-threshing which was devastating winter employment as sailors and soldiers flocked back from the wars. Many East Anglian districts which escaped the 1816 mobilisations were disturbed by fiercer recurrence in 1822, and in 1829 parts of Essex experienced identically-motivated rioting. The physical demolition of machinery was utterly unambiguous: the issue united labourers, craftsmen and small farmers, and at Winfarthing the crowd in 1822 was led by carpenters. An open meeting of labourers assembled at Hoo formally resolved that any farmer who persisted in the use of threshing and the drilling machines and mole ploughs, which had also figured in 1816, would have his property fired. The same message was also delivered through the medium of threatening letters, while Essex farmers were warned off mechanised threshing by graffiti chalked on barn walls.[106] The owner of the first machine used in Surrey was threatened with arson in 1791, but south-eastern protests against threshing-machines were relatively muted because reduced corn acreages discouraged investment in them during the depression. In 1800 food prices motivated arsonists at Downland East Dean: in 1805–6 they discussed whether incinerating an oat-rick would also destroy a machine in an adjacent but locked barn. After 1815 mechanised threshing provoked a series of incendiary attacks.[107]

By the late 1820s, hostility to technological innovation was universal in England, and if a minority of labour aristocrats benefited, outside their privileged ranks hostility was peaking and transmuting itself into sheer hatred. A symbolic expression occurred in 1829, when a 'steam carriage' careering along from London to Bath was attacked at Melksham by a crowd 'impressed by the notion that … [it] was calculated to reduce *manual* labour; and cries were set up "We are starving already, let's have no more machinery!" "Down with the machinery!" "Knock it to pieces".' Other rural observes confirmed the 'blind fury against machinery, which is characteristic of the present times'.[108]

Violent resistance to migrant Irish harvest labour increased in rough proportion to their incursions. Although there were wartime precedents for hostilities in the Fens, after 1815 further violence was probably experienced somewhere in most years, though the press played it down before the late 1820s. Then the succession of light harvests commencing in 1828 seriously aggravated the problem. In 1829 the 'unusual number of Irish harvestmen' in Lincolnshire drove down piece rates, which 'in some cases … produced ill-treatment of the Irish' and escalated to 'murderous attacks' across the Rutland border.[109] Similar events occurred in the south-east before 1830, when ethnic violence intensified.

The Old Poor Law

Recurrent machine-breaking and the rising intolerance of Irish harvesters reflect the vulnerability of both to direct action. However, the issues of work, wages, and allowances were inextricably juxtaposed: 'it was too generally the practice to beat [labourers] down so low, as well in wages as in parochial allowances', with repeated downward revisions of both in tandem. The vestries' extended role turned poor-relief into a gigantic theatre for fierce conflict. Strife was multi-dimensional, with vestrymen, who had never achieved much of a reputation for politeness either between themselves or with claimants, often locked in vitriolic exchanges, replete with expletives. Commentators dubbed them 'bear gardens', lamented interjections made without 'regard to courtesy', and castigated frustrated vestrymen who made 'public censure on the Parochial Authorities' on leaving the meeting. In the 1870s one some-time official recalled the 'stormy, angry vestries held' during 'the great agricultural depression'.[110]

Vestries were repeatedly besieged by stone-throwing crowds and occasionally literally invaded by substantial groups of protesters. Officials were regularly assaulted. In one typical revolt, at Crondall in Surrey, roadworkers refused to execute the prescribed number of daily trips with wheelbarrows loaded with stone from the village pit, where-upon the vestry mulcted each protester's pay, reaffirming that three journeys comprised the stipulated daily task. Individuals protested over numerous issues, none more poignantly than Thomas Culver whose 'threat ... of leaving his Wife and family to the Parish' was made over the withdrawal of all relief on his refusal of summertime farm-work at the derisory weekly rate of 7*s*. Some vestries adopted self protective strategies, ranging from Easebourne's instructions that women were not to lobby the meeting, to Heathfield's practice 'to decide in the absence of applicants for Relief & for them to be told on the following morning by one of the Overseers'. This shielded vestrymen at the expense of inflating the role of officials in claimants' minds. But employers were expected to make representations on their labourers' behalf, reflected in one of the many complaints against 'yeoman' Farndell of Bosham, who 'never attended the Vestries'.[111] Inadequate representation and secrecy contributed to the extension of conflict up the administrative hierarchy, notably with collective remonstrations, some of them violent, at Petty Sessions where individuals also protested, many of them vehemently.[112]

The complexities of causal issues generating this protest can be explored through case studies. Claimants Charles Weston and George Eastwood of Burwash were subjected to universal economising mea-sures imposed by their vestry and were in perennial conflict with its officials after their relief was repeatedly curtailed and suspended for refusing instructions to cease keeping dogs and, in Weston's case, maintaining adolescent daughters at home. This broke instructions to make them available for parish-directed employment, an offence aggravated by their being 'dressed in a manner superior to their condi-tion'. After one altercation with the domineering overseer, farmer Flurry, the pair allegedly fired his barn. Flurry represented traditional overseers drawn from the more substantial employers serving their year, whose property was vulnerable. But his targeting might have owed as much to his profile as an underemploying farmer as his present term as a parish officer. The fact that the two ostensibly had personal grievances against him, deriving from his latter role, constituted a critical part of the prosecution's case, but motivational ambiguity was an element in the jury's acquittal.[113]

Most assistant overseers were not exposed in the same way, but they were open to terrorist tactics. Thomas Abel, of Brede, whose duties included supervision of roadworkers and residential governorship of the workhouse, together with the equally vexatious task of collecting the rates, was subjected to numerous threats and at least one assassination attempt when a gun was discharged through his bedroom window. This assailant was never identified, though Abel's multifarious duties spawned enemies from virtually all social groupings. Suggestions that the culprit was a smuggler in this location increased rather than reduced the numbers of suspects. Magistrates were targeted too, and again evidential legal imperatives turned on identifying suspects with personal grievances derived from their subjection to judicial functions. The prosecution of William Edwards of East Grinstead for firing Justice Cranston's property followed his worship's patient explanation that two magistrates were required to uphold an appeal against select vestry decisions, prohibiting unilateral intervention to overrule Edwards' daily receipt of only 1*s.* 6*d.* for roadwork. This case failed as well, as jurymen appreciated that active justices were exposed to what was described in a previous unresolved case as the 'atrocious attempts of roguery to wreak vengeance upon Magistrates'. Claimants at Mayfield subjected to the parochial economising directed by the youthful utilitarian squire, William Day, were aware of the principal source of reduced benefits. But Day's campaign against parish subsidies of plebeian cottage rentals also alienated numerous petty landlords. The author of an anonymous letter threatening to murder Day was never caught, despite his orchestration of a vestry reward for information, and whomsoever was responsible no doubt took satisfaction at the restoration of subsidised rents.[114]

These cases, and the previous evidence of poor-law administration being engulfed by conflict, derive principally from south-eastern parish and Petty Sessional archival sources between 1815 and early 1830. Historians' assertions that they were not experienced in East Anglia are questionable on evidential grounds.[115] Protests reveal that claimants resented reductions in benefits which cut their living standards and were equally opposed to usage of relief mechanisms to enforce discipline, subservience and, through them, social control. Unemployed farm-workers clearly expected labouring work to be organised by local authorities with pay on a par with their counterparts who secured jobs with the farmers. Attempts by the latter to drive wages down, in cahoots with vestries which withheld benefits or work from those who refused to accept derisory rates offered by parsimonious private employers, were perceived as immoral. Under- and unemployed rural artisans bitterly resented being reduced to labouring under parish auspices. Moreover, all categories of claimants ultimately expected protection from the Bench against parochial cheese-paring backed by disciplinary measures, as reflected in the considerable resort to appellant proce-dures, and were distressed once magistrates abandoned their customary role as the preservers of the poor's rights. The Bench also incurred opprobrium from the ranks of non-claimants, including those gravely disadvantaged through being forced to support relatives from whom public aid was withdrawn, and those who also benefited from the recip-rocal arrangements found at village levels, especially cottage landlords.

All of these features represent the centrality of the poor law to parochial rural economies. It was a mechanism for a restricted redistribu-tion of wealth rather than a simple device by major farmers to subsidise their wage bills. For many working-class families, their entitlements to multifarious benefits and employment were crucial to their existence, and these were seen as sacrosanct; hence the vigour of protests when they were threatened, infringed or negated. In cash terms, workers were the greatest beneficiaries, and there were psychological elements too which cut both ways. A surprisingly high proportion of village resi-dents benefited to degrees, though this is not to claim that all ratepay-ers profited. In fact, given the complexities, it would be difficult precisely to demarcate net gainers from net losers. Given the interplay of rights and customs which the poor law embraced, moral considera-tions were manifest during the 1820s once determined campaigns to reduce costs were coupled with the system's manipulation to enforce social discipline. Captain Swing categorically restated claimants' and others' objections to both.

Captain Swing

However Swing is characterised, the protests represented a calculated strategy for the ultimate objective, namely the restoration of rural com-munities' economic and social equilibrium. Every issue which had provoked previous protests was readdressed. Swing's attempted reorder-ing of socio-economic relationships constituted the most powerful coherent and concentrated expression of countryside moral economy. The staggered start by farmworkers and others in Kentish localities to address their multifarious grievances in 1830 as the summer passed into autumn initiated the subsequent series of mass risings which literally swept through the cornlands to reveal local and regional differences of emphasis and, in some places, additional issues, including political ones. The politics, however important, need not detain us here.[116]

In Cobbett's account, the revolt commenced in July 1830 with the violent expulsion of Irish haymakers from the Isle of Thanet. With the third consecutive thin cereal harvest in prospect, coincident with an unprecedented build-up of Irish labourers, violence between English and Irish harvesters flared in Kent and Sussex. For Lincolnshire, a distinguished local historian has revised Hobsbawm and Rudé's count of three anti-Irish riots to 21. When Kentish incendiarism commenced in earnest in September 1830, the immediate victims were exclusively those who had employed the Irish. Sussex Justice Sanctuary, who played a major role in Swing's suppression in the Horsham district, unequivocally told Home Secretary Melbourne that 'The employment of the Irish Labourers in England is a great evil & ... ought to be reduced.'[117]

According to Cobbett's explanation of Swing's trajectory, Kent protesters, having expelled the Irish, progressed to wholesale destruction of threshing machines. These commenced in Downland Upper Hardres, a typical 'close' village, but it bordered Stelling with its squatter community on Minnis Health. As cereal prices began to rise, Upper (and Lower) Hardres farmers used their own and hired machines to speedily thresh newly-harvested corn to catch rising markets. In late August, after extensive planning and threats against their use, a major assault was launched. The crowd 'appeared not to be all of the labouring Class – Some appeared above', including butcher Carswell and blacksmith Arnold. At least one small farmer was involved in the planning, a feature by no means confined to south-eastern Swing.[118]

Cobbett was adamant that the speedy reversion to hand threshing generated work and reduced the numbers 'doing useless work with half a belly full ... crushing stones': 'it was in vain to argue with the labourers that the destruction [of threshing machines] ... did no good, for ... they knew that one ... machine did the work of ten men.' Cobbett made no observations on the well-known fact that hundreds of village artisans played a major role in cornland Luddism. Others emphasised this phenomenon, including Colonel A'Court at the Wiltshire Special Commision, who stated that at Heytesbury a machine 'was broken in a minute, evidently by persons who understood the trade. I should think by blacksmiths and carpenters.' Carpenter Cooke, of West Grimstead in the same county, was said to be 'the instigator of others, and had lent them his tools'. Since many a country gentleman not only professed a profound ignorance of why such men participated, and compounded this by discriminating against artisans when deciding who should be prosecuted, a spirit echoed by professional judges when sentencing, Cobbett's silence is surprising.[119]

Swing's protests exuded many features of 'collective bargaining by riots', juxtaposed with elements of the strike, reinforced by terrorism, principally arson. A south Dorset observer simply said that 'There has been what is termed "a strike for wages" in almost every village hereabouts', which embraced all labourers, including George and James Loveless at Tolpuddle. Samuel Selmes, the biggest tenant farmer in south-east Sussex, reported on 9 November that 'Peasemarsh Rye Udimore Northiam Tenterden & Rolevenden are all struck from work this day.' A Berkshire roadworker asserted that he had as 'much right to strike' as those in farmers' employ.[120] The 'pressing' of all workers, including journeymen, was very common, if not universal.[121] Wages and levels of employment were important issues almost everywhere. Several Swing assemblies articulated customary adages that the 'Labourer is worthy of his hire'. A written statement, addressed to the 'Gentlemen of Burwash', insisted that the considerable assemblage 'come this day to meet you with good Intent although you may think otherwise ... wishing for nothing but a fair living by our own Industry in a Land of great plenty'. Daily, rather than weekly, rates were *the* principal concern, reflecting the realities of labour casualisation, not its acceptance: the logic of demands for more employment suggests the opposite. So too does the agreement, secured in places, that labourers should not be turned off during wet weather, a common post-1815 practice, but provided with alternative tasks.[122] The precise levels of demanded wage increases reveal little ostensible consistency, even between neighbouring parishes, though sometimes labourers determined against this situation.[123] Wage agreements had a snowball effect. As one labourer said, he 'wanted his wages advanced as well as those in other places'. Overall demands for adult daily rates ranged from two to three shillings, and more generally reflected existing regional disparities. The revolt also coincided with the traditional period when lower wintertime wages were about to be, or were in the process of being, determined at parish levels. This underpinned Swing's capacity to sweep the cornlands. A Sussex farmer who had 'lowered wages ... since Michaelmas' sought to appease the crowd by paying the difference to the workers involved.[124]

However, this device was inadequate. Many labour negotiators insisted that summer rates being paid in 1830 were increased by around $12\frac{1}{2}$ per cent, with provision for a higher rate, usually of about 20 per cent, to come into force at Easter 1831. At Etchingham on the East Sussex–Kent border, the 'United Petition of their body' assembled on 10 November stated that married men were to have a daily wage of 2s. 3d. rising to 2s. 6d. on 1 March 1831, while single men were to receive 2s., again rising to 2s. 3d. To these were subjoined stipulated revised rates for younger workers under eighteen using the customary categories, those aged sixteen and seventeen, and adolescents of fourteen and fifteen. This petition contained a more generalised refinement, namely that children aged over twelve were to receive a 'proportion' of the bachelors' wage, individually tailored to reflect not just age but also capacity, a normal criterion. In places, piece rates were added; usually these were to be 'raised in [the same] proportion' as daily wages. The Etchingham proposals were unusual only in their apparent acceptance of differential rates between bachelors and family men and reflects the negotiated outcome. More often, attempts by farmers to maintain this convention were vigorously resisted, revealing the determination of younger men to be paid the going rate, irrespective of their domestic responsibilities, and reflecting their significance in Swing crowds, both numerically and especially as a source of militancy.[125]

Hobsbawm and Rudé identify 'simple wages riots' as central to a 'wages movement', at its most pronounced in Essex where Swing represented a 'straight' fight over this single 'issue … between the labourers and their employers'. But wage rates were also understood to apply to workers directly employed by the parish, though it was not invariably stated even where roadworkers were leading protesters. It was dramatically reinforced at Hadleigh, Essex, where these authors report 'a wages strike of the unemployed'. Equally unrepresented both in the papers drafted by labourers' leaders for employers and vestrymen to sign, and in formal agreements listing wages, were those for journeymen craftsmen, despite their strong presence in mobilisations. Occasionally, journeymen demanded the restoration of wage differentials: if labourers were to get the revised daily rate of 2s. 6d. from Ladyday 1831, then '3s. 6d. for tradesmen' was appropriate, according to the Kintbury wheelwright, Oakley. Some master craftsmen also combined to agree minimum prices and threatened those who undercut them.[126]

Demands for more employment were of course organic to the universal attack on threshing machines. Although one prisoner in

Berkshire stressed that 'all they wanted was to break the Machines', in 1830 rural Luddism comprised the essential complement to wage demands and explains the repetitively close correlation between machine-breaking and wage-negotiating crowds. Indeed, the veteran East Anglian labour historian, A. F. J. Brown, argued that over much of that region the destruction of threshing machines followed resistance to increasing wages. Swing's insistence on greater employment was often expressed in general terms, without specific arrangements to enforce it. The Etchingham labourers tellingly accepted an almost customary vestry calcualtion, that if every occupier employed one man per £20 of ratings, with those small farmers rated under that sum employing proportionately, it would 'prevent any surplus hands being left to work for the Parish'. The negotiated agreement based on Henfield labourers' written terms, that no man was to be unemployed, may have been a common outcome. This reflects a number of assumptions, especially that farmers would farm more intensively, and therefore absorb more labour, once their non-labour costs were reduced by lower tithes and rents, to which we return. Nevertheless, in places greater employment was effected immediately, symbolised by the response of one particularly unpopular farmer at Steyning, who pacified the crowd 'by taking six more men at one farm' alone. Some specific demands in a consequential number of locations included not simply guarantees against the further employment of itinerant labour, which was not restricted to the Irish, but also the reservation of all work for the parish's settled inhabitants: the employment of 'persons not belonging to the parish' was one of the other complaints against Bosham farmers, while Lord Sheffield's 'foreign' steward and bailiff on his Sussex estate were specifically denounced by a pseudonymist. Cobbett disapproved as it 'narrowed the market for labour, making the labourer almost the slave ... by confining him in his own parish'.[127]

Swing, despite rhetorical flourishes, accepted that landworkers' wages could not be expected to meet the living costs of family men, irrespective of the numbers of young children. The Etchingham wage rates were linked to required child allowances; 1s. 6d. was paid weekly for the third and each subsequent child. Across the parish border, the somewhat higher wage demands presented at Burwash were in part compensated for by the identical 1s. 6d. child allowance commencing with the fourth. These should not continue to be 'struck of[f] under 14 Years ... for a Girl & 12 for a Boy For under that age they are not able to support themselves & the parent is not able to do it', unless the offspring were in permanent work, which of course was difficult to secure.

The Berkshire Swing leader, roadworker Sadler of East Haghorn, 'required the price of two loaves and One shilling a Week for himself… his Wife a loaf and a half and his Family the price of a Loaf for each Child'. The fact that he 'was a Criple', and therefore less likely to secure farmwork, may have conditioned his demand for the restoration of almost the classic Speenhamland sliding scale.[128]

Sadler also demanded 'his Rent paid' by the parish, but overall attitudes to rents were ambiguous, despite one Surrey JP's claim that farmworkers were 'maddened by oppression… chiefly from the high Price of Cottage Rents'. The Burwash petition stipulated that the minimum weekly income of 12*s.* for married but childless men, mostly aged workers, would enable them 'to live and pay his rent as [they] ought to do'. Elsewhere cottage rent reductions were sought, including Goudhurst and nearby parishes in West Kent, Framfield and Mayfield adjacent to Burwash, and by a huge crowd from several villages which lobbied an MP at Hungerford. One of the Shelleys halved his cottage rents at Warnham. At Overton, Hampshire, the crowd insisted on farmworkers' wages being raised to 12*s.*, with house rents paid by employers, already part of a package agreed at Amport. Farmworkers accepted tied houses, though these were Downland communities where scarce housing was owned by farmers' landlords; the agreement constituted the regulation of an existing system.[129]

Swing's intervention over poor-law matters was not restricted to benefits as protesters seized the opportunity to reform its administration. One expression of this was the number of annual overseers whose properties were targeted by arsonists, a clear adoption of terrorism to soften them up. Where assistants were employed, their dismissal was demanded as a precondition for the restoration of more generous relief and better treatment of claimants, notably the end of punitive initiatives taken by these fellows. Their ceremonial removal is well-known, as at Henfield 'so that… he shall be neither justified nor authorized to domineer or bullyrag over the poor'. Taking them across the parish boundary symbolised the fact that they were outsiders, though Assistant Barron at Ticehurst pre-emptively fled over 30 miles to Rochester. Specific additional symbolism included the giant wooden scissors paraded at Ninfield, where unmarried mothers had suffered the indignity of having their heads shaved. Symbolisation in villages near the coasts, where beach pebbles for road mending had been loaded into carts and pulled by parish employees, was achieved through using the same vehicles to convey the assistant over the border. At Fawley, Hampshire, the crowd seized the offending cart, threatened to destroy it unless the vestry promised that it 'should be drawn by horses and not by men … old and young and boys' and 'particularly Jane Stevens, an idiot'. The Ringmer poorhouse grindstone, used to punish insubordinate parish employees, was 'pulled … down to the yells of the mob'. These and other close ties between workhouse administration, enforced residence therein, assistant overseers, make-work schemes and punitive systems naturally varied, but precise local grievances sometimes also led to direct attacks on workhouses.[130]

Greater employment at enhanced wages, with more generous poor-law benefits, subjected all ratepayers' (and especially farmers') liquidity to further strains, and some realistically claimed that bankruptcy loomed. This comprised the economic rationale behind the widely-reported 'junction which the Farmers have latterly formed with the labourers', in the words of a Norfolk clerical magistrate, to demand tithe reductions, which was extended to lay proprietors. These 'symptoms of combination' were usually impossible to prove for prosecution purposes although, as the same parson emphasised, one major reflection was the refusal of farmers to enrol as special constables, a feature not restricted to East Anglia. It should be noted that Swing coincided with annual tithe audits, which took place publicly with tithe-owners traditionally providing a dinner at inns, events facilitating protesting assemblies. Where collected, tithes united communities, especially in the south-east and particularly in the Weald, where insolvency had made small farmers 'quite reckless'. Farmers, particularly smaller farmers and tradesmen, widely exploited the tithe issue where relevant. Acrimony recurred when tithe-owners offered 10 per cent reductions, as these represented major savings for big farmers but minimal cuts in small farmers' business outgoings.[131]

Substantial farmers figured in demands for rent reductions, as exemplified by the tenants on the Corfe estate in Dorset who were 'refusing all assistance' to authority 'unless' their landlord 'promises a reduction in rent, in proportion to the increases of wages demanded'. Although labourers and some farmers followed Cobbett's automatic linkage of tithes with rents, cuts to the latter were not widely demanded, according to Hobsbawm and Rudé, implying that most major estate-owners were thought to have already made sufficient downward adjustments, though Swing encouraged something of a further round.[132]

In some localities Swing sought a fundamental solution through broadened demands. The Amport package included 'a portion of fuel' supplied by the parish. Reduced fuel prices were demanded at Goudhurst and at a Hernhill pub the 'general conversation' focused on

a local wood dealer accused of monopoly.[133] South Hampshire protesters incinerated toll-gate keepers' cottages and threw the gates into
the flames. However, these incidents do not represent a reincarnation
of earlier eighteenth-century hostility to turnpikes by country folk
infuriated by the *de facto* privatisation of roads and the payment of
tolls for a previously free public facility. Keepers were recent recruits in
the war against smugglers, and these protests appear to have comprised
opportunistic attacks on the excise's new allies.[134] Elsewhere, smugglers
used their organisational prowess and their famed bludgeons to join
crowds in securing Swing's main objectives.[135]

Finally, Swing's onslaught against threshing machines extended to
the premises of agricultural engineers, iron founders, paper-millers and
other technologically-driven enterprises, among them saw-millers.
In Hampshire a crowd raised by 'Ruffians, strangers', attacked the
Tasker Brothers' Upper Clatford iron foundry, which they 'completely
destroyed leaving a melancholy wreck'. Craftsmen, among them the
ruined Tangley blacksmith Carter, were principally responsible. Another
exclaimed that he 'should like to be down with all foundries ... Some of
them said that the foundry was ruining every one – carpenters, and
wrights, and weavers, and every body ... they could not live for it, and
that therefore the factory must come down.' Saw-mills were attacked in
Hampshire, Berkshire and Wiltshire. In East Anglia timber-merchant
Calver's wind saw-mill in St Clement's parish, Norwich, was fired after
the sawing machinery was destroyed. Owners of the 'principal factories
about Greenwich and Deptford' were threatened by 700 men from the
Sevenoaks district, reputedly organising to 'destroy ... all descriptions of
machinery', a mobilisation accompanied by an 'immense number
of ... threatening letters sent' to proprietors of advanced mills in the
'environs of London'. Commissioner Rowan of the Metropolitan Police
reported that his men neutralised 'about one thousand' intent on
'burn[ing] all the Machinery of the Saw mills' on the South Bank.[136]
Swing also released antagonisms in Kent and Hampshire against substantial printers who had installed steam presses and millers using
steam-power.[137]

Considerable damage was inflicted on paper-mills, notably in the
vicinity of High Wycombe, where new machinery was being installed.[138]
In Norfolk, at Lyng paper mill, a crowd armed with 'axes, hammers,
bars and bludgeons' inflicted £748 worth of damage to recently-
mechanised rag 'chopping machines'. Other paper-mills in this district
were also attacked, with sectors of these crowds proceeding to adjacent
villages to demolish threshing machines. Norwich weavers, involved in

a fierce industrial dispute and democratic politicking, sacked a silk factory and also participated in arson attacks targeting threshing-machine owners in nearby villages.[139] In Wiltshire, too, Swing reignited long-standing hostilities to textile technology, with a flood of 'anonymous Letters sent to the principal Clothiers threatening their machinery'. The 'carding and other machines' at Quidhampton woollen manufactory, near Wilton, were destroyed and its counterparts at Mere saved only through the intervention of the Wiltshire Yeomanry. An anticipated assault on Trowbridge mills did not materialise, surprising one resident who ascribed it with some 'reason … [to] some of our worst Characters … gone from the Town & neighbourhood to assist the discontented' in their attacks on threshing machines in nearby villages.[140]

The New Poor Law

The foregoing evidence can be woven into an identification of the principal components of a countryside moral economy, when tested against immediate post-1830 rural developments. This chronology commences with Swing's suppression from October 1830 to mid-1831. That repression, after a bewildered and incoherent start, was utterly ruthless, due to the new Whig-dominated government's undisguised opportunism to prove to its vociferous critics that commitment to parliamentary reform did not mean ministers were in hock to rural mobs. Swing also provided much of the empirical evidence which was equally opportunistically seized upon to promote a radical revision of the Old Poor Law.

Many of those who caved into Swing's demands consciously and semi-successfully bought time. In places, reneging on these agreements began almost immediately, as in Wiltshire, where by 18 December 'the farmers … began to back out of their compulsory bargains with the labourers'. Once the columns of *The Times* filled with accounts of the Special Commission trials shortly before Christmas, farmers in many locations 'having recovered from their fright … began to lower the Wages', according to the King's private secretary. Cobbett predicted the resultant intensification of incendiarism, and in February 1831 claimed that 'country newspaper' editors were ordered by local grandees not to report arson, a fact admitted candidly but privately to the Home Office by a principal insurer.[141]

However, the determined suppression of the riots and militant reactions to broken agreements must not disguise the fact that the rising evoked considerable sympathies for the plight of rural workers at all

244 Moral Economy and Popular Protest

levels of society, revealing close parallels with the responses to food riots from a similar social mixture identified by Thompson. Grandee hostility to threshing machines found an early apogee in Sir Edward Knatchbull's notoriously lenient sentences imposed on the first batch of Kent machine-breakers in October. Some Norfolk magistrates formally published advice to farmers to cease machine-threshing. Reports of other landowners' instructions to tenants to desist made the newspapers. When the Battle Petty Sessions convened on 8 November, the Bench coupled its denunciation of incendiarism with the powerful recommendation to all vestries to arrange full employment 'at proper & sufficient Wages'. The Earl of Chichester made an unprecedented visit to chair Hellingly vestry on 25 November and, in the presence of an equally unprecedented attendance of 32 men, piloted through a scheme extending the Roundsman system to *all* ratepayers in the interests of full employment. Privately the Earl believed that grandees 'can give no stronger authority... that... wages are insufficient than by sanctioning... allowances' in aid thereof.[142] Others were less pragmatic, including the 'very old and very intemperate' Justice Willis when chairing Ringwood Petty Sessions on 2 December. Informed that Ibsley Parish Officers reduced allowances, thereby neutralising a niggardly wage increase, Willis denounced them, adding that such conduct encouraged incendiarism.[143] This went unreported to Whitehall, but the Reverend Fowles, who prevailed on a farmer to pay a crowd £10 towards members' lost wages, was sternly rebuked for exciting 'irritation and disorder'. 'Gentleman farmer' Rush of Dawling Hall, Norfolk, found himself in the Assize dock for directing his labourers forcibly to release arrested machine-breakers.[144]

Nassau Senior asserted that Swing's demands were 'repeated... by the farmers, the clergy, the magistrates, in short by all the ignorant and timid throughout the country'. Economic realities meant that such people's politics soon consigned them to minorities among hard-pressed employers and ratepayers. This paternalistically-driven outlook put them on a par with their earlier counterparts when they invoked the law against forestalling. Just as the latter, in the face of hostile receptions from *laissez-faire* ideologues and authoritarian Home Secretaries, had engineered more generous poor relief and charitable schemes, after Swing they orchestrated adoption of the Labourers' Employment Act and reinforced philanthropy, most notably with allotment provision. Squire Methuen of Lyneham, Wiltshire, very tellingly took 70 acres from two large farms to 'let to the poor inhabitants, in lots from a quarter of to $3\frac{1}{2}$ acres, according to the largeness of their family'. Montague-Burgoyne of Essex typically believed that 'the Peace & Safety of the Country depends on the System'.[145]

The press teemed with reports of the prodigal productivity of spade husbandry and with it opportunities to reduce poor-law expenditure. Farmers remained opposed, convinced that allotments gave labourers an independence that was destructive of industrial discipline. Ironically, the feared loss of all poor relief constituted a major objection from the labourers themselves. Moreover, many providers not only discriminated against workers with compromised reputations, but subjected allottees to irksome conditions, including loss of land for dishonesty, drunkenness, non-attendance at church and even unabated claims on parochial funds. It is surely significant that demands for allotments are absent from the substantial documentation of cornland anti-New Poor Law riots in 1835–36.[146]

The causes of popular hostility to allotments reinforce the argument that countryside moral economy embraced the right to work and/or relief. Farmworkers continued to struggle for better wages between 1831 and the 1835 implementation of the New Poor Law. Further localised adoption of striking can be found in the early 1830s in response to traditional autumnal downward wage revisions. East Anglia saw 'large scale strikes' for wage increases in the spring and summer of 1832, some of which ended with a curious combination of imprisonment and fines for violence and exhortations from the Bench for employers to abandon 'irritating and insulting language' in their dealings with labourers.[147] More ambitious movements affected other districts, including parts of Hampshire in 1832 and south Dorset in 1833–34. Both ended in failure, spectacularly in the latter, with the Tolpuddle Martyrs. However, the Dorset activists had key links with some of the craft unions powering the emergent Grand National Consolidated Trade Union which aimed to unionise farmworkers.[148] The Hampshire movement was spearheaded by Cobbettites. The evidence is inadequate for any confident assessment of the distribution of such politicised groupings, though an informed guess is that they were numerous.[149]

Those responsible for the intense incendiarism in the immediate post-Swing era saw arson as a means of increasing wages. Events in Berkshire at Lambourn in 1832–33 are revealing: several firings of individual farmers' properties failed to prevent savage downward adjustment of wintertime wages, and it was said amongst agricultural labourers 'employed partly on the roads' that 'there would be no good times at Lambourn till there had been a good fire'. The latters' definition was revealed on 19 November with an attempt to 'fire the town itself' through simultaneous blazes started by rags soaked in inflammatory liquid. The fire did considerable damage, burning horses alive at the Red Lion, and an investigation by Bow Street police officers produced five arrests. One prisoner cracked on interrogation. His evidence proved that the arsonists' 'object was to intimidate the Farmers ... to raise their wages'. The incident was used immediately in a spate of anonymous letters eleven miles away at East Henney, after unsuccessful appeals to Wantage Petty Sessions for higher allowances. Once again an approver revealed details normally unavailable;

> Their reason for writing were that they had been beaten down in their wages, and could scarcely live. The letters referred to the fires at Lambourne, and threatened that they should be served worse ... if they were not better to the poor ... they did not intend to set fire to the property ... only ... to frighten the farmers to get more money.

Other cases revealed that agricultural 'Labourers have regular meetings to discuss the utility to them "of having a fire" ... if their grievances were not redress'd'.[150]

In July 1831, Cobbett claimed that 'there are no more' threshing machines 'to break ... or at least, so few in number as not to be worth speaking of'. In fact, Swing's triumph was less complete. Further machine-breaking occurred in Kent in 1831, in response to rumours that previous offenders had been wrongly convicted: these rumours were scotched by more trials. Some Norfolk farmers reintroduced them in 1832, though in most of Suffolk hand-threshing was restored until the mid-1840s, when the reappearance of machines contributed to very fierce incendiarism.[151]

The implementation of the Poor law Amendment Act 'created ... an undefined terror'. Sheer disbelief greeted the new Relieving officer on his first visit to Mountfield. A crowd, 'mostly women', exclaimed 'that there was no act of Parliament for striking off their relief but that it was done by the Board of Guardians ... there was no act or order of the kind ... it was an alteration made by the farmers who wanted to starve the poor.' A copy of the Act was hastily but pointlessly procured: labourer Hilder declared that 'they did not mean to have their children taken from them'. The Officer 'was dragged out of the [Parish work] house by a number of Women', dumped in a cart with 'a Hankerchief tied to the top of a Hop Pole' and drawn out of the parish. Similar scenes were common. At Willingdon, Sussex, the Relieving Officer was perceived to have 'come down there to starve them', and his counterpart, accompanied by the overseer at Bapchild, 'were forcibly expelled ... & their Papers & Books torn to pieces'. Ringmer ' Paupers were very abusive to [Relieving Officer] Bull and said he had no business there, and [they] did not want any body out of the Parish.'[152]

This destruction of parochial autonomy was an important feature in many anti-poor law protests,[153] including those over workhouses. One resolution passed at a rally at Jevington on the South Downs stipulated 'that no Pauper should be obliged to go into any Workhouse out of his own Parish', and women gathered at Uckfield 'to resist the introduction of the paupers of one parish into the Workhouse of another'. Although the Jevington protesters also passed an 'unanimous determination to resist the separation of man and wife' in the huge existing workhouse at Eastbourne, adequate to effect classification, that could be achieved in many Unions only through distributing the elderly, the children, the able-bodied males and their wives to different present parochial workhouses throughout the Union. This meant not only separation, but location of dismembered families miles apart from each other. Implementing this arrangement sparked considerable protests by current workhouse inmates, among them those at Steyning, where fist fights commenced between male inmates and a pugilistic magistrate, who was worsted before the army rescued him. Soldiers escorted different categories of inmates to redesignated workhouses in Horsham Union.[154]

However, these initial, and principally overt, protests were crushed more easily than their Swing antecedents.[155] The Amendment Act was imposed on a 'half-starved, miserably clad, wretched, and discontented' workforce. A radical southern journalist opined that 'The cure for all [these] evils lies in ... *competent wages* and *full employment*', the precise objects of a new trade union, United Brothers, formed in the Rye region early in 1835. They received financial aid, advice and speakers from unions in London, Manchester and Birmingham, expanded rapidly along the Kent and Sussex coasts, and began to penetrate the interior. One local compaigner, speaking at Heathfield in the High Weald, argued that:

> Your Labour is exacted by the ... Tyranny of the Farmers ... The Labourer is worthy of his hire ... I call upon you like Men in defence of your rights not to be led by these petty Tyrants ... By uniting with us we are determined to stand by each other in defence of our Rights & Liberty ... We have got Reform have your expectations been realised [The] first reformd parliament passd the poor Law Bill

places & punishment assign'd you directly you become poor and you are punished a[s] a common fellon.

But the Brothers were defeated by a vigorous lock-out within six months, precluding their intended strike at the 1835 harvest. Similar fates befell the Essex 'County Union' in 1836 and, in 1838, a remarkable reignition of trade unionism in south Dorset, Tolpuddle country, orchestrated by Robert Hartwell, the London compositors' union leader. In all of these struggles, employers exploited both the New Poor Law and surplus labour. Unionists were sacked and faced incarceration in workhouses. Alternative workers were easily procured in a buyer's market.[156]

The last recorded major act by the Brothers comprised a mass lobby of the Battle Board of Guardians. The unionists knew the army was on the alert and in this dilemma could only petition, replete with highly symbolic pleadings central to our identification of rural moral economy:

> That your Servants and Labourers view with much alarm the fearful infringements which this Bill is calculated to make upon their right and Liberties; that your Servants and Labourers have always been willing to work for their Bread; and to use their utmost exertions to maintain their Families; and that your Petitioners are determined not to let the Law of God be torn assunder by the Laws of Man, which will be the case if the present system is acted upon; Your petitioners therefore humbly request that relief may be given them as heretofore and that your Petitioners may not have their wives and families taken from them when they are thrown out of employment or overtaken with sickness or casual Misfortune: but that they may live as they have hitherto done in their own humble cottages and in the Bosom of their Families.

The Board's contemptuous dismissal of this plea for the maintenance of all the benefits derived from the Old Poor Law, on the grounds that they were not going to be 'intimidated' from the 'performance of their duties' by an 'illegal assembly', equally speaks for itself.[157]

The process of implementation also revealed powerful hostility from lesser ratepayers, which endured. Those without a secure financial base felt as vulnerable as their labouring neighbours. As we have seen, many master craftsmen and independent jobbing skilled men were beneficiaries of those aspects of the old system now specifically outlawed under the new, among them the payment of rent for cottages, parish contracts for services and goods, and subsidies for those tottering on the edge of insolvency. Small businessmen, including rural shopkeepers, were disadvantaged in the fierce competition for Poor Law Union contracts, which favoured grander operators exploiting economies of scale. Moreover, small ratepayers also faced the not inconsiderable costs of paying their contributions to funding new workhouse erection and the eradication of parochial debts. There were compensations, including the usually overlooked Act of 1835 permitting the sale of parish properties to help cover this capital expenditure. The impact of this legislation warrants detailed analysis, but it certainly facilitated considerable speculation for those with even modest sums to invest. In this context the New Poor Law's initial disadvantaging of cottage landlords was reversed.[158]

Medium and substantial farmers benefited handsomely. They fully exploited the continued bloated labour force, now living in the workhouses' shadows. Some farmers pushed wage levels down further. Employers claimed that labourers worked harder and calculated that their men's new determination to keep their jobs meant per capita productivity increases of around 25 per cent.[159] This, together with the huge savings for big ratepayers, more than compensated for the loss of wage supplementation represented by the end of allowances in aid. The return of agrarian capital's profitability at the same time formed the final ingredient in the equation.

However, agrarian capital did not have everything its own way. Incendiarism achieved unprecedented peaks prior to 1850 over much of the cornlands and was not exclusively East Anglian: neither was animal maiming. Arson was routinely given as one explanation for many southern Unions' refusal to accept or abide by imposed formal Prohibition Orders against outdoor relief to the able-bodied, though the sheer scale of under- and unemployment, which varied considerably, was another factor along with its corollary, the huge costs of maintaining especially large families in workhouses. The tacit continuance of disguised forms of outdoor relief is well-known. Many of the most pauperised villages additionally exploited their retention of autonomy over the roads to maintain traditions of putting the unemployed to work, and they boosted public employment by quarrying their materials from pits hired out of the highway rate. In February 1839 the Salehurst vestry convened to consider 'the best method of Employing or Relieving At the Parish Expence such labourers As Are not in the service of Any Private Individual And whose families would be Destitute without Parochial Assistance of some kind.' They decided on road improvement schemes which were renewed during successive winters.

Other parishes raised voluntary rates to similar ends, including winter-time outdoor relief. Cornland perceptions of Victorian workhouses began to change once rural depopulation and a buoyant agrarian economy, often in conjunction with roadworking, restored some basic equilibrium between labour supply and demand. Hated they remained, but from the 1850s workhouses acted more as receptacles for the aged: as an emigrant from Caistor wrote home from New Zealand in 1875, there was no Antipodean equivalent to Lincolnshire, where when 'you are worn out from old age, [you are] sent to the slaughter house, as my poor old father was at that cursed union, where he pined to death. I would rather die in a ditch.'[160]

Conclusion

How, then, is the moral economy of the English countryside to be reconstructed? What are its components? The formation of that moral economy represented a response to, and indeed a not unreserved accommodation of, socio-economic rural change over about three-quarters of a century. The intensification of agrarian capitalism and the proletarianisation of the bulk of the rural labour-force constitute the principal germinative themes. Proletarianisation reduced labour to virtual total dependency on the market, at least in the theoretical sense. That dependency, *and popular attitudes to it*, revealed itself in any number of ways.

First, rural workers visibly supported fair-price notions, with district consumers having a priority for locally-grown foodstuffs, as opposed to their neglect by farmers and merchants exploiting higher prices in distant markets. This proves the ubiquity of the Thompsonian moral-economic outlook over living costs. But it was of reducing significance for farmworkers from the 1790s, and after the last great subsistence crisis in 1816–17 it became of even more restricted import. However, concepts of fair market prices did not evaporate. If traditional *taxation populaire* and food blockading were virtually absent during Swing, surviving fair-price concepts resurfaced in the Captain's demands for lower cottage rentals and cheaper fuel.

Farm labourers, service and other rural industry workers attributed critical importance to the wage: all categories responded to wartime inflation in the 1790s by the adoption of collective action to achieve increases adequate to living costs. Such agricultural labourers who were able to exploit wartime labour markets to their advantage did so, notably through migration after better-paid work, insistence on piece-rates and by jettisoning customary live-in service in favour of pure cash wages at market rates. The latter phenomenon proves young workers' resentment over the restraints of annual service, especially the rigours of living in the employer's house, and its non-embrace by moral economy. Wage considerations endured. Swing made that clear, an attitude speedily reinforced once the Amendment Act and its implementation loomed. Hence the resort to trade unionism between 1832 and 1838, and hence too the timing of much arson when farmworkers' wages were altered at Easter and Michaelmas. Nassau Senior commented to Lord Chancellor Brougham that:

> The riots and still more the fires of 1830 was a practical lesson on the rights of the poor and the means of enforcing them, *the fruits of which are far from exhausted.* That wages are not a matter of contract but a matter of right, that they depend, not on the value of the labourer's services, but on the wants, or his expectations ... [they are] monstrous and anarchial doctrines.

We are indebted to the famous economist for such an eloquent expression of this component of countryside moral economy.[161]

However, farmworkers, in contrast to their skilled neighbours, accepted that labourers' wages adequate to the support of families, irrespective of size, were impossible. Although there is limited evidence of hostility to any need for regular parish aid, acceptance of regular *de facto* child allowances occurred speedily, initially attributable to the impossibility of large families surviving the famines without such payments. The subsequent enhancement of 'casual' one-off payments for all manner of essentials constitutes a progression. Therefore recourse to both regular and occasional wage supplementation was well-established and essentially accepted before Napoleon's final defeat.

The depression, and the grossly inflated rural labour supply, put as much pressure on securing work as an adequate return for it, even when supplemented. Statute law directed parish authorities to find work for the unemployed: once faced with both under- and unemployment, labourers looked to their vestries to honour that commitment. Skilled men, when identically placed, had little option, short of migration or emigration, other than to emulate their labouring neighbours. Opportunities for direct action to increase the demand for labour were very restricted, except over threshing machines and migrant labour. But resistance to these indicates, together with demands for work, that full employment, even if that meant parish work for at least parts of the year, was embraced by countryside moral economy. Moreover, threshing machines ensured that the technology issue was of major significance for all countryside workers, and many other categories of inhabitants, and served to unite considerable majorities against inventions destructive of the economic equilibrium of their communities.

Wages and work also reflected in popular attitudes to both tithes and farm rentals. The fact that farmers during Swing encouraged labourers to campaign against current tithe levels proves farmworkers' rudimentary economic understanding, namely that tithe payments diminished that wages fund and jeopardised poor-relief funding. Most Anglican clergymen visibly lived relatively affluent lives and to all intents and purposes put little of real value back into their communities. Moreover, in many, though not all, counties, they constituted a considerable proportion of the most active magistrates and, if some were more generous over poor-relief appeals, any positive features deriving from this activity were more than dissolved by their criminal adjudications.[162] Landowners were in a roughly parallel position. Rentals were second to tithes in Swing's estimation: neither were to remain at levels incommensurate with an agrarian economy in which labour received its just desserts. The moral economy demanded appropriate adjustments to ensure that the impact of unfavourable economic conditions was borne by all.

The right to poor relief, and more especially adequate public assistance, was jeopardised notably in the 1820s by local authorities' determination to reduce expenditure. This proved a complex task, owing not least to the conflicting economic interests of different categories of ratepayers. The adverse context in which the attempt was made was aggravated by the use of the benefit system to discipline recipients. However, relief had become part of the moral economy. It was central to Swing's negotiations, whatever the incidence of regional variations, and embraced work, weekly incomes and a whole range of allowances, especially with respect to children under the age of being able to obtain work in the depression, rent and, where appropriate, public provision of housing. And, as the treatment of assistant overseers revealed, recipients refused to have these benefits conditional on subservient conduct. Benefits comprised rights, and their centrality to moral economy was unambiguously re-articulated by protesters against the Amendment Act, and almost pathetically reaffirmed by the United Brothers once staring defeat in the face over wages. The enduring character of incendiarism and animal maiming was at least partly oriented to preserve a viable remnant of entitlements under the Old Poor Law, underwriting Cobbett's stance that the latter was 'the Magna Charter of the working people'.[163]

However, Cobbett also defended moral-economic concepts pertaining to what historians have dubbed 'social crime', a defence which by implication went beyond that definition. 'The Labourers know as well as I do that, if they are unable to obtain bread for *work*, they have a RIGHT to it without', and 'if refused [poor] relief, a *right* to *take the food where they find it*'. Among those *articulating* the right to steal was the farmworker forced to accept vouchers in lieu of money wages for exchange at the village shop for goods at inflated prices, and who responded by realising cash through the sale of a farming implement stolen from the employer.[164] The perennial thieving of corn from their employers by English farmworkers, especially for pig and chicken rearing, was notorious but, even if there were thousands of prosecutions, many farmers turned a blind eye so long as theft levels remained moderate. Both sides regarded handfuls of barley, or pocketfuls of potatoes, essentially as perks and legitimate whatever the law formally decreed.[165] In these contexts it is possible to detect linear developments whereby proletarianised labourers retained a tokenised toehold on the production ladder, a particularly powerful symbol where wastes and commons had been appropriated through enclosure. The privatisation of traditional communal rights over such land, to which woodlands should be added, like the *de facto* transformation of game into personal property, reveals parallels in the contexts of wood stealing and poaching. The right to glean was a technical victim of case law and, where attempts were not made to completely eradicate it, the ancient custom was transmuted into a parochially orchestrated concession and restricted to designated categories of the 'deserving poor'. Recurrent village disputes to protect unregulated gleaning rights for all locals indicates that it, too, constituted a part of moral economy. Those excluded gleaned illegally, if at all, and therefore resorted to theft to compensate for what several historians have calculated as a valuable component of family income.[166] Where such infractions of redefined private property rights become endemic, pilfering from employers' stockpiles, raiding woods and pulling sticks from hedges for fuel, like the trapping of rabbits for the pot and poaching more valuable game for sale on the black market, become integral components of the moral economy of the poor. The Amendment Act made it an even more important component of that moral economy, symbolised by the very marked intensification of sheep-stealing after 1835: usually this meat was for consumption by workers in their families, rather than for sale along with game on the black market.[167]

Cobbett's ultimate answer to rural under- and unemployment, and poverty, turned not on the preservation of Old Poor Law entitlements but on agrarian economic and social restructuring to recreate a traditional world. The economic implications behind its social gradations reflect another perception of moral-economic principles, ultimately focusing on universal access to land. Cobbett's dreams were undoubtedly shared to degrees, but, if we can detect their application of sorts in multifarious brands of social crime, access for all to the land had been largely driven out of moral-economic perceptions by the realities of capitalist cornland development. That development was underpinned by theorists, and supported by the state, the great majority of substantial landowners and their tenants. The final acceptance of allotments represents part of a desperate attempt to come to terms with the loss of pre-1835 benefits, while allotment provision was an equally desperate attempt to deploy paternalistic devices to protect capital from incendiarism. Allotments, of course, endured and were central to attempts to sanitise the cornlands. But Swing, and to some extent the Amendment Act protesters, also reveal degrees of politicisation among the rural poor. Labourers, and their allies (most notably the journeymen craftsmen), also articulated their identification that taxes impoverished, while enriching sinecurists, placemen and those comprising the uppermost layers of the English ancien regime. However, the political route to change was blocked repeatedly by the realities of radical weaknesses and reverses which were particularly poignantly experienced in the cornlands.[168]

Ironically, it was the market, not the reformed parliaments, that marginally improved the lot of farmworkers after 1850, and the principal ingredient was rural depopulation during the age of profitable high farming. The latter once again disproportionately benefited the craftsmen. But their brief alliance with the labourers between the mid-1810s and the late 1830s seems to have invoked their own variant of moral economy, as producers in times of crisis, which reveals an ideology underpinning custom and practice at no great remove from that identified by Professor Randall among West Country woollen workers. In the final analysis of countryside moral economy, technologies which profited the few, at the direct expense of the many, had no legitimate place.[169] The same must be said of most other means whereby capitalists profited from cutting and paring plebeian living standards, especially by multifarious manipulations of the labour market, and then through reducing poor-law benefits. Only access to land was not unambiguously embedded in, as opposed to being refracted by, the moral economy.

Access to land became more visibly embraced by moral economy once survival dictated acceptance of allotment provision in the unprecedented circumstances imposed by the Poor Man's Robbery Act.

No historian, least of all the present author, should underestimate the enduring impact of the New Poor Law. Nevertheless, it is not insignificant that, first, its principles were considerably modified in practice, and, second, the attempt in the 1870s to reinvigorate the strict application of those principles had a particularly muted effect in the cornlands. The financial implications of the workhouse test, especially when imposed on men with large families, of course constituted a major disincentive to apply it invariably. However, there was more to the issue than costs. Aversion to incarcerating elderly labourers and their wives once they were past supporting themselves was not confined to the potential or actual victims, but was widely shared in cornland communities. Even the particularly unpleasant utilitarian enthusiasts who dominated the notorious Andover Board of Guardians paid *de facto* pensions to the aged and, moreover, 'did not take much notice' of the residual earnings of such folk from weeding gardens and scouring the roads for dung to sell,[170] while more liberal Boards condoned any number of devices for aiding those in temporary difficulties out of the house. Some went further. 'We consider that an honest man, with large family, is entitled to an order' for weekly food allowances 'if he does not earn so much a week', stated chairman Robert Wells Eyles of the Croydon Union in 1844.[171] This perversion of post-1834 medical relief entitlements is itself an eloquent testimony to the persevering spirit of rural moral-economic precepts. These were embedded, and at times reflected, in the very language. As the veteran chairman of the Uckfield Union mused in 1904, 'people talk of getting "Parish Pay" instead of relief', just as they had on his initial election in 1858.[172]

Notes

1. E. P. Thompson, 'Moral economy reviewed', in Thompson, *Customs in Common* (London: Merlin, 1991), esp. pp. 336–40; K. D. M. Snell, *Annals of the Labouring Poor* (Cambridge: Cambridge University Press, 1985), pp. 99–103. In his original article, 'The moral economy of the English crowd in the eighteenth century', Thompson observed that the mere 'disposition to riot' – let alone mass mobilisations – 'was certainly effective as a signal to the rich to put the machinery of parish relief and of charity…into good repair': 'Speenhamland' was a noted exemplar, but at this point Thompson withdrew, saying that an 'examination of such measures would take us farther into the history of the poor laws than we intend to go'. These comments imply that Thompson perceived that poor relief was indeed part of populist

moral economic *mentalité,* and not something magically separated from it. Reprinted in Thompson, *Customs,* pp. 242–3.

2. Thompson, 'Moral economy reviewed', p. 340; emphasis added.

3. Essentially, east and south of a line from the Wash to the west Dorset coast. I have included Lincolnshire, but not the East Riding of Yorkshire.

4. The case for an agricultural revolution, greatly focused on this period, has been powerfully restated by M. Overton, 'Re-establishing the English agricultural revolution', *Agricultural History Review,* 44, 1 (1996); Overton, *Agricultural Revolution in England. The Transformation of the Agrarian Economy 1500–1850* (Cambridge: Cambridge University Press, 1996), *passim.,* but esp. pp. 7–9 and ch. 5.

5. C. Tilly, 'Contentious repertoires in Great Britain, 1758–1834', in M. Traugott (ed.), *Repertoires and Cycles of Collective Action* (Durham, NC: Duke University Press, 1995), pp. 15–42.

6. For example, at North Creake, Norfolk, T. Harrison to Earl Spencer, 9 December 1794 and June 1796, BL, Althorp papers, G16; G33.

7. Notably the exemplary local study by J. M. Martin, 'Village traders and the emergence of a proletariat in South Warwickshire, 1750–1851', *Agricultural History Review,* 32 (1984).

8. For exceptions see esp. G. F. R. Spencely, 'The origins of the English pillow lace industry', *Agricultural History Review,* 21 (1973); P. Horn, 'Child workers in the pillow lace and straw plait trades of Victorian Buckinghamshire and Bedfordshire', *Historical Journal,* 17 (1974).

9. Sir Charles Willoughby, Oxfordshire, to H. Dundas, 19 November 1794, Scottish Record Office, Melville Mss GD.51/1/372.

10. E. J. T. Collins, 'Harvest Technology and Labour Supply in Britain, 1790–1870', Unpublished PhD thesis, University of Nottingham, 1970, pp. 162–3 and notes 1 and 8; A. Armstrong, *Farmworkers. A Social and Economic History, 1770–1980* (London: Batsford, 1988), pp. 48–52; and the even more convoluted hedging in Armstrong, 'Labour I: rural population growth, systems of employment and incomes', in G. E. Mingay (ed.), *The Agrarian History of England and Wales, VI 1750–1850* (Cambridge: Cambridge University Press, 1989), pp. 702–6; E. L. Jones, 'The agricultural labour market in England', *Economic History Review,* 2nd ser. xvii (1964), pp. 323–5; R. Wells, 'Tolpuddle in the context of English agrarian labour history, 1780–1850', in J. Rule (ed.), *British Trade Unionism 1750–1850. The Formative Years* (London: Longman, 1988), pp. 101–2.

11. A. F. J. Brown, *Essex at Work 1700–1815* (Chelmsford: Essex County Council, 1969), p. 131.

12. Wells, 'Tolpuddle', pp. 101–2; R. Wells, 'Migration, the law, and parochial policy in the eighteenth and early nineteenth centuries', *Southern History,* 15 (1993), pp. 107, 114.

13. For example, a Wrotham labourer, working predominantly on piece rates, was joined by his fourteen-year-old son; the latter received 8*d.* daily with the promise of annual increases on his birthdays; settlement examination of John Lawrence, West Malling Petty Sessions, minutes, 2 May 1795, Centre for Kentish Studies, Maidstone (hereafter CKS), PS/Ma4.

14. Wells, 'Tolpuddle', pp. 102–3; for the later eighteenth-century decline, see esp. K. D. M. Snell, 'Agricultural seasonal unemployment, the standard of

living, and women's work in the south and east, 1690–1860', *Economic History Review*, 2nd ser. xxxiv (1981).

15. Wells, 'Tolpuddle', pp. 101–2; and sources cited there.
16. D. E. C. Eversley, 'The home market and economic growth in England 1750–80', in E. L. Jones and G. E. Mingay (eds), *Land Labour and Population in the Industrial Revolution* (London; Arnold, 1967).
17. *Sussex Weekly Advertiser*, 2 April 1792, 14 April 1794, 19 and 26 September 1796, 24 August 1801 and 21 July 1806; letter from the Rev. W. Densham, Petersfield, 31 October 1800, Dr Williams Library, New College Mss. 41/78; British Parliamentary Papers (hereafter BPP), 'Emigration from the United Kingdom' (1826), vol. iv, p. 137.
18. A. Young, *An Enquiry into the Progressive Value of Money in England* (1812), pp. 90–1; Young, *An Enquiry into the Rise of Prices in Europe* (1815), pp. 175, 210; T. R. Malthus, *A Letter to Samuel Whitbread MP* (1807), reprinted in D. V. Glass (ed.), *Introduction to Malthus* (London; Watts & Co. 1953), p. 201.
19. R. Wells, 'Social protest, class, conflict and consciousness, in the English countryside 1700–1880', in M. Reed and R. Wells (eds), *Class, Conflict and Protest in the English Countryside, 1700–1880* (London: Cass, 1990), p. 129.
20. East Grinstead vestry typically appealed to all ratepayers to 'use…most strenuous endeavours to find employment for the Poor actually belonging to this, and not employ those belonging to other Parishes'; farmer Longley of Lydd, who employed the migrant 'honest, sober and industrious' labourer Bayley, acknowledged that 'all the rest of our Parishioners employ their own people'; East Grinstead vestry minute, 25 March 1827; Longley to Winchelsea Parish Officers, 27 January 1825, East Sussex County Record Office (hereafter ESCRO), Par. 360/13/11; 511/35/1/243; Wells, 'Migration', pp. 114–15.
21. See esp. B. Short, 'The decline of live-in servants in the transition to capitalism; a critique of the Sussex evidence', and M. Reed, 'Indoor farm service in 19th century Sussex: some criticisms of a critique', *Sussex Archaeologial Collections*, 122 and 123 (1984 and 1985).
22. J. Archer, *'By a Flash and a Scare'. Arson, Animal Maiming and Poaching in East Anglia 1815–1870* (Oxford: Oxford University Press, 1990), pp. 31–3; *Kent Herald*, 11 June 1835; *Stamford Mercury*, 29 July 1831; Earl of Northbrook (ed.), *Journal and Correspondence of Francis Thornhill Baring, Lord Northbrook* 2 vols (privately printed, Winchester, 1905), I, p. 102; *The Times*, 5 January 1831; *Maidstone Gazette*, 27 February 1831.
23. See esp. M. J. T. Edgar, 'Occupational diversity in seven rural parishes in Dorset', *Local Population Studies*, LII (1994), pp. 48–51; but cf. E. A. Wrigley, 'Men on the land and men in the countryside: employment in agriculture in early nineteenth-century England', in L. Bonfield, R. M. Smith and K. Wrightson (eds), *The World We Have Gained* (Oxford: Oxford University Press, 1986), pp. 295–6, 302–3, 335–6.
24. BPP, House of Commons Select Committee report, 'Emigration' (1825–6), vol. v, Question (hereafter Q) 1057; cf. Brede, 'overdone with Carpenters'; overseers to their St Thomas a Beckett, Lewes, counterparts, 10 May 1829, ESCRO, Par.253/12/1.
25. BPP, House of Commons, Select Committee reports, 'Agriculture' (1833), vol. v, Qs 9919–21, 10094; 'Agricultural Distress' (1836), vol. viii, Qs 903–6,

914, 3084; R. Wells, 'Rural rebels in England in the 1830s', in C. Emsley and J. Walvin (eds), *Artisans, Peasants and Proletarians 1760–1860* (London: Croom Helm, 1985), pp. 129–30; *The Times*, 25 December 1830.

26. Blacksmith George Carter was born, bred and married in Tangley, Hampshire, and by 1830 had ten children under working age: according to his wife, 'We lived confortable by ... his Trade'. Later, the 'principal farmer in Tangley', Richard Fortescue, explained that Carter

    > once had two small freehold Cottages and a little forge ... but that from the falling off of Business and this very ... heavy and yearly encreasing family He was obliged to part with them [the cottages] to the Parish and obtain relief. Since He has worked as a Labourer and on the Road as the Officers directed and had Parish Pay and was glad in the Evingng to do any little Smithis Job He could procure.

    Fortescue to J. Wilks, MP, 25 January 1831 and Mary Carter's petition, n.d., PRO, Home Office (hereafter HO), 17/46. pt. ii.

27. One classic dual-occupationist, a fellmonger-farmer, bought a piece of waste in Ashdown Forest 'to build some Cottages', as running them up was one of the very few 'modes of investment' for 'small freeholders' to circumvent the depression. Elizabeth Beard, Keymer, to S. Peskert, 14 August 1836, ESCRO AMS. 5774/4/9; cf. R. Buchanan, Shere, to a Mr White, 16 July 1830, Guildford Muniment Room (hereafter GMR) PSH/SHER/28/10.

28. S. MacDonald, 'The progress of the early threshing machine', *Agricultural History Review*, 23 (1975), esp. pp. 49–50, 66, 75.

29. D. Grace, 'The agricultural engineering industry', in Mingay, *Agrarian History*; R. E. Morris, *The Royal Dockyards during the Revolutionary and Napoleonic Wars* (Leicester; Leicester University Press, 1983), p. 60; F. Hull (ed.), 'A Kentish holiday, 1823', *Archaeologia Cantiana*, LXXXXI (1967), p. 116; A. Somerville, *The Whistler at the Plough* (1848; new edition, ed. K. D. M. Snell, London: Merlin, 1989), pp. 371, 377–8; Archer, *By a Flash*, p. 43; L. T. C. Rolt, *Waterloo Iron Works: a History of Taskers of Andover 1809–1968* (Newton Abbot: David & Charles, 1969), chs 1–3; *Sussex Weekly Advertiser*, 9 July 1810; J. Peniston, Salisbury, to W. Lambert, Bath, 28 January, to Charles Baker, Southampton steam saw-mill owner, 26 August and 22 November 1828, and to a Mr Jones, Birmingham, 19 May 1829: M. Cowan (ed.), 'The letters of John Peniston, Salisbury architect, Catholic, and Yeomanry Officer 1823–1830', *Wiltshire Record Society*, vol. 50 (Trowbridge, 1996), pp. 84, 111, 115, 134; *The Times*, 29 November 1830.

30. D. C. Coleman, *The British Paper Industry 1495–1860* (Oxford: Oxford University Press, 1959), pp. 147, 151–5, 212–3, 219–21, 230, 258–9, 264–7, 286–7; *Herts Mercury*, 20 November 1830; *The Times*, 12 January 1831; Peniston, to Greenwich engineer Penn, 1 July 1827 in Cowan, 'John Peniston', p. 73.

31. R. Wells, *Wretched Faces: Famine in Wartime England, 1793–1801*, (Gloucester: Alan Sutton 1988), *passim.* and esp. ch. 17.

32. Wells, 'Social protest, class', pp. 135–8: Wells, 'Tolpuddle', pp. 101–7: Wells, 'Migration', pp. 107–18.

33. This argument's most recent major reiteration underpins G. R. Boyer, *An Economic History of the English Poor Law, 1750–1850* (Cambridge: Cambridge

University Press, 1990), esp. pp. 143–4, 216; however, this theoretically driven volume, for all its econometric sophistry, is characterised by a staggeringly profound ignorance of the English countryside. For a more sensitive appraisal, albeit a synthesis, see J. P. Huzel, 'The labourer and the poor law 1750–1850', in Mingay, *Agrarian History*, pp. 772–92.

34. Wells, 'Social protest, class', pp. 137–8.
35. Ticehurst vestry minute, 17 January 1822, ESCRO Par. 492/12/2/5.
36. 58 Geo. III c. 69 (amended by 59 Geo. III c. 85) and 59 Geo. III c. 12.
37. 'A Girl of 14 would go into service: a Boy of 14 would be allowed on the roads, 3s a week; and a Boy of 11, 2s 6d': BPP Report of the Royal Commission on the Poor Laws, 1834, Appendix B, p. 520.
38. R. Wells, 'Social conflict and protest in the English countryside in the early nineteenth century: a rejoinder', reprinted in Reed and Wells, *Class, Conflict*, pp. 69–70.
39. 'Putting the poor to lodging like horses to grass'; Colonel A' Court, to the Poor Law Commission (hereafter PLC), 28 September 1835, PRO, Ministry of Health (hereafter MH), 32/56; Dr Black expressed surprise at the number of relatively affluent individuals at Farningham prepared to take such lodgers for the small allowances, but this reflects many farmers' and others' need for income from any source in the depression. S. B. Black, *Local Government, Law and Order in a Pre-Reform English Parish, 1790–1834* (Lampeter: Mellen, 1992), pp. 233–4; Wells, 'Social protest, class', pp. 139–41.
40. Goudhurst, list of relief recipients, 1834–5, PRO MH 12/4911. Depositions against East Grinstead Swing protesters, November 1830; Burwash vestry minute, 5 March 1831, ESCRO, QR/E807; Par.284/12/1; Snell, *Annals*, pp. 265–6.
41. BPP, 'Emigration', Qs 1145–6; Wells, 'Migration', pp. 103–7.
42. A. M. Urdank, 'The consumption of rental property: Gloucestershire plebeians and the market economy 1750–1850', *Journal of Interdisciplinary History*, 21, 2 (1990), pp. 262–7.
43. Most detailed vestry minutes reveal such assistance; for just one example see Crondall, 16 March 1829, GMR PSH/CRON/8/1. B. Reay, *The Last Rising of the Agricultural Labourers* (Oxford: Oxford University Press, 1990), p. 53; for farms, see P. Lucas, *Heathfield Memorials* (1910), pp. 137, 149.
44. S. G. and E. O. A. Checkland (eds), *The Poor Law Report of 1834* (Harmondsworth: Pelican, 1973), pp. 183–5, 192, 457–8.
45. Compaigns were waged in hundreds of places against paupers tippling; but the inadequacies of attempts to prevent it through the 'Brighton plan' (which had pre-war precedents) whereby the names of all relief recipients were printed and published weekly, as a warning to licensees and to invite exposure by ratepayers, had a limited effect, and claimants also traded in tickets for flour to secure cash for drink. *Maidstone Journal*, 9 May 1786; *Sussex Weekly Advertiser*, 28 June 1819; cf; vestry minutes, Midhurst, 2 January 1818, and Ticehurst, 1 October 1819, W[est]SCRO Par.138/12/1: ESCRO Par.492/12/2/5.
46. R. G. Cowherd, *Political Economists and the English Poor Laws* (Athens, OH: Ohio University Press, 1977), pp. 72–3, 76–7; J. S. Taylor, *Poverty, Migration and Settlement in the Industrial Revolution*, (Palto, California: 1989), p. 100 and note 5; D. Fraser, *Urban Politics in Victorian Britain* (London: Macmillan,

1979 edn.), pp. 26–8, 33, 38–40; B. Keith-Lucas, *The English Local Government Franchise: A Short History*, (Oxford: Oxford University Press, 1952), pp. 23–7; P. Hastings, 'The old poor law 1640–1834', in N. Yates, R. Hume and P. Hastings (eds), *Religion and Society in Kent, 1640–1914*, (Woodbridge: Boydell and Kent County Council, 1994), pp. 133–4; Weale to the Duke of Richmond, 10 April 1834, WSCRO Goodwood Mss, 669, enclosing statistics revealing annual reductions from £1848 in 1829–30 to £1287 in 1833–4, underscored by additional figures relating to individuals, including payments to a bricklayer reduced from £10 to £5 17s. across the same period.

47. The expression used by a hostile 'country surgeon' when writing to the press, and – amongst many others – by a labourers' petition to Lord Gage, principal proprietor at Ringmer; *The Times*, 25 November and 6 December 1830. The officer was 'To make himself fully acquainted with the character and circumstances of each claimant', in the perception of legislators; BPP, House of Commons, Select Committee, 'Poor Laws' (1817), p. 21.

48. *The Times*, 25 November and 6 December 1830; at Bearsted, Kent, when Mrs Hewitt's labouring husband was ill, she obtained a 'little work from the Mill at my house', otherwise 'my family would very much have suffered', but the assistant 'had the impudence to ask' the mill owner 'himself what I earned', and cut their relief by that amount: Prosecutor's brief against William Dyke, Kent Winter Assize, 1830, PRO Treasury Solicitor (hereafter TS), 11/943/3412.

49. Cobbett repeatedly attacked these practices after the adoption of the Sturges Bourne Acts; *Political Register*, 22 December 1821 and 6 March 1824; cf. *Brighton Herald*, 20 November 1830; *Brighton Gazette*, 19 December 1833; Wells, 'Social conflict, class', p. 145; *Sussex Advertiser*, 8 August 1825.

50. P. Mandler, 'Tories and paupers: Christian political economy and the making of the New Poor Law', *Historical Journal*, 33, 1 (1990), p. 93.

51. Among the most informative examples are the Battle Petty Sessions minutes covering most of the years from 1815 to 1832, ESCRO, PS/BA, 2, 3, 4, 5, 7.

52. The Battle Bench unequivocally ruled in November 1821 that thereafter 'orders to be made on Parents & Grandfathers to maintain there Children & Grand Children wholly so long as they have any Property'; subsequent orders reveal policy enforcement, ESCRO PS/BA, 4. This policy, which was certainly not an East Sussex idiosyncrasy, was overlooked by one recent enthusiastic discoverer of the fact that some *menu peuple* owned a little real estate, which is marshalled behind claims of entrepreneurial plebeians' 'market orientated values', and their concomitant hostility to moral economic notions; Urdank, 'Consumption of rental property', *passim*. Victims of such parochial and judicial rulings might think they were ruined by blatant fracture of moral-economic values.

53. Bourne to the PLC, n.d. but 28 October 1834, PRO MH 12/4911; *Brighton Gazette*, 10 January 1833.

54. The case at its most extreme was seen in 'a Farmer who rents at £1000 p. an. is master of all the Markets within his reach; a few of these will be withholding their Corn raise the price ... to what they please': J. Montague, near Chippenham, to the Secretary of State, 31 October 1766, PRO State Papers Domestic, 37/5, ff.258–60. Cf. *Lloyds Evening Post*, 6, 8, 27 and 29 October 1766; *London Chronicle*, 9 December 1766.

55. *Debrett's Parliamentary Register*, XLIV (1796), pp. 213–15.
56. F. G. Stokes (ed.), *The Bletchley Diary of the Rev. William Cole 1765–7* (London; Constable & Co., 1931), p. 41; Hooper to James Harris MP, 26 October 1766; Third Earl of Malmesbury (ed.), *Letters to the First Earl of Malmesbury ... 1745 to 1820*, 2 vols (1870), I, p. 114; H. C. Henderson, 'The 1801 crop returns for Sussex', *Sussex Archaeological Collections*, XL (1952), p. 57.
57. A. Young, *An Inquiry into the Propriety of applying Wastes to the Better Maintenance and Support of the Poor* (Bury St Edmunds, 1801). For the parliamentary campaigns, see J. R. Poynter, *Society and Pauperism. English Ideas on Poor Relief, 1795–1834*, (London: Routledge & Kegan Paul, 1969), pp. 98–104.
58. G. Spater, *William Cobbett: the Poor Man's Friend*, 2 vols (Cambridge: Cambridge University Press, 1982), II, p. 349; *Political Register*, 24 March 1832; *Brighton Gazette*, 19 and 26 August 1830.
59. Cobbett denounced what he clearly saw as a dependency culture as early as 1808: *Political Register*, 16 July 1808; T. Rudge, *A General View of the Agriculture of the County of Gloucester* (1805), p. 346; A. D. Gilbert, 'Methodism, dissent and political stability in early industrial England', *Journal of Religious History*, X (1979), p. 386.
60. *Cambridge Chronicle*, 8 January 1830; *Political Register*, 26 May 1821 and 11 September 1830.
61. Manifested in East Anglian youths' dislike of the 'regularity of life'; cited Archer, *Flash and a Scare*, p. 30; for a classic eulogy on the system, see *Brighton Gazette*, 5 November 1833, cited Wells, 'Tolpuddle', note 27, and cf. Cobbett, *Political Register*, 22 December 1832; B. Reay, *Microhistories. Demography, Society and Culture in Rural England, 1800–1930* (Cambridge: Cambridge University Press, 1996), p. 33.
62. BPP, House of Commons, Select Committee reports, Emigration', Q 1208, and 'Poor Law Amendment Act', (1837), vol. xvii, Qs 3008, 14905; draft reply to the PLC, from G. Courthope, Ticehurst, n.d. December 1832 or Janurary 1833, ESCRO SAS. Co/C/230.
63. See esp. Wells, 'Migration', p. 94. The oft-remarked endurance of live-in service establishing a settlement thereby legitimating a removal into the 1830s and beyond, is a chimera. This was long after the principal period of corn-land resort to removals, namely 1815–20. Sometime live-in service remained one of the few legal grounds, other than the father's (or even grandfather's) settlement, for older people domiciled away from their parish of settlement after the 1820s, if and when their removal was determined upon. Legislators recurrently shied away from major alterations to the law, and in our context it is significant that the Poor Law Commissioners' doctrinaire demand for its abolition in 1832–34 was reflected in the fact that live-in service for future settlements was one of the few and minor changes to settlement criteria the Commissioners succeeded in achieving under the Poor Law Amendment Act itself: 4 & 5 Will. IV c. 76, sections 33, 55, 64–7 71, 84; J. Tidd Pratt, *The Act for the Amendment and better Administration of the Laws relating to the Poor in England and Wales* (1834).
64. J. Neeson, *Commoners: Common Right, Enclosure and Social Change in England 1700–1820*, (Cambridge: Cambridge University Press, 1993); E. P. Thompson, *The Making of the English Working Class*, (Harmondsworth: Penguin, 1968 edition), pp. 240–1.

65. The obvious contrast is with Ireland; the literature is vast, but for a recent brief historiographically-oriented discussion, see R. F. Foster 'Introduction' to C. H. E. Philpin, *Nationalism and Popular Protest in Ireland* (Cambridge: Cambridge University Press, 1987).

66. The encolsure of Wilbarston in Northamptonshire ran into trouble after the first two meetings of the Commissioners were forcibly obstructed. The account of the crushing of overt resistance is instructive. The authorities decided to confront the anticipated third intervention 'by a tumultuous and disorderly concourse of people' with the Volunteer Cavalry. The nearest troop was not used in favour of two others whose men did not have local connections, but were typically drawn from the more affluent farmers, who were 'very eager for the service & seemed delighted' at the opportunity of active service against obdurate commoners indignant at the relatively poor quality land earmarked for their small portions. Captain Cartwright, JP reported that:

> the whole neighbourhood was terrified, & so much at [Market] Harboro[ugh] that we could not prevail for a while upon any one to drive the Waggon with the Posts and Rails ... Upon our arrival on the ground, we found a good many people assembed, & some of them obstructed the way into the field, where the poor's allotments were to be marked out ... & they were so far obstinate & troublesome, as to make it necessary to read the Riot Act ... A bonfire had been cunningly made just at the entrance ... which they thought would frighten our horses, but it had no effect. We took two or three of the most clamarous (for they were abusive in their language), & having punished them by making them assist in putting in the Posts & Rails we released them ... It has had the good effect of showing the alacrity of the Yeomen.

Cartwright to Spencer, 21 and 26 July, and reply, 22 July 1799, BL Althorp papers, G32.

67. The famous Otmoor enclosure has been recently subjected to an excellent re-examination which also reveals that enforcing the Act required a policing operation as prolonged as it was unprecedented: D. Eastwood, 'Communities, protest and police in early nineteenth-century Oxfordshire: the enclosure of Otmoor reconsidered', *Agricultural History Review*, 44 (1996).

68. A. J. Peacock, *Bread or Blood* (London; Victor Gollanz, 1965), pp. 17–18, 20, 62, 69–70.

69. E. J. Hobsbawn and G. Rudé, *Captain Swing* (London; Lawrence & Wishart, 1969), esp. pp. 111, 147–8, 158.

70. Ibid., p. 16.

71. To give but two examples: when Wellington, as Lord Lieutenant, investigated claims that Swing in Hampshire was orchestrated, an analysis of villages rising on the first days of concentrated mobilisations, 19–22 November, identified 27, four of which are not even identified as Swing parishes, with three more listed only as experiencing arson in Hobsbawm and Rudé's tabulations: G. Hollis to Wellington, n.d. received 22 December 1830, Southampton University Library, (hereafter SUL), Wellington Papers, 1/1157/2. The private papers of the East Sussex Curteis family likewise reveal several unlisted places with specific risings (ESCRO AMS.5995/3/1–14) and this evidence together with Home Office materials also indicates that

the mobility of itinerant crowds ensured that no parish over most of Wealden East Sussex escaped from both indigenous risings and intrusions by parties from the neighbourhood.

72. B. Bushaway, *By Rite: Custom, Ceremony and Community in England, 1700–1880* (London: Junction Books, 1982), pp. 180–1.

73. W. G. Hoskins, *The Midland Peasant: The Economic and Social History of a Leicestershire Village* (London: Macmillan, 1957), p. 245; Neeson, *Commoners*, pp. 5–6, 41, 52, 59, 142, 158, 172, 284–5, 297, 324–7; I. Dyck, 'Towards the "Cottage Charter": the expressive culture of farm workers in nineteenth-century England', *Rural History*, 1 (1990); I. Dyck, *William Cobbett and Rural Popular Culture*, (Cambridge: Cambridge University Press, 1992), pp. 51–60, and appendix I; I. Dyck and A. Howkins, 'Popular ballads, rural radicalism and William Cobbett', *History Workshop Journal*, 23 (1987).

74. Stokes, *Bletchley Diary*, p. 41.

75. For some details of purchases by Lewes-based businessmen see C. Brent, *Georgian Lewes 1714–1830. The Heyday of a County Town* (Lewes: Colin Brent Books, 1993), pp. 10, 31–3, 51; Wells, 'Social protest, class' p. 124.

76. BPP, House of Commons, Select Committee report on 'Agriculture', 612 (1833), vol.v, Qs 12774, 12780; *Sussex Weekly Advertiser*, 2 October 1815 and 21 January 1822.

77. Prosecution of wagoner Church of Heyshott, Sussex Summer Assize, *Sussex Weekly Advertiser*, 8 August 1825; indictment, PRO Assizes (Assi), 35/265/5. However, farm labourers who were kept on could be disadvantaged by a new farmer in ways other than by dismissal. Farmer Sharp of Henley was denounced in a threatening letter after taking over from his deceased predecessor, Freeman, for saying that he 'would fetch the fat off…Freeman's men': *Reading Mercury*, 29 November 1830; see also Reay, *Microhistories*, pp. 18–19.

78. Neeson, *Commoners*, pp. 265, 270; *Hertford and Ware Patriot*, ns. xxviii, (n.d. but probably 1834, copy WSCRO Goodwood Mss 1474). The feelings of those who did not join the 'small farmers' who emigrated to escape penury and degradation at parish expense from the Guildford area in the late 1820s can only be imagined. One of the two vessels leaving Rye for Australia in 1828 contained East Sussex farmers and their husbandry 'implements', the other labourers: *Sussex Advertiser*, 5 May 1828; BPP, 'Agriculture' (1833), Q 131.

79. *Sussex Weekly Advertiser*, 10 June 1793, 24 September 1810, 14, 21 and 28 January, 4, 18 and 25 February and 1 April 1811, 22 February 1812, 13 and 27 May, 5, 12, and 26 August, 16 and 23 September 1816.

80. Cited Hobsbawm and Rudé, *Captain Swing*, p. 339, note 34.

81. *Political Register*, 4 December 1830; T. Sanctuary, Horsham, to Peel, with enclosure, 18 November 1830, PRO HO 52/10, ff. 536–7; *Maidstone Gazette*, 11 January 1831.

82. A. M. Colson, 'The Revolt of the Hampshire Agricultural Labourers and its Causes 1812–1831', Unpublished MA thesis, University of London, 1937, pp. 94–5.

83. J. Hasted, *History of Kent*, 13 vols (1797–1801; 1972 edition, ed. A. Everitt), I, p. xix; VIII, pp. 78–9, 118; IX, pp. 46, 304; Young, *An Inquiry*, pp. 67–8,

83–6, 95–6, 101; *Political Register*, 25 June 1821; Reay, *Microhistories*, pp. 20–1, detects marked resort to squatting during the Napoleonic Wars.

84. Neeson, *Commoners*, pp. 28–34; BPP, 'Reports of the Poor Law Board on the Laws of Settlement and Removal of the Poor', 1850 (1152), vol. xxvii, report on Surrey and Sussex by Capt. Robinson, composed 1848, p. 81; BPP, House of Commons, Select Committee report, 'Commons Inclosure', (1844), vol. v, Qs 5330–54; *Sussex Agricultural Express*, 17 February 1877.

85. M. Chase, *'The People's Farm': English Agrarian Radicalism 1775–1840* (Oxford: Oxford University Press, 1988); M. Chase, '"We wish only to work for ourselves": the Chartist Land Plan', in M. Chase and I. Dyck (eds), *Living and Learning* (Aldershot: Scholar, 1996), pp. 133–43; R. Wells, 'Southern Chartism', *Rural History*, 2, 1 (1991), pp. 52–3.

86. Thompson, 'The moral economy', p. 189.

87. J. Stevenson's revised synthesis in his *Popular Disturbances in England 1700–1832* (London: Longman, 1st edn 1979, 2nd edn 1992), ch. 5, offers a review of some of this literature, but he overemphasises the later eighteenth-century refocusing of this category of protest on the industrial Midlands and the North, invoking my work in support: p. 124 and note 29. I was impressed by the very wide geography of food rioting in the wartime famines of 1794–6 and 1799–1801; Wells, *Wretched Faces*, part II, and cf. Wells, 'The revolt of the South-west 1800–1; a study in English popular protest', *Social History*, 6 (1977), which Stevenson chooses to ignore; see also A. Randall, A. Charlesworth, R. Sheldon and D. Walsh, 'Markets, market culture and popular protest in eighteenth-century Britain and Ireland', in Randall and Charlesworth (eds), *Markets, Market Culture and Popular Protest in Eighteenth-Century Britain and Ireland*, (Liverpool: Liverpool University Press, 1996).

88. D. E. Williams, 'Morals, markets and the English crowd in 1766', *Past and Present*, 104 (1984); D. Gregory, '"A new and differing face in many places": three geographies of industrialization', in R. A. Dodgshon and R. A. Butlin (eds), *An Historical Geography of England and Wales* (London: Academic Press, 2nd edn, 1990), p. 354 and esp. note 10.

89. R. Wells, 'Counting riots in eighteeth-century England', *Bulletin of the Society for the Study of Labour History*, xxxvii (1978), pp. 68–72.

90. D. Vaisez (ed.), *The Diary of Thomas Turner, 1754–1765* (Oxford: Oxford University Press, 1984), pp. 82, 107; *York Courant,* 21 October 1766; indictments of seven 'labourers'; depositions of two butchers, a grocer and a blacksmith, Berkshire Lent Assize, 1767; Sussex Summer Assize 1757, indictments, PRO Assi 5/87; 35/197/10.

91. P. Reynolds, Huntingdonshire, to W. Frend, 31 July 1795, F. Knight (ed.), 'Letters to William Frend', *Cambridge Antiquarian Records Society* (1974), p. 14; Wells, *Wretched Faces*, pp. 108–11, 128, 161–2, 274; K. D. Bawn, 'Social Protest, Popular Disturbance and Public Order in Dorset, 1790–1838', Unpublished PhD thesis, University of Reading, 1984, pp. 13–15; Peacock, *Bread or Blood*, pp. 76–8, 83–5, 88–91, 95; *Sussex Weekly Advertiser*, 27 May 1816; *The Times*, 14 October 1816.

92. Harrison to Spencer, 13 and 15 October 1795, BL Althorp papers, G.19; Wells, *Wretched Faces*, pp. 165–8, sources cited there and table 13; Watts, London Fire Office, to the Home Secretary, 1 November 1800, PRO HO 42/53.

93. M. Clarke, 'Crime in the Sleaford division of Kesteven, 1830–8', *Lincolnshire History and Archaeology*, xviii (1983), p. 18.

94. E. F. Genovese, 'The many faces of moral economy; a contribution to a debate', *Past and Present*, 58 (1973).

95. In 1732 live-in servants in Kent insisted on improved premiums and the Bench castigated farmers for caving in owing to labour scarcity; N. Landau, *The Justices of the Peace, 1679–1760* (Berkeley, Cal.: University of California Press, 1979), p. 247.

96. *Sussex Weekly Advertiser*, 26 November, 3 and 10 December 1792, 24 November 1794 and 19 January 1795; West Sussex Quarter Sessions minutes, January 1795, ESCRO QO EW 31; C. Emsley, *British Society and the French Wars 1793–1815* (London: Macmillan, 1979), p. 31; Brown, *Essex at Work*, pp. 130–1; Wells, *Wretched Faces*, p. 163.

97. Ibid., pp. 163–4; Mrs D'Arblay, West Humble near Dorking, to Dr Burney, 4 and 22 March 1800, in J. Hemlow (ed.), *The Journals and Diaries of Fanny Burney* (Madame D'Arblay), 4 vols, (Oxford: Oxford University Press, 1973), IV, pp. 401, 407; *Kent Chronicle*, 10 March 1801.

98. Wells, *Wretched Faces*, p. 164; *Sussex Weekly Advertiser*, 10 June 1805, 11 July and 1 August 1808.

99. An argument predicated on London and the industrialising regions, though even here the case is evidentially inadequate; but see J. Moher, 'From suppression to containment: roots of trade union law to 1825', in Rule, *British Trade Unionism*, pp. 84–6.

100. Poynter, *Society and Pauperism*, pp. 59–61; Wells, 'Tolpuddle', pp. 106–7.

101. Strikes by cornland town artisans were periodic, and often seasonal, exemplified by those resorted to by Hastings builders and Lewes bricklayers; *Sussex Weekly Advertiser*, 24 April 1823 and 14 March 1825.

102. Exampled by four Burwash labourers' summary convictions on 12 September 1826 for harvest contract breaking; summary returns, ESCRO QR/E790.

103. *Sussex Weekly Advertiser*, 28 September 1801 and 7 October 1822; both involved hopping.

104. H. Shadwell, Lewes, to the Duke of Richmond, 5 and 15 February 1801, PRO HO 42/61; *Sussex Weekly Advertiser*, 2, 9 and 16 February, and 16 March 1801; West Sussex Quarter Sessions rolls, indictments, 1794–5, WSCRO QR/W608, ff.58, 62, 609, ff. 51–3.

105. Hence a discussion between two labourers at Bearsted; 'Stokes…does not employ many people…Mr Wise was a good kind of Man and employed a many and paid them better than ere a Master in the parish'; prosecutor's brief against William Dyke, Kent Winter Assize 1830, PRO TS 11/943/3412.

106. Peacock, *Bread or Blood*, pp. 27, 49, 69–70, 73, 75, 102; P. Muskett, 'The East Anglian riots of 1822', *Agricultural History Review*, 32 (1984); A Charlesworth, 'The development of the English rural proletariat and social protest 1700–1850; a comment'; Wells, 'Rejoinder', reprinted in Reed and Wells, *Class, Conflict*, pp. 60–2; 78; Archer, *Flash and a Scare*, pp. 76–7, 81–3; T. L. Richardson, 'Agricultural labourers' wages and the cost of living in Essex, 1790–1840: a contribution to the cost of living debate', in B. A. Holderness and M. Turner (eds), *Land, Labour and Agriculture, 1700–1920* (London: Hambledon, 1991), p. 86.

107. *Sussex Weekly Advertiser*, 14 April 1800, 11 November 1805, 7 April 1806,
      1 April, 11 and 25 November 1822, 12 and 19 October 1829; King and
      Fell, Lewes, to J. Hitchens, London, and to E. J. Curteis, 10 and 15 May
      1822, PRO HO 64/1, ff.205–8, 246–7; depositions of labourer Cheesman,
      and farmer Hobson, 28 September, and 8 October 1813, ESCRO QR/E737.
108. *Salisbury and Winchester Journal*, 3 August 1829; *The Times*, 2 December
      1830; H. Drummond, Albury, Surrey, to Peel, 17 November 1830, PRO, HO
      52/10, ff.199–200.
109. *Kent Herald*, 4 September 1828; *Stamford Mercury*, 14 and 28 August, and
      4 September 1829. Oddly the Irish make no appearance in Peacock, *Bread
      or Blood,* and but once in Archer's index, *Flash and a Scare.*
110. Dundas to Willington, January 1830, cited M. Neuman, *The Speenhamland
      County: Poverty and the Poor Laws in Berkshire 1782–1834* (1982), ESCRO
      Par.372/12/1; 1834 Poor Law Report, appendix C, p.138. *Sussex Advertiser,*
      15 October 1873.
111. Crondall vestry minutes, 1 July 1822, 16 June, 22 September, 2 and
      17 November 1823, and 23 February 1824, GMR PSH/CRON/8/1; vestry
      minute, Easebourne, 13 May 1822; deposition of farmer Farndell, Bosham,
      18 November 1830, WSCRO, Par.86/12/1: Goodwood Mss 1477a;
      Heathfield overseer Barrow's deposition, 30 October 1834, ESCRO QR/825;
      The Times, 2 December 1830.
112. For such incidents, see Wells, 'Tolpuddle', pp. 116–18.
113. R. Wells, 'Crime and protest in a country parish: Burwash, 1790–1850', in
      J. Rule and R. Wells (eds), *Crime, Protest and Popular Politics in Southern
      England 1740–1850* (Rio Grande, Ohio: Hambledon, 1997), pp. 204–5.
114. Brede vestry minutes, 15 March and 21 May 1829, ESCRO, Par.253/12/3;
      Sussex Weekly Advertiser, 1 and 15 February 1802, 11 March 1808, 12 May,
      22 and 29 December 1823, 4 and 18 January 1825; Edward's indictment at
      Sussex Winter Assize, 1823, PRO Assi 35/263/4; Mayfield vestry minute,
      3 January 1825, ESCRO Par.422/12/1.
115   Archer, *Flash and a Scare*, pp. 84, 143, 258–9, but cf. 76, 88–9; A. Digby,
      Pauper Palaces (London: Routledge & Kegan Paul, 1978), pp. 258–9, nei-
      ther of whom cite similar sources.
116. For which see Wells, 'Rural rebels', pp. 131–43; Wells, 'Social protest, class'
      pp. 183–91, and esp. R. Wells, 'Mr William Cobbett, Captain Swing and
      King William IV', *Agricultural History Review,* 45 (1997).
117. 'What business had they to give their work to a parcel of Irish laborers
      when their own countrymen were starving'; *Maidstone Gazette*, 24 August
      and 28 September 1830; *Political Register,* 4 June 1831 and 24 March 1832;
      Sanctuary to Melbourne, 20 January 1831, Bodleian Library, Ms. Tap.
      Sussex C2, ff.61–2. S. Barber, 'Irish migrant agricultural labour in C19
      Lincolnshire', *Saothar,* VIII (1982), p. 16 and esp. note 19; Wells, 'Social
      protest, class', pp.159–61; R. Russell, *Three Lincolnshire Labourers' Move-
      ments* (Barton on Humber: Workers' Educational Association, 1994), ch. 1.
118. *Political Register,* 4 June 1831; depositions, Francis and Richard Castle, John
      Cramp, George Youens, John Jeffreys, 19 September 1830, CKS Q/SBe/120;
      Maidstone Gazette, 7 September 1830; *Norfolk Chronicle,* 15 and 22
      November 1831, covering the trial of a 'cowman' sentenced to seven years'
      transportation for heading a crowd, but not actually assisting in the

destruction of threshing machines. Near Stelling, Henry Atwood 'keeps 2 or 3 Cows... he has a little land' but 'no ploughing land'; cf. A. Randall and E. Newman, 'Protest, proletarians and paternalists: social conflict in rural Wiltshire, 1830–1850', *Rural History*, 6, 2 (1995) p. 209.

119. *Political Register*, 6 June 1831; *The Times*, 23 December 1830 and 5 January 1831; Wells, 'Rural rebels', pp. 136–7.

120. W. Maitland Walker, 'An impartial appreciation of the Tolpuddle Martyrs', *Proceedings of the Dorset Natural History and Archaeological Society*, 55 (1933), p. 62; Frampton, re. Tolpuddle, to Melbourne, 2 April 1834, BL Add. Mss 41567, f. 163; *The Times*, 6 December 1830; Selmes, Beckley, to H. B. Curteis, 9 November 1830, ESCRO AMS.5995/3/11.

121. Hawkhurst events were typical, with one man saying that he 'would go out sooner than be ill treated as I was a pressed Man', while on an attempted desertion the crowd called out 'strip him, black him and make him walk in front'. The Rye crowd 'forced Millers from their Mills, & blacksmiths from their forges'; prosecution brief against five Hawkhurst men, Kent winter Assize, 1830, PRO TS 11/943/3412; H. Mascall to H. B. Curties, 10 November 1830, ESCRO, AMS.5995/3/14.

122. Burwash petition, n.d., forwarded by the vestry to H. B. Curteis, 9 November 1830, ESCRO, AMS.5995/3/12; *Brighton Herald*, 27 November 1830.

123. An undercover policeman infiltrating plebeian pot-houses in East Kent, said that 'all the... talk is about the wages, some give 1s8d per day some 2s some 2s3d and they say they want 2s6d... and they shall be comfortable'; D. Bishop, Deal, to W. Rowley, 11 November 1830, PRO, HO 52/8, ff.148–9.

124. *Brighton Herald*, 27 November 1830; *Morning Chronicle*, 24 November 1830.

125. Etchingham, resolutions of thirteen occupiers, chaired Joseph Hyland, 10 November 1830 and sent to H. B. Curteis the same day, ESCRO, AMS. 5995/3/14; *The Times*, 28 December 1830; *Brighton Herald*, 27 November 1830.

126. Hobsbawm and Rudé, *Captain Swing*, pp. 102, 108, 118–19, 128–31; *The Times*, 28 December 1830.

127. Deposition of special constable Keeling, Wallingford, and cf. J. Mills, Ringwood, Hampshire to Melbourne, 23 and 26 November 1830, PRO, TS 11/849; HO 52/7, ff.21–3; A. F. J. Brown, *Chartism in Essex and Suffolk* (Chelmsford: Essex County Council, 1982), pp. 24–5; Etchingham agreement, 10 November 1830, ESCRO, AMS.5995/3/14; *Brighton Herald*, 27 November 1830; Farndell's deposition, Bosham, 23 November 1830, WSCRO Goodwood Mss 1477a; *The Times*, 22 December 1830; *Political Register*, 4 December 1830.

128. Letters to Curteis, from Burwash, and Etchingham, 9 and 10 November 1830, ESCRO AMS. 5995/3/12, 14; deposition of James Fuller, 22 November 1830, PRO TS 11/849.

129. H. Drummond, Albury, to W. Bray, Shere, 24 November 1830, GMR. E list 46; Sir C. Webster, Battle, to Peel with enclosure, 12 November 1830; prosecutor's brief against W. Martin and others, Sussex Winter Assize, 1830, PRO HO 52/10, ff.397–8; TS 11/1007/4051; *Morning Chronicle*, 23 November and 6 December 1830; Wells, 'Rejoinder', pp. 69–72; *Reading Mercury*, 3 January 1831; BL, Place Newspaper Coll. vol. 21, f. 90; Colson, 'Revolt', pp. 94–5.

130. Hobsbawm and Rudé, *Captain Swing*, pp. 18, 78, 91–2, 122, 221; *Brighton Herald*, 27 November 1830; *Rochester Gazette*, 16 November 1830; E. J. to H. B. Curteis, 10 November 1830, ESCRO, AMS.5995/3/13; *Salisbury and Winchester Journal*, 3 January 1831; Colson, 'Revolt' pp. 116–20; W. Cowburn to Baron Vaughan, copied to Wellington, and his reply, 1 and 7 January 1831, SUL, Wellington papers, 4/1/3/4/4.

131. Dallington farmers' petition, cited Hobsbawm and Rudé, *Captain Swing*, p. 83; *Norfolk Chronicle*, 1 January 1831; *The Times*, 12 November and 31 December 1830; E. J. Curteis to H. B. Curteis, 10 November 1830, ESCRO, AMS.5995/3/13; Courthope, draft return to the PLC, n.d. (December 1832 or January 1833), ESCRO, SAS. Co/C/230.

132. Earl of Uxbridge to the Home Office, 26 November 1830, cited Bawn, 'Social protest', p. 86; Hobsbawm and Rudé, *Captain Swing*, esp. pp. 83, 121, 130; Randall and Newman, 'Protest, proletarians', p. 211; *Political Register*, 4 and 11 December 1830.

133. Colson, 'Revolt', pp. 92–5; prosecutor's briefs against W. Standen and others, West Kent Epiphany Quarter Sessions, 1831, and the arsonist Packmen brothers, Kent Winter Assize, 1830, PRO TS 11/943/3412; for Hernhill, see also Reay, *Microhistories*, pp. 75–7.

134. The crowd which unusually mobilised on a Sunday at East Dean 'declared their intention of destroying all "… excisemen and turnpike gates"'; *Salisbury and Winchester Journal*, 29 November 1830; cf. R. Foster, *The Politics of County Power. Wellington and the Country Gentlemen, 1820–52* (Brighton: Harvester, Wheatsheaf, 1990), p. 69; for earlier incidents, W. Albert, 'Popular opposition to turnpike trusts in early eighteenth-century England', *Journal of Transport History*, ns. 5, 1 (1978), and A. Charlesworth *et al.*, 'The Jack-a-Lent riots and the opposition to turnpikes in the Bristol region in 1749', in Randall and Charlesworth, *Markets, Market Culture*.

135. Hobsbawm and Rudé, *Captain Swing*, p. 247.

136. *Salisbury and Winchester Journal*, 29 November and 27 December 1830, and 24 January 1831; *Southampton Mercury*, 27 November 1830; *The Times*, 29 and 30 November, 3, 22, 23 and 29 December 1830, and 3 January 1831; Rolt, *Waterloo Iron*, pp. 44–6; *Bury St Edmunds Post*, 8 December 1830; Anon., London, to Wellington, and Colonel Rowan to the Home Office, 4 and 9 (6.30 p.m.) November 1830, PRO HO 40/25(1).

137. *Kent Herald*, 16 September 1830; W. Taylor, Euston Sq. to Peel, 4 and 7 November 1830, PRO HO 40/25(1), ff. 31–2, 93–4; *The Times*, 6 December 1830; BL Place newspaper coll. vol. 21. f. 78.

138. Hobsbawm and Rudé, *Captain Swing*, pp. 114–15; *Herts Mercury*, 20 November 1830; *Morning Chronicle*, 29 November and 1 December 1830, *The Times*, 12 January 1831.

139 *Morning Chronicle*, 2 December 1830; *The Times*, 6 December 1830; *Norfolk Chronicle*, 4 and 18 December 1830, 9, 25 and 29 January, 26 March, 2 and 16 April, and 9 July 1831; *Norwich Mercury*, 30 July 1831; *East Anglian*, 12 April 1831; Archer, *Flash and a Scare*, p. 174.

140. G. Bush, Trowbridge, to Colonel A'Court, Heytesbury, 27 and 29 November; A'Court to Colonel Moir, Salisbury, 30 November 1830, PRO HO 40/27(5), ff.378–80; *Salisbury and Winchester Journal*, 29 November 1830 and 10 January 1831; J. Peniston to the Marquis of Bath, 25 November 1830, Cowan, 'John Peniston', pp. 221–2.

141. R. Withers, Cambridgeshire, to Hardwicke, 26 November 1830; Hobhouse diary, 17 December 1830, BL Add. Mss 35691, ff. 297–8; 56555, f. 76; Sir H. Taylor to Wellington, 26 December 1830, SUL Wellington papers, 1/1157/1; *Political Register*, 12 February 1831; Secretary, County Fire Office, London, to Peel, 12 November 1830, PRO HO 64/1, f.293.

142. Thompson, 'The moral economy', pp. 207–12, 226–8, 241–6; Hobsbawm and Rudé, *Captain Swing*, pp. 75, 123–5, 199–200; Lucas, *Heathfield*, pp. 148–9; Hellingly vestry minute, 25 November 1830; Chichester to Courthope, 2 April 1831, ESCRO, Par.375/12/6; SAS. Co/C/230.

143. J. Mills (a Volunteer Officer who rejected negotiation in favour of a military 'offensive' against Swing), Ringwood, to Wellington, and reply, both 3 December 1830; Wellington said that only the Lord Chancellor could remove a JP when convicted of crime; as Lord Lieutenant, the Duke would 'endeavour to discover who are the friends of … Willis, and I will thro' them remonstrate with him': SUL, Wellington papers, 4/1/2/2/42–3; Mills to Melbourne, 26 November 1830, PRO HO 52/7, ff.21–3.

144. Phillipps to Fowles, 26 November 1830, PRO HO 41/8, pp. 138–9; *East Anglian*, 22 March 1831; *Norwich Mercury*, 26 March 1831.

145. Senior to Lord Chancellor Brougham, 14 September 1832, cited by P. Dunkley, 'Whigs and paupers; the reform of the poor laws 1830–1834', *Journal of British Studies*, 20, 2 (1981) p. 139; Montague-Burgoyne to Richmond, 13 September 1831; Labourers' Friend Society Prospectus, 1831, WSCRO Goodwood Mss 636; 1474; Chichester to Sanctuary, 14 January 1831, Bodleian Library, Ms. Top Sussex, C2; Chichester to Courthope, 29 March 1831, ESCRO SAS. Co/C/230; *Hampshire Chronicle*, 8 October 1832.

146. *Sussex Advertiser*, 28 February and 21 March 1831; Chichester to Sanctuary and to Courthope, loc. cit. Memorial, Kelvedon Hall, Essex, March 1831; Midhurst Spade Husbandry, printed accounts, 1831–4; Montague-Burgoyne to Richmond, 16 March 1834; Labourers' Friend Society, prospectus 1834, WSCRO, Goodwood Mss 636; 669; 1474; *Hampshire Chronicle*, 8 October 1832; *Kent Herald*, 14 March 1833; *Brighton Gazette*, 14 March, 16 and 30 May, 27 June, 5 and 12 December 1834; Randall and Newman, 'Protest, proletarians', p. 212.

147. Wells, 'Tolpuddle', pp. 120–1; *Bury St Edmunds Post*, 18 April, 6 June and 9 August 1832; *East Anglian*, 30 October 1832; Archer, *Flash and a Scare*, p. 98.

148. The 1832–34 period requires systematic study aimed at cornland interactions between market and other town trades unionists and rural workers of all hues. To give one additional example, at Yeovil in January 1834, 'Operatives in the Glove Trade have thought proper to form a Union on the same basis as the other Trades' Unions in different parts of the country', which provoked a lock-out; in April 'Upwards of 150 agricultural labourers' came to Brighton 'to join the Union Societies established there'; *Poor Man's Guardian*, 18 January 1834; *Brighton Gazette*, 17 April 1834; Frampton to the Earl of Digby, 30 January 1834, and 4 February; Digby to Frampton, 3 February; copy of a handwritten paper outlining Union policy, circulated Haselbury, Dorset, enclosed G. B. Portman, Byminster, to Frampton, and reply 1 and 3 March 1834, BL Add. Mss 41567, ff. 121–2, 127–8, 132–4, 150. For an initial broader contextualisation, see Wells, 'Tolpuddle', pp. 120–5.

149. Dyck, *Cobbett*, pp. 198–9; Wells, 'Social protest, class', pp. 189–93.
150. *Hampshire Chronicle*, 31 December 1832; *Reading Mercury*, 7 January 1833; *Berkshire Chronicle* (which did not report the fire at the time), 16 March 1833; W. Rowland, JP, to Melborne, 24 December 1832: PRO HO 64/3, f. 244; Lord Teynsham, Brighton but re. Kent, to Richmond, 26 December 1831, WSCRO, Goodwood Mss 636.
151. *Political Register*, 30 July 1831; J. Partridge, Barton, Kent, to the Rev. Chetwyne, 10 April 1831, CKS U239/Z4; letters to Melbourne from Deal JPs, 5 and 8 August, and Clerk of the Peace, New Romney, 16 August 1831; Justice Bradley, Sittingbourne, to Camden, 6 August 1831, PRO HO 52/13, ff. 70–6, 81–2, 87–9; *Maidstone Gazette*, 12 July, 9 August and 6 September 1831; BPP, 'Agriculture', (1836), Qs 7385–6; Archer, *Flash and a Scare*, pp. 44, 98, 140; D. J. V. Jones, 'Thomas Campbell Foster and the rural labourer: incendiarism in East Anglia in the 1840s', *Social History*, 1 (1976).
152. W. H. T. Hawley, Battle, and Clerk, Uckfield Union, to the PLC, 27 April and 1 June; Rev. Poore, Murston, to Russell, 3 May, and deposition of W. Bray, Ringmer, 28 May; depositions of farmer Daws and T. Barham, Battle Union, both 21 July 1835, PRO MH 12/12854, 13157; HO 52/26, f. 130, 52/27, f. 192; Assi 36/2. *Brighton Patriot*, 26 May 1835; cf. Digby, *Pauper Palaces*, pp. 222–4.
153. Though parish claimants in such Gilbert Unions which functioned up to 1835 were more accustomed to dealing with officials resident elsewhere.
154. *Brighton Patriot*, 15 and 22 September, and 29 December 1835, and 19 January 1836; *Sussex Advertiser*, 14 September 1835; Petworth jail calendar, Michaelmas 1835, WSCRO, QR/W779; cf. J. Knott, *Popular Opposition to the 1834 Poor Law* (London: Croom Helm, 1986), pp. 71–2.
155. R. Wells, 'Resistance to the New Poor Law in Southern England', in Rule and Wells, *Crime, Protest*, pp. 98–101, 108–10; cf. Digby, *Pauper Palaces*, p. 23.
156. Wells, 'Rural rebels', pp. 144–7; T. P. Durrant, JP, Mayfield, enclosing spy's report from Heathfield to W. Day, 25 July 1835, WSCRO, Goodwood Mss 1575; United Brothers' handbill, 8 May 1835, PRO HO 52/26, f. 168; *Brighton Patriot*, 14 July 1835; Wells, 'Tolpuddle', pp. 124–6; R. Wells, 'Southern Chartism', in Rule and Wells, *Crime, Protest*, pp. 129–30.
157. Bellingham, Battle, to Russell, 25 July 1835, enclosing Board minutes, PRO HO 52/27. ff.212–13A.
158. 5 and 6 William IV c. 69, as amended by 7 William IV & 1 Vict. 50. The Act is apparently unknown to Urdank, 'Rental property'; his argument might be fortified by it, although in places the wealthy craftily blocked purchases of almost invariably dilapidated buildings, to prevent small investors packing these hovels with marginal folk; alternatively, they were demolished. However, some parishes simply permitted residents to go on living in these places, though they were not repaired; Wells, 'Social protest, class', p. 149; BPP, House of Commons, Select Committee report, 'Andover Union' (1846), vols 5 and 6, Qs 10819–20, 17566–72, 17744–8.
159. Wells, 'Tolpuddle', pp. 110–1.
160. Wells, 'Resistance', pp. 120–5; Randall and Newman, 'Protest, proletarians', p. 215; R. Arnold, *The Farthest Promised Land: English Villagers, New Zealand*

Immigrants of the 1870s (Wellington, NZ: Victoria University Press, 1981), p. 157.

161. Senior to Brougham, loc. cit.

162. E. J. Evans, 'Some reasons for the growth of English rural anti-clericalism, 1750–1850', *Past and Present*, 66 (1975).

163. *Political Register*, 20 December 1828; cf. W. Apfel and P. Dunkley, 'English rural society and the New Poor Law; Bedfordshire 1834–47', *Social History*, 10, 1 (1985), pp. 54–5; and F. Driver, *Power and Pauperism. The Workhouse System 1834–1884* (Cambridge: Cambridge University Press, 1993), p. 114.

164. Unsigned, undated letter, but re. conviction of Burwash labourer John Clifton, March 1818, ESCRO QR/E755; *Political Register*, 22 December 1821, 20 December 1828, and 24 March 1832.

165. Cobbett made observations about pilferage, 'taking things in kind', itemising 'pocketfuls of wheat' lifted almost daily by farmworkers, but did not condemn it; *Political Register*, 17 March 1821; in Hampshire, the Rev. Butler took a relaxed view of 'how very uncommon strict honesty is among the lower classes', adding that 'things may occur without my knowledge…a farmer may detect a man in stealing turnips or cutting wood' but his reverence would remain ignorant 'unless the man is brought before a magistrate': BPP, House of Commons, Select Committee report, 'Poor Law Amendment Act' (1837–8), vol. XVII, Qs 5013, 5408.

166. P. King, 'Customary rights and women's earnings: the importance of gleaning to the rural labouring poor, 1750–1850', *Economic History Review*, 44 (1991); P. King, 'Gleaners, farmers and the failure of legal sanctions, 1750–1850', *Past and Present*, 125 (1989); Wells, *Wretched Faces*, p. 305.

167. Wells, 'Social protest, class', pp. 179–80; cf. Knott, *Popular Opposition*, p. 78 and table 3/1.

168. See esp. Wells, 'Southern Chartism', *passim*.

169. A. Randall, 'The industrial moral economy of the Gloucestershire weavers in the eighteenth century', in Rule, *British Trade Unionism*.

170. BPP, 'Andover Union', Qs 11068, 17454–80, but cf. Qs 161, 1220; for the attitutde of the Union's first chairman, the Rev. Dodson (1836–46), see esp. Qs 263–4, 3182, 3415, 3483–4, 3561, 3975–81, 4371–6, 4419–20, 4787–8, 4856–8, 5003–4, 5040.

171. BPP, House of Commons, Select Committee report, 'Medical Poor Relief' (1844), vol. 9, Q. 5545, and cf. the returns of Lincolnshire Poor Law Unions to Chadwick's 23 January 1844 circular, requiring explanations of rising outdoor relief expenditure, esp. that from the Clerk to the Louth Union, 12 March 1844, PRO MH 32/86.

172. *Crowborough Weekly*, 16 July 1904.

Index

Abel, Thomas   234
A'Court, Colonel   236
Acts of Parliament, 12,
    George III c.71   97
Adams, John   154
agrarian capitalism   210–19, 250
    critics   219–21
agricultural revolution   209–10
agricultural workers,
    wages   212, 229–31,
    237–8, 250–1
Alfriston   229
allotments   244–5, 254
America, colonial   149–52
American Revolution   152–6
    economic crisis   156–8
Andover   255
Annam   193
apprenticeship   22, 79, 173
Armytage, Sir Samuel   62
Arnold, David   13, 24, 123
arson   200, 240, 243, 245–6
artisans   22–3, 79
Assize of Bread   16, 68, 76, 77, 103
authorities, local response to
    riot   10–11, 71–3

Bacon, Matthew   99–100
bad name   196–7, 199
badgers   10, 61, 81, 96, 97
Bailington   63
bakers   8, 14
Balasore   136
bankruptcies   224–5
Banks, Thomas   81
Barrington, Daines   100
Bath   5
Battams, Thomas   106–7
Beadon, Sir Cecil   130–1
Belcher, Andrew   148–9, 152
Bellary   128, 133
bells, regulating markets   14–15
Berg, Maxine   182

Berkshire   7
Birmingham   106
blacks, colonial America   149, 150
Blackstone, Sir William   99
Bloch, Marc   187
Bohstedt, John   4, 9, 11, 17,
    55, 168, 180
Book of Orders   34, 57, 77–8, 80
Bordeaux   35, 42, 43, 47
Boston (Lincs), food riots   34, 36,
    40, 41, 44
Boston (Mass.)   151
    American Revolution   153–5
    food riots   148–9, 152
Boston Massacre   154–5
Boston Tea Party   153
bread, prices   230
Bread or Blood protests   210
Bristol   8, 14, 16, 48, 69, 177
    food riots   34, 35, 42–3, 44
Brougham, Lord Chancellor   251
Brown, A.F.J.   239
Buckingham, Marquess of   106–7
Bures   63
Burke, Edmund   96, 97–8, 102–3,
    104, 109
Burma   187, 189, 190, 191, 192,
    193–4
Burton, Captain   62
Burwash   239, 240
butchers   102–3, 104

Calais   43
calico-printers   169
Campbell, Bruce   36–7
Captain Swing   23, 210, 224, 225,
    235–43, 250, 252
carcass butchers   102, 104
cash crops   139
Casse, William   35, 42, 43, 47
Charlesworth, Andrew   1, 183
Chayanov, A.V.   187
children, work   216

China 124
Chingleput 129
Chippenham 11, 14
cholam 127, 128, 129
Christian, Edward 99
Cinque ports 41
Cirencester 7
Civil War, US 159
Clare, John 224
cloth-dressers, industrial
 action 168–9
clothiers 243
Cobb, Richard 4, 187
Cobbett, William 24, 210, 219–21,
 226, 236, 237, 239, 241, 246,
 252–3, 254
Coke, Sir Edward 99, 104, 113
Colchester 63, 65, 67, 68
Colley, George 70
colliers, food riots 5–6, 64, 67–8, 69
colonial state, taxes 191–2, 193–4
Combe, Alderman 104
Combination Acts 230
 repeal 168
combinations, illegal 171–2, 174–5
combine harvesters 200–1
commons 80, 225, 226, 253
Company of Weavers, Fullers and
 Shearmen 178
Conway 67
Cooke, Carpenter 237
coolstaffing 178, 179
Cornwall 9
Countryman, Edward 24, 147
courts, attitude to marketing
 laws 98–100
Coventry 16
craftsmen, incomes 213
Crediton 178
crime, famine-related 135–7
Cuddalore 130
Cuddapah 129
Cullompton 181
cultivation practices, peasants 189–90
Culver, Thomas 233
customs, moral economy 194–5
customs officials 39
 colonial 153–4
Cuttack 130

dacoity 136–7
Dallaway, William 5, 7
Day, William 234
dealers, grain 13, 132–3
Dean, Forest of 10, 13
dearth 4, 24, 45
 1346–47 36–7
 1766–7 219
 1795–6 105–7
 social protection 58
 starvation 79
Declaration of Independence 158
demographic growth 13, 211
depopulation, rural 254
depression, post–Napoleonic wars
 212–14, 251
Derby 66–7, 69
Devizes 11
Dewsbury, food riots 61–3, 67, 68,
 74, 81
Dobson, Rodney 182–3
Dongan, Governor Thomas 148
Dorking 230
double-cropping 199, 204, 205

East Grinstead 216
Easebourne 233
Eastwood, George 233–4
economic crisis, revolutionary
 America 156–8
Edward I 44
Edward II 44, 45
Edward III 36, 40, 45, 49
Ellenborough, Edward Law, Lord
 108, 111, 112
Elton, Sir Abraham 97
Ely 38
employment, rural 231–2
enclosure 13, 211, 220, 223–7
engineering agricultural 214
engrossing 8, 57, 61, 69, 79, 93,
 95, 96, 97, 98, 99, 101, 102,
 109, 110, 148
enlistment 211
entitlement thesis 2, 25, 137
Erskine, Thomas 108
estates, consolidated 210–11
Etchingham 238, 239
Evans, John 70

Exeter 49, 177
  food riots 170–1
Eyles, Robert Wells 255

factors 10
famine
  1315–22 36–7, 45
  India 135–8
  Napoleonic wars 228, 230
Famine Code 134
farmers 10
farms
  consolidation 219–20
  larger 211
Fawley 240–1
Federal Constitution, USA 153, 158
fiscal system, colonial state 191–2
Fisher, William 73–4
Flanders 39
Flurry, Farmer 233–4
food distribution 193–4
food prices 211, 227–9
food riots 1–2, 9, 57–60, 124–5, 166,
    201–2, 210, 227
  1347 34–6
  1550–1650 57
  1560–1740 57–8
  1740 60–8, 78
  1740–1820 59–60
  assumption of royal power 44–5
  'classic' 11–12
  counting riots 9, 59–60, 84, 227
  criminality 6–7
  decline 24
  Dewsbury 61–3, 67, 68, 74, 81
  Exeter 170–1, 180
  India 127–31, 133–4
  King's Lynn 34, 35–6, 40–1
  medieval England 3
  moral economy perspective 3–12
  parliamentary patronage and 68–71
  riotous communities 9–10, 67–8
  tradition 60–8
  violence 6, 62–3
food supply 227–9
forestalling 8, 14, 33, 40, 44, 49, 50,
    57, 61, 68, 69, 79, 93, 95, 96, 97,
    98, 99, 101, 102, 104, 105–6,
    107–12, 148

Fox, Charles James 104
Framfield 240
France, military campaigns 40
fuel prices 241
Funtingdon 229

game theory 187
Gandhi, Indira 123
Gascony 35, 36, 37, 37–40, 43
Genovese, E.F. 229
George III 108
gleaning 59, 253
Gloucester 42, 43, 48
Gloucestestive 5, 7, 20, 21, 24
Godstone 226
gossip 196
Goudhurst 216, 225, 240, 241
grain
  government intervention/
      non-intervention in trade 16,
      131–2, 140
  India 127
  local measures 15–16, 75
  marketing, India 125–6, 132–3
  prices 228–9
  release to market 11
  rise of national market 12–13
  shipments to Gascony 37–40
  in transit 13–14
  transport 38
  Tudor and Stuart regulation 33–4
grain exports 13–14, 59, 60, 63–4, 78
  licences 47
  prohibition 43–7, 58, 61, 78
Great Depression 192
Grenville, William, 1st Baron 104
Grose, Mr Justice 109
Grosvenor, Sir Robert 70
guilt 198

Ha-Tinh 193–4
Hadleigh 238
Hanoi 193
Harrington, James 157
Harrison, Richard 228
harvest failure 37, 57
Haverfordwest, 5
Hawkins, Serjeant William 99,
    104, 113

Hay, Douglas   18, 20, 93
head tax   191–2, 194
Hearn, Major C.S.   129
Heathfield   233, 247–8
Hobsbawm, Eric   224, 236, 238
Holland, Henry Fox, 3rd Baron   104
Holywell   67
horse thieves   7
Hoskins, W.G.   174, 224
Hue   193
Hull, grain shipments   37, 39, 40, 41
Hungerford   240

India   13, 123–4
   food riots   24, 127–31, 141
   philanthropy and paternalism
      138–41
   pre-colonial 125
Indian Famine Commission   134
industrial disputes
   moral economy and 21, 166–9
   shipwrights   169–71
   woolsorters   171–6
industries, rural   212, 214, 216
inflation, America   156, 157
Ipswich   48
Irish, harvest labour   220–1, 231,
   232, 236
iron foundries   242
ironworkers   69
Isle of Thanet   236

jobbers
   butchers 102–3, 104
   cattle   11, 95–7
   corn trade   8, 95
journeymen weavers   178
journeymen woolsorters   171–6

Kadir, Haji   196
Kaye, Sir John   62, 68
keelmen   69
Kent, food riots   34, 36, 41–2
Kenyon, Lord   95, 101, 104–5, 107,
   107–12
Kettering   63
King's Lynn
   food riots   34, 35–6, 40–1, 44, 78
   grain shipments   37–9

Kingswood (Bristol)   5, 68
Knatchbull, Sir Edward   244
Krishna 129
Kurnool   129, 136

labour combinations   60
labour consciousness   171, 176
labour demand
   agriculture   211
   paddy harvesting   202–4
labour force, casualisation   213
labour markets   183
Labourers' Employment Act   244
laissez–faire   18, 21, 24, 183, 205, 244
Lambourn   245–6
land, access to   223–7, 254–5
land tenure   202
   impact on peasantry   190–1
landless labourers   191, 205
landowners   10, 14, 190, 195, 196
   grain shipments   38
   labour relations   203–4
law
   attitude of courts   20, 98–100
   food marketing   20, 44, 94–5
   repeal of old laws on food
      marketing   97–8
Lechmere   220
Lemesurier, Alderman   103
Lewes   227, 231
Lewes, Sir Watkin   103
liberties, American Revolution   158–9
live-in service   222–3, 251
Liverpool, Charles Jenkinson,
   1st Earl   104–5
localism, grain trade   13, 15
lock-outs   248
London   60, 61
   Common Council   96, 102–3
   grain shipments   37, 39, 40, 43
looting   130
   grain   129
Lorimer, Saier   46
Loveless, George and James   237
Luddism   63
   rural   236, 239

machine–breaking   200, 231–2,
   236–7, 238–9, 242–3, 244, 246

Madras 139
  famine crime 136–7
  food riots 127–31,135
Madurai 136
magistrates 6
  poor law appeals 218
  response to food riots 10–11,
    61–2, 64, 68–9, 71–3, 74–5, 106
Maidenhead 227
Mainwaring 104
make-work schemes 215
Malaysia 195–202
Malcolmson, Robert 168, 171
Maldon 40
Mallard, George 65
Manchester 101, 102
Manningtree 63
Mansfield, William Murray,
  1st Earl 98–9, 100, 101, 112
manufacturing 214
market economy 2, 56–7
  innovations 75–7
market regulation 14–15
  colonial New York 148, 149
  corn measures 15
  Tudor and Stuart 33–4, 58
marketing offences 93–4
  Courts' response to 98–100
  local enforcement 100–5
  parliamentary attitudes 95–8,
    104–5
  Waddington and Rusby
    cases 107–12
  see also engrossing; forestalling;
    regrating
markets
  market experience 17–18
  national 12–13
  non-intervention 24, 131–2
  pitching 14–15
  regulation 43–8, 76
Marx, Karl 168
Maryland 157
master-shipwrights, wage cuts 169–71
master-weavers 178–9
Mayfield 240
mechanisation 195, 204, 205
Melbourne, William Lamb,
  2nd Viscount 236

Melchebourn, Thomas de 47
merchants, grain 13
Methuen, Squire 244–5
middlemen 13–14
middling sort, moral economy 8
migrants, Irish labour 220–1, 231,
  232, 236
migration, agricultural labour
  211–12, 250
military operations, grain
  shipments 40, 47–8
millet 127
mills
  bolting 63, 75
  demolition 61, 242
miners 9
Minnis 226, 236
mob
  English 111–12
  Indian 129
Mold 67
monsoon failure 127–8, 135
moral economy 1–3, 147
  countryside 209–10, 245, 250
  food riots 3–12
  and industrial disputes 21–2,
    166–9, 182–3
  North America 24, 148–9
  peasant societies 25
  peasant villages 194–202
  as value system 19–25
mortality, famine-related 138
Mostyn, Sir Thomas 70
Mount Vernon 149–50
Munro, Thomas 140
mutuality 201
Mysore 139

Naxalite 123
Neeson, J. 223, 224, 225
Nellore 129
New England 150, 151
New Poor Law *see* Poor Law, New
New York 148, 151, 155
Newbury 5
Newcastle upon Tyne 64–5, 67–72
Newport Pagnell 66
Nghe-An 193

Norfolk 48
North America, moral economy 24
North Arcot 129
North Carolina 157
North Curry 225
North-Western Provinces, India 139
Norwich 8, 16, 66, 68, 72, 242–3
Nottingham, food riots 63

Oastler, Richard 24
Orissa 130, 135, 136
Oundle 213
outdoor relief 249–50
Owen, William 71
Oxford 5, 7, 16, 75 101, 102

Paine, Tom 150
paper mills 242
Parliament 153
  debates on food marketing 95–8,
    104–5
parliamentary enclosure 13, 211,
    223–7
parliamentary patronage, food riots
    68–71
paternalism 20, 24, 33, 34, 49,
    79–81, 93, 138–41, 189, 202–6
Paul, Sir G.O. 79
peacekeeping, food riots 71–3
peasants
  India 124
  moral economy 25, 194–202
  subsistence 189–92
Pembroke 67, 71
Pennsylvania 157
personal grudges 7
Peterborough 65
Philadelphia 150, 155
philanthropy, India 136–41
piece-work 211, 212, 250
pitmen, industrial culture 183
Pitt, John 10–11, 20
Pitt, William 'the Younger'
    103, 104, 111
plantations 149, 150
poaching 253
political economy 12, 17–11, 96,
    98, 131

politics of justice 73–5
politics of reputation 196–7, 199
Poole, Steve 8
poor
  hostility to grain traders 132–3
  provisioning 19–20
  subsistence 195
  survival strategies 137–8
Poor Law 58, 80, 214–19, 223,
    232–5, 243
  New 210, 242, 243–50, 255
Poor Law Amendment Act 252
poor relief 232–5
  extension 214–19
  protests 240–1
population
  decrease 214
  growth 211
  increase 57
Porteous, Captain John 73
Portland, William Bentinck,
    3rd Duke 104
posse comitatus 71
Pownall, Thomas 97, 104
pragmatic economy 55
Price, Richard 167
price riots, revolutionary America
    156–8
price rises 4
prices
  grain 128–9, 228–9
  setting 77–8, 130
private tithes 199–200
production relations, Malaysia 202–6
property of skill 79–80
prostitution 219
protest, types of 9–10
provision politics 55, 56–60
public assistance 215–16
punishment, food rioters 73–5
purveyance 41–2, 43

ragi 127, 129
Ramsey Abbey 38
Randall, Adrian 1, 21, 166, 168,
    182–3, 254
ratepayers, small, hostility to poor
    law 248–9
real wages, farmworkers 212

regrating 8, 14, 57, 61, 93, 95, 96,
    97, 98, 99, 101, 102, 106–7, 109
    110, 148
relief, outdoor 249–50
Renton, Simon 8
rents 190, 240
reputation, attacks on 196–7
Rhuddlan 64, 70
rice 128
    India 127
    price-fixing 130–1
Richardson, Ebenezer 154
Richmond, Charles Lennox,
    8th Duke 104
Ridley, Alderman Matthew 69, 70, 72
Riot Act 71
riots, anti-New Poor Law 247–9
risk aversion, peasants 189–90
Rudé, G. 224, 236, 238
Rule, John 17, 21, 22, 79, 166
Rusby, John 107–12

sabotage, combine harvesters 200–1
Sadler 240
Saffron Walden 63
Saigon 193
St Albans 227
Salisbury 11
salt tax 192
Sanctuary, Justice 236
Sandwich 41, 47
saw mills 242
Saya San rebellion, Burma 193, 194
Scott, James C. 2, 25, 137, 187
    The Moral Economy of the Peasant
        188–9
Seer, Isaac 229
Selmes, Samuel 237
Sen, Amartya 2, 25, 137
Senior, Nassau 244, 251
shame 198
Sharp, Buchanan 3, 20, 33
Sheffield, Lord 239
Shelley, Sir Timothy 225
shipwrights, industrial disputes
    169–71
Shrewsbury 105
silk weavers, Spitalfields 22
Silvester, Eusebius 63

skilled labour, casualisation 210, 213
slavery 149, 150, 152, 159–60
small farmers 224–5
smallholders 191, 205
Smith, Adam 18, 96, 98, 108, 131,
    168, 176, 180
Sneider, Christopher 154, 155
Snell, Keith 23, 209
social control 204, 235
social crime 253, 254
social ostracism 197
social sanctions, village life 196–9
South Arcot 130
South Carolina 149, 157
Southwold 48
Speenhamland system 214–15
squatting 226
Stamp Act 1765 153
Statute of Artificers 1563 79
Stelling 226, 236
Stockton 64, 67, 71–2
Stone, Lawrence 166
strikes 168–9
    Captain Swing 237
    East Anglia 245
    rolling 174
Stroudwater 7, 10
subsistence, peasants 189–92
Suffolk 48
sugar 152

Tamworth 49
Taunton 177, 178, 181
taxation populaire 228
taxes 190
    American colonies 153
    colonial state 191–2, 193–4
tenancy
    by forms of 190–1
    of transfer 205–6
tenants, outbidding 197–8
Tetbury 15
Tewkesbury 43
Tharrawady 194
theft
    by farmworkers 253
    of paddy 199–200
Thetford 36, 38, 41
    food riots 34, 36

Third World　2, 20
Thompson, E.P.　12, 137, 171, 193,
　194, 226, 244
　Customs in Common 2, 19, 138
　Making of the English Working Class
　19, 187
　moral economy 1–3, 33, 55, 56, 75,
　78, 93, 123, 124, 130, 147, 166,
　187–8, 201–2, 209, 227
　Whigs and Hunters　189
threshing machines　231–2, 236–7,
　238–9, 242, 244, 246, 252
Thwaites, Wendy　7, 76, 80
tithes　241, 251
Tiverton　177, 178, 180–1
Tolpuddle Martyrs　245
Topsham　169–71
trade clubs　177–9
trade union consciousness　179
trade unions　172, 176, 247–8
tradesmen, incomes　213–14
transport　13–14
troops
　British, in America　154–5
　food riots　6, 72–3, 74, 111

United Brothers　247–8
United States　153
Upwell　65, 72

Vale of Clywd　67, 70–1
vandalism　200
Vellore　131
Vermont　157
Vietnam　187, 189, 190, 191, 192,
　193–4
Virginia 149

Waddington, Samuel　18, 98, 107–12
wage-cuts, shipbuilding　169–71
wages
　agricultural workers　212, 229–31,
　237–8, 250–1

　reduction　169–71, 243, 249
　regulation　22, 79
　weavers　180
　woolsorters　171–6
Walker, Patrick　155
Walter, John　57, 58
Washington, George　149–50
Weale, Robert　217–18
weavers　21, 79, 177–81
　wages　66
Wellingborough　65
Wells, Roger　7, 23, 76, 209
Wesenham, John de　35, 47
West Indies　149, 152
Weston, Charles　233–4
wheat　127
　prices　179–80
　release to market　11
Willan, T.S.　38
William Wynn, Sir Watkin　70–1
Williams, D.E.　9, 17, 227
Williams, Gwyn　4
Williams, Ned　70
Williams, Neville　38
Willis, Justice　244
Wiltshire　5, 7, 10, 11, 13, 21
Winchester　49
Winchester measure　15
Wisbech　65, 72, 74
Woollstaplers Society　172
Wolverhampton　106
woolcombers　173, 177–81
woollen industry　21, 178–9
　regulation　15
woolsorters, industrial disputes　171–6
workhouses　216, 234, 249
Wynne, Sir George　70

Young, Arthur 220

zamindars　138–9
Zola, Emile　193